"*Big Motorcycle* is a wild, mystic-linguistic hybrid about war and peace--both of which yet rage in the mind of F.X. 'Fussy Frank' Donner."

> --Konomi Ara, Tokyo-area writer / translator, has numerous books to her credit.

"The startling underworld of outcasts, losers, malcontents and sociopaths that lurks beneath Japan's stoic and buttoned-up veneer comes to life under F. J. Logan's bloodstained pen. It takes an informed outsider--a *gaijin* with street cred--to tell this story, because no Japanese writer would dare. Logan unveils a secret world, passionately, vividly, relentlessly."

> --David Benjamin, author of *Life & Times of the Last Kid Picked,* etc., former editor, *Tokyo Journal.*

"Relentlessly verbal, outrageous, unashamed, funny--a joy to read, page by clever page."

> --Terry Caesar, author of *Conspiring with Forms,* etc., and, most recently, *I Wouldn't Want Anyone to Know: Stories of Teaching in Japan.*

"Logan's potent style drives us into a culturally confounded world inhabited by intricate characters that showcase the noblest and the basest facets of the human psyche. *Big Motorcycle* is a fascinating read."

> --Jefferson Cronin, writer / actor / media personality, winner of the Guamanian Maga'lahi Award for Performing Arts, and former editor of *The* (Elkins, W.Va.) *Tygart Valley Press.*

Big Motorcycle

A Story of Tokyo

By

F. J. Logan

ISBN: 1-4033-9828-3 (E-book)
ISBN: 1-4033-9829-1 (Paperback)
ISBN: 1-4107-0227-8 (Dustjacket)

This book is printed on acid free paper.

1stBooks – rev. 05/08/03

For Gillian

Friday, 12:23 P.M.

Where is the fucking *soup?*

Coming, no doubt. On the way. Like every other god damned thing.

Or in the mail. Donner snorts. Tall and slightly stooped, neatly bearded brown and gray, balding though now he simply avoids mirrors, sharp-featured, irritable, childless (thank Christ), needing glasses to read and drive, still strong but no longer agile, Donner glances up from the red-scored student essay and purses his lips and frowns at the old waitress, who squeezes between packed tables, sets a steaming bowl of *miso* soup in front of him, and smiles—a smile wide and toothy, a literal stunner of a smile: her upper left central incisor, gold-jacketed but otherwise unremarkable, flashes and blinds him to everything else, hits him like Private Nguyen's boot to the head, knocks and drags and sucks him right out of his forty-something body, out of his orderly Tokyo present, and twenty years back to the bad north bank of the stinking Song Cai.

Thick heat, flies, the club of the sun. A POW transit camp, just a little clearing, screened from the air by the over-arching palms. Dust in the dry season, mud in the rains. Two hootches. One for the guards, one for the patrols which came, sometimes with prisoners, and went. A half-ton carryall parked under a large, many-rooted tree dripping with vines. Cages there also, but rotted and rusted, useless. Six steel stakes in the center of this compound, hammered three meters apart and deep into the earth. Two meter-long chains welded to the top of each stake, one prisoner locked to the end of each chain by a cuff around his left ankle. Six stakes, two chains, twelve men. Seldom fewer, never more. Sgt. Thuong saw to that. Thuong, with a gold incisor just like the waitress's. Donner stares at hers, not seeing it or her or the room, while he fingers the slight familiar bulge beneath his shirt where, on a thick gold chain, hangs Thuong's.

Who hasn't needed that or any tooth for twenty-five years. Who had been their interrogator, Donner's and Buddy's. They and all the rest, Thuong said, should have been grateful, after the ambush. Grateful *for* it. Yes, because they were POWs instead of KIAs, which they surely would have become if left to their own devices. And because they had a chance to learn the truth about the brotherhood of man, about historic inevitability. Here was opportunity. Did they not realize this?

Well, no, they didn't see it that way at all. But Donner and Buddy—that is to say, Francis X. Donner, 2nd lieutenant, and Franklin D. Nakamura, 2nd lieutenant, United States Army—kept their views to themselves. They told Thuong everything else, however. Name, rank, serial number, you bet. Old battle plans, troop placements? Sure. Then every other possible thing he might want to know, and a great many things he probably didn't. The idea was to keep Thuong talking.

"What is Viet Cong? Not exist I tell you. That American invent, as invent son of a bitch Diem. We not Viet Cong, because no such thing. We Viet *Minh.*"

"Right," said Donner.

"You historian you say," said Thuong.

"Yes," said Donner.

"So I tell you something history now. This war to liberation. First we kick out French, now we kick out you, China help us, we happy, not your business."

"True," said Donner.

"Then fucking hell what you are doing here?"

"Drafted. No choice."

Which was partly true. Buddy was a West Pointer, but Donner had in fact been drafted, a week after graduation from his little suburban Chicago college. Boot camp at San Antonio, then officers' candidate school, trying to drag things out, playing for time. At OCS unaccustomed freedom, exhilarating. No Martyr Ice Queen of a mother, with her slow psychic surgery, no Momster. But then suddenly Saigon, and Buddy, and the jungle. Patrol after patrol, lock and load, lock and load, coming together in a haze of numb terror and exhaustion as one endless patrol, stalking and being stalked. Death riding them all, every minute, whispering to them and bathing them with its breath of steamy rot, and finally claiming most of them the morning of the ambush.

"I helping you stay live, officer and gentlemen. Suppose be intelligent. You think Hanoi will bomb San Francisco? Maybe we sneaking up out of ocean and stealing TV sets of you?" The flush was spreading up Thuong's neck, across his snub-nosed baby like face. His scalp, clearly visible because of his brutally short weekly haircuts, was reddening as well. "No? You not think that? Then fucking hell what you are doing here?"

4

That was the question all right. Donner saw it in his mind's eye looming huge, hewn in mountainous block letters. It was what Donner asked himself a thousand times a day, looking out over the dust and filth and chained men. Over the months, as the beatings and starvation shattered his nerve, he came up with many answers, none of them good. The truth was, he didn't really know what he was doing there, and suspected they had all been suckered. Donner and Buddy didn't really understand anything about the war, either, didn't know what if anything Westmoreland and his generals had up their ornate sleeves, had never been in on the Big Picture.

But the Little Picture, ah. The prisoners' war was now tiny, immediate, intensely personal. Their crucial piece of enemy intelligence concerned Thuong's bottle of Cutty Sark: down to half full, no problem. Like many short fleshy men, Thuong, tipsy, was a jolly fellow—good company, almost. A newspaperman in civilian life, he was amiable, a good talker, fairly well informed on a range of subjects, a good listener. But when the bottle was empty and Thuong was full, then the men knew that at least one of them was probably going to die.

"Why? Why? Why? Why? Why not America jus' fuck away?"

Thuong, howling. Early on, a bespectacled corporal had tried to answer the question: "You don't know it, but we're here to help. To save democracy. If this country falls to the communists then that will be the end of free speech on this planet. Mr. Nixon explained all about that." The corporal's skull, spectacles stapled awry, festooned with colorful taped-on memoranda, now reposed on Thuong's camp desk and functioned as paperweight and ashtray.

"Why you here?" Thuong would roar, then smile, and continue in the soft voice of reason, "Actuarry, I know why. Because you are stupid."

"Stupid!" Donner and Buddy in unison.

"Stupid!" the others, pfcs and noncoms, chorusing.

"Or jus' maybe God and country?"

"No!"

"Pie of mom?"

"No!"

"Love Diem, so nice Catholic, go to the haybone?"

"Fuck no!"

"Save world?"

"No! No! Just stupid!"

"Ronald Reagan say one time could pave onto whole country, then paint for parking stripes, no probrem, you could home by Christmas."

"Reagan is an asshole! They're all assholes!"

"Then why you listen them?"

"Stupid!"

"Jus' only stupid? No more other reason?"

"That's it!" screaming, not looking at each other, competing. "Stupid!"

"How... stupid?" Thuong would ask quietly, smiling wider, the gold incisor glinting, his eyes squeezed nearly shut from the pressure of his fat cheeks, easing his Bowie knife from its sheath, starting forward. "How, exactory?"

"Really stupid!"

"Too stupid go to Canada?"

"Yes!"

"Too stupid be C.O., talktalk, nice jail having color TV, watch *Girrigan?"*

"Yes!"

"Too stupid jus' cut triggah fingah?"

"Yes!"

"But much smottah now, I think."

"Much!"

"Would cut fingah now?"

"Yes!"

At this point Thuong might hand a boy the knife, and say, "Okay, do, please," and the boy would, gasping and sobbing. Afterward, Thuong retrieved the knife. He might stroke the flat side of the blade against the boy's throat, to clean off the blood, then pick the finger from the dust and say, "I gonna mail draf' board for you, maybe not too late. You are nothing to lose, right? It couldn't hurt."

And sometimes that was enough. Thuong would shuffle back to his tent, sleep, lay off the Cutty for a week or ten days. But usually there was more. When the finger lay in the dust Thuong, giggling, would say to the boy, "How morale?" or, "Are you plan for home by Christmas?" and then stroke the boy's throat with, not the flat of the blade but rather its edge, jumping back from the jet of blood.

In time the dust around the six stakes became soaked and caked, thickly carpeted with flies. The blood stank worse than the urine and feces, worse even than the gangrenous leg of a Huey pilot who, half delirious and begging for death, Thuong was doing his best to keep alive.

Thuong's men complained about the stench, so he modified his routine. He quit executing prisoners in the

8

compound and then trucking them, with the rest of the garbage, down the road to the deep erosion gully. Instead, he began dumping them in the gully first, and then clambering down to execute them. Thuong didn't mind the smell. But one day a river rat took a chunk from his chubby ankle, and he scrambled back up to the truck, bawling for his fourteen year old, eighty pound driver, Corporal Trac. Back at the compound, Trac poured Cutty Sark on the rat bite, and Thuong sat wincing, deep in thought.

Next time, he chose four prisoners, two pairs of stake-mates, then had them bound two and two, face to face with their arms around each other, and slung into the back of the truck. On arrival at the gully, Thuong took his time, hauled the two pairs of men off the flatbed, offered them all a drink, a puff on his Marlboro. He told a few stories, let the four men look down into the bone-strewn gully, at the tangle of skeletons picked clean, at the fresher skulls still alive with maggots.

"So," Thuong said toward the end of the Cutty Sark, "Trac come here." Trac flicked away his cigarette, stood, and ambled over with his pride, an American M16. "Time for serious. Playing Viet Minh roulette. You like, it fun. One only bullet, see? Then spinning cylinder, completely fair. Now I'm throwing coin which you must call it in air." Quick prods from Trac's rifle muzzle. "You and you, call!"

"Heads!"

"Tails!"

"Ah, it is tails. Therefore," he would say, addressing the prisoner who had made the right call, "your team win, get to play some more. Other team get nothing till next time, too bad for them, got to go back to camp, tell everyone 'bout new game. Losing team, step back please with truck. Now again I am throwing coin. Call in air. Call!"

"Tails!"

"Heads!"

"Good! Two times row, lucky. So you first. I hold pistol your head, like this, don't worry jus' a little pistol, only kill you little bit, and pull trigger. Like this. Ah, it is click not boom, too bad. But we are must not cheating, so now we hold pistol head your friend, like this, pull trigger, like this. Ah, once again it is click, so now is more your turn, you have again chance, bullet could be anywhere, pull trigger to you, and is… *click* one more time, I'm sorry, but still you could win, now pull trigger to friend, and is… *boom.*

"Well, too bad, he winnah you losah. He go to the haybone. No, not necessary hold friend body. Trac help you down to ground. Now Trac fix arms and legs with rifle butt. Trac?... Ah, that good screaming. Now Trac roll you two in ditch. Could give friend little hug now, nobody evah know it. Even kiss. You have mosquito lotion? You have lotion to the cobrasnake and rats?"

So that became standard operating procedure for executions. Thuong never tired of it. Usually, the loser lived a day or two, with the sun and rats, his embrace tightening around the bloating winner, his world shrinking to a tiny center-point inside some huge and brilliant scream.

While the screams continued, Thuong pottered about sober and smiling, looking like a Buddha in khaki. And all the rest of the men were safe, chained in the compound, with the two hootches to look at on the road side and jungle creeping up on the river side, and nothing more to worry about than the routine beatings, dysentery, starvation, lice, and jungle rot. They squabbled over blackened grains of rice scraped from the guards' mess kits and prayed for the screams to continue. Big Buddy Nakamura, in between bouts of malaria, down eighty pounds from three months

11

earlier, prayed. Donner wept and cursed and prayed. Just one more scream, please, and after that another, and another.

"Bud," Donner whispered one execution-evening, still curled and rigid from a clubbing that afternoon, still breathing in sips but no longer sobbing, "let's play a game. Try to imagine doing something to Thuong."

"Something bad? Given the opportunity?"

"Given the opportunity. Something too terrible."

They lay, as always on such nights, listening to their thoughts and to the screams. Pitying the screamer, willing him to continue. But then the intervals would grow, the screams would weaken, become faint, finally stop, and the waiting would begin. For Thuong to pop another bottle. All agreed, that was the worst. The clammy night fogs, the thick baking endless days, the boots and rifle butts in the ribs, the huge hunger, the malaria that shook them the way a terrier shakes a rat: these things didn't begin to compare with the waiting. Donner waited and trembled and wept.

"Donner," Buddy said one night, embarrassed, "crying doesn't help."

If the waiting was unbearable, however, the bugs were relatively bearable. In fact, Buddy discovered that the larger insects, beetles and millipedes, were part of the solution and not the problem.

"Squash its head, pop it in, down the hatch. Vitamin pill."

He and Donner began telling each other about the nutritiousness of bugs, whispering together about amino acids. Passing the time, blocking the gully. They got so they could snatch a droning June bug out of the air and swallow it alive and then make their joke about butterflies in the stomach. The other POWs would see them do this, but the odd bug was hardly worth a betrayal. Buddy and Donner were the Bugmen of Alcatraz. Body vermin too. If beetles and grubs were okay, and they definitely were, why not lice?

"Billion baboons can't be wrong," Donner said, as he and Buddy searched each other's scalps and armpits.

"Mm*mm*," Buddy would say, finding a fat louse, cracking it with his teeth.

"Mom's cootie pie."

"What we're fighting for."

Once, just after sunset, with a breeze moving down from the hills and along the valley, and the jungle quickening, Buddy caught a little tan snake and gave Donner half, and Donner had wept in silent gratitude for an hour before he fell asleep. Another time a river rat strayed too close to Donner's dark perimeter, and they shared that too, flipping bits of fur and bone into the bush just before sunup. The drying rat blood on their faces blended with their own. Buddy and Donner lay in the dust, waiting out the nausea, pulsing all that day with magic acids.

Rat night was a watershed. After that, they took the initiative. They still-hunted every night. Four-hour shifts, one sleeping, the other at the limit of his chain, waiting to pounce. There was a surprising amount to pounce on, humble fauna drifting across the compound. They got moths and strange stick like insects and praying mantises. (One mantis had a giant jungle roach in its mandibles, a bonus.) They got pill bugs and dung beetles, and one night a swarm of white creatures that looked like termites. A sick pigeon had tumbled in and flopped close enough. There was a gecko, some sort of newt, several dozen cicadas and locusts and a huge bug that looked so much like a leaf that's what they thought it was till it moved. And, one moonlit night, an eerie silvery rippling, a migration of tiny toads.

"Bite size," said Buddy.

"Doing okay," said Donner.

"Still losing weight."

"But we can think. That's a plus."

"Can do better, though," said Buddy. "We can start a trapline."

The guards made a practice of throwing their used chewing gum into the compound then laughing as the closest POWs kicked and gouged each other. Buddy got lucky one afternoon and caught a wad of gum in the air, clapping his hand to his mouth. Twenty minutes later he looked up and winked at Donner: *Buddy hadn't eaten the gum.* He palmed half and passed it to Donner, and on the following three nights they rechewed the two small wads to keep them juicy, then set them as close as possible to the bush.

"How it all started," said Buddy.

"Caveman digs a pit, throws in his Juicy Fruit."

"Here comes the mammoth, says, What *is* that luscious fresh fruit smell?"

"Game over for the mammoth."

The first two nights, nothing. But on the third a giant amber ant appeared, circled each wad in turn, clambered over them, nudged and palped them, then crawled back into the bush.

"Doesn't like Juicy Fruit?"

Buddy shrugged.

But ten minutes later a column of these ants appeared. As fast as they reached the gum wads, they were lifted off, crushed, eaten. That night, after at least a hundred ants each, Buddy and Donner retrieved their bait and popped it back in their mouths. The remaining ants broke ranks, milled about, then dissipated. But the following night they were back, and the night after that. Following their leaders to destruction.

"Ants," said Buddy. "They never learn."

"Yeah, well," said Donner, chewing, "they're army ants."

The gum finally disintegrated, but by then the friends had each consumed, by Buddy's reckoning, the nutritional equivalent of a Big Mac.

"Tasted good," said Buddy. "Like raspberries. It's the formic acid, which is very good for you. Ants are full of it."

"Pretty soon we're into the rains. Means leeches. Like oysters, in a way."

"Leeches are almost pure amino acid."

"Fact of science," said Buddy. "Leeches to the slaughter."

"Mary had a little leech. Gonna say, Oh, god, get this human offa me."

"Gonna have leftovers."

"Gonna get fat."

Maybe it was the scraps of protein, maybe just the novelty of doing rather than being done to, but the friends eased back from some dark place in the mind. Buddy rallied, remembered he was an officer, kept a flow of grim wisecracks in whispered circulation among the men: Bob Hopeless. And Donner at least had fewer fits of rage and terrified weeping. One night Buddy woke and whispered to Donner, who had a big scorpion at bay against the stake, "Donner?"

"Fierce little fucker. What'll he taste like? Shrimp?"

"Donner. I don't want to die."

And for a while longer—because they were officers? because Thuong wanted someone to talk to? because he hated them worst and wanted them to wait longest?—they were all right. Relative newcomers died. Donner and Buddy became the camp veterans. Four months, still breathing in and out. But then one afternoon at the end of the dry season, they found themselves trussed face to face and bouncing along on the carryall's flatbed. Wood smoke in the air, shafts of late sun reaching through the high emerald canopy, red dust over everything, stillness.

En route to the gully. Bouncing along with them an artillery sergeant and the Huey pilot, similarly bound. The pilot's leg was wrapped in a plastic garbage bag to contain the stench, the top of the bag secured by a wire tourniquet biting deep into his thigh. Perhaps this wire had slowed the gangrene, but now he was clearly dying: face white and oozing cold sweat, eyes sunken, breathing shallow. At the gully, Buddy lost the toss, or rather won it, so he and Donner, jerking and sobbing, were shoved back against the truck while the others finished the game.

"Buddy," Donner whispered, his throat thick with terror, "who won?"

"Artillery man," said Buddy. "Had to play lying down."

"Buddy," said Donner, weeping. "Buddy."

"Get this. Trac is breaking the gangrene leg. Huey's right out of it."

"How drunk is he? Thuong, I mean. How drunk is Thuong?"

"He's drunk. Laughing like hell. We got to do something."

"Buddy, I'm shaking. I can hardly stand up."

"Got to, Donner. This is it."

"Got to." Donner drew a long ragged breath. His teeth chattered. "That's right, we got to. Okay, count of three, we jump sideways right onto Trac. Like a square-dance where they do that bit. Ready?"

"Nothing fancy," said Buddy. "I'm telling you."

"Forget about Thuong," said Donner. "Go for Trac. Only thing in the world is that rifle. Count of three. One. Two. Three."

Buddy and Donner were emaciated, but together they were still three hundred pounds, or almost, and they were weak, but when they landed on Trac they knocked the air from his lungs, and Buddy got both hands on the rifle barrel, and together they proved stronger than the eighty pound corporal, for when they rolled off Trac and scrambled to their feet, stumbled, then scrambled back, it was Buddy who held the rifle, but by the barrel, and therefore had to swing it by the barrel using only his wrists and a little body english to catch Trac in the throat. Then Thuong was closing with them, drunk and staggering, the pistol coming up, so Donner, tears of pure terror rolling down his cheeks, waited till the distance was right and placed a weak kick in Thuong's groin, giving Buddy's hands a few seconds to work their way down the rifle barrel to the stock and then the trigger, and finally swing the muzzle around on Thuong, who had raised the pistol again, to the level of Buddy's heart for a sideshot, and squeezed the trigger, once, twice, and then frantically several times more.

"No rounds," said Buddy. "Remember? It is click not boom. Now lie down there by Trac. On your stomachs, hands behind your back and grab your belt." Thuong hesitated. Donner kicked him again in the groin, harder, and, as Thuong grunted and went down, twice more: a careful kick in the kidney, then, after some maneuvering, one in the temple.

"Don't shoot him," Donner hissed. "Whatever you do."

"Rifle shot they'll come running."

"He's gonna figure that out, real soon. Trac too."

"What's Trac doing?"

"Sweating. Grabbing his belt. Knows English."

"Keep him covered. We'll squat a little, then you sort of keel over onto Thuong so I can grab the knife, then we roll up again."

"Getting late. They'll be wondering."

"I know. Okay, over onto Thuong, and… *got it.* Now up."

"Got the knife? That's great."

"I got the knife." Donner's voice quavered, broke. "But what am I gonna do with it? I can't reach the cords!"

"Oh, Jesus."

"Can't reach the fucking cords, so what good is the knife?"

"They're gonna be here. Something's up. All this time, no screaming."

"So scream."

Buddy screamed.

"Good. Keep it up. Louder. Imagine what they'll do to us."

Buddy screamed and screamed.

"Give the knife to Trac, tell him to cut me loose, no no, forget I said that, all right here's what we do. Slow and careful across the road. Cover 'em, don't take the piece off 'em, if you have to shoot one, shoot both. Okay, now I'm holding it by the blade, I'm gonna back you right up against the cutbank, stick the handle in the dirt."

"Don't drop it, Donner. Don't cut yourself."

"Okay, now I'm rubbing the knife against the cords, but I have to go easy because the dirt is crumbling. Knife is sharp, but I have to go slow."

"Jesus. I can't shoot, and you can't cut."

"I'm cutting, I'm cutting." Donner sawed at the cords.

"Jesus."

"Okay, hold on."

"Thuong's coming around."

"Just a minute. There! There! Hah!"

Donner brought his elbows together then jerked them up and apart, and the frayed cord snapped, freeing his wrists enough so that he could jerk them back and forth, and slough off the rest of the cord. Then he yanked the knife from the cutbank, grabbed the handle in his right hand, and brought the blade between them, cutting the cords that bound them at the chest, then hunching his shoulders and dropping to his knees, slipping from Buddy's embrace, twisting, in time to see Thuong now up on all fours and Trac with his hands palm-down at shoulder level on the ground and muscles tensed. Donner dropped the knife and snatched the rifle from Buddy, striding over and kicking Trac in the ribs, bringing the rifle up and then down with all possible force catching Thuong at the base of his skull with the butt, then up and down again, this time between Thuong's shoulder blades, then rushing back, retrieving the knife, cutting Buddy's cords.

"I hear them," said Buddy. "They're coming. I hear something."

"I don't," said Donner. "Oh, Jesus, maybe I do."

"We need some real good screaming, right now."

"Well," said Donner, handing knife and rifle to Buddy, "we got Thuong." Donner rolled the dazed and gasping man onto his back. Straddling Thuong's chest, Donner drove his thumbs deep into the inside corners of the man's eyes, curled his thumbs and scooped out both eyeballs, which then hung from the sockets by shreds of nerve and muscle. Thuong bellowed, rolling in the dust and clawing at his face, eyeballs flailing wetly at his temples. "That's good screaming, Sergeant," said Donner. "Keep it up."

Donner retrieved Thuong's Cutty Sark, took a drink, handed the bottle to Buddy, who also took a drink. Their trembling slowed. The jolting panic eased. Turning to Trac, holding out the quarter-full bottle, Donner said, "Finish this." Trac did, then dropped the bottle and stood, swaying. "Now," said Donner, "get in the truck."

Trac climbed in but fumbled so badly with the seatbelt that Donner went around to the passenger's side and fastened the buckle just as Trac fainted. Climbing out, Donner noticed Trac's musette bag on the floor, in the litter of caked mud and dead leaves and cigarette butts. And, beside the musette, a dirty-white five kilo bag, secured at the top with a twist of rusty wire.

"Yahoo! Rice!"

"Rice? Where?"

"Here," said Donner, grunting, dragging the two bags from the truck. "Our lucky day. Now for Trac. Roll his window up a little bit, pull his head out."

"Like this?"

"That's right," said Donner, joining him. "Now we grab his hair and yank down. One, two, three, yank."

Trac's neck broke with a liquid snap.

"Bottle in the cab. Thuong's hat and sunglasses in the cab. Now the river."

Donner—when had he ever thought this fast in college?—switched on the ignition and depressed the clutch pedal with his hands. Buddy shifted to first, Donner eased out the clutch. The vehicle bucked once and the engine died.

"This time," said Buddy. "Let's take off the brake."

Donner released the hand brake, they repeated the process, and the truck gave a gentle lurch, began rolling down the track toward camp, gaining speed as the downgrade steepened, veering to the right and scraping against the cutbank and sheering off its passenger mirror, slowing, nearly stopping, then clearing the cutbank as the track curved right, then jouncing straight across the ruts and off the road to the left and down the river bank, tumbling twice end over end and finally coming to rest upside down with its rear end in the cocoa colored water and its cab in the mud. No fire.

"It is splash not boom," said Donner.

"Well, gah-ly." Mimicking Donner's Chicago nasals, Buddy raised his hand to shield his eyes and peered down. "Looks like a terrible accident. Probably Trac there couldn't hold his liquor, and you and me and Thuong got thrown into the river and drownded. Especially you and me got drownded, tied together like that. And of course he was too drunk. Bodies are way downstream by now."

"Gonna be a problem for someone."

"Sure will," said Buddy. *"Our* problem is walking out of here. I can barely stand up. No way can we carry those bags."

"So it's lucky we have Thuong," said Donner. "Strong as a buffalo, Thuong, just needs a little direction. If you'll help me take down his trousers, like

25

this, I believe we can cinch this cord around his balls, real *tight,* and then—"

"Really is a screamer, isn't he?"

"He surely is. Now we just haul his pants back up and leave this little piece of cord dangling from his fly. See? Like a bridle. Tug to the right, tug to the left, no problem. Try it. Yank straight up, see what happens. Get him on his feet."

"Worked."

"Like a charm. Musette on his shoulder, rice in his arms. Got the rifle, the pistol, the knife. Let's go."

Buddy pursed his lips, looked down. "There's Huey."

Donner stood for a moment, looking down at the Huey pilot lying on the edge of the gully, conscious now, writhing and working his mouth, locked in the arms of the dead artillery man. In breaking the pilot's gangrenous leg Trac had torn the garbage bag. The stench leaking from these tears was almost palpable. Donner quickly knelt and lay the knife point just below the pilot's left armpit then pushed. As the blade entered his heart the pilot quivered then lay still. Donner rolled them into the gully with his foot. He and Buddy stood for a moment looking down. Then Buddy turned to Thuong. "Let's go, motherfucker," he said, giving the cord a vicious tug.

"Great screamer," said Donner.

"First rate. But." Buddy bent and picked up a fist-sized chunk of rotting tree limb and, yanking Thuong's head back, jammed the wood into Thuong's mouth. "Enough is enough."

They shuffled through the weeds between the dusty wheel ruts, Buddy leading Thuong, stride after stride away from camp. Donner, bringing up the rear, dragged a thorny little branch. Just before sunset they left the track and followed a game trail angling up into the hills. They moved cautiously in the darkness. They stopped to rest, and Buddy said, "Poor Huey."

"Better than the rats."

"What'll they think, search party?"

"Knife wound showing?" Donner asked.

"Couldn't see it in the dark anyway. By morning, well."

"Doubt if they'll climb down and check."

It was at that moment Buddy found the chocolate.

"Well," he said, rummaging in the musette, "what have we here, Thuong?"

"He can't talk too well with that log in his mouth."

27

"I know, but I think he's trying to tell us about the chocolate. Yes, truly. Half a big Hershey. For you and for me. Only a little bit melted. Eat it slow. Suck on it. Ever taste," said Buddy, and his voice cracked, "anything like that?"

"Never. You want some, Thuong?"

"Says, no thanks. Says we can have his."

"So good it hurts."

"Moon's up, lock and load."

Moonlight and a dusting of stars, the smell of wood smoke. But then the soft night thickened with clouds, and a nervous wind gusted up the trail past them, gusted again, steadied and strengthened. Twice Buddy nearly lost his footing. Twice Thuong stumbled and dropped the rice bag.

"Lose that bag, Thuong, and you're dead."

"Lose it, we're all dead," said Buddy. "How far, d'you think?"

"About as far as we're going to," said Donner, noticing as he spoke a looming mass ahead and to their right: a granite outcrop with a yard of overhang. Several large bamboo had lodged against this outcrop, partially concealing it. The wind picked up, humming through the bamboo, twisting the long delicate leaves this way and that. A fat raindrop struck Donner's cheek. "Could creep in there," he said. "Make a little fire, cook some rice."

"Cook some rice," said Buddy. "Cook… some… *rice.*"

Crawling, Donner gathered twigs and dry leaves, assembled them, lit them with Trac's matches, fed the flame with more and bigger twigs. Buddy sloshed water from Trac's canteen into the dead boy's messkit saucepan. Outside the ring of firelight Thuong lay quivering, tightly curled, humming and growling against his wooden gag. While the water heated Buddy undid the wire on the rice bag and poured a little into the saucepan, frowned, tested a handful with his tongue. Donner watched while his friend sagged against the rock. "Hey. Hey, Bud. What is it, moldy? Listen, this is no time to be—"

"Not moldy. Not rice."

Salt. In a rice bag. Why? They'd never know. They crept a little apart, each with his hunger and his disappointment. Donner felt a bitterness at the back of his throat. Absently he fed the fire as the desolation eating through him worked itself to rage. He grabbed the bag, emptied it on the rock, pawed through it: all salt. He upended the musette: box of matches, moldy socks, more wire in a coil, a hank of the same nylon

29

cord that had bound them, a bundle of letters held together by two cracked and faded red rubber bands, a spoon, an envelope containing four photographs—Trac and family, Trac and schoolmates, mongrel bitch with pups, Trac saluting Thuong—a few grubby piastres, one US dollar, six rifle cartridges, two green plastic garbage bags, a dented and scuffed flashlight, an amulet.

Trembling, Donner threw down the empty musette.

"No!" he shouted.

He cut a ten inch length of bamboo, wrapped some of the extra wire around Thuong's right leg above the knee, stuck the bamboo underneath the wire and twisted, hard, once around, twice, three times, then bound the stick in place with more wire. Dull-eyed, Buddy watched him work. Thuong squealed into the gag, arched his back, clutched the wounds where his eyes had been, seeming to understand before Buddy did. But then Buddy got it too.

"Donner!"

There was surprisingly little blood. Donner made a shallow cut along Thuong's calf, then ripped skin from muscle, which he severed at its insertion point behind the knee, then carefully cut away from the bone, and finally sliced free. He held up the calf muscle: a fibrous mass like a little red and white coconut.

"No, Donner."

"Protein."

"Never."

"Well, fuck that." Donner lay the meat on a bamboo windfall and began slicing furiously, dropping slices into the now boiling water. "Die if you want, you dumb shit. Some of the slime you ate in camp." Donner stirred the mixture with Trac's spoon, sliced and added more meat. "Hey, pinch of salt."

"Donner."

"Didn't you ever cut your finger and suck it? You come this far to die on a hilltop? Do that, Thuong'll know. He'll laugh. He's laughing at you now."

Buddy, shaking his head.

But by then the salt water and muscle tissue had begun a transformation. Pungent steam, mostly lost to the wind—but a wisp or two tickled their nostrils and kicked cramps into their stomachs. They watched the broth darken, saw a hint of golden oil droplets at the surface, felt saliva welling.

"We need," said Buddy thickly, "more firewood."

When he returned, the two plates from Trac's mess kit were each half-full of cooling soup. Fortunately they had to share the spoon. They were forced to eat slowly. After the fifth spoonful Buddy looked up. "All that Cutty, Thuong kind of marinated himself, didn't he?"

"Who'd have thought he could be so sweet and tender?"

"Should kill him. Put him out of his misery."

"Can't," said Donner. "No fridge. Got to recuperate."

Buddy nodded. "Long ways to Saigon," he said, drawing the back of his hand across his mouth.

Four days on the hill. Weather turning dank, chill. It rained off and on, so Buddy cut arm and head holes in the two garbage bags. Ponchos. The friends took turns sleeping and standing guard, risking the fire, grateful for its warmth. The soup they simmered for hours, down to a thick bouillon. Buddy, foraging for firewood, also dragged in some dead wrist-thick bamboo. Donner leaned these against the outcropping. They now had a sort of burrow. On the afternoon of the third day Buddy said, "You lifted that bamboo one-handed."

"So I did. How're you feeling?"

"Terrible," said Buddy. "Maybe even awful. Anyway, much better."

"That's good. Thuong, on the other hand, is not."

By the afternoon of day four Thuong had a wire tourniquet above each knee and elbow. Below the wire, lengths of lucent bone swarmed with ants. The once-fat ruddy face was drawn and waxy. Every few seconds a gentle tremor rippled through him. Leeches pulsed and glistened in his eye sockets.

"We should, you know, put him out of his misery," said Buddy.

"If it'll make you happy."

"Got leeches in there sucking on his brain."

"All right," said Donner. "Do him."

"Look like black squirmy eyeballs. It's disgusting."

"So do him," said Donner. "Do unto others. Here's the knife."

"I never killed anybody before, you know. Like that."

"So you want to kill him because that's nice, but I should do it because—"

"Hey, Donner."

"—because *you're* nice?"

Buddy blushed, tried to smile.

"Okay," said Donner, no sarcasm now. "Don't worry about it. Maybe you could pack up the musette. I'll step over, have a word with the sergeant."

Up close Thuong was difficult to look at. So Donner looked at the knife blade while he spoke. "Thuong, Thuong, what in hell you are doing here? You can't see it, but I've got your knife, and I'm going to shove it through your heart. More'n you'd do for us. You fuck. Are you reading me, Thuong?" Just then, Thuong twisted his head toward Donner, and Donner caught a glint of gold. Thuong's jaws still gaped around the wooden plug, lips gnawed back. His teeth, especially the gold incisor, seemed huge.

Well, why not? Donner raised the knife, sliced at Thuong's mouth, wrenched at the gold tooth till it was in his hand. He wrapped the tooth in one of Trac's old socks and stuck it in his pocket. "Bye, Thuong," he said, easing the knife point in under the man's left nipple. Then Thuong did a startling thing: he threw his head and shoulders back and arched his spine like a woman in ecstasy, transfixing himself on the blade and making a high sound.

Half way down the hill Buddy said, "Why the tooth?"

"Don't know," Donner said, and it was true. "Souvenir, maybe." He shook his head, shifted the rifle to his left hand. "We should stay alert here, Bud. Maybe they're still looking, who knows."

They weren't still looking, however. There were three sets of rain-blurred bootprints on the river bank, by the upside-down truck, and Trac's body was no longer in the cab. Buddy and Donner waited out the daylight in the tall grass. That night they found a half-dozen big pieces of drift and lashed them together into a raft that didn't look like one. This they dragged out into the current and clambered onto. The silvery tangle of roots and branches screened them.

They drifted that night and all the next day, hungry and thirsty, speaking little. At dusk they heard the rotor blades for perhaps thirty seconds before the Huey swooped around the bend in the river and blasted overhead. Buddy was ready with the flashlight. When he pressed the button, however, nothing happened. He smacked it into the palm of his left hand and was rewarded with a feeble gleam. Instead of trying an SOS, he swung the flash in an arc above his head. The chopper reared like a suddenly reined-in horse, then eased back and down, close enough so that Buddy and Donner could see the faces staring into their own.

Three minutes, they were aboard, the gunner clambering down and dragging them up the ladder, two trips, the Huey then racing back along the Song Cai to

Nha Trang on the coast. Twice Buddy woke and said, "The camp! Men in the camp!"

And Donner said, "Upriver to the truck."

Two days later, six gunships made a pivot-turn at the upside-down truck and found the camp. First they strafed the hooches. One of the guards, perhaps wounded and enraged, opened up on the prisoners in the compound, killing six of them. Learning of this, Buddy and Donner told each other that half was better than none. They were two days at Nha Trang, a week at the base hospital at Cam Ranh, three weeks in Saigon, a week in Tokyo, at the New Sanno Hotel. R&R, but Donner couldn't rest or relax. He was afraid of everything, afraid of his own fear.

"What are you going to do now?" Buddy asked.

"Don't know," said Donner. "I'm not going back."

"I don't want to go back, either."

"I didn't say, don't want to, Buddy. I said, *won't.*"

Two days later a visitor, a brigadier. Short, thick-waisted, hard-jowled, bald. Late fifties. Eyebrows big and black. Hair covering the backs of his hands and the first two joints of his fingers, bursting from ears and nostrils, curling up past the knot of his tie. Five o'clock shadow, oh nine hundred.

Salutes.

"My name," said the brigadier, "is Tynan. My son was in that camp, a lieutenant, like you men. Took two rounds in the leg."

"How is he, Sir?" asked Donner.

"He'll be all right. He's stateside now. He's out of it."

"So am I, Sir."

"Oh." The brigadier's eyebrows shifted upward very slightly. "I didn't realize you were wounded."

"I'm not, Sir."

"Ah. Well. What are you talking about?"

"General," said Donner. "Did your son tell you about Sergeant Thuong?"

"Mentioned him."

"Thuong didn't make it."

"Can't say I'm sorry."

"No, Sir," said Donner, pouring a cup of thick black coffee for the general. "Nor me. Thuong was a hard man to like. But he was also a hard man to argue with. He said, 'Would you cut off your trigger finger *now,* save your life?' And we all said, yes, and we all meant it. So he said, 'Why you not do that *before* you drafted? Maybe you much smottah now.' And it was true. We're smarter now, much. *I* am, anyway."

"Well, it hasn't been easy. Not for any of us. But you men should know that General Westmoreland has stated positively that the end is in sight. Mr. Komer says the same thing, and Mr. Lodge. There's light at the end of the tunnel."

"I can't see it, Sir," said Donner.

The General sighed. "You sound like John Vann, who is back in Washington right now. Son of a bitch says the light is a freight train coming right at us. What do you think about that? Tried to tell it to the Joint Chiefs, to their faces. What in the world do you think about that?"

"I don't know Mr. Vann, Sir," said Donner.

"Sugar, General?" asked Buddy. "Cream?"

"Who does Vann think he is, anyway? He's not even a colonel anymore. Whose side is he on? I don't see any call for that kind of talk."

Donner looked up sharply. "I don't see any light, Sir."

"Would you really cut off your finger?"

"No question, Sir." said Donner. "A million times I wished I was back at the draft board with a good sharp knife. But then of course it was too late. Now suddenly it's not too late again. I could shoot some Novocain in there first, call some reporters. I know a few."

38

"Pure cowardice, Lieutenant. And it would mean a ruined life."

"I could take you back, General, show you a whole gully-full of those."

"I see. And what about you, Lieutenant Nakamura?"

"Sir, I'm an Army man. But this war, well, we're losing, and that's a fact."

"We're winning, and that's a fact. I could show you the figures, show you the maps, the overlays. It's not wishful thinking. If you had the big picture, you'd know. We've got the data. You can't ignore facts, Lieutenant."

"Yes, Sir."

"We've got the hard data and the firepower."

"Yes, Sir," said Donner. "But then you don't need us."

The General glared at them then sighed once more. "My son owes you, I owe you." Turning to Donner, "You want out? You're out." Turning to Buddy, "You want reassignment? How's Germany?"

"Germany is wonderful, Sir."

"Good morning, gentlemen. As you were."

"Good morning, Sir."

Salutes.

The door not quite slamming.

Standing for some seconds by the table. Eggs and bacon in a pool of sunlight. Orange juice glowing.

"Donner, would you really cut off your finger?"

"No."

"Why not? Are you afraid?"

"Would *you* cut off *your* finger?"

"No," said Buddy. "Might hurt."

"Seriously."

"Seriously," said Buddy. "It wouldn't be right."

"It wouldn't be right. Oh, Buddy."

"Are you afraid to cut off your finger?"

"More coffee?" asked Donner.

"Half a cup. Well, *are* you? Are you afraid?"

"Buddy," said Donner, "we'll stay in touch."

And they had: Buddy through his string of postings and promotions, Donner through his ambitionless globetrotting journalism. Donner gradually came into a little money; Buddy made his own. Donner lifted weights, angrily, took vitamins, had checkups. He finally more or less settled in Japan. He married, bought a house, worried about termites. He went for long resentful runs along the Sakai river. Fearful of his own anger, he seldom questioned himself closely, but he knew, he knew. There was certainty in the tight, sick feeling of his chest: he'd been robbed in some animal way. Part of him, the best part, was still trapped in the jungle. Buddy seemed not to share this vague outrage, which Donner had tried to find words for on several late alcoholic phone calls. Donner quit drinking; his wife began. Donner lost his shakes—at least the ones you could see.

Never closer than a thousand miles for the next twenty-five years, they suddenly found themselves neighbors. Buddy was now commander of the Sagamihara depot camp in Kanagawa, a ten minute walk from Donner's house. They ran together, drank mineral water, went to the *dojo* on Wednesdays and worked on their *kata.* Their wives even got along— Donner the Irishman married to a Japanese; Nakamura married to a freckled and rawboned Scots-Irish MP from Palo Alto. So what more could Donner ask? Because he and Buddy were together, and Buddy was the best friend he ever had and ever would have, and, God damn it, Donner should have been happy.

His waitress is back. She smiles again, reaches toward his still-full bowl, looks at him, concerned: was the soup perhaps no good?

"*Ie,*" said Donner, looking at her tooth. "*Miso-shiru wa daijobu desu.*"

True enough, the soup—then or now—is not the problem. The problem is with Donner, and he knows it without knowing that he knows it: all the vitamins in the world, all the workouts and saunas and *shiatsu* massages, all the desperation and scrambling of those postwar years, will never give him back what he never had much of anyway, his courage. It's locked inside there, frozen, with himself.

Friday, 12:25 P.M.

Pity the poor *chinpirra,* lowest of the low, not even a *yakuza* at all, really—just a sort of would-be apprentice, striving always to perfect his menacing slouch, his malevolent stare, his overall junior gangster style. Which would set him apart from the thousands of other *chinpirra.* Which might cause him to be noticed.

Pity Uchiyama Masaaki, of the Araddin pachinko parlor in Asagaya, because nobody ever noticed him. No underboss, or even under-underboss. Uchiyama's immediate superior, Suzuki Makoto, is little more than a *chinpirra* himself. Of course, the pachinko parlor is *yakuza*-owned, everybody knows that, even the stupid schoolboys who loiter there and give the place such a bad name, but Uchiyama has never seen an actual *yakuza*—only, now and then, their sleek black Lincolns and Mercedes ghosting in and out of the Araddin's parking lot. The men behind the smoked windows of those cars had paid no attention to *him.*

But they should have. They should have noticed, asked around, made an effort to comprehend some of Uchiyama's true potential. They have no idea what is right under their noses, because Uchiyama is no ordinary punk. He has The Look: thin, wiry body—short, but he wears those elevator shoes with the pointy toes—thin lips and western-looking eyelids and very little forehead, punchpermed hair, tight black trousers and shirts, wraparound sunglasses. Real Foster Grants. Hardly any pimples anymore, just on his cheeks and forehead, and mostly not the huge purple kind. In fact, Takeshi, who is very good-looking himself, once told Uchiyama that he'd be quite handsome with just a little more chin.

Yes, he has The Look, and he has the moves. True, he can't enlarge his chin, but he can and does make the most of it by keeping it up and sneeringly to the right and speaking in a sinister near whisper. No question, he's intimidating. He has, well (and his mirror tells him that it's true), *presence.* He also has a knife, and a solid gold ring in the shape of a skull with two ruby eyes. Anybody gives him trouble, he'll punch them out, and that ring will be the last thing they'll see for quite a while. And smoking, always smoking. Like James Dean, Uchiyama Masaaki is a rebel. So Uchiyama smokes Deans, and he smokes them in a special way, a way that is his trademark. Lighting up, he never looks at cigarette or lighter. Then he leaves the cigarette in the corner of his mouth, contemptuously, scorning to squint against the smoke.

Scorning also to notice the swarms of schoolboys. These infest the Araddin, horsing around in the bright gold-and-glass cavelike entranceway, or, if they actually happen to have a few hundred yen, playing the stupid video games and ignoring the real pachinko machines in the main hall. Video games are not life. The schoolboys don't realize this, but he, Uchiyama Masaaki, very definitely does. He understands life as few understand it. So the schoolboys are not even an annoyance, really, because they are so far beneath his notice. He leans against the big plastic harem girl, not noticing them. Disdainfully he jets smoke from his nostrils, glancing up every thirty seconds or so from the thick *manga* adventure comic book in his hands, keeping his eyes half-closed and his gaze on the middle distance, alert for trouble.

Alert and ready for it, eager, impatient. Today as always, however, there is not the faintest indication of anything like trouble. Today as always, the Araddin is depressingly tranquil, if you don't count the raucous schoolboys, as Uchiyama definitely doesn't. Just the soft, boring *pachinpachinpachin* of the machines. Is it his fault that trouble never comes his way? Hardly.

45

Probably the sheer menacing force of his personality keeps it always at a distance. But how frustrating! He wishes that anybody—yes, even the nothing schoolboys—could see him in action. But there is never any action.

Sighing, his coffee break now over, he flips his Dean into the street and, comic under his arm and fists jammed into front trousers pockets, ambles back over to the *sendenkaa,* the sound truck, trying not to look at it. His lot in this bitter life, until he is finally noticed and rewarded for the courage and zeal which are his, is to drive this vehicle all over the Asagaya district of western Tokyo, ten hours a day, seven days a week, while the taped message blares away from the speakers on top and slowly destroys his fine mind.

MAIDO ARIGATO GOZAIMASU! ARADDIN PACHINKO WA TOTEMO TANOSHI DESUYO! MINA SAMA! KYO ASONDE KUDASAI! MAIDO ARIGATO! A thousand thanks, honored people, and please come play pachinko at the Araddin, and we'll all have fun, fun, fun

Over and over, an endless loop—and *loud,* way above the legal decibel limit for *sendenkaa,* but what good are the police? They know who's really in charge. Hasn't he, Uchiyama, made several dozen calls to the police, cleverly disguising his voice, complaining about his own *sendenkaa?* To be told, naturally, that there was nothing they could do. Well, true enough. And the message, the message. That hysterical female voice with the horrible tune from Mary Poppins jangling. Earplugs, no good. Nor those big plastic earmuffs that shooters wear. Nothing helps. Uchiyama Masaaki has never told anyone, not even Takeshi, that now, after two years of that tape, he hears it all the time. When he's working and when he isn't. Waking and sleeping. The tape is embedded in every cell of his brain. He'll never be rid of it, not until he dies. If then. Is it any wonder he drinks?

Oh yes, he hates this sound truck more than any other single thing in the universe. It is a Nissan S-Cargo, and it does indeed look like a snail. Suzuki Makoto purchased it and is very proud of his choice. And, yes, it is roomy in back, plenty of headroom, excellent gas mileage. It is also perfect, as Suzuki Makoto often points out, for transporting *hanawa,* those huge artificial floral wreaths on tripods displayed at parlor openings and at funerals. And so forth. Granted, it's a totally practical machine. *But it looks like a fucking snail*—round-backed, bug-eyed, rose-hued, absurd, the very last vehicle Uchiyama would have chosen to drive. A clownmobile.

What would he have chosen? A Cadillac! A Benz! Or even a Rolls! Huge, jet black, no chrome. No chrome on the car at all, except for the hubcaps and the hood ornament. And windows tinted just as black. He could see out—except why would he want to, who was there to notice?—but nobody could see in, disturb his privacy. And he would sit in the back wearing his million yen mohair suits from Seibu, and his Foster Grants. He'd be talking on the telephone—do this do that—he'd light a Dean with his solid gold lighter, and the rotten schoolboys would finally start to realize the true facts. Because he'd be a boss, maybe even the *oyabun* himself. And he'd get respect.

Not like now, when everyone laughs at him. Yes they do, and Uchiyama knows it. They laugh at the *sendenkaa,* and they laugh at him, never looking beyond the appearances of life, never taking him seriously for one minute, never considering that he too just might have human feelings which could be hurt. To everyone else in the world he is a joke. They don't know he knows it, but he knows that and a lot more besides. The time will come, though, when they will laugh no more. Once one of the schoolboys actually called him a *bakayaro,* and what did Suzuki Makoto do? Laughed too! Said take it easy, they're just children, not to mention customers. Bought him a can of Pocari Sweat, said relax, forget it.

Relax! Forget it!

Uchiyama, hearing a snicker behind him, whirls. But the schoolboys are innocently at their video games. Except, as he well knows, they aren't. He takes another step toward the S Cargo and the laughter sounds again, softly. Feeling his neck hot, the rage building, he walks stiffly to the little truck, not looking at it, not looking at the horrible pink cuteness of it with Snoopies dressed up like Arabs and plastered all over the doors and back panels. He gets in. As he drives away the schoolboys appear at the Araddin entrance, arms around each other's shoulders, squeaking out the Mary Poppins refrain. They do this every afternoon. It's the high point of their day. How he pities them. Uchiyama sees the schoolboys in the rearview mirror, but pretends he doesn't. He won't give them the satisfaction. But if could he'd kill them all.

Flipping his *manga* comic into the back with the hundreds of others, giving the ignition key a vicious twist with his right hand, Uchiyama Masaaki gropes with his left for the can of Pocari Sweat—which, little did they know, really contains pure vodka!—raises it to his lips, and treats himself to a healthy slug. He revs the tiny engine, popping the clutch and squeaking the rear tires, lurching out onto the road, heading west. Dreading, loathing, hating, despising. The afternoon run is never less than brutal, especially now, in simmering autumn. Heat coming off the cars and trucks and buses in waves. Hondas and Toyotas and buildings and people all jammed together and turning gray together in the sooty unbreathable fumes. All the way down to Kichijyoji station then all the way back to Asagaya, fighting the noontime crowds and later the five o'clock rush, taking every possible detour. Looking like a snail, moving like one.

Is today worse than usual, or does it just seem like it? *Maido arigato gozaimasu,* stop start, stop start, and wouldn't you know, the Yamazaki Bread van in front of him pulls over and its blinkers come on. The son of a bitch has just parked, in the middle of the fucking road, while he runs around back and humps his trays of bread into the 7-11 store, does the paperwork, maybe has a coffee and a smoke with the counterman, they're laughing in there all right, having a good time. Well, that's just what Uchiyama needs when he's so far behind schedule anyway. He can't get around the truck, though, can he? There's nothing he can do, except have another sip of vodka and try to calm down. But when the van finally zips around the corner and down a side street, the S-Cargo is still stuck, behind a bus, and the whole line of traffic is backed up at a red light.

Is this a road or a parking lot?

Seething, Uchiyama drinks vodka and looks around. Across from the 7-11, to his right and just ahead, is a temple, standard model. Green copper roof in a peak, demons by the entrance, gong, swept mud. And the cemetery. Big dark family stones, wooden *sotoba* markers sticking up like giant tongue depressors. What's the point? You're dead, you're dead. Superstitious assholes putting down flowers, lighting incense, leaving glasses of sake on the tombs. Waste of good liquor. Uchiyama has another drink. Some old guy—a priest?—praying with a couple rich guys, clapping their hands, bowing. What are they praying for, more money? They need it, with that Benz, and the chauffeur. Look at those suits. What do they know about being poor? What do they know about anything?

Uchiyama could tell them a few things about poverty. Working like a slave in his father's *sakana-*

ya, always smelling like a god damned fish, and for what? Cigarette money, and everything else into the special tuition account. University. How wonderful, he could go to the university and stay bored shitless for three or four years and then go back to the fish shop for the rest of his life. Work right alongside the old man, listen to him. No thanks. His father, a real *bakayaro,* completely unsophisticated, doesn't care about prestige or the emperor or anything except the fish shop, although even Uchiyama's little pink truck is better than the *sakana-ya,* as anyone with half a brain would realize. Well, the old man is old.

Nearly as old as that shiny pink old clown kissing his magic charm. Praying for hair? Old-timers, who can figure them out? Uchiyama checks his own hair in the rearview. Perfect: Michael Jackson, a little Elvis, but curlier. The girls like that. Though to tell the truth Uchiyama doesn't give a damn about what girls like or don't like, or about girls, period, because, face it, that's what they are. Always sort of soft and damp and unrealistic. (Once he touched Miki's breast purely by accident, and it felt squashy and gassy, like the belly of a cat.) Never stop giggling, never shut up. They come into Araddin after school too, shrieking, and in

Uchiyama's opinion they are worse than the schoolboys.

Both are the exact opposite of Takeshi, who is already assistant manager of the Convenience Mart and Uchiyama's special friend. Well, not friend, exactly, but sometimes Uchiyama comes into the store very late, maybe for a hot can of Boss coffee. He and Take-*kun* smoke together, silently, on either side of the counter, saying nothing because at such times words are not necessary. The two young men understand each other, know their destinies if there were any justice in the world. Take-*kun* would become president of the Convenience Mart chain someday. Uchiyama would begin his rise through the ranks of the *yakuza* just as soon as his leadership qualities came to the attention of his superiors. This is understood. Uchiyama feels the powerful bond between them. Two winners, smoking quietly, looking out at the street. Separated by the counter but still close. They use the same ashtray. That means something. And they both smoke Deans.

Finally the light changes, finally he can get moving, get on with it, get on with his god damned life—what now? The bus creeps over to the curb because it's a god damned fucking bus stop about two meters from the traffic light, that's great planning, and of course there's about twelve old farts from the lawn bowling club, and they take about five minutes each to climb in, good, all aboard, finally, the door closes, maybe we can actually get through the light.

No.

The door is opening again and this tiny *obaasan* is climbing down, six hundred years old, almost completely dead, all crippled and bent over like a pretzel. No teeth, face like a walnut down there around her knees, maybe three hairs on her head. Doesn't she know how bad she looks? Or doesn't she care? Why are they allowed out in public? Creaking this way slowly, slowly. Missed the light again, so take your time, old crock. Hobble around behind the bus, that's it—no, better not start across the street, because the light is about to change. Well, she *does* start across, and the light *does* change, and the bus moves off, and here's this crazy old piece of shit crossing against the light but stopping right in front of the S-Cargo. She's looking it right in the headlight. Is she grinning? Is she laughing? Is she standing there doubled up and laughing, god damn it?

"Get out of the fucking way, you crazy old bitch!"

That's it, the last straw, he doesn't have to put up with this. Uchiyama Masaaki hits the horn, pounds with his fist on the dash, leans far out his window cursing the old woman over the *MAIDO ARIGATO GOZAIMASU, ARADDIN PACHINKO WA,* and then Uchiyama, shaking with fury, drops back into his seat and further enrages himself by knocking his Pocari Sweat can of vodka from the console to the floor, and so punches the roof three times, full force, before he finally loses patience completely and scrambles across to and climbs half out of the passenger window, the S-Cargo bouncing and leaning this way and that, and screams at the old woman and hammers on the passenger door with all his might. Here it is, then, *trouble,* and he's ready for it, because they think he'll take anything, but he won't, how wrong they are, and soon the world will notice him, understand that he, Uchiyama Masaaki, exists, and they'll appreciate him, realize their big mistake, when he's finally got their terrified attention.

"Rotten old whore! Rotten old bitch! Rotten old whore-bitch!"

Across the street, in the act of raising to his lips again the golden amulet, the dignified and priestlike old man, tall, full-bodied, shaven-headed, permits himself a faint frown, then turns his head slightly to behold the *sendenkaa,* then slowly turns his head back the other way, regarding the slender and elegant man to his right and raising almost imperceptibly his left eyebrow. In six strides the slender man is beside their automobile, is being handed the telephone by the stiffly bowing chauffeur, is jabbing at it with his forefinger.

Finally, *finally,* Uchiyama Masaaki gets moving, still trembling with rage. The carpeting is squishy with vodka. There is a little left in the can, and savagely he drains it. He should be at the train station by now, of course, and making his turn, but he's only just coming up on Joshi Dai Mae—huge high wall, trees, shiny white buildings like it's maybe heaven—where all the rich little bitches go to school, and play tennis in the sun with their University of Tokyo boyfriends, and live happily ever after. Probably they all laugh at him too. Sure they do, but, frankly, Uchiyama doesn't care about their opinions. Because, one, they're girls, and, two, they're all stinking rich.

Therefore what do they know—about reality, about life? If they happen to want *go man* yen, what do they do? Get a job, do a little *arubaito* like a normal person? Fuck no. They just say to their fat daddies, who never had to work in a fish shop, who are all high school principals and *butchos* and sales managers, "*Oto-san,* could I please have some money?" And that's all there is to it—never mind the millions of honest people who have to sweat night and day and work like dogs for every single yen, which the government taxes out of them anyway and gives to places like this where nobody does anything but read English books and flirt around with foreign teachers who know nothing at all worth knowing, and have fun. They have parties and dances and concerts, and they think that's life, they really believe they're better than he is, because all Uchiyama ever got from *his* old man were cuts all over his hands and the stink of fish. The *sakana-ya*—that was *his* university. How he hates, hates, hates all the rich little bitches, spoiled and rotten.

There's one now, leaving the restaurant, waving to her friends across the road by the gate, laughing, thinking how beautiful she is, tall and graceful with her long glossy hair and designer clothes and probably Italian shoes and handbag with the tennis racket handle sticking out of it, *of course,* and gold ear-hoops sparkling in the sun. Now she's starting across the road—like it's *her* road, which maybe someone gave her for her birthday. She's smiling, her friends are smiling, the guard at the gate is smiling. Well, maybe it's time to wipe those smiles right off their faces, have a little fun himself.

Donner, hunched and tense as always, moreso after his worst Namwarp in years, emerges from the restaurant into the noon glare and the sudden snarl of a small engine at high revs and a blur of pink as a strange little truck races past and toward a student screaming with her hands up in the middle of the road, and there is the smell and feel and sound of tires locked and burning against the pavement as the little truck or van swerves to a stop just inches from the screaming girl, and there is the driver, a god damned zit-crusted punk, red in the face and laughing, laughing with his eyes squeezed shut and head thrown back, and the Donner who has become Donner gets blasted by a huge red rage, and even before the truck stops completely Donner finds himself moving, head down, charging the thing, attacking it and hitting it with his shoulder, slamming into it sincerely and pushing it up on two wheels then scrabbling, scrabbling, getting his fingers under the rocker panel on the driver's side and then just straining up with everything he has and more, *willing* the thing up and over with back and thighs and a huge grunting exhale, beating the awful weight of it, lifting, shouting with the raw crazy effort of the lift, tilting the god damned thing, feeling finally a sweet subtle shift in the center of gravity, and then the truck sways for a second, begins to topple over on its side while Donner screams from deep in his belly and gives the truck a push, hearing the very final-sounding, metal-against-concrete *crump.*

MAIDO ARIGATO GOZAIMASU! MINA SAMA, ARADDIN PACHINKO OH ASOBI-NI ITTE KUDASAI!

More or less back in control already and taking deep deliberate breaths, Donner regards the pop-eyed and spittle-foaming punk trying to climb out of his seat harness and through the passenger window. Donner yearns to grab fistfuls of greasy hair and give a strong enough yank to snap the punk's neck. Instead, he leans close, nose-to-nose almost, feeling Thuong's tooth on its chain swing free of his ruined shirt, seeing it bounce glistening against his tie. Alcohol sweetness billows from the cab. He gives the kid his very worst smile.

"Hi there," says Donner. "Have a nice week-end."

Donner hears high relieved laughter gusting around him and sees the punk's eyes roll back in his head, the

59

kid apparently going into some sort of seizure and subsiding back into the cab. As Donner walks through the gate with the still-trembling student and her friends, the guard says to no one in particular but loudly, *"Sugoi!* Lose control, has tip his truck! *Taihen deshyo."* And they all laugh and say, That's it, *sho ga nai,* tough luck. "Because," says the guard, "I had seen him many time so drunk."

"Yopatta," Donner agreed. *"Zannen desu ne?* Isn't it a shame?"

Late for class, Donner lingers inside the gate as three gleaming and immaculate police cars finally ease up, and six perfect police officers drag the thrashing punk from the cab of his little pink truck which looks like a snail, and handcuff him doubled over and retching, wild-haired and hoarsely gibbering. Donner listens as each officer in turn earnestly explains to the others why his own pristine vehicle is not appropriate for transporting the *yopparai.* They shake their heads and start to fill out forms, muttering, disgusted.

But Donner himself, how about him? He's late for class, disheveled, bathed in cooling sweat. He stinks. His shirt is a write-off, but never mind the shirt, it's the suit he's concerned about. His favorite, a rich tan with red and blue pins to give it life, Italian wool, put together five years ago by the best tailor in Seoul. Four fittings. Well, it appears that the jacket is ripped at midseam, between his shoulder blades. Also at the left armpit. And where is the middle button? Ah, in his hand. Both jacket and trousers will need special cleaning, too. Dust, grease, crud. So what's his reaction to that? Furthermore, his right shoulder is throbbing, and his lower back feels like hot concrete. He'll be half-paralyzed tomorrow, may be gimping around for a week. How does that make him feel? And are his hands sore? And is the nail on his right index finger broken and bleeding? And is middle-aged Donner shivering from some kind of shock, numb and aching at the same time, but grinning? Grinning like a fool? Yes, and yes again. Though you'd think he should feel pretty bad.

Friday, 6:26 P.M.

In the considered opinion of Colonel Franklin Delano "Buddy" Nakamura, F.X. Donner, the Colonel's best friend for three decades, has always been a bit of a flake. Nor is Donner mellowing with age—the reverse, if anything. Hype, hyper, hypest. And stranger. But subtly. No, it's not just the constant yapyapyap with Ruriko, who puts away her share of the gin, true enough, but married to him that's understandable. The scrapping is a symptom, however. Of what? Wired too tight, looks like he's cold most of the time. Basically a loose cannon on the deck. You'd have to know him as long as Buddy to realize just how loose.

Like that business today with the van. Pure Donner. Perk along okay for a few years, everything superorganized, lists and schedules and every waking second accounted for, right on track, neurotic as hell but rational, then boomo. Out of the blue, something like that. Because of his domestic situation? Because now he's a quote unquote professor? Because of Nam? Buddy isn't buying. Donner was Donner before the classroom, before the war. Thing is, he doesn't need a reason. Donner: a closet flake in Flake City.

Hey, read the papers—the *Mainichi,* the *Times,* whatever. Weirdies creeping and slithering out of their closets every day. The commies, trying to blow up the Emperor every couple months—never mind that communism is dead everywhere else in the world except maybe certain ritzy areas of Beijing, these people haven't got the word. Then of course there's your fascists, blowing up anybody who might *criticize* the Emperor, suggest that his daddy might have had something to do with wasting vast multitudes fifty years ago. And let's not forget the gangsters, and the kid-killers, and all the religious gonzos like you wouldn't believe. Donner wrote a piece about the gonzos, and it was better than his usual magazine stuff. Buddy actually enjoyed it. Waco wackos? Nothing on Tokyo.

Special clubs here, superexclusive, *big* yen to get in, guys can dress up like Shirley Temple and sit around sipping lemonade, bat their eyelashes at each other. Great. And slasher porn, video supermarkets full of the stuff, fun and games for the whole family. And those big fat comics where the hero gets to put everyone else in a meat grinder, nipples and organs and G-strings all over the place, baseball bats in various unlikely orifices, blood and more blood.

Manga, they call them. Sick stuff. The sort of thing you wouldn't bring into a Saigon cathouse, selling like mad here. Umpteen million salarymen slaves with their noses buried in that shit every day of their lives, riding the trains, drooling.

So sick. Just like New York or L.A. Nothing different about Tokyo. A little more discreet is all. That sadoporn shit, supposed to make them *less* weird, *less* crazy. Sublimate out all those dark urges, become shiny and wholesome, a real asset to society. Social science, Buddy has to laugh. Deviance is okay. Gang wars, any kind of aggression, is normal, healthy. Evil is good. Well, Buddy isn't buying. Professors. Broadcasting bullshit blithely. Why? No payback. They don't have to take any consequences. But someone does. And every wacko that comes out of his closet, every one you read about, there's more that don't. Thousands.

Still, most people, East or West, what you see is what you get. Pretty well. They're consistent, the same all the way through. Not Donner. He's layered, like an onion. Top layer is his charm, considerable but very thin, and beneath the charm is all that impatience because everything has to be perfect and right now, and beneath these is the very thick layer of rage and fear that surfaced in the camp, but way deep, down near the center, the rage and fear give way to a sort of black amusement at life, and, finally, right at the heart of Donner, is a sort of homicidal indifference, a void.

Or so Buddy imagines. Maybe not, however. It's all pretty fanciful, and Buddy's no shrink. But get behind all the fussiness and tics and twitches and compulsions, and then you better watch out. Donner's a killer. That's not theory. That's fact, and a very good point to keep in mind when dealing with him.

Nakamura himself, professional warrior and so forth, sort of helped kill Trac, the little driver, but never killed anyone else except in combat, and maybe not even then, because there's nothing quite as confusing as combat, and, anyway, they used to fudge those kill ratios outrageously. Called it Creative Writing 101. Buddy has to laugh. If you believed the kill ratios, there were a couple hundred thousand Wyatt Earps in khaki stalking around in the Delta, which, face it, wasn't the case at all. But it was the case with Donner—who surely is not an evil man. In the right circumstances, however, or rather the wrong ones—what? The necessary thing, that's it. Donner does the necessary, no hesitation. Instinct, an extra chromosome. Donner always has one more option than most people. Push him too far, he'll rip out your heart and eat it.

A natural killer and a weirdo, going around imitating a college professor these days, and Nakamura thinks it's pretty funny. Sure, Donner disgraced himself in the camp, lost it completely, an officer yet, weeping and sobbing most of the time which really got on Buddy's nerves. *But* it was Buddy who gave up. Forget all the blubbering, concentrate on the essential point. It was Donner who got them out of there, saved their lives. Maybe the Brigadier was right about him: no balls. Maybe Donner even agrees. But Buddy doesn't think it's that simple. Nothing is simple with Donner—he stood up to the Brigadier, didn't he? A lieutenant eyeball-to-eyeball with a general officer: *I don't see the light.* No, Buddy has given Donner a lot of thought over the years, and this is his conclusion: it all depends on which layer, which *Donner*, you're dealing with. Which Donner, which situation.

Something like that would account for the latent flakiness. But, what the hell, Donner makes sense most of the time. Also, he doesn't look all that bad, if he'd just shave off that stupid beard and stand up straight like a man and quit shuffling around all the time like he just caught one in the grapes. Bad back, all right,

Buddy'll give him that, but why the bad back? Attitude. Brain all knotted up, back muscles all knotted up. That's the long and short of it. But don't try that psychosomatic stuff on Donner.

Still, credit where credit is due. Donner has a hell of a nice slender build, strong, good proportions. Nakamura, by contrast, is no longer slender. Hasn't been, since the camp. Well, he's fleshed out in twenty years, gotten a bit thick-waisted. Some people—Janey—might say obese. But so what? Most guys fill out with age. Besides, he's six-four and carries the weight well and still looks damn good in his uniform. Imposing. Buddy's father and grandfather were imperial marines, right there in the palace guard, the toughest of tough guys, and his more remote ancestors had all been soldiers of one kind or another. Far back as the records went. *Samurai.* It's funny, posted here in the good old homeland, looking like some giant economy size native, but having nothing more in common with them than a bunch of Martians. Polite, smiling, skinny little rascals—except for those sumo guys with their giant asses hanging out of their diapers, he has to laugh—whereas Buddy Nakamura is none of the above. Flab? Okay, sure, but by God he still knows how to hold himself like a man. How to stand, move, walk.

How to run.

"Where we headed?" asks Donner. "How far?" They are southwest of Tokyo, moving along the north bank of the Tama, below Noborito. It's their favorite route. They'll do a few more miles, to the storm drain or a little beyond, then double back to Buddy's car, meet Janey and Ruriko in from shopping at the big downtown stores, Shinjuku or Ginza, then the four of them will go someplace for dinner if Ruriko isn't too smashed. They'll head back to Kanagawa after the rush hour. Their Friday routine. "Storm drain?" says Donner. "What're we running to?"

"Flab," says Buddy.

"That's a pretty good joke," says Donner, looking out over the river.

"You didn't laugh, however."

"No," says Donner, his stride stiff and jerky, "but I'm thinking about it. Maybe I will, if you don't do your cannibal joke. *Mm*-mh, *lookin' good, sweetheart,* when you see a fat chick. That one, especially. I'm tired of it."

"Cannibalism isn't funny."

"My point," says Donner. "And anyway we never ate him. Just *parts* of him. Not the same thing at all, really. Like his calves, which is basically veal."

"Hey, you don't laugh at my jokes, I won't laugh at yours. But why don't, you take off, that stupid tooth? I hate it." Buddy is huffing audibly now. "I said, I hate the fucking, tooth."

"I heard you. I wear it as a reminder."

"Of what?"

"I forget."

"You wear it, for amusement," says Buddy. "So you, can say stuff, like that. Think it's amusing, wear a dead man's tooth. What do you, *talk* to it? Say, Ha ha, Thuong, got the last laugh? You think it's funny. Well, you're wrong." Buddy's face is a furnace, sweat-slick, his breathing harsh. "I said, you're, wrong. I said, the tooth is, not funny."

"I heard you."

"Lots, of things, aren't funny." Buddy, puffing and scowling.

"You're right. I'll make a list. Everything isn't funny, I'll put it in there."

"Then, here's something, for your list. Should go, right, at the top. Old guys, tipping over kiddy cars, scaring the shit, out of people."

69

"How'd you hear about that?"

"I heard about it," says Buddy. "Don't worry."

"How'd you hear about it?"

"I *heard* about it. Tip the thing over, coulda landed on somebody, gas tank coulda blown. Did that, ever cross, your mind? Back's fucked already, so you say. Did you think, that would help it? I notice, that your stride, is pretty ragged"

"Minor stiffness."

"You're limping."

"And you're practically having a heart attack. You are digging your grave with your fork. Cholesterol. *And* booze. *And* cigarettes."

"Don't smoke," says Buddy. "Quit. Three days. Not one. Cigarette."

"All that sweat? It's your body trying to get rid of the poison."

"Not one. Few puffs. That's all. Race you to the gingko tree."

Race. Donner snickers. Can that lardass make it as far as the tree?

At this point, the river path below the retaining wall and the highway above it converge and run parallel for about three hundred yards, past the old, carefully twine-wrapped and pruned and propped-up gingko tree, past the storm drain channel with its bridge. Around them are the last of the day's picnickers, Frisbee-throwers, grade school excursionists. There are the usual shutterbugs snapping the autumn lilies and the bridge and the sunset river and each other. Buddy and Donner come abreast of the wall, its concrete blocks set meticulously in a diamond pattern, course after course, up to a height of perhaps thirty feet and topped with a metal railing now edged with red-gold from the setting sun. The wall is to their right. Suddenly, Donner and Buddy are in cool shadow. In a sort of sound shadow too. That is, they can feel vibrations, but the horns and engines and whine of the tires overhead seem remote, like a train whistle wind-borne across some midnight vastness. Also, from their angle the traffic is invisible.

"Thing is, Donner, you're dangerous, you're a flake. Don't you ever stop—"

"Okay, to the gingko. Take you that far just to stop all the meat."

"—ever stop, and *think?*"

"Go."

71

Up above, Kawakami Yukio, a prominent member of Japan's new ultra-right, is racing along on his beautiful Kawasaki motorbike. Yukio's thoughts are vengeful and bloody. How, he asks himself for the thousandth time, could his tiny country harbor so many traitors? The mayor of Nagasaki saying in public, *on television,* that some responsibility for Japan's involvement in World War II must be borne by those then prominent in the Showa court! Why not just come out and accuse the *Emperor?* That mayor earned his bullet in the back. And Yukio's own father, the so-called historian—well, Yukio doesn't want to think about the old man. And what's his name, the Minister of Education, who wanted to put the same kind of treasonous garbage in a high school *textbook.* Till he found himself hacked to bits on the steps of the Diet building—hacked to death, with, as a matter of fact, the same sacred *katana* which Yukio now draws from its scabbard as he catches sight of his quarry's wide back.

Kawakami Yukio's quarry is a fat and famous history professor, a radical, Yamamoto Koichiro, waddling along behind his short fat wife—necessarily behind her, because they are too thick-bodied to proceed side-by-side on the narrow walkway—talking,

72

laughing, looking down at the river at the sunset, enjoying themselves in the open air and thick exhaust fumes as they do almost every evening in good weather. The wife carries a fat-looking child on her back, *ombu*-fashion. The professor carries in his arms a fat foreign dog.

Yukio cannot see the dog, but knows that it is there, a dachshund or some such, gross-bodied and senile, for all practical purposes legless, nestled like some nightmarish infant between the professor's meaty breasts, occasionally lowered to the sidewalk for a piss against the green metal railing or a large thorough shit on Yukio's country. All that loathsome tissue, pampered and pink, undulating along ahead of Yukio. A parade of decadence. A vile symbol of everything wrong with postwar Japan.

What would the *shogun* have thought of such a family? Yukio snorts, cranks on the accelerator. How long would they have lasted with the Fujiwaras? As a matter of fact, the *katana* which he now brings aloft is a Fujiwara blade, and famous, once the personal weapon of the favorite nephew of Yoritomo himself, a sword of legend, nearly a thousand years old. The one they called *Mitsumasa.* Bright Justice.

How appropriate.

Justice is flashing down upon Yamamoto Koichiro, that diseased pear of a man with his jelly waistline slopping over all around his enormous belt—what a contrast with Yukio! Whose own waistline is sixty-eight centimeters, never more, whose belly is ridged and rippling with corded muscle from his daily five hundred sit-ups on the inclined board. Yes, how utterly different in all things. Is there room enough in Japan for both of them? Yukio thinks not. He thinks the professor might agree—though probably not with Yukio's conclusion.

There, closer every second, unmistakable, the squashy back and bald head with its fringe of greasy hair straggling over his collar. Degenerate, perverse, obscene Yamamoto, woman-hipped, far-left-of-center. Kosei University hotshot, well-known and soon though very briefly to be much moreso. And smart as smart could be—but not smart enough! These geniuses, they never learn, it seems, because Yamamoto's new World War Two book is full of the same slanders and half-truths that transformed the Education Minister into human *sashimi* and will have the same effect on Yamamoto himself in about fifteen seconds.

Why? Two excellent reasons. First, simply to get rid of Yamamoto, irresponsible at best, because Japan will be much better off without him. Second, to make his, Yukio's, mark in the Organization. If he were completely honest, this second reason is nearly as important as the first, and Yukio has to admit the electric thrill he felt when fat Yamamoto's fat book hit the stands: *here was Yukio's golden opportunity,* to distance himself from the microphone men—that whole soft flock of strutting, posturing, orating New Rightists—and achieve instant recognition.

And distinction. Because Yukio is a leader, not a follower, wise beyond his thirty-three years, and bold, and a patriot of the sort that seems to be dying out— even, let's be honest, within the Organization itself. Had he gone through channels, proposed the execution at a formal meeting, done everything by the book, what would have happened? Maybe they'd actually do something, put a bullet in the ceiling—what was *that* supposed to prove?—like that foolishness with Hosokawa. But probably they wouldn't. It would be talk and more talk, his enemies finding fault with the idea, picking it apart, doing their coward best to scuttle it and him. Debates, resolutions back and forth, millions of words. Result? Zero.

Or, if they actually sanctioned the killing, there was no guarantee that the honor would be Yukio's.

There are, after all, more senior men. And they would have talked too, about tactics and contingencies and weather conditions and timing, shut Yukio out, then as likely as not decided at length that the timing was bad, it was too late, Yamamoto was *passé,* and the herd of little yes-men would agree, finally, that it was best to refrain, and then, savoring this consensus and glowing with a sense of accomplishment, they would all have trooped contentedly back to their black sound trucks blaring martial music, back to their beloved microphones.

Well, Yukio is tired of microphones, tired of all the booming, empty words. It is pure noise. So he took the initiative, consulted no one, determined to act. Actions speak louder than words, as the Americans say, and his action this afternoon would speak loud and clear to the Organization and to the nation, would signal a major change in attitude. In the future, big issues and questions would be less muddled with greed and cowardice. Japan would be less mired in the squalid daily money-grubbing clown-act of Democracy. In the future, great issues would be honorably addressed, clearly defined, sharper—as sharp as the *Mitsumasa* which now holds above his head, naked and gleaming in the rich sunset-light.

The *Mitsumasa* which, granted, his Organization does not realize is in his possession. Oh yes, he is taking a fearful chance, but when he has cleansed the nation of Yamamoto, and cleansed the sacred blade of traitor's blood with a silken cloth, and returned blade and cloth together as is their way, remarking softly that he thought they need concern themselves no further about Yamamoto Koichiro, then he would see the faces of his enemies blanche with envy. Yukio would be a made man. The Organization would take on a new vitality, would participate in the life of Japan with a virile new aggressiveness. And he, Kawakami Yukio would become at a stroke someone to be reckoned with, a mover and a shaper, a figure for the next century's history books. Books that would be written with—Yukio would see to it—a proper regard for *moral* truth.

Six times Yukio sat entranced through the movie *Black Rain,* deeply impressed especially by the scene wherein the motorcyclist-avenger—a common *yakuza,* but a man who knew how act—closed with his victim, touched *katana*-tip to pavement and drew sparks just before the decapitation. Yukio knows that the sparks were a little bit of Hollywood; no one with a proper respect for the blade would dream of desecrating it in

77

that way. But the rest of the scene he considers a primer for the perfect assassination: silent lightning-blade, motorcycle for a split-second attack and escape, helmet and leathers guaranteeing absolute anonymity. Perfect. Foolproof.

Why even bother to escape? Good question. Why not just wait defiantly for the police, as Kunihito did on the Diet building steps, standing above the soggy mess of the Minister? It is tempting—let the world know immediately who is the traitor, who the patriot. But the problem is propriety. Kunihito was arrested, inconvenienced in a hundred small ways, subjected to their dismal charade of a trial, declared insane, and shuffled off center stage. Democratic/bureaucratic game-playing. In Yukio's opinion most unseemly, even degrading. That perfect act, so clean and beautiful, subsequently tarnished—by Yamamoto and others—blurred in the popular mind, cheapened, debased.

But not this time. Yukio's ruggedly handsome features—strong chin, high cheekbones, fine tall nose, deep frown-lines in a V between his eyebrows, military crewcut—are hidden by the full Arai helmet, and his powerful body is encased in tough, double-thick leather: jacket, trousers, gloves, boots. These he will discard afterward. No need to discard the Kawasaki, however, his pride and joy, his second love, because the gleaming ivory metal-flake gas tank and fenders, always highly waxed, are overlain with red tempera paint which will wash off in about two minutes. Furthermore, the Kawasaki now bears license plates which were, until yesterday, bolted to the rusted hulk of an old Honda 50 delivery bike moldering behind the Nakamori *sushi-ya* in Iidabashi where Yukio works.

Where he used to work. Yes, though educated—some might say highly educated—but far too impatient to wait around for diplomas from universities which are themselves a big part of the problem, Yukio is a *sushi* chef by trade, a good one. He knows how to wield a blade, all right. And up ahead is his fat poisonous *fugu* fish.

Yukio flashes past a university couple holding hands, mincing along behind the Yamamotos. Unisex, the *An An* look. Same book bags, same pastel-framed eyeglasses. Are they *douseiaisha*, homosexuals? If not, which is the boy, which the girl? Presumably they can tell the difference, but Yukio can't, not for sure. He knows, however, from having riffled disgustedly through *An An* and *Brutus* and a few other slick wads of garbage, that the boy is likely the more vivacious and feminine of the two—long permed hair, frilly orange blouse, baggy shorts, fuzzy pink knee-socks and pink thick-soled shoes—and the girl is probably the one with the short hair and the necktie.

Yukio knows them, knows their type, recognizes them as children of the postwar middle class, the lifestyle people, sunk in their mindless hedonism and acknowledging no imperatives higher than those of their own soft flesh: comfort, ignoble ease, titillation. He is aware of their utter self-absorption, their lust for fashions and cosmetics, their other infantile concerns. Babies in the bodies of adolescents, a disgrace to their country, the end product of all the Yamamotos' lousy liberalism. How he despises them, the *wagamama*.

Yukio resists the urge to behead them too, pushes them from his mind, as he throttles back, the supertuned engine now whispering as he covers the final meters to the object of his hate, bringing the blade down in a perfect right-to-left arc, his timing exactly right—*as sweat-drenched Yamamoto bends in the act of lowering the dog, and Bright Justice whistles over Yamamoto's head and his wife's head, the stroke throwing Yukio off balance off the motorcycle seat cartwheeling over the street-side railing slamming him into the wife crushing him against her against the*

*river-side railing as something snaps and the woman
screams and the bike caroms off the street-side railing
then spins showering sparks and flurry of red paint
flakes on its side and into oncoming traffic.*

Disaster!

But Yukio has not relinquished his grip on the
sacred *katana.* Instantly he wriggles free and aims
another stroke at Yamamoto's rosy bald crown, but the
stroke, which should have split the man like a *hirame*
fish, merely causes Yamamoto to blink and push his
heavy black-rimmed glasses back up on his nose and
widen his eyes as comprehension and a terrible rage
begin to bloom behind the thick fogged lenses and the
dog in his arms starts a low tearing sound deep in its
throat and the woman at the railing screams and
screams again and Yukio draws back his arm for one
more stroke even as his eyes tell him and he begins to
understand that the sacred blade is *broken,* that
somehow in the fall it snapped in two, and what Yukio
holds in his hands is a *stump,* and he begins to
understand further that this sacrilege is *his,* that all is
lost, and that there is only one way even to begin
making atonement, and that is by the supreme act of
seppuku, ripping open his own belly right here and

gasping out his life as so many other great *samurai* have done.

So, ignoring the shouts the squealing brakes the screaming woman, ignoring the animal savaging the leather at his crotch and the professor's fat wet fingers yanking the helmet from his head then tightening on his throat, ignoring all of it and emptying his mind, stilling his mind, as the way of the soldier, the *bushi-do,* requires, Yukio brings the maimed blade up and then down with all possible force into his stomach, and feeling the pain, worse than he imagined or could have imagined, but realizing even in his agony that it is the pain of a kick, a punch, an assault with a blunt instrument because the flat stump-like blade has failed to penetrate the leather jacket just as the dog's teeth have apparently failed to penetrate the leather trousers, and when the full horror and cruelty of this final trick of fate is clear and real in his mind Yukio sobs aloud.

His sobs, however, are strangled because he himself, mouth gaping and jaws working, is nearly strangled by the professor, Yamamoto's berserker strength digging both big thumbs into Yukio's windpipe, and Yamamoto's giant bulk showering him with drops of perspiration, pressing him back onto the concrete, pinioning Yukio's arms and the dog at

Yukio's groin, and bringing his face up to Yukio's, sickening him with long shuddering blasts of scalding *tonkatsu* breath from huge hairy nostrils. Yukio hears a strange humming and notices that shimmering black spots now swarm at the periphery of his vision, swarm and grow and interconnect and threaten to swallow him in darkness, but then the fat maniac's flat mad eyes with their pinpoint pupils suddenly widen further, actually bulge, seem ready to pop from his fat purple head, then just as suddenly roll back in their sockets as the professor begins to vomit pork cutlet and rice and half-digested egg into Yukio's face, into Yukio's mouth, disgorging torrents while beginning to convulse on top of him, then releasing his hold on Yukio's throat and clutching desperately at his own chest, scrabbling at it as though mad to rip it open and fix something terribly wrong within, arcing his torso up and off Yukio's, bucking like a walrus, then shuddering, shuddering again while time seems to stop completely, then collapsing back onto Yukio and finally rolling off him, shuddering once more, a final spasm, as the professor fetches up against the green iron railing, stone dead, as everything for Yukio goes dead-black.

Yukio—*how much later?*—is galvanized to consciousness and action by the smell and vile taste of acid death-vomit and by the woman's screams which have grown into one long wrenching howl of loss and by the crushing fire at his groin and by the faint still-distant sirens. He grabs the railing and hauls himself to his feet. He grasps the dog by its hind legs, and, unmindful of the agony, unmindful now of everything but escape, with all his might rips the animal's jaws from the gnawed leather at his private parts, then, sobbing with pain and revulsion, flings the animal over the river-side rail, and hears its high-pitched shrieking yipyipyip diminuendo as he vaults the street-side rail, dodges cars trucks scooters and scuttles over to the big Kawasaki, rights it, hits the starter button, hits it again—nothing!—grabs the bent handlebars and runs with the bike, runs desperately because the sirens are close now and he knows his Organization will never shield him from the police but rather help them and then exact some terrible punishment of their own, it is from the Organization he is running, hoping the engine will catch—it starts! But then coughs and dies. Yukio runs harder, through traffic, around the corner as the engine catches again and he feeds it more gas, then vaults onto the seat and immediately shrieks as his outraged scrotum is bruised further by this contact, so he pops sobbing from the seat and stands on the pegs, hunched over, steering the bent and broken machine along on its rackety smoky curiously eccentric bobbing wobbling very slow course toward what must be, *must* be, escape.

Buddy and Donner, Donner in the lead and both running hard, hear the woman's scream not as a scream but as some first voice, felt more than heard, prolonging itself out and down, loud but insubstantial, like something torn from a dream's underside, and they all—picnickers, photographers, black-uniformed high school students, Buddy and Donner—react as one organism in the charged panic-medium, all snap their heads around and up, see something, a scrap of white and pink, soar over the river-side railing and hang in the bright air for a drawn-out microsecond while it registers that this something is a some*one,* a baby, gathering per second per second momentum down and outward, its arc of fall taking it beyond the bridge across the storm drain channel and into the dark of the dry channel itself, twenty feet below the river-path and fifty feet below the highway, and onto rocks and jagged chunks of rusted junk and a faintly luminous carpet of broken glass.

"No!" Buddy and Donner shout.

Donner, sprinting past the gingko, feels the inrush of a huge ecstatic wind which fills him, pulls and pushes him until the falling infant seems to slow, descend in measured clicks like the second hand of a watch, increase in size like some cinematographer's trick, and Donner at the center of this rushing dream of force knows nothing that his bones and muscles don't.

"No!" Buddy shouts again.

Donner hears him. Some tiny part of Donner understands the shout but disregards it as he is seven then five then three strides from the edge of the storm drain channel then pushing off from the flagstone edge of it, leaping, and not just with his legs, lofted by the power, because he knows the channel is too wide but also that it isn't, can't be, and his arc intersects the baby's as he takes her on his fingertips like a football, pulls her in, curls his body around her and rolls in the air, as the blank faces and huge eyes on the bridge to his right blur and pinwheel, rolls as his shoulder then head hit the flags on the far bank, rolls and rolls into the dark.

The darkness thins, dissipates, and there is Buddy's face, mouth working but no sound except the woman's scream around it, the scream smelling rough and red against the light, which thickens again, swallowing him deeper than before. But far down in the throat of nothing he spins a flashing dream of sirens, of screams harmonizing with them, of Buddy's face, of figures in white.

Of a microphone in his face: How does he feel?

Friday, 6:41 P.M.

Kobayashi Miyuki likes her job at *Nihon Terebi.* Likes it? She loves it. Well, almost of the time. It is more than job, TV work. It is adventure. Three years, and still it is exciting. Not the studio. That is just office politics. But being out, all over Tokyo, that is *subarashii*—wonderful. Listening in on police and fire bands, racing patrol cars and ambulances to the scene, getting to there ahead of uniforms, sometimes. She loves that, being first. Then getting the story, taped and into the can, while uniforms still are huddled around their shining vehicles, talking, smoking, getting ready to do what they do not want to do, because that means risk. Few police officers willingly risk their lives or even their upholstery. But Miyuki is different. Her NHK van is scratched and dented. But it is sheet metal only. Miyuki is a risk-taker.

Who? What? Where? How? When? Why? Interviewer's questions applying to her. Probably, was American School of Japan. Good old Yamamochi-mai. Expensive, mediocre, trendy. Full of tiny blond barbarians in Miki House outfits. (Diplomatic kids were worst.) Of course, she was the *ichiban* shy little girl there. And most self-conscious teen later on. Other

Japanese at A.S.O.J. called her *Ka,* mosquito, because
of her voice. All she wanted was to disappear, curl up
tighter and tighter until she was gone. Last thing she
wanted was eyes turned her way. Public speaking?
Debate? Class play? These words made her sweat and
tremble, made her stomach churn. Attention, the
thought made her to shudder.

Still, she forced herself. Did things one year which
were unthinkable the year before. Receiving much
encouragement from Uncle Makoto. Learning from the
Americans, absurd as that sounds. Because, ignorant as
Americans are, they at least know that they exist, as
persons. Her American classmates had opinions—
mostly wrong, mostly stupid, but theirs. And so,
gradually, Miyuki began surprising her family and
herself. Winning prizes, even valedictorian. She was
not only a someone, but (it slowly dawned to her)
someone special.

So why did she take that stupid office lady job? No
choice—or, rather, no awareness about there could be
a choice. Everybody said, Oh, *Nishinihon Denki,* how
wonderful, you are so lucky, they are such a big
company. Big, yes. But so what? When she thought of
the years she wasted to there. Miyuki the sweet little
OL, pouring tea and smiling—and bowing! Perfectly!

As they taught her to do with the bowing machine! A cute robot, for all those petrified *wagamama.* And some oily little *chikan* too, licking their lips, shifting around their eyes, putting their sweaty hands to her. Well, as the Americans would say, fuck that.

Thanks to the Buddha, she finally got up her nerve to quit—and didn't her father have *takusan* to say about *that?* "You are twenty-five! Stale Christmas cake! Who will marry you? Nobody! How will you then live?" And her mother, "Oh, if you could only have found any nice boy at *Nishinihon Denki.* Such a stable company, such stable young men. Those are ingredients for stable marriage."

Stability, their god. Every day like the one before, so you could sleepwalk through them all. Miyuki said *kekko desu,* no thanks, went back to school, took some real courses, finally got on with NHK. As a gopher, but so what? Better a gopher than a robot, as Uncle Makoto said. Anyway, she was not a gopher for so very long. And now she travels—Los Angeles, Beijing, Seoul, Paris, Moscow, Hong Kong twice—she questions, interviews, does what she has to do. She gets the story. She makes the news, in some sense. She goes to meetings, and men ask for her opinions. And listen to them. Senior men. And office ladies pour tea for *her.* Yes, thanks to the Buddha. Being noticed, that was her girlhood definition of hell. Now, however, three million Tokyo-*jin* notice her at least once in the day, and it is heaven.

Though not entirely. Most newsy news is often unpleasant, sometimes horrible. Like the monster. Eighteen months, five baby girls gone, three returned in bottles. Ashes. Last week, the note, *Love has freed Yoko.* How do you deal for that? By, Miyuki supposes, not dealing for it at all, by blocking it, not thinking about it. You just hold your breath, knock on the door, do the job. Like removing out your own appendix. You ask the questions which are moronic—*How do you feel about finding your baby's ashes on your doorstep in an old whiskey bottle?*—then jump into van and back to studio. Stop along the way perhaps to smoke and tremble. But never cry till after work.

On the bad days Miyuki almost, *almost,* wishes she was back pouring tea for old Oikawa, with his sick grin and his hand moving up under her skirt like some small animal which is so frightened. Dealing for Oikawa would be a sort of fun now, on the very bad days, because she has learned so well about human bodies are fragile. Miyuki knows that she and everyone is an individual, absolutely alone. So easy to kill, so

91

horribly hard to die. So full of blood. Miyuki looks at humans and sees shimmering bubbles, red, ready to burst. She no longer goes to movies. Rambo, pow, boom. She sees the schoolboys and salarymen reading their fat sick *manga* on the trains, and she wants to stop and explain to them concerning the pitiful delicacy of human flesh. She has an ulcer. Has had, for eighteen months. They slid a thick black rubber tube down her throat while she gagged, and they said, "Hmm," and later they said, "Maybe too much stress." Well, they were right. Too much stress from too much knowledge.

From knowing what really happens when human flesh is shot, stabbed, bombed, dropped from some thirty storey *tatemono*, crushed and cremated in glowing wrecks, left in shallow graves for weeks or months, pulled from Tokyo Bay finally. Ugliness of death. Her first real story: next-door neighbors in a *manshon*, paper-thin walls between to the apartments, so one couple gets a noisy dog which *wanwanwan-suru* all night until neighbor husband crushes in and throws dog off to the balcony. Eighteen stories, messy, woman was hysterical completely. Other husband grabs dog-killer and throws *him* off balcony. When finally they got there even uniforms started to vomiting.

Or how about Rush-hour Ripper. Keio? Odakyu? Miyuki doesn't recall which train line, and it doesn't much matter because all are the same, especially at eight A.M. Crammed with suffering *sararimen* wedged in tight enough to hurt. So every day for months or years some young executive—eager to be first off train, first at work, first period—fights his way for the front and jostles one poor little... what the Americans call a nerd. Every morning. Nerd apparently broods. One day nerd is waiting with a butcher knife. The word was disemboweled, but it is just something you read and doesn't even begin to give you that rich sweet mess.

Flingers, rippers, poisoners, men who shot women for their car keys, who beat babies to death with shovels for a few thousand yen. And so forth, all of the year through, no end to it. Oh, it could have been worse. She could have been in New York or Sarajevo or Bogota. But even in Tokyo and in just three years she has become expert on mortality. She knows about brains on the wall, blood and shit all over everything. She has seen death, smelt it—you don't get that from newspapers or *terebi,* that stink—touched it. And this intimacy always moves her. It is all so… butchery.

This time too. Scene on the bridge, medium-bad at least, dusk, a little breeze, leaf-smoke. They pull up, Miyuki and Hiroji her cameraman. First ones there, sirens in the distance, what did they have? A fat dead man wedged against the railing and covered with vomit, a dead-pale pudgy woman with an empty *ombu* on her back, screaming, looking down at the river then over at the dead man, whipping her head back and forth. Small crowd forming. People pointing, shouting. Strange man on a smashed-up motorcycle. Honda? Kawasaki? Old, anyway. Red. Bad paint-job. Horns beginning to sound. Miyuki, feeling the first twinges in her stomach, tries a few questions. But no point, the woman is hysterical, doesn't even see Miyuki. The woman, sobbing and moaning, kneeling and shaking the dead man then jumping up and leaning over the rail and screaming.

"Hanako. Hanakohhhh."

The scream drawing itself out into a wail. Miyuki looks over the railing herself, and there below is another strange scene: a tall bearded foreigner in a gray sweatsuit and curled up on the path—drunk? heart attack from running? epileptic?—a huge *Nihon-jin* in an orange sweatsuit bending over him and shouting something. Did the huge man kill the foreigner in a fight? The foreigner is America-*jin*. How does Miyuki know? She knows. Crowd around them, more people rushing in from upriver and down. Three old men taking pictures, flashcubes going off like *hanabi*. Behind them, in the channel of the storm drain, broken glass, an old rusted bicycle frame, and a dead... dachshund?—like a fat hot dog with *takusan* ketchup. So what happened? Did the foreigner fall? Perhaps. There is blood. But he is alive, he is moving his head, he could not have fallen so far. Or could he? He is an American, after all. They are both looking up here— why? And what is he holding?

"*Hanakohhh.*"

Miyuki asks Hiroji to get some footage of the woman and the dead man, and of the police when they arrive. Then she pulls Hiroji down the long flight of stone steps angling across the retaining wall to the river bank. She pushes through the crowd, kneels by the bloody tall foreigner no longer curled on the flagstones, now being held sitting by the huge Japanese runner with the terrible haircut. Male sweat, steaming, strong enough to make her eyes water. She gets the mike past the huge man's ear and into the *gaijin's* face:

95

"How are you feeling?" she says—well, she can make a pretty good guess how he's feeling, but of course she has to ask—"What happened?"

The foreigner's eyes roll up, head falls back. Out.

Miyuki turns to the huge Japanese: *"Doh sh'tan desu ka?"*

"Dough what? Listen, please keep back. We have a situation here."

"You speak English." Miyuki is surprised.

"Wakarimasen," says the huge man. "That's all the Japanese I know. My friend jumped over that," jerking his head back toward the storm drain channel, "and landed real hard, hit his head. That's all I know. Picked up some glass."

A Japanese who can't speak Japanese. *Nisei?* Sounds like Los Angeles, but he looks like a *sumo* wrestler, like Chiyonofuji—except for that scrub-brush haircut. Upper arms larger than Miyuki's thighs.

"Donner," says the man. "Hey."

Flash, goes a camera, silvering the dusk.

"Ha... na... kohhhh." From above, the wail, moving coldly out and down like ink in water, spreading urgency, dread.

"Okay," the big man shouts, craning his head around and up. "All right!"

"Who is all right?" Miyuki asks, then, peering around the huge man's shoulder catches a glimpse of pink ribbon and wide terrified eyes, shining like black glass, and tiny hands clutching at the bloody foreigner's old T-shirt: *Bushe & Quayle, Foure Mor Yearse.*—Ribbon, eyes, hands: *baby.* What is this man doing with a baby? Is she his baby? How could that be? Or was he stealing her? Is this American the monster? Or, more likely, did he jump over the channel like a fool and land on the baby, and crush her? Or did the baby crawl through the railing above and fall onto this foreigner? Miyuki tightens her abdominals against a rippling ulcer-pang. The camera is rolling. She touches the huge man's shoulder. "Whose baby?"

"Ambulance," he says.

"It is on the way," she tells him. "But what—"

"I don't know," he says. "We're running along, we hear a scream and here comes this kid sailing over the rail. That's all I know. My friend here caught the baby, could be her mother up above. Really, that's all I know. Get those people back with their god damned cameras."

Flash, flash, flash.

"Man down, man down, please get the fuck back."

"Ohhh, Ha... na... kohhhhh."

97

"Lady!" shouts the big man, craning around again, his bristly thick neck creasing, reddening. "The kid is okay, I said! Come on down and get her, god dammit! Understand? Okay?... *Daijobu!*"

The bearded American opens his eyes, mumbles, "What." He runs his tongue along his lips, lifts his head slightly and shakes it, spraying Miyuki with sweat and blood. She looks at the camera, sees a droplet of blood near the center of the lens. That will look bad. The foreigner blinks rapidly, shakes his head again. Miyuki shrinks back. "Hey," he says thickly, "what... what," as his head drops again onto the big man's shoulder, jostling the baby who begins a breathy high-pitched scream, her rosebud mouth opening and closing, her tiny chest expanding and contracting violently and finally forcing out the word:

"*Maamaa.*"

"*Hanakohh.*"

"Easy, Donner."

Flash, flash.

The screaming woman pulls herself along the rail till she is directly above them. "Hanako," again, but the scream is tinny now, little more than a whimper, barely audible above the sirens. The woman's arms reach out and down. The woman's jaws move, her mouth gapes, lips form the syllables, "Ha. Na. Ko."

"It's *daijobu,* isn't it? Doesn't that mean basically okay?" the big Japanese-looking man, the *nisei* or whatever, is looking directly at Miyuki, wanting the word, then catching her slight nod, turning as they all turn, to see white uniforms behind the woman, all the figures in near-silhouette against the golden sky and backlit by flashing blue lights. Uniforms are pulling at the woman, who grips the rail and lowers her head, slowly rolling it from side to side. She opens her mouth again. The big man shouts up to her, *"Daijobu!"* and then, at three uniforms moving down the steps, "You men! On the double! Officer down!"

"Buddy," the man mumbles, cradling the baby, "Hey Buddy, I."

Miyuki cups her hands around her mouth, feels the fire in her stomach, feels the hot prickling of tears as she calls up to the woman. *"Akachan wa daijobu deshyo! Bikkuri dake shika to omou."* I think the baby is just frightened.

Flash, flash.

But the woman seems not to hear or see Miyuki, seems to see and hear only the baby. Woman twists away, right then left then right, slipping the hands from her shoulders, leaning further over the rail, opening then closing then opening her mouth, lips forming an O, no sound coming now as the woman's features crumple, mouth trembling open wider now, wider, woman's tongue so bright unrolling from her mouth, amazingly long and like a tiny carpet of red, impossibly long, until finally, half of a second later, everyone realizes that of course it is not her tongue and what really it is, and cringes as it widens, nears, splatters the gravel path their clothes their faces, the sunset firing all these ruby drops to gold.

Flash.

Friday, 7:22 P.M.

Tanaka Hatsue feels political oppression like a physical weight. Each morning she wakes gasping and cursing beneath the sheer planetary mass of human vileness. Each breathless day she spends reviling the immensity of human exploitation, raging at it, screaming it out in a voice now ragged and hoarse with the desperation of knowing in her blood and bones that it is snowballing, this aggregate of evil and woe, that, yes, every day, hour, minute it is growing, accelerating, thundering down upon them, the people, and soon would crush them all. Twitching and simmering, Hatsue fights back, fights the hydra-headed foes of global Communism, but utterly without hope.

Tanaka Hatsue is tough, sour, crabbed, hate-full. Twenty-nine years old, still a Kosei University student—technically, anyway—tiny, rodent-faced, chinless and bucktoothed, lank-haired, bespectacled, she lives at home, subsists on her tiny campus radical stipend. Once a month she treats herself to some good *sushi* or *sashimi*. All the rest she saves. Her mother is dead, finally, two years ago. And her father. One after the other.

It is just as well. Though frightened by Hatsue's fury, her mother never quit trying to find a husband for her. "Hat-*chan*, why don't you put on your special kimono, and we can have your picture taken for *ohmiai.*" Hatsue hated and hates the idea of arranged marriages, *any* marriages, anything and everything else about the sick middle-class lifestyle. She never wore a kimono in her life—not even for *Shichi-Go-San,* girl's day. She wears Edwin blue jeans rolled at the cuff, a canvas jacket, heavy leather boots. On student demonstration days she adds a white helmet with a white hand-towel across her mouth and tucked behind the straps, and round John Lennon prescription sunglasses. Only her nose shows, and Hatsue wishes she could cover that too. Her nose is like a miniature gardening implement.

"But *why*, dear?" her mother once wailed, objecting to the concealment. "You have such a *pretty* face." And that time Hatsue attacked her physically.

Hatsue's mother had a sort of Sanrio world-view. Everything in her mother's world was *furi-furi fua fua:* fluffy and dreamy. She read *So Big Comic for Lady*, a *manga* inane almost beyond belief, and believed every word. She watched the *terebi* where everything is rigged to look like Fantasyland on a good day. Except for the news, of course, which is a little more realistic. Her mother was secretly in love with the newsman Ozawa, that slick smug bastard with a different suit from Seibu every day. Her mother commented on Ozawa's comments (*"Taihen, desu ne?"*), bobbed her fat head in agreement with every oiled lie that slid from his ever-smiling mouth.

Why did the old lady love Ozawa? Because she had no longer existed for Hatsue's father, probably, a liitle man of iron and ice-water, a *tochikorogashi,* one of Tokyo's real estate tiger sharks, an embidiment of The Enemy. He had the teeth for it, big, blue-white and perfect, always on display. Hatsue despised her mother but profoundly hated her grinning father all those years she worked in his office. Her father never perspired, never fidgeted, never stumbled or fumbled. Her father, that diamond-hearted gambler. And when the old bastard gambled once too often and ate some *fugu* fish *sashimi* with a bit too much of the lip-numbing poison dripped back on, Hatsue cheered and sobbed aloud.

Hatsue's father, still stinging her eyes with tears.

Her mother, still able to curl Hatsue's lip in a sneer. The old cow, in love with Ozawa, wrote letters to him, praised him. Praised even that mindless little microphone girl, Kobayashi Miyuki, said approving things about her makeup. Makeup. Well, that was a good metaphor, was it not, for her mother's mind? The superficial was all, the real nonexistent. Hatsue's mother smiled and pottered through all the nice pastel days, oblivious to the war of good against evil, unaware of The Enemy's crushing juggernaut weight, daring once even to defend the Showa Emperor: "But dear, what did Tenno Heika ever do to *you?*"

Hatsue could almost have pitied her, had not such softness been long since purged by hate. Hatsue pits her strong hate against all oppression—of Jews by the Russians, of Palestinians by Jews, of Croats by Serbs, of Kurds by Iraqis, of half the world by the Americans, of Blacks by Whites, of East by West, of Japanese women by Japanese men, of her campus radicals by the police, of Left by Right, of ying by yang.

She rages. Now and then the rage swells so as to catch in her throat and choke her. At such times she can do nothing but go to her room, take up her *kendo* stick, and lunge-feint-block-parry for hours with unflagging brilliance and viciousness, dripping vinegar sweat, glimpsing at times in the full-length mirror of her *tansu* the quicksilver countenance of the Enemy, the pitiless Oppressor, eclipsing her own. Brilliance and viciousness… and thickly mounting passion.

Hatsue's mother wanted her to see a psychiatrist.

There is an irony for you.

Ironic because, in these decadent days, she is not sick enough, or in the right way. Who does Hatsue hate worst? All foreigners everywhere. All domestic political groups but her own. By turns and fitfully, unwilling to risk overlooking any, she hates them all, but her purest detestation she reserves for the brutal new ultra-macho Ultra-Right. Oh, how she loathes them. When she sees them in their huge black buses with the speakers blaring she wishes for bombs, bazookas, laser-guided anti-tank weapons. Anything at all to shut them up for good.

Yes, every girl has a dream, and hers is to kill as many as possible of them, the neonazis, grandsons of those wonderful strutting bullyboys who brought World War II to the Pacific. ("But dear," said her mother once, "That was a long time ago, before you were born. Why don't you and that nice Yuji go to Disneyland and just have fun? We are living in the 90s. And we are so very rich.") The Right, *Ouyoku* pigs, who every day bring their crushing numbers and money and arrogance down a little harder on the Left. Her father, a fascist in every atom of his being, funded no fewer than six such groups. Well, she had put a stop to that before his ashes cooled.

Yes, the New Right are fanatics, and Hatsue lusts not merely to cut off their money but their balls. And their lives. She will, too. Perhaps an entire stage-or bus-full. She has been saving and investing for years. Plastic explosives? Rocket launchers? She has not decided, has not yet made a solid Red Army connection. But she will acquire something significant and therefore expensive. Hatsue has the means, she is a realist. She will fight capital with capital.

Parents dead, grandmother senile and irrelevant.

Hatsue is free to do as she likes—and what is that?

Fight, struggle, go down kicking and screaming.

But not, it seems, tonight: cool, clear, breezy, quiet. The Left, her people, "radicals" to the zombies and fascists, called a student strike at the Ichigaya campus of Kosei University, a moldering concrete jumble, grimy blocks squatting absurdly on a wedge of land worth trillions. They are protesting the Emperor. He did or did not do something—what? Whatever, it was oppressive. Comrades manning the picket lines. Mochizuki-*san* on the bullhorn. Good speech, floodlights, posters—

BRING YOUR ROCKS AND GASOLINE BOMBS!!!!

—burly police in lovely brutal pairs, murmuring into their helmet mikes, in touch with the huge grey armored buses, their field headquarters. Many of these police are in riot uniform—chest armor, helmets with face protectors and neck-flaps, shin-guards—and carry the huge exciting metal shields. The police are there in case of trouble, and so is Hatsue. Trouble is what she passionately desires.

She knows, however, admits bitterly to herself, that trouble is highly unlikely. Why? Student apathy. She looks at the well-dressed-well-fed students milling around the campus, smoking, laughing, reading their fat *manga*, utterly ignoring the speaker and the strike. To them, to everyone, her people are a joke. (One foreign journalist even wrote an article about them, "Japan's Radical Left-Overs," and Hatsue would like to finish that *gaijin* too, ship him back home in a box.) Undergraduates. She shakes her head in disgust. This is the raw material of revolution? These so-called students who don't care about anything but their own comfort and amusement? Half the boys are business majors. Yes, little human calculators with tiny pathetic bank accounts. And the girls—mindless! *Yakyuu*

107

cheerleaders mincing around, flaunting their painted faces and their bodies. The world to them is one big game of baseball. One giant ongoing disco. Hatsue tries and fails to find some pity in her heart for these campus queens strutting and caroling, exulting in their power, sunk from sight in their own perfect flesh.

Oh, Hatsue knows her undergraduates, knows their infantile concerns, their dilettante interests. Cosmetics for every occasion including synchronized swimming. A little art, less science, a few remembered scraps from their lying history books—*Karl who?*—and their capitalist sociology and economics textbooks, maybe opened and glanced at just before a test. Jazz dance, soft tennis, and *eikaiwa* with that fat stinking foreign *sensei*, Duck. And sex.

Always sex. Undergraduates are disgustingly sexual, though not in any obvious way. Fixated on each other carnally. *But how many undergrads are interested in or even happen to notice the iron heel of oppression that is grinding the entire world into the dust, that is raping yes raping everyone, that is picking all their pockets, that is ripping the last pitiful shreds of food from the frozen bleeding mouths of the starving poor?* Easy, Hatsue. Try to relax. All right. But, ah, how she despises undergrads. They have no class consciousness at all, these children of the new middle class, two generations from the rice paddy and the *jinrikisha.* What do such rabble have to do with global questions of principle, with ideology? She curls her lip. Well, their herd-mentality should not surprise her. What does she expect from a bunch of proletarians?

Contemptuously, Hatsue turns her back on them.

And sees him.

Imagine her feelings of warrior joy, when, on this third day of the strike and having almost given up hope of contact but experiencing still an itchy sort of anticipation, like a young girl before her first date, she looks up from her post at the *uramon,* the rear gate, and sees him, all alone. Hatsue, with her sweet Secret concealed by towel and helmet.

Oh, she thinks, oh come to me.

It is hate at first sight. If he isn't a right-winger then nobody is a right-winger. He has The Look: bulgy muscles, crew cut, arrogant mouth, beautiful tall nose. Crazy for glory, total fanatic, a real goose-stepper. Probably has pinups of himself all over his room. Riding a smashed-up old motorbike, no helmet, some kind of *unchi* all over his leathers. He is one of Them, all right. Hatsue stiffens, quivers. Her nostrils flare.

She feels sweet rage begin to build, to throb and tingle, feels it like the first touch of a new lover.

Kawakami Yukio has done it! He's gotten away from that scene at Noborito, eluded the police even though his poor battered Kawasaki is now belching oily purple exhaust and can't make more than twenty kilometers per hour. Yukio has been devious, cleverly taking mostly side streets to Iidabashi then doubling back behind the communist university toward his place in Yotsuya. He is feeling much better. The pain in his throat, stomach, and groin has subsided. More importantly, his womanish panic has evaporated. Yamamoto is dead, after all—hardly in the way Yukio wished, but dead is dead. And Yukio has escaped, is almost home. So his only problems are the helmet, which has his name in it, and the sword, Bright Justice, both lying back there on the walkway above the river. Clues for the police, for the Organization.

But are these problems really so bad? Yukio is beginning to think not. He is, after all, a leader—tough, resourceful, highly intelligent. No, Yukio is far from beaten. He'll just ditch the bike somewhere—an alley, a vacant lot—then report everything stolen. Bike, helmet, leathers. Certainly, he'll have to talk to the police about it eventually. Certainly, they'll have their suspicions. But so what? What could they prove. What harm could the *police* do?

As for the sword, there is a whole museum full of ancient and sacred blades, all but indistinguishable from *"Mitsumasa,"* nearby in Toronomon. He will go there and steal one first thing tomorrow, then sneak it back into headquarters and replace it in the case. Nobody will know the difference. Problem? What problem? Yukio is grateful for this opportunity to show what he can do. And he has nothing to be ashamed of, *honto ni.* Just give it time. Twenty years from now he'll take that replacement sword from the case and tell them all the story, and what will they do, his disciples? Laugh, complement him on his nerve and quick wits, be even more awed by his prowess.

Yukio is laughing to himself as he judders and sputters past the rear gate of Kosei Daigaku, the communist university—why was he nervous before, why upset, why even considered quitting?—when he sees the tiny figure in jeans and canvas jacket: white helmet, white towel, Lennon sunglasses in the middle of the night. Holding a thick bamboo straight up and down, *kendo*-fashion. Another traitor. Yukio's reaction is automatic and instantaneous. He feels the stirring

111

bristles on the back of his neck. He feels his back and shoulder muscles knot with fury. He swerves and rides right up to the radical *bakayaro,* the Enemy.

"*Aka!*" Yukio shouts. "Red!" and aims his devastating straight right at the midget radical's ugly little nose. "Terrorist!"

"*Ouyoku!*" Hatsue squeaks, "Nazi!" She glides beneath his lumbering punch, in her element now, planting her feet, already establishing rhythm, feeling the oppression lift, her terrible weight of being lighten. Oh, this is good, this was worth waiting for.

Hatsue gives him quick lateral strokes along either side of his handsome jaw, waits two pulsebeats, her timing perfect, then angles the bamboo down across the bridge of his nose, which is now and suddenly no longer beautiful, no longer much of a nose. Oh, wonderful. He grabs his face, blood blooms between his fingers, he's helpless, arched backward on the seat and elbows to the sky, scream just starting. Hatsue moves in, uses the bamboo like a spear, gets every gram and erg behind it, buries the tip in the pit of his stomach. He's down, off the bike, gasping, blubbering, rolling on the ground, doubled up like a stuck grub.

Thank you, Lord Buddha.

How are you feeling now, Mr. Wonderful?

Hatsue waits three beats, flicks the bamboo down between his legs, sees his eyes bulge and his mouth gape, waits another beat then lays into him with a lightning series of verticals. It does seem as though she might really kill him. Hatsue is breathing heavily, and not just from the exertion. Yes—why deny it?—she is excited, aroused, as hot with desire and longing as she can ever remember being. Stroke, stroke, stroke, now deep and gutful.

"Police!" he screams. "Help! The *aka's* killing me!"

But Hatsue can't stop, wouldn't if she could, she's on fire, raining the long strokes down over his entire gorgeous repulsive masculine body, feeling the shock travel back through her muscles and tiny bones right to the core of her, to her loins, her center.

Oh, oh, this is it, this is wonderful, this is what makes it all worthwhile—but suddenly she too is down, on her stomach, arms pinned, and the huge weight is back, but this time it's a physical weight, a real man, a policeman. She glimpses the blue fabric of his sleeve, feels those rough thick arms close around her, feels whiskers against the side of her neck, hears the deep grunts, curses, creaking of leather, and smells aftershave and tobacco and that rank male sweat-stink that she hates more than life itself. That smell, more than anything else, is driving her mad, crazy, right out of her mind.

Oh, oh, now he's turning her over, arms twisted up behind her back and her whole front exposed. Hatsue loses control absolutely, abandons herself, screaming, kicking, biting, working one arm free and dragging the ragged bitten nails across his face. Hear him growl at that! Feel him crush his face against her chest and tighten his hold. He's strong! She can hardly breathe. A pounding running of boots. A pain explosion in her right thigh—oh, *so* good—and her helmet and scarf are yanked off, her sunglasses sent spinning. Now they're looking, all those men, they have to, they have no choice. They must see her Secret: eyeliner, eyeshadow, blush, and luscious carmine gloss on her bitten lips. She has it now, has all that male attention, and she's almost there.

Hatsue twists and gets a thumb into her man's eye, hears the scream, hears from above a rough grunt of astonishment—"*Onna desu!* It's a girl!—and almost laughs. Then those yellow buck teeth close on her man's ear, and she whips her head from side to side, feeling the lobe rip free, feeling the man convulse and hearing the yowl, tasting the blood of the Oppressor.

"Rape!" she screams, feeling the ecstasy mount, crest. "Oh, rape!" Feeling also those steely arms tighten in rage and pain—did they ever hold so close any wife, any sweetheart on a date?—as she jams herself helplessly against him, thrusts and thrusts again, her pelvis battering his, stroke after stroke, and she feels it then, feels it drenching and flooding her, and she knows that she has won, and that there is no stopping. And then sobbing and snarling she just lets go completely. "Oh," she moans, "how I hate you. Oh, oh… ohhhhh!"

Yukio can hardly believe the pain, can hardly believe that no bones are broken when it feels like they all are. Then the monster in his testicles wakens and subdues all secondary agonies, even the terrible black-feeling jaggedness in his abdominals. But then the first numbness in the center of his face gives way to nestled white layers of living agony, and he wishes he were out cold, dead, anything, because no human could tolerate these levels. He can hardly see, right there beside him, three big policemen grappling with the murdering little radical, one of them using his club, one of them taking a twist around his long hair—*her* long hair! A little female rat-radical! All painted up like a Soapland whore! They're all looking at her. No one is looking at him. Yukio somehow rights the Kawasaki. Weeping, he drapes himself over it and pushes it staggeringly off toward the Yasukuni shrine. Sags and limps inchingly along while his mind tries to compass it: the person who nearly killed him is a *girl*.

First a fat professor, and then a girl!

Yukio rounds the corner, leans against the wall, weeps long and bitterly, curses, bleeds and vomits down along the Kawasaki's bent front wheel-fork, hears the shouts, the sirens, metal doors chunking shut, some deep booming bullhorn-voice. And he wonders, *why?* Then finally silence and deeper darkness, a fractional ebbing of the agony. Yukio walks then trots the bike, hits the starter, eases himself onto the saddle, then wobbles sputters fizzles away.

Why?

Down the twisting back-alleys, into Yotsuya, passing the Organization's headquarters, still with body on fire and brain ice-numb. He glances down and sees it, sees the white helmet dangling from the chin-strap around his left wrist. *He has kept the helmet.* He blinks, peers in at the characters on the liner. The *kanji*

blur then clarify. 田中初枝 "Tanaka   Hatsue."
This is her helmet with her name in it. And then Yukio
has his idea, his best one ever. Battered and bleeding
as he is, he has an idea worthy of Napoleon or Julius
Caesar: *he will bomb his own HQ.*

That's all. No more thinking. Time to act. There—
there in the wire mesh *gomitokoro* by the alleyway, an
empty sake bottle. Retrieve it, take the siphon tube
from the bike's tool-pouch, fill the bottle. Unzip the
leather jacket, rip a chunk from the stupid T-rrific T-
shirt which is part of his disguise, and jam it in the
mouth of the bottle. Wait while the gasoline soaks up
through the rag. While waiting, take out his Swiss
Army knife (it even has a tiny but functional saw and
scissors), and carve a little message on the door:

OUYOKU BUTA!!!!

Right-wing pigs! That looks authentic. Then light
the rag and flip the bottle through the little window.
Duck back, wait. Yukio flinches at the crump and roar,
volume enough to wake fat Yamamoto, almost. And
now the final touch: drop the helmet in the alley.
Yukio sputters away, triumphant, riding on fumes but

he doesn't doesn't have to get far before he ditches the bike. He is almost home.

Oh, masterly. Napoleon? Caesar? Fujiwara? Gazing down, applauding. At a stroke, Yukio has turned the tables on everyone, put the dice back in the cup for a whole new game. Which he is now winning. He has covered his tracks with the missing sword, shamed his lukewarm comrades, galvanized the rest of them to action, brought all possible vengeance down on radicals generally and especially on this one, this Tanaka Hatsue, this *girl.* For the third time that evening, Kawakami Yukio chuckles, but now very softly, because of the pain.

Kinoshita Kunihiko? Kinoshita Kunihiko. It has a familiar ring. Cuffed and helpless, Hatsue looks at the sergeant's name-tag and thinks. Ah.

"Kinoshita Kunihiko, *desu ka?"* she says. "Tamachi Heights, *desu ka?"*

"Shizuka ni," the sergeant growls. "Quiet. Throw the little bitch inside."

"Tamachi Heights, *desu ne?"* she says. She was right! She has seen the name. "That is your home. And every month the rent goes to Tanaka Holdings."

"How do you know that?" The sergeant, puzzled and angry.

"To Mitsubishi regular account number 893427115."

"How do you know that? Are you also a spy?"

"Oya desu. I am no spy. I am your landlady."

"Uso! It's a lie!"

"Tanaka Holdings, that is me. Look in my wallet. Use your telephone."

"Uso." The sergeant, rubbing his chin, blinking rapidly.

"Give me a cigarette... Light it... *Arigato."*

The sergeant turning away, telephone jammed to the side of his head, grunting and nodding. The wounded parolman shuffling up to the riot bus, supported at each elbow by brother officers, holding his ear and grimacing, regarding Hatsue and her cigarette, leaning down to peer at her wide-eyed with rage and bewilderment. Hatsue takes in a grateful lungful of the smoke, blows it in the man's face, half closes her eyes, smiles.

"Chidzu," the man hisses. "Cunt."

"Maido arigato," she says, husky-voiced. "To you a thousand thanks."

Friday, 8:12 P.M.

Again the microphone, words all syncopated, reverberating in at him from someplace behind when— Donner, with but a slippery and liquid-bright shimmer- surfacing access to this situation. Which seems to be coming together around his slowly coalescing self in the present. He looks straight ahead: ceiling. Ah, that tells him something. Behind his head a raised softness. Pillow. He looks down at the smooth length of himself beneath a light green sheet. At the wood grained metal foot of the bed, for bed it is. He looks left: window, dark. He looks right: tubes and wires protruding from beside the headboard, walls white and green, shiny floors, the queasy lingering aftersmell of institutional food, the hospital hush.

All right, he can handle it, things are coming under control. Back to the doorway. Three figures in white, a man two women, hesitating there at the threshold, heads close, whispering. Buddy and Janey sitting to his left. Buddy like some boulder or swollen redwood stump. Janey—tall, dark, blue-eyed, freckled, a real Celtic warrioress—leaning slightly forward in her chair and peering at him. That clear, hard, cop stare. Because Janey *is* a cop, an M.P. at the Sagamihara housing unit, where nothing ever goes really wrong, and she is bored, a black-belt, fourth *dan,* but nobody to use it on. Janey killed a man once, a drunk Marine. Knocked his piece to one side and punched him in the throat. Smashed his larynx. Couldn't breathe, went into convulsions, died before the ambulance got there. Donner has always been very simpatico with Janey. He gives her a smile.

Even closer, up by his left shoulder, a starchy white nurselike presence connected to the damp infant warmth and weight pressing there. The baby. Right.

Ruriko, irritated still or again about something, sits huddled toward the foot of the bed, looking down and massaging her forearms. Thirty-nine, just two years older than Janey—hard to believe. Ruriko: some lines, lots of gray in her thick glossy hair, but it's a nice gray, silvery. High strong cheekbones, full lips, figure thickening only a bit. Still lush and lovely. But the emphasis on lush. Donner senses it through the fog. Ruriko needs a drink. Or, rather, another. Several more. Doubles.

Crowding in close on the right, some newsgirl and her cameraman, the girl pale and trembling. NHK? Was she somehow familiar? He looks again at the mike, then down along the right sleeve of her blouse, sees the brownish blotches, and understands that these are bloodstains.

Bloodstains from.

Ah. Was this newsgirl in the ambulance too? Donner thinks so. Did she croon to the baby, keep her arms around Donner's? He out cold completely, so he believes, or at least not for very long, but all recentness feels curiously smashed and jagged. There were some roaring brown intervals during which everything seemed to shrink back and stipple over with a sort of flat monochrome irrelevance. Shock, he supposes. He lost it there by the river, confusing the Tama with the Song Cai, and some weird fog sucking him back to that gully full of slick red skulls. No good, no good. He lost it again in the ambulance and once or twice since then, when lights cut through the rushing sepia smog-tones, when brusque actions were taken which had tugged and hurt sharply. Shock, for sure, but the situation is now easing and clarifying. Control—isn't that what Donner's all about?

Donner is doped against pain, but not, it seems, heavily. He has no sense of chemical well-being, only areas of ominous numbness—his left eyebrow, shoulder, and hip, and the outside of his right thigh— which speak as yet abstractly to his brain. Donner can now think, but has a hard time rummaging around and hauling out words for his thoughts, then pushing these big fuzzy words out of his mouth and toward the surrounding ears. Even small words—*a, the, we, run*—seem the size of gerbils. Even his very simple message for the television girl: *Go away.*

But, but. A lovely girl, looks like just out of her teens. Obviously suffering herself—deadline pressure? Pain? Pity for the baby? *Gaijin* fever, because he's a foreigner? Donner feels badly for her, watches a tear well on her eyeliner, slip to her cheek, and roll slowly down, a wet streak narrowing through her makeup. The tear expires at the curve of her jaw. She swallows once, twice. Donner watches the muscles working in her throat, her tongue moving over her lips. Clearly, she would prefer to be elsewhere but is gamely doing her job. A journalist himself, Donner can see that she is doing it well, asking the right questions, rephrasing the difficult ones. Her English is good. Methodically, she goes after the *who, what, where, when* of Noborito.

If not the *why.*

Most questions, Donner just waves a hand at Buddy or Janey or Ruriko. Let them handle it. Especially Ruriko, with her perfect Japanese and her perfect public self, her universe of private grievances.

But never mind Ruriko. Donner has his hands literally full with the baby who, since they made contact in mid-air, has clutched his beard, hair, T-shirt—and simply clung with the strength of terror. A strong baby, clinging still, trembling and weeping. Her tiny vertical ponytail with its pink and blood-speckled ribbon brushes against and tickles his nose. He remembers whose blood it is and again feels the seep of pity. Donner cradles the baby in his left arm, feeling foolish.

"This," he says, "… baby."

"Yes," says Ruriko. "Of course."

"Until," says the newsgirl.

"Whenever," says Ruriko, giving Donner a look. *"Itsudemo ii."*

It's starting again, the room unmooring itself and echoing. Donner focuses on the clear plastic tube snaking from the square of tape on the back of his right hand. Focusing helps. But the monochrome velvet wind noise is seeping back in with all its nibbling warmth, infiltrating all around the edges of his awareness. The moment is once more outpacing him. Ruriko needs a drink—and a baby? Is that it? Is that the essential point here? Donner does what he always does when trying to concentrate. He moves his right hand to Thuong's tooth on its gold chain. But tooth and chain are gone.

"Got 'em," says Buddy. "All your stuff, right here."

Moods of the room: Buddy semijocular, Janey solemn, Ruriko angry, newsgirl pained, medical people concerned and alert. Donner watches the newsgirl's bobbed hair bounce minutely as she speaks. Her lips move, he sees her little *doracura,* those pronounced upper canines. Donner can also hear her, hear the soft staccato Japanese and the more oblong English words, plosives and fricatives coming rapidly with no spaces in between, so before he can sort the words for comprehension, can line them up in his mind and bear down on them, they seem to overlap and finally swallow each other in a rippling sweep of syllable-chords. Donner shakes his head and shrugs.

"She says, 'What happened?'" Buddy repeats, slowly.

"Don't," Donner croaks. The nurse holds a bent glass drinking straw to his lips, which feel cracked and dry, as though he has been to a dentist. He runs his tongue over them, then sips ice water and tries again. "Don't know."

"Says, 'How did the baby fall?'"

125

"Don't know," says Donner.

"Says, 'What if the baby has no relatives?'"

"Then we keep her," says Ruriko.

"Don't know," says Donner.

"Then we keep her," says Ruriko.

"Says, 'Where do we live?'" says Buddy. "Right out there by Hashimoto, ma'am, Sagamihara Depot Camp."

"Let me hold her," says Ruriko.

"I live in the Camp," says Buddy. "Donner and Ruriko are sort of right around the corner."

"Good idea," says Donner. "Shoulder's... wet."

"Lady says, 'When you—'"

At Ruriko's touch, the baby trembles. As Ruriko tries to lift her the baby screams high and wild in total panic and clings frantically to the collar of Donner's hospital pajamas, rips out a tiny fistful of his beard.

"Wow," says Buddy. "Quite a grip. Quite a screamer."

"You'd scream too," says Janey.

"What's the matter?" asks Ruriko.

"Don't know," says Donner.

"Look," says Buddy, pointing a corrugated-banana forefinger. "She's even hanging on with her toes.

Never saw that before. Curly pink toes, just clamped right on there. Better leave her be, Ruriko."

"I wasn't going to *hurt* her."

"Leave her be. Donner? Lady wants to know, when're you getting out?"

"Don't," said Donner. "Tonight?"

"No chance, Francis," says Ruriko. "Look at yourself." Then, "Why doesn't she want me to hold her?"

"Don't touch the baby, Ruriko. Wait till she calms down," says Donner, now in a lucid space, feeling a small hot whiskerless patch on his cheek. "Tonight, tomorrow for sure. Lots to do."

"Maybe I don't think so," says the nurse suddenly. "Three day at least. Maybe four, five. Depend on a doctor. Depend on a cat scan."

"Depends on me," says Donner. "Tomorrow morning. Where am I?"

"Hospital, town of Fuchu. By the river."

"Good. Close to home."

Camera, oh, yes. The little red light winks out. The cameraman backs toward the three figures in white still nodding and whispering in the doorway. The newsgirl leans against the foot of the bed, sighs, then looks up.

"Mr. Donner," she says, slowly, "you should listen to your doctor. You should get some sleep."

"Why *can't* I?" says Ruriko, now plainly aggrieved. "Why *can't* I hold her? I'm certainly not *drunk,* if that's what you think."

"Baby is nervous," says the nurse.

"Is traumatize," says the man in white.

"I *know* that. I wanted to comfort her, give her a little hug. That's all. Just one little hug. Is that too much to ask? What about *me?*"

"I hate this damn snuff," says Janey, touching the slight bulge in her cheek. "Wish I had a smoke."

"Me too," says Buddy. "Leave the baby be."

"I knew it," says Donner. "Smoking."

"Not your business. Not at all."

"You'll never quit."

"My business," says Buddy.

"No balls."

"Two balls and two lungs. All of 'em my business."

"Never catch any babies that way," says Donner.

"Cross that bridge when I come to it."

"Consider your health," says Donner, perking up. "Consider your loved ones. Don't you ever stop and *think?*"

"That's the problem," says Buddy. "I think too damn much. Got to take my mind offa things. Offa these *plump, luscious nurses.*"

"I'm going out," says Janey. "Spit this goo. Get a little fresh air."

"I'm going out, period," says Ruriko. "I am *not* drunk."

"Mr. Donner," says the newsgirl. "That was a pretty good thing, which you have done by the river. We have a picture, you know."

"How," says Donner, suddenly tired again. "Could?"

"One man who already was there. Photographer."

"My name is Donner."

"Yes," says the newsgirl.

"What's-your-name?"

"Miyuki. Kobayashi Miyuki *desu.*"

"*Hajimemashite,*" says Donner.

"Not really the first meeting," says Miyuki. "But, *yoroshiku.*"

"*Yoroshiku dozo.*"

"So sad, by the river."

"Yes," says Donner. "And before that, I've seen you, I think."

"Yes," says Miyuki, reaching out, touching the baby's shoulder. "Ah, the poor little *akachan.*"

"On TV."

"What is going to happen to *her?*"

"Don't know," says Donner. "Relatives? Some agency?"

"To tell the truth, Mr. Donner, you should listen your doctor—"

"I *am* a doctor."

"—*Doctor* Donner—"

"Call me Donner."

"—you should listen your doctor, Donner."

"You don't have to call me Doctor Donner."

"Ah, so, a joke. Your are feeling better."

"Not too bad."

"Still you had better to listen your doctor. You need the rest."

"Yes," said Donner. "But so do you."

"Maybe we could do another interview," she says, to Donner, but keeping her eyes on the baby. "Later. Now I must to return back, to studio."

"Sure," says Donner. "Take it easy."

"When you are feeling better."

"Actually, I don't feel too bad."

"That's good."

"I mean, considering."

"That's good," she says. *"Ki o tsukette kudasai,* please take care."

"Hai," says Donner, scrabbling for the words, getting them, very pleased. *"Ki o tsukemasu,* I surely will take care. I always do."

Friday, 10:31 P.M.

Youth, health, strength, superb physical conditioning—these all make a real difference in terms of recuperation. And of course courage. And, well, painkillers and alcohol. Kawakami Yukio, home, finally, and, after half an hour of alternately soaking in the hot *ofuro* and soaping under the shower, now sits with an icepack on his nose and washing down the Norshin tablets with cup after steaming cup of sake. With every cup, his vitality of mind and body comes surging back. What were agonies are now dull pains and will soon be half-pleasurable twinges and soreness. Or entirely pleasurable. Yukio's lip curls at the feebleness of a little invigorating pain against the power of his fixed purpose. Discouragement? Absurd.

Yes, Yukio is safe and mending fast. He allows himself a chuckle and another cup of sake, while looking around at his room, with, as always, satisfaction. Yukio is lean and compact; his room is small and uncluttered. No 4LDK for him, even if he could afford it. He neither wants nor needs a separate living area and dining area and kitchen. He is a soldier, not some middle-class housewife. A palace? Fine, if all his aspirations are realized. A barracks? Fine, in the mean time. But never, not ever, some *furi furi fua fua* middle class luxury nest a la Yamamoto.

Ah, Yamamoto. Rest in peace, Professor Dumpling, Professor *Daifuku.* Yamamoto, Wagamamamoto, Squashimoto. Yukio grins, pours another steaming cup. No, the good professor would not have been happy in Yukio's unliberal home, would have panicked at the absence of creature comforts. No soft thick foreign carpets, no hundred electrical gadgets to save his precious time, to spare him all exertion, to encourage his soft and effortless regression to gross fetushood. To indulge his putrid liberal flesh.

None of that here. Just as well he's dead, old Commietraitormoto, because this room, Yukio's, is Japan's Room of the Future. The keynote here is not luxurious weakness but Spartan strength. Bath-toilet. Living-dining area. Period. Two burner *gasreinji,* tiny sink with the water heater above it, tiny *reisoko* for the beer and sushi. Battered *kotatsu* to stick his legs under on those winter mornings and evenings while he eats, reads, sips the *ocha* and the sake, writes the endless memoranda (which he never mails) to their Leader, the head of Shining Mist, his organization, which is much more than that. Shining Mist is Yukio's life.

And the Leader, Nakatani Taro, is more than Yukio's Leader. Nakatani-*san* is his spiritual father, replacing Yukio's pathetic actual one, another so-called historian, a zealot, a devil for "facts." Yukio downs a bitter cup. Ah yes, the old man. Who wrote a scandalous high school textbook slandering Nippon in the name of "accuracy": World War II had been "hyped as some kind of jihad or holy war"; the incidents at Nanking and Bata'an and elsewhere were "atrocities, completely covered up." He actually wrote that. Fortunately, a government committee cut and rewrote that passage and 290 others, because it looked like treason to them. And to Yukio's classmates. And to Yukio.

Yukio, who was trying to hold his head up at school. At his mediocre school, which is all his bar hostess mother could afford, because the old man's money went for lawyers. Fighting for his vile book. Stubborn old bastard, in and out of the courts for most of Yukio's thirty years—but the old man finally lost! Something else to celebrate. Just last week, Yukio read about it, the Supreme Court. A clear, hard, realistic ruling. The state has the right to do whatever it wants to a textbook so that teaching can be "neutral and fair." Yukio will drink to that. The old man is still pottering around up there in Takasaki, writing letters to the editor, but he hasn't got many years left. Yamamoto is waiting for him in hell.

What a contrast, both of them, with Nakatani Taro—may he live forever! Yukio drinks liberally to the Leader's health. The Leader, who was actually here once. Who graced Yukio's home with his presence, sat on that very cushion, looked around, nodded. The nod was in approbation, Yukio knew. Wordlessly, perfectly, the Leader praised Yukio's asceticism. Yes, that nod, that moment, is a flashing diamond of memory.

Yukio tosses back his sake in tribute to it, pours himself another.

Praised him, yes, and rightly so. True, the Leader's sense of duty requires that he visit all the comrades. But Yukio could tell how specially pleased the Leader had been in this room, how regretful that he'd had to leave after only a few minutes. But those few minutes were enough to perfect the soldier's understanding between them. The Leader ran his white-gloved hand around the door frame molding, over the topmost row of books, then, smilingly, like the Buddha proffering the lotus, presented his open palm for Yukio's own inspection. Immaculate. As white and shining as the tough martial spirit which they shared.

"I'm cold," the Leader said. "Where is your heater?"

"Resting," said Yukio, risking levity, relishing the Leader's characteristic deadpan wit. As though the Leader could care whether a room were freezing or broiling! Or even notice! No, the Leader is far above such things too. Yukio's ancient kerosene room-heater is for use on the coldest days only. The rest of the year it stays wrapped in plastic and tucked into the *oshire*, beneath his *fouton* and blankets. His old Sony black and white is for watching the news and nothing else. The rest of the time it is off. His clothes-rack holds only his uniform, a few shirts and trousers, a brown leather bomber jacket. The bookshelves behind him hold works on political philosophy and nothing else, except a few volumes by Mishima. And, well, a few stacks of *manga* for his lighter moments. (*Manga*, but serious ones, which speak to his own situation, boldly illustrated sagas of the struggles and trimuphs of the Right.) His tea-chest holds underwear, sweaters, handkerchiefs, a very expensive Masamoto sushi knife, small but beautifully tapered and honed, and a small, round, flat metal box with the word "Kotobuki" on the lid. The box once held cookies. Now it contains his few valuables and papers. Period.

No wife, no squalling brats. Nothing soft.

Yukio drains his sake, decides he's had enough.

Oh all right, one more, but only one. Yes, he has those few possessions and nothing else. A man is free in proportion to the number of things he can do without. So Yukio's criteria are necessity and sufficiency. For him the question is, How much for the body? And the answer is, Enough that the Work may go forward. And no more. Frills and decorations? None. Above his bookcase, a formal photographic portrait of Tenno Heika in imperial robes, a shot of Yukio and his comrades, and a framed Special Order of Merit from Shining Mist. On the far wall, a calendar with today's date circled in red.

No, nothing here to coddle or distract. Yukio does an hour of calisthenics every day, finishing with twenty one-handed pushups, left and right. In winter, he skips rope barechested in the snow, until his corded body glows and steams. Then, like the Danes in their saunas, he whips himself all over with a fistful of knotted nylon twine. Stinging welts, blood to the surface, that feeling of such intense *vitality*. (Whipping and manipulating often to the point of, well, ejaculation—but so what? Whose business is that? It is a warrior's way, private, efficient, at once mortifying the flesh and easing it.) Afterward, winter and summer, always an icewater shower. Yukio has never had a cold in his life. He is a real soldier—a supersoldier, since he imposes this training on himself. He is his own drill sergeant, and a brutal one at that. In the entire Organization, only Yukio keeps to such a high hard regimen, keeps to it gladly, knowing as he does the unimportance of *having,* the overwhelming importance of *being.*

Being what? What *is* Yukio? Well, he is a hero. That is the correct word. Let us use it. He has put everything on the line for Principle, has long sacrificed his comfort, stood ready to risk his life, for the greater good. Is there some better definition of hero? Yukio thinks not. He has this night taken chances which the normal man would not have contemplated. He has sustained wounds in battle. By killing Yamamoto, or providing at least the occasion for his death, Yukio has covered himself in—in glory. Those are the true facts. That is the real factual situation, shorn of all emotionalism. So that is the proper term for Yukio on this night of pain and high hazard: hero.

Certainly, Shining Mist could use a hero or two. Several months ago at a rally the Leader hinted as much to Yukio. The Leader looked around at all the preening chorusing yesmen in the hall, then favored Yukio with a wry smile, which Yukio had been quick to interpret. *Don't be like them,* the smile said, *like the strutters and fashion-plate orators, with their sparkling brass buttons and their brassy young women, because the future of our group and our country is in the hands of doers, not posers.* That was the message of the smile, another diamond moment, and Yukio knew he read it properly. What would the Leader say right now, if he could look into Yukio's mind and heart? If he were suddenly in possession of all the true facts and details and motivations concerning this epic Friday evening?

Yukio has another drink and ponders. He sees the Leader in his wisdom smiling again. *Yuk-kun, he might well say, you have been rash. You have acted without consensus or approval. But you have* acted. *That is the essential point. You made mistakes, but you have also made history. All those others, the jealous ladies' men, who say you stink like a fish and think like a fish, they will never make mistakes because they will never take risks. Don't concern youself about them. They are followers, and nothing can alter their essential nature. As a group, they may seem formidable, but I assure you that individually they are afraid of their own shoelaces. Such men, if we may call them such, are easily expendable.*

Expendable—has Yukio has drowsed for a split-second?

He is hyper-alert once more.

Expendable, yes, hard but true. Yukio drinks, nodding profoundly, humbly acceding to the sheer mass of solemn truth borne by the Leader's words. Expendable, all of them, exactly right. Yukio couldn't have put it better himself. *Such men,* the Leader would surely say, *such men are absolutely interchangeable, perfectly mediocre. They think with their glands, like their girlfriends, and, like them, are at best decorative. Such so-called men are mere flesh—creatures of the physical, prisoners of the superficial, slaves to the appearances of things. In fact they are no great improvement over the traitor Yamamoto-sensei. Whereas we, Yukio, you and I, are concerned with the reality that resides beyond mere flesh. Yes, our concern is with the spirit. With, in short, the reality of the spirit.*

Yes!

And the spirit of reality.

Exactly! Yukio nods, pours.

The spirit of Yamato!

Banzai! Yukio downs the sake manfully and at a gulp.

Therefore we, Yukio, you and I, are essential to the Mission. They are not. They are easily replaced. As easily as burnt furniture and scorched timbers. More easily, in fact, than the sword. But swords too are replaceable, Yukio, so do not worry. A sword is a piece of metal. Old katana are valuable of course, but chiefly as symbols. Of what we as a people once were and will be yet again. Symbols, relics, material things. Not our first concern. As you and I know very well, we are concerned ultimately with the spirit, with the mind and heart of Dai Nippon. And that spirit, my son, burns most brightly now in you.

Yes, yes, yes. Simply… yes. Yukio, nodding again beneath the weight of Truth, feeling the hot tears welling, refilling his cup and drinking a silent toast to Nakatani Taro. To such a Leader. A Leader who could at any time have Yukio's life for the asking. That is the depth and power of Yukio's love.

And does not Yukio himself participate in this greatness? The answer again is yes, and to a very considerable degree. True, the potential to realize personal greatness lies within the power of all, if they would simply reach out, grasp, hold fast. But potential remains merely that. Few dare to realize it. Yukio is one of the few. Not a boast: the simple truth. He has this night proved himself a cunning and remorseless foe.

And how are they faring, his enemies? No doubt blubbery Yamamoto is on ice somewhere, his fat wife blubbering, their foreigner-loving liberal friends all frightened and huddled together like a bunch of flabby degenerate rabbits. And that is the desired response after all, terror being the appropriate emotion for traitors.

And the radicals! Yukio chuckles again, briefly, until his belly muscles cramp and double him over in his chair. Oh, that little hell-bitch! But Yukio thinks of her, crushed and helpless beneath the weight of the big policeman, and his belly muscles relax, and he can breathe again. He smiles. Yes, that was only the beginning for her. Soon she and all her traitor-comrades would be crushed and pulverized—gasping, screaming, protesting their innocence—beneath the massed weight of the police and the entire right wing and the whole fat stupid middle class. Protesting their innocence—truthfully! That is the delicious part! Truthfully and futilely protesting their innocence of the evening's typically radical outrages. Theft, mayhem, assault, firebombing. Shame on them.

And then the weaklings and appeasers in his Organization, the pitiful *wagamama.* The ones who said, *No violence, no direct action, let's refer everything to a subcommittee, let's form a study group, let's order some pizza, let's get home in time to cuddle up with our wives and sweethearts.* Well, they'll lose face, won't they? A lot. And maybe have some trouble with all their posturing and parliamentary nonsense in a hall of charred timbers, ankle-deep in a cold slush of ashes. Fair enough, they'll be shown up for what they are, the microphone men. They'll be on the sidelines where they belong. And his few real comrades will be strengthened. And his own path to power swept clean. Real power. In the Organization and soon in the entire Right and therefore Japan itself.

And therefore the world.

Napoleon *would* be proud.

All right. Tomorrow, the doctor, fix the nose. Take a week or so—Yukio no longer has a job, nor any regrets about that—so he can lie low here, rest, let nature do its work. He can watch the news, observe his strategy as it bears its inevitable fruit. Disaster? Yukio smiles. What disaster? He is happy things turned out this way, ecstatic. This evening will mark the beginning of the beginning of Japan's long climb back. This evening will take form as one of the standout early chapters in his autobiography, which schoolchildren in the not too distant future will be obliged to read, for inspiration and guidance.

Yukio raises his cup, toasting Napoleon, his great Leader, himself, spilling hardly a drop. He chuckles, winces, does something unusual for the comfort-scorning soldier he has become: he reaches for the television's remote control device, and thinks, chuckling, then laughing out loud despite the pain, *Don't want to use this thing too much, get soft like Yamamoto.*

Click.

No news yet. Nothing till eleven.

Click.

Oh, all right, one more.

Friday, 11:02 P.M.

Teshima Tadao seldom pays much attention to the news. He either knows about it beforehand, whatever it is, or he is uninterested, or both. Usually both. It is his business to know things. He is an important man, *oyabun* of a major Kanto group. He is very old but not elderly, tall, thick-bodied, strong, heavy-featured, shaven-headed. Teshima has three senior *kobun*—Eiji, Tetsuo, Akio—and perhaps a thousand middle-and junior-level men. Managers, workers, soldiers. And if you count *chimpira* and other hangers-on, fringe types and hopefuls, then that figure would double. If you count them. Teshima does not, because they are nonentities, clowns.

Like that young imbecile in the pachinko truck this afternoon—

Never mind.

Teshima would like to take that punk, and—

Never mind.

As the masseur works on his back, gorgeous with gryphons and dragons, Teshima lies, eyes closed, half-listening to the television beneath the big faded sign:

TATOOED PERSON'S NOT ALOWED ON PREMISIS

145

He and the senior *kobun* and the guards, all lavishly tattooed, are where they always are in the early evening, in a sauna above a theater which—to Teshima's private amusement—shows mostly yakuza movies. It is near Ikebukuro station, on the Yamanote line, in northwest metro Tokyo. It is in the shadow of Sunshine City, that colossal pile—how many stories? How many people could it hold? Thirty thousand? More, maybe. Teshima has a large piece of it, of course. The theater building he owns outright. He likes the sauna, likes Ikebukuro, likes being in the heart of the grit and glitter, the noise and fumes, the money.

He, Eiji, Tetsuo, and Akio are getting their nightly *shiatsu* massage. Teshima loves *shiatsu,* credits it with his remarkable vigor. *Shiatsu* hurts. *Ah!* As the man's iron hands twist and knead, Teshima exhales sharply then sucks in a big lungful of the good steamy-cedar smell. He moves his cheek slightly over the perfect white cloth which covers his pillow, savoring the linen caress.

Oh yes, savoring it. Teshima is an ascetic, as everyone knows, because he wants them to know that. But he can take enormous pleasure from the sensations of everyday: the smell and underfoot springiness of fresh *tatami*, his mossy rock-garden with its *koi* pond, morning birdsong, a woman's soft laughter, good green tea properly served, the sweet healing steaminess of his evening *ofuro*, the delicious pangs of *shiatsu*. So in many respects he is no ascetic but rather a sensualist, even a voluptuary. But, pleasure or pain, he gives no sign. His inner state is his business. Teshima is a man of secrets.

Indeed, one of his life-strategies has been to discover as much as possible about others while giving away as little as possible about himself. Consequently, he has whole floppy-disc libraries on the major figures of the age. Useful information, much of it: potentially embarrassing or incriminating. But they, the competition—police, rival gangs, politicians, big business types—have nothing on him beyond a contradictory mass of misinformation and a few biographical guesses. As DiGiralamo used to say, *Nobody has a handle on Tod.* Nobody knows him. Has he vices, superstitions, weaknesses, loved ones? No one knows. Nor will they, ever. His friends are long-dead, most of them, but certain abstractions—Courage, Duty, Honor, Patience, Justice, Courtesy—have become his daily companions, have taken on substance, personhood. Their counsel is invariably good. Taken together, they constitute *giri-ninjo,* that

147

blend of obligation and humaneness that ennobled the lives of many a samurai.

And many a true yakuza too.

People call them gangsters, hoodlums. The policeman Ishimura, for example, is always talking about the need to sweep Japan clean of them. Well, Teshima knows it is all talk, and he knows Ishimura's Chief, a much more reasonable man. But Teshima dislikes the names. Punk. Underworld scum. *Gyangu.* Because he calls the yakuza mother, father, brother.

Before he was born, Teshima lost his biological father, in the last week of the *Nichi-Ro Sensoh,* the Russo-Japanese War. He lost his grandmother and mother in the flooding of a very bad typhoon in 1916, and everyone else in the cholera that followed the floods. Then *Kanto Dai Jishin,* the Great Kanto Quake, destroyed his orphanage in 1923, reduced it to a dusty heap of brick and mortar, put him out on the streets of Shinagawa, Omori, Kamata, Kawasaki. He begged, stole, sometimes worked for 30 or 40 *sen* per day. Real labor—unloading trucks, stevedoring, warehousing— whatever nobody else would do. Labor that burned more calories than it would buy at the noodle shops. Young Teshima, working like an animal. Eating, sleeping, living like an animal. Thinking like one.

Not a stable boyhood. No notion that there could be such things as stability, continuity—anything beyond the rubble-strewn present.

Then everything changed for him. Born in 1908, he came into existence in 1925, on a steel-bright New Year's afternoon in Yokohama. He had been picking pockets at the shrine, tried to pick the pocket of a slim young man in Western *yofuku*: homburg hat and thick tweed suit with a gold watch-chain across the vest-front. As he probed for the man's wallet, however, Teshima felt a steel band around either biceps. Hands. And he no sooner realized what was happening to him than it happened. The young man turned, slowly it seemed, and gracefully, so that the full skirt of his jacket flared, and, smiling, he hit the seventeen year old Teshima between the eyes.

Consciousness. Vibration, movement, motor-car. Back seat. Hard-bodied men on either side. They sat, hands on thighs. Teshima's head ached. Outside, dusk, the western clouds reddening. Too cold to stick and melt, snow brushed against the windscreen. They were passing an unfamiliar stretch of rubble, brick and stone: scorched half-walls of warehouses, power poles rusted and leaning: the legacy of the Quake. Through the gaps Teshima glimpsed gray reaches of harbor water. He turned his head, concentrated on the men in the front seat. The driver, big, steering them around the holes and piles of rock with quiet concentration. The slim man, the one who had struck Teshima, lounging in the passenger seat, smoking a cigarette, letting the smoke trail out his vent window. Teshima looked again at the men flanking him, their fingers splayed on the stretched fabric of their trousers. He noticed that the fabric was good, heavy and tight-looking, the creases sharp from the knees down. He noticed that the man on his left wore a plain gold ring, and that the man on his right seemed to have something wrong with the little finger of his left hand. Teshima looked again. Yes: no first joint.

"What kind of auto-car is this?" The slim man, his face now in profile to Teshima, was, it seemed, addressing him.

What kind? Well, it was big. It smelled new. Leather, cologne or hair lotion, tobacco. A good smell. Teshima sniffed, looked around. Glass, bright chrome, gleaming whiskey-colored wood with a tight spiral grain. Engine quiet and powerful. But what *kind?* He had no idea. He was riding in an automobile-car, truly inside one, for the first time in his life, and looking out. That much he knew, but that was all. He tried to think, but his thoughts skidded from kinds of automobile-car to kinds of death. The men would probably kill him. There was nothing he could do to save himself. He knew it, but, as the knowledge grew, it brought a strange dawning lightness and sense of relief. Was life so wonderful, after all? As for the car, well, he knew of course that there *were* different kinds, but that was all. He shook his head, shrugged.

"*Shirimasen.*"

"Don't know? Well," said the man, "this is a Packard."

A Packard!

"A new one," the man added, expelling small smoke-puffs with each word.

Teshima Tadao was riding in a new Packard automobile-car!

"Do you know who I am?"

Again, Teshima shook his head.

"I am a Packard owner."

All four men laughed briefly, soft little barks of amusement. Then the man at the wheel and the two in back resumed their former blank expressions, as if powerful rubber bands beneath their skins had snapped back into place. Teshima noticed that the one on his left, the one wearing a ring, was blind in one eye. It was milky-blue, like a marble. The slim man retained his smile.

"I am a Packard-owner, and my name is Moriuchi Tadamasa."

No! Death, then, certainly. Moriuchi Tadamasa—ah, Teshima had no luck. Moriuchi, who would go on to become an intimate of Kodama, Taoka, Kishi. Who was already a local power. Trying to pick the pocket of Monster Moriuchi. Why not try to steal the tonsils of a wolf? Teshima could only sigh and gaze down at his old cracked shoes. Well, what did he have to look forward to? Another seventeen years like the first? Had he anything to lose?

Moriuchi was no longer smiling. His voice was hard. "Beg for your life."

A pause, three or four heartbeats, then once more Teshima shook his head.

"Good!" Moriuchi seemed delighted, was smiling again. "It was our little test. If a man will whine and plead when he is not even in pain, then he will do anything, and you can never trust him. You would be surprised how many do beg. Tough men. Unfortunately for them." Moriuchi reached over the back of the seat, held out his leather-bound cigarette case, the leather patterned in shiny irregular squares, the skin perhaps of some strange animal. "Smoke?"

"Arigato," said Teshima, thank you.

"Anyway, this is how we recruit."

Thus began his real life. Moriuchi was, had been, everything to him. Friend, boss, teacher. Forty years later, Moriuchi-*sensei* died, and Teshima inherited the 250 man organization which, in another twenty years, quadrupled. One thousand good men, dedicated, sworn. That was enough. Of course, there were many larger combines in Japan—the gigantic Yamaguchi-*gumi,* for example, of Osaka-Kobe. But size isn't everything. Man for man, Teshima's was the most efficient operation of its kind on the Pacific Rim, or so he believed. And it was his, absolutely. He never had to second-guess some super-*oyabun* like Inagawa, never had anyone breathing down his neck. When, for example, he decided that his people would pull out of drugs and prostitution, well, that was what they did. No discussions, no lamenting lost revenues. And what a good decision that was, financially and spiritually.

Oh, yes, Teshima Tadao is a spiritual man, or has over the years become one. Shinto, Buddhism, Christo-*kyo*—he saw no great differences. Toward the end, Moriuchi-*sensei* had been uneasy, had advised

153

Teshima to phase out the drugs and women if possible. Teshima did so. Of course, many women went into prostitution voluntarily. But many did not—those little Thais and Philippinas, for example, whose families sold them. And who wants to be constantly trying to separate the entrepreneurs from the slaves? Not Teshima, not when he could be making money. Drugs, same thing. Except of course methamphetamines, which were hardly drugs at all, more like solid-state coffee. Teshima noticed that, sooner or later, drugs turned everyone, dealers and users alike, into beasts. Dead ones.

Teshima knows of no exceptions. That gross Escobar, the former ultrabillionaire? Latterly a fugitive, desperate, living as Teshima himself used to. Now dead, shot to pieces. One example of many. Therefore, in the long run at least, drugs and whores are bad business. And, very possibly, terrible karma. Call that superstition, Teshima does not care. The point is, no women and no narcotics, for it has been so decided.

Gambling? Fine. Clients are adults. If they want to pit themselves against the odds then that is their problem. Loan-sharking, same thing. Nobody drags Teshima's borrowers in off the streets and forces half a million, a million yen on them. Gun-running? Not so terrible. More often than not it simply helps maintain a balance of power, helps prevent wholesale destruction of one side by the other. Teshima is old. He believes in good and evil. But he is very skeptical about—as DiGiralamo called them—*good guys and bad guys.* DiGiralamo, his old partner, an exception: one of the very good guys.

Protection, extortion, blackmail? Hard words for frequently beneficial activities: checks and balances for the power-mad, a redistribution of funds for the disadvantaged. Teshima rebuilt his old orphanage. He maintains a dozen scholarships, although he has no very high opinion of universities. He put Eiji, his number one, through law school. Teshima is no Gautama, nor does he pretend to be. But, catering to the darker impulses, Teshima has now and then managed to harness them for the common good. Even so-called labor racketeering has its points, and thousands of marginally employable men have Teshima to thank for their paychecks. Management too. Teshima's unruly *sokaiya* specialists have caused the speedy adjournment of many a vast and tedious annual meeting, to the satisfaction of everyone—or almost.

And so forth. Teshima is the man, and has been for fifty years, who can get things done. His people thrive in that rich narrow field where *thou shalt not* overlaps *I will.*

Surely, they have their detractors, but these are all comfortable people, are they not? Soft, thickly muffled with ideals, swaddled in comforts and advantages. Like a shepherd toward his fattest sheep, Teshima holds the middle-class in affectionate contempt. Daily he thanks his gods that he is what he is, that his life has been as it has been. He loves the yakuza, their traditions and history, all those centuries of itinerant gamblers and peddlers and masterless samurai. Outcasts, barred from society's rewards—but some yakuza have nonetheless done their best to safeguard that society. Occasionally at the expense of their lives. Have not his men functioned as auxiliary police? They have. They have broken strikes, battled the Reds, stood firm between the Imperial family and those who meant them harm. Is Japan once again wealthy and powerful, standing tall in the councils of nations? Yes indeed, and much credit should go to the forces of conservatism and stability. To Japan's right, of which the so-called gangsters were such a vital part. Scratch a yakuza, get beneath that tattoo, and you'll find a patriot. So Teshima makes no apologies, suffers no guilt, has few regrets. He has triumphed where others would never have survived.

And Teshima Tadao has known love. A love named Hanako, who bore him a son, almost forty-eight years ago. Sweet lover, the wife of a friend, true—but a friend who had shipped out to Luzon at the start of the War, and of whom there was subsequently no word. Well, they both thought he was dead. But no, he staggered out of the jungle a full three years after the armistice, his uniform in tatters, and his reason. So Teshima took care of them both, all through the postwar horrors. Thousands lived in the subway stations—Ueno, Kanda, Ginza—but not those three. Thousands scrounged and starved, but Teshima kept Hanako and her husband in, if not luxury, then at least comfort. A nurse for the husband, and, for Hanako, Teshima.

Thirty-seven years old, a brilliant black marketeer. Sponge-like he soaked up the millions of tiny details— names, faces, prices, strengths, weaknesses—learning every day from Moriuchi-*sensei* and from DiGiralamo, the quartermaster sergeant. DiGiralamo had the instincts. He could steal anything from anybody, sell anything to anybody, but had never made so much money so fast as they had in the hot sun and stinking rubble around Akihabara, and, later, after some bad territorial battles, Ochanomizu. How many cartons of Luckies and Camels had they vended? How many Hershey chocolate bars? Zippo lighters, Schaeffer pens, Bulova wristwatches, Zenith radios? Too many to count. These were the crucial nouns in the language of the Occupation, trade the crucial verb, supply and demand the new grammar.

Nylon stockings, a Mount Fuji of nylons. And good rye whiskey, an ocean. Even Jeeps! Yes, truly—and more than once. Always they got a good price. Everybody knew Teshima. He was everywhere on his huge Harley-Davidson motorcycle—the 61E model no less, the true Knucklehead—and wearing his aviator sunglasses. He was the expediter, the middleman, the doer. He brought Americans, officers and enlisted men and swarming civilians, with all their urges and their massive purchasing power, together with his army of variously-skilled acquaintances. He knew them all, and they all knew him. Except that none of them really did.

Only Hanako. His supreme secret and the main reason for all the others. Yes, those were the days, life sung in his veins then. Everything he did, it was for her. Well, now she is with the ancestors, and their boy too. But the boy's child, Hatsumi, Teshima's granddaughter, has survived. True, she married a left-wing intellectual, a fat professor-clown, a person beneath all notice. But they have a child, just two, whom Teshima has never seen (for they are all his secret). From the photographs, however, a beautiful child: Hanako. His line. War, fire, epidemic, earthquake, typhoon—all the demon jests, surviving them. His line, his blood, infant Hanako.

And does he not have the first Hanako, still, in his heart? Does he not, constantly, breathe the special life of remembrance into her spirit? And pray daily for her and all of them at the shrine? Are not their ashes in the ornate *butsudan* in his home, and will not he, in a year, or five, or ten—it makes no difference—join them there? And did he not love her every second of every minute of their lives together, and absolutely? And, having had such love, is he not among the luckiest of men? Yes. Yes, of course. But still, after thirty-five years, the black times come, eclipsing her luminous memory. Well, they have to be got through, so get through them he does, those days and hours and minutes of scalding grief. Of which he gives not the slightest outward sign. Teshima is in control of himself; controlling everything else is easy.

He has by now an almost mystical feel for the requirements of a given situation, a perfect sense of timing. Zen, something like that. A natural killer, natural strategist, he does what is necessary, no more or less, at the right moment. He is the pure instrument of his own policy. Minimum effort, maximum effect.

His lieutenants, the three *kobun* and others just below them, believe that he is perpetually testing them. He is. He tests them with his silence, his periods of seeming obliviousness, which can stretch for days. He tests them by observing the quality of their repose as he strums upon his old *shamisen*, which is a normal *shamisen* except that the stretched cat skin beneath the strings bears a tattoo, a small coiled dragon. (Well, perhaps the cat skin did not come from a cat.) Strumming, plucking, musing, meditating. Then suddenly Teshima will snap his head up and whisper a question, and the question will be unerring, perfect, the last question some of them want to hear, because arrowlike it will lodge in some tender area of bad planning or sloppy administration.

Or theft. There was that time in spring 1979 when he skewered young Gen with such a question, unfortunate Gen who had managed to skim a hundred million or so. Oh, yes, that kept them alert, the nerve-

160

wracking silence followed by the arrow-question. Then more silence. Sometimes they would come forward voluntarily, unable to stand the strain, and tell him things he had not known. When they did this he merely nodded.

True, he is a manipulator. But not just negatively. When his people act intelligently and speak to the point and remember *giri-ninjo* then he rewards them lavishly. All three current *kobun* have, and know they have, a higher net worth than himself. Teshima saw to it, that close evening in the fall of 1988—he still wants to laugh—when there were five remaining *kobun,* and Teshima suddenly demanded all their assets (which he knew to the yen). Three signed everything over. One, Taro, sought to conceal half. And one, Noboru, resigned. Teshima then presented the three obedient *kobun* with doubled fortunes, from his own assets, at Noboru's retirement party.

The look on Noboru's face. And Taro's. Well, Taro was too fast. He bolted, dove through the window and out into the hot cloudy night. He escaped, took over a right-wing group, in effect surrounded himself with bodyguards. So Taro is not yet in the Bay with Gen. Taro is a loose end for Teshima, who will have to do something about him sooner or later, to save face. But there is no hurry. And, in the meantime, Taro is not getting much sleep, moving from cot to cot, alternating, trying to keep Teshima guessing. Teshima has no need to guess. Teshima knows.

So too bad for Taro and Gen, but Noboru's fate has been, to Teshima's way of thinking, worse. Noboru sentenced himself to life: playing golf, playing at business, getting fat. Anyway, Teshima is rid of the three bad ones and has bound the three good ones even more tightly to himself. And cheaply at the price. What does Teshima at his great age need with vast sums of money?

Teshima has power, much better than money in the long run, and he has his organization. Every man in it knows that, without him, they would be merely a group of superior individuals. That, with him, they are a whole which is more than the sum of its parts. They know it, he knows it. Of course, the top three are competing to succeed him. That is as it should be. But they seem in no particular hurry. So when they drink his health at dinners and parties they seem sincere. And they mean it when they say, "Live a hundred years!"

Well, perhaps they are thinking, "ninety-five." But Teshima will settle for that. He swims, he goes for walks, he mostly eats the vegetarian *shojin ryori* of those ageless Buddhist monks, he drinks ginseng tea, and he hardly smokes at all these days. Teshima is still strong, too—big-boned, heavy-muscled—still tough. And not make-believe tough like today's *gyangu*, those greasy boys in black who see too many movies, and go around frightening schoolgirls and office ladies on the train, and think they are heroes. That *gurentai* in the pachinko *sendenkaa* this afternoon. Teshima contented himself with merely firing him, but—

Forget the punk.

Remember control. That is Teshima's strength and the source of his power. Personal and corporate, through good times and bad, in life and death. These bland days, everything is in the computer: accounting, planning, strategy sessions, important decisions, operating procedures, goals for the next ten years or ten hours, everybody's birthday. Everybody's favorite cigarette, after-shave lotion, *manga*. Files for everything, control by microchip—well, why not? Teshima even has a Death File, a disk in an envelope in his safe: itemized lists of people and agencies to notify, things to do, last wishes. Hit a button, there it will be. Control continuing when he is a double handful of ashes in an urn right beside Hanako's and the boy's and Moriuchi-*sensei's.* Meanwhile, his life is one continuing celebration of decorum, a daily ceremony as perfect in every respect as he can make it.

Ah, but sometimes, sometimes. It comes out of nowhere and hits him like a blow, the old rage and sorrow at her death, undiminished. The curve of a woman's neck might trigger it, or a woman unseen in a crowd but wearing that special perfume, or the rustle of a kimono. Fleeting sights, smells, sounds: they have the power to send him reeling back, helplessly recalling the deep clarity of her eyes, the down on her forearm backlit by the setting sun, the music of her voice. Her totality, sharp and thrilling as on the day they met. Dreams too, now as always nearly every night, although they seem too real for dreams. Visions, maybe? Anyway, his bedroom door is oak and steel with deadbolt locks, the room itself soundproofed, because, when he wakens with her name on his lips— well, that is for no one else to hear, an old man calling out in the night like a lover.

Is that why he got out of prostitution, the real reason? He admits the possibility: prostitutes are women; Hanako was a woman; whatever sullies women sullies her, her blessed memory. Not rational, no, but—

"Dead are Professor Yamamoto Koichiro and his wife Hatsumi—"

Teshima's eyes open on the television.

"—he of an apparent heart attack, she of a stab wound inflicted by—"

"Turn it up," says Teshima. "Listen."

"—survived by their infant daughter, who fell or was thrown—"

"Call the station," said Teshima. "Discover what is going on."

"—eyewitnesses report—"

"Tell them I want to know."

"—caught by an English teacher, who was slightly injured when—

"Probably nothing. But strange, don't you think? Find out where he lives."

"—police are looking for a motorcyclist—"

Teshima reacting nonchalantly, issuing orders at a measured pace, exchanging a glance with Eiji, his number one. Teshima *oyabun* is seemingly once more relaxed and sighing with pleasure-pain under the hands of the *shiatsu-shi*, and nothing in the dignified planes and angles of his face suggests the magnitude of his alarm, suggests that this old stoic is no stoic. Oh! Oh, Hanako!

Friday, 11:02 P.M.

Takeshita Satoshi's life is religion, and that religion is himself. Some Buddhism, a little Shinto, a hint of *Christo-Kyo*. But mostly his own insights which, to him and his followers, are Truth. Tall, fleshy, generous-hipped, richly-bearded, he has come to believe that the Other speaks through him, and, that being so, and the Other being by definition infallible, the matter is beyond argument. The Other which is the All which is the One. *Is,* not could be. Takeshita is therefore no debater. He is not interested in dialogue. Instead, he is accustomed to rap out flat declaratives punctated with rhetorical questions:

"Peace wants us."

"Wealth is damnation."

"Where is our faith in faith?"

Takeshita is an expert on faith. At one time or another he belonged to a half-dozen *shin-shin shukyo,* the so-called "new-new religions" in Tokyo. But all of them, in his opinion, had a crucial weakness: they all neglected the divine-human nexus, generally, and, specifically, this nexus as applied to himself. That is to say, he, Takeshita, had made Contact, yet few heeded him! So he moved from group to group, taking with him each time a dozen or so other disaffected. Soon these numbered over a hundred, were a tiny new religion in their own right, with Takeshita where he belonged, finally, at the heart of things. They call themselves *Zenbu-Kyo,* Universalism, because they are not just another religion. No, they are the essence of all true religions, which essence is the unquenchable longing of all human hearts for the Absolute, the Other, the One.

Possessing Truth, they seek to share it. They stand patiently in train stations all over the city, wearing their famous "rhino hats" (the rhinoceros is for them sacred, its irresistible strength and single horn a potent symbol for that Unitary Creative Force). They distribute their leaflets, side by side with the pathetic *Watchtower* people. They advertise in the more affordable tabloids. They swarm out, ring bells, pound on doors. They use their own aggressive proselytizing technique, *shakubuku,* a relentless questioning and answering intended to draw prospective converts out of their old easy attitudes, to shake them, to bring them in line with the Truth of their fierce new faith.

"In hell," Takeshita tells his people, "the chains are made of gold."

That is not opinion but rather revealed fact, revealed to and through Takeshita himself, who greatly favors these lost ones of the world by sharing this and other revelations with them, unworthy as they are. They are of course free to accept the Truth or reject it.

A gratifying number have accepted it, persuaded largely by Takeshita's indifference to persuasion. The group now has its own headquarters in the Urawa district, north of metro Tokyo. They have a temple, a dormitory, and an administration building. All this cost a great deal of money. Members are therefore regularly challenged to contribute as much and as often as possible.

"Discard your materialistic security blankets," Takeshita exhorts them scornfully, the "fearful ones," those who have not yet earned their rhino horns. "Grow to adulthood in the Spirit of the One, laugh, and live free."

Takeshita is specially contemptuous of the middle- and upper-middle-classes, the "portfolio people." They have been given the Truth; collectively they have the means to bring this Truth to the entire world. But what do they do? Whine about retirement fund tax laws. Snivel about funds "out of reach" in trust and escrow accounts. They make him ill. So there are regular expulsions for miserliness, *Zenbu-Kyo's* cardinal sin. Once expelled, the fearful ones are assessed twice the usual fee for readmission—or, rather, for the opportunity to enter a probationary period, at the end of which they *might* be permitted to *reapply*. Those fearful ones who do not reapply, or whose reapplications are refused, are eradicated from the Rolls and consequently from the Heart of the One.

They cease to exist. Takeshita, as Great Healer, can do nothing about it. His power is as nothing to that of the All. Indeed, no power on earth or in heaven can save these "nonexistent ones"—unless, in His boundless mercy, the One Source of All True Religion were to inspire them with sufficient grace for a true act of supreme penitence. Such an act involves shaving the head, dressing in coarse robes, and becoming, for a period not less than five years, temple functionaries. And, to prove contrition, they are obliged to sign over to the Temple *all* their assets.

Nothing could be fairer. These fearful ones had the nearly inconceivable good fortune to encounter the freedom of Truth. Which they had then spurned, preferring the burden and confinement of their gaudy yellow chains. For such insane wrong-headedness could any punishment be too harsh? Takeshita thinks not. He points out, frequently, that he expells the fearful ones for the same reason that a physician seeks to expell disease from the physical body. And, truly, these expulsions do have a tonic effect on the others— mostly lower middle-class and not yet dead in sin— who offer up their savings accounts, mortgage their homes, cash in their insurance policies. Competing with each other, they beggar themselves materially and thereby enrich themselves spiritually beyond measure. "Cast off your golden fetters," Takeshita urges them, "even the slenderest, most gossamer." And they do. Takeshita knows they do because he is also, despite his multitude of other heavy tasks and endless responsibilities, the group's treasurer.

Now and then, however, one or another of the portfolio people defies Takeshita and the One, and departs permanently. A small group of these even hired a lawyer in the hope of somehow recouping their paltry contributions. The sum was negligible—Y60,000,000 or so—but their effrontery was vast. They accused Takeshita of extortion and fraud! They proposed to drag the Great Healer into a criminal court! Thus they repaid his efforts on their behalf. Well, they succeeded not in their blasphemy. The lawyer was warned. The warning was ignored. Then he and his family, as the newspapers put it, "disappeared." Takeshita and three senior rhinos know with certainty that these enemies of Truth will not reappear. Not in this life. Thus was the One appeased.

But at great cost. The putrid mass media of this degenerate age loved the whole episode, of course took the part of the venal lawyer, howled for months about the so-called "crime," which had been nothing more or less than simple justice. The government couldn't make a case, but the journalists and the mindless television people tried *Zenbu-Kyo* in the court of public opinion. The verdict, guilty. And they would *not* leave it alone. Still, after eighteen months, scribblers reheat the stupid non-story again and again, smearing the faithful with innuendo and wild speculation, staying just this side of libel. Worse, fallen-away fearful ones, no longer fearful, are selling their lurid stories to the tabloids. The result, predictably, a period of negative growth for *Zenbu-Kyo:* the number of converts dwindling, apostasies increasing, vital monetary contributions greatly diminishing.

Furthermore, the local people here in Urawa have erected an observation tower just outside the temple grounds, and from this tower mount a twenty-four hour guard—as though over a pack of criminals! And there

171

is nothing Takeshita can do about it, because, in a sense, everyone in Japan is watching them. One more negative incident—never mind whose fault—and *Zenbu-Kyo* will be through.

As matters stand, he and his get little respect. Indeed, Takeshita reflects, bitterly, the ignorant masses have begun openly deriding his faithful, subjecting them to rude catcalls— *"Where is the lawyer Iidzuka and his family,* bakayaro? *What did you do with the baby Iidzuka? How did you pacify him?"* One group of drunken, late-returning salarymen actually micturated on three of the faithful. A contest. Their hilarious object? Damnable defilement: to reach the rhino hats with their arcs of stinking urine. Where were the police during this outrage? Where indeed? Unavailable, nowhere to be found, no doubt in the back room of their *koban* slapping their thick thighs with mirth. Yes, the sacred headgear has become the butt of much coarse merriment. In fact, all Tokyo is laughing at the rhino hats.

Takeshita finds this laughter galling. *Tokyo This Month,* a vile rag, recently ran a particularly vile article, "Oh, Come Now, All Ye Faithful." Purportedly a study of the *shin-shin-shukyo,* it is instead superficial and cretinous attempted satire. There is a sidebar devoted to *Zenbu-Kyo,* and every time he rereads this piece of slander his rage grows. It is the writer's tone of studied insolence, his cruelly casual mockery—his devilish cheerfulness!—that makes Takeshita's fingers itch to strangle "Oswit Nan, Ph.D." The article has been translated and widely reprinted. Every Japanese adult has, it seems, read it or heard of it. The whole country is, it seems, laughing—no; worse: snickering.

Well, the Great Healer knows how to bide his time. He has taken no action thus far. But this piece of slander he will not overlook. He has vowed that, if and when he penetrates the writer's absurd pseudonym, he will permit himself the luxury of exacting a terrible vengeance. Which will look like a terrible accident.

The Healer scowls.

But now imagine the great man's astonishment and delight as he raises his eyes from "Oswit Nan's" smirking photograph on the *TTM* contributor's page and beholds the same stupid face—same fussy little beard, same sparse hair, same sharp cheekbones—on the television screen! That same face—but no longer smirking—and wonderfully bloody!

"—report screams, confusion. The baby was caught by an English teacher, who was injured when

they hit the far bank of the drainage channel. There was some broken glass."

Oswit Nan is an English teacher. What is his stupid name?

"—Ara!" says the newsgirl as the camera cuts back to her. "Ki o ushinaimashita."

Who? Who fainted?

"—caught, just on time, by F.S. Donnell-sensei," says the girl.

"Donner," says a big man, holding him up. "F.X. Donner."

Thank you. Thanks to the Buddha. All gratitude to the All.

"Professor Donner," says the girl. "Of...?"

"Kanagawa," says the big man, whose English is excellent, as good as Takeshita's. "Works at that women's college, I forget the name. Something to do with Mr. Reischauer, when he was ambassador, or his father? Nice place, trees, maybe somewhere around Mitaka? Out there on the Chuo line anyway."

"Edo Joshi Dai?" the girl asks. "In Kichijyoji?"

"Could be, sounds right. Listen, he's hurt, not too bad, but I think—"

"Ah, daijobu," *says the girl.* "Ima, desu ne? Kyukyusha ga kimasu."

"What?" says the big man with the bad haircut.

"Ambulance. Now is coming."

"Ah, right, good," says the big stupid man, who sounds like an American even though he looks like a Nihon-jin. "Ambulance."

An ambulance today…

The Great Healer smiles.

Tomorrow a hearse.

Friday, 11:02 P.M.

Sawada Ginroku hardly ever watches the *terebi,* really watches it: *no time.* Ginroku's time is precious. He must squeeze the seconds and minutes into diamonds. Time is money, as the Americans say, truly. But he sits in front of the giant-screen Sony as much as possible when home, partly because of an agreement with his wife: when the set is on, she is off, silent. *Shizuka*—which happens to be his wife's name. What a laugh, as the Americans would say. A wife named silence who never shuts up, not even in her sleep, though the television has a quietening effect. Even so, the poor bitch forgets, starts bouncing around during the commercials—*tsumaranaimono,* really boring garbage—but she gets all excited about the latest twelve-speed fingernail polish dryer or some other *bakamono* gizmo, starts to squeal and coo, keeps it up, louder and louder, so that Ginroku finally has to shout, "*Kudoi!* Enough!" Then he usually just tells her to order one, whatever it is, get it, *katte kudasai,* but please let him watch his program in peace. So the *terebi* doesn't really give him much of a rest from his wife, but still it's time well spent. Why? Because the terebi-clowns sometimes give him ideas for T-shirts.

T's, *honto-ni.* Ginroku is the king of Japanese novelty T's. Waking, sleeping, putting it to his bimbos, he's in a T. Even on formal occasions, with a tux, he wears a T-shirt, and the wilder the better. Why not? As he often says, it's the perfect advertising at the perfect price. True, these Ts, flapping at the arms and shoulders but stretched taut across his belly, seem to emphasize his vulgarity and oafishness. But so what? Ginroku doesn't give a shit. He loves his shirts, his money, his own abundant flesh.

His favorite shirt, he adores it, wears it only a few times a year and the rest of the time it's right there in the *kashikinko*, to which only he has the combination. Because the shirt is priceless. On the front, a huge picture of himself. Big wet grin, perfect hair, little eyes squeezed almost shut, sweaty forehead, rosy cheeks and chins. Face like Ampan Man, the kid *manga* hero. What's he wearing in the picture on the shirt? The same shirt! With the same picture, only of course a bit smaller. And so forth. Diminishing self-images, but an infinite number of them, at least theoretically. Once he wore it when he took one of his little sales cuties to Korakuen first, to the fun house, the Hall of Mirrors. They walked in—*banzai!* Ginrokus everywhere, an infinity of infinitudes, a universe of himself, at the

177

center and to the farthest reaches. Floor, ceiling, walls, all him. He just stood, rooted to the spot, grinning and grinning at all the millions of grinning Ginrokus. Finally the cutie dragged him out of there—but *sugoi!* As the Americans say, a real peak experience.

T-shirts are Ginroku's life. Well, they've been good to him. He started with a second-hand thermal printer in his garage, the kind you mashed down on each individual shirt while you looked at the second hand of your watch for what seemed like forever. What fun that wasn't. But now it's a different story. Three big fully-automated Toshibas churning out hundreds of shirts an hour. All his designs are completely original, adapted from the cleverest British and American ones (he has all the catalogues, don't worry) and, in his opinion, often improved. And do they sell! Some big new rock group has a concert one night. The next afternoon half the greasy punks and pouty little *burikko* in Tokyo are strutting around in a commemorative T: rock-clown bent over backwards and screaming into the mike, green face purple hair orange bass guitar. Or purple face and green hair. All basically the same of course but not to the punks and bimbos. And for those few days and hours, the new shirts *move.*

Thousands and tens of thousands, mounds and bales and truckloads cycling through his sales-tents in Harajuku, Yoyogi, Roppongi. The teen meccas. Which are crawling with *gaijin* punks too—Yanks, Brits, Aussies, the odd Frog. He's grossed over a million yen a day on a hot new item. One single item, is the point—*per day*. Like the first time "Guns 'n Roses" was in town. Or that "Bushe & Quayl" gag he borrowed from Crazyshirts in '92—every foreigner in town was smirking around in one of those beauties. And he's had these strokes of genius consistently since the early 60s. That's why he's king.

Furthermore, his gross isn't that far off his net. His overhead is almost nonexistent. He has two wholesalers, a Taiwanese and an Indonesian, both greedy *bakamono*, but they have to compete. He buys their plain white shirts, for what? Maybe 97, 98 yen to the shirt. Good enough quality, pure cotton, nothing really wrong with them. But cheap. And he has a line of credit with them, so none of his own hard-working money has to get involved. Then Ginroku sells the printed ones for 1,000 or 1,500 yen apiece. Sometimes more, if the suckers are really biting. Figure the markup, figure the volume. He pays his *burikko* the minimum, 800 yen an hour, and in that time they can

179

and often do sell a hundred shirts each. (He gives them big discounts on Ts for themselves, they're thrilled, truly they are mindless.) *Okane ga takusan kakaru-yo,* the money really piles up

Ts are a goldmine. His.

Expensive rights? Listen, that's the best part, the funniest. He drops in on the *tarento*—wrestlers, actors, rockers, it makes no difference, they're all clowns— and he says, all humble, *"Etoh ne?* Every other kid in the city walking around and wearing your picture—*do desu ka,* how does that grab you?" It almost always grabs them. They almost always go for it. So Ginroku, instead of having to *buy rights, sells advertising.* They pay him to make money off them! Ginroku works it both ways, just like those Frog designers! If he came up and tried to buy the rights to their stupid faces, they'd tell him *sayonara,* or they'd try to pry every possible yen out of him for that great privilege. But sell them something, make it seem like a wonderful opportunity for them—which in a way it is!—and that's a different story. He has three companies: T-rrific to move product, Sawada Communications to pitch ads, and Silver Six Market Surveys to prove how T-rrific Ts are the perfect venue for any big name talent as well as any up-and-comer.

Smiling, lightly stroking his belly, Ginroku lies beside his whispering wife. He punches a few buttons on the arm of his recliner-massage chair, feeling it start to work now on his lower back. His wife looks over, quickly punches the same buttons on her chair.

Ginroku breathes a little sigh of contentment and thinks about the up-and-comers—who are really down-and-outers in brief disguise, all of them. The rockers especially. Make a little money, go to L.A., stick every dime up their noses, get busted, return to Tokyo, discover that they are yesterday and nobody remembers them. End of "career." Elapsed time maybe fourteen months. Then work as a parking attendant or some such for the rest of their lives, plotting their comebacks which never happen. Has-beens at nineteen. Ginroku always has numbers of them selling Ts. It gives them a chance to wear shirts—hand-washed, cared for like some relic of the Buddha—featuring guess who. Themselves, of course, when they were *yumei*, names.

Drunky Brains Oh! I'll! Gig Hokkaido Tour.

Pathetic.

Ginroku grins. Now and then some very young schoolgirl wanders in, under the awning, and gets big eyes, says to the clown, Oh, *sugoi,* you are so-and-so.

And that's the has-been's big moment for the week. Or the month. Tell her how they're getting a new group together, real serious, and the minibimbo says wow *subarashii.* Ginroku pays these clowns straight commission; they maybe make enough to eat cheap soba and share some dry place at night with the spiders and the *gokiburri.* Ginroku grins wider. No more cockroaches for him. No indeed. He runs a hand over his opulent belly and breasts.

Why should he mind dealing with the clowns? He doesn't. When they're names, they make money for him. When they're nobodies again, they'll probably wind up behind one of his counters, making money for him. They can have their moment of glory, their cocaine and studio limos. Ginroku will take the money. That's the bottom line, as the Americans say. When the show's over, the dust has settled, everybody's finally asleep, who has the money? Most have lost, a few have won. Because money is the point. Ginroku has lots of it now—if you ask him how much, he'll tell you—and he wants lots more.

So none of it sits around idle. Real estate, stocks and bonds, term deposits, money market—he dabbles. But most of Ginroku's money is out on the streets, working really hard and bringing in ten percent a week from numerous little short-term lending arrangements. Call it loan-sharking if you can't think of some better term, but it's almost legal, and as easy as adding a column of figures. Figures with a lot of zeros.

Loans began as a sideline. One of his teen has-been counter-jumpers asked him for *hachi man,* eighty thousand yen, he'd pay it right back, blahblah. Ginroku told him, go to the bank, told him he wasn't in the lending business, so forth, but the kid said banks wouldn't even talk to him. Interesting. Ginroku'd known it, of course, but never really thought about it: a whole sub-population that couldn't go to banks, had no credit. So he thought, Why not? He said, *Mondai nai,* no problem, and made the loan. The kid signed everything Ginroku stuck under his nose. Result? Interesting again. The kid, who is now pushing thirty and no longer a kid except of course mentally, never missed a payment on the interest. Or no, he did miss a few that first year—just to get himself in a little deeper?—but after that, just like a machine. Every Monday, there he is, reaching for his fat wallet (fat with old yellow press clippings, which he *reads,* over and over when business is slow, handling them tenderly). The kid even seems to draw some weird comfort from his weekly obligation. And—here's the funniest part—although he has now repaid his loan seven and a half times, he's never managed to pay off any of the principle.

None of it, not one yen. Because the kid is such a loser he has to have numerical proof that's what he is? Because he needs at least one regular human arrangement? Because he can't see any farther ahead than the weekend? For a while Ginroku was intrigued. Once in a roundabout way he raised the subject, wondered aloud why the kid didn't look out for *ichiban* like a normal person and retire the principle. *"Dekimasu-yo,"* the kid answered with a sort of shy pride, like they were both on the same team. *Dekimasu. I can handle it.* Well, of course he *could* handle it—a few thousand yen a week, that's all—but why *should* he? Ginroku still doesn't know and doesn't really care. The point is the kid is now a regular tiny source of income. More than that: the kid now belongs to Ginroku, will do anything Ginroku tells him to, is a sort of slave.

Who wants a punk-slave? Who cares about one pathetic little sucker? Nobody, of course. But there's one born every minute, as the Americans say—and not just in America. Tokyo is full of them. That's the delicious fact. All looking for God, Truth, the Big

Secret. Shopping for crazy religions. Looking for the Way Out, the Way In. Or at least for some stern *otosan*-figure, someone to give them a fatherly pat on the head when they pay, someone to rebel against, someone to blame for their lives, someone to plead with for forgiveness. Ginroku sees to it that they find him.

And it never fails to thrill him when they make those first tender moves. When they miss payments, ignore penalties, "forget" to figure in the interest on the interest. Then he knows they're his, part of that twenty percent or so who'll never get near the principle. He lends to anyone, the stupider the better, the real bottom-feeders as the Americans call them. He used to think rockers were the biggest cretins, but now he knows it's the *gyangu,* the little yakuza gophers and wannabes. They don't even pretend to read the contract. Whatever it is, they just have to have it, and right now. Rolex? Okay, here's a million yen. Third-hand Mercedes with the smoked windows and everything needs an overhaul but that magical three-pointed star? Okay, *dozo,* take the money. And they're his. One little clown, no chest, no chin, pimples on his pimples. What did he want? Plastic surgery? No, this kid absolutely needed a big gold ring in the shape of a human skull, rubies for eyes. Rubies, what a laugh, gold. Ginroku actually tried to talk him out of it. Of course the thing turned green. Also of course the kid is still paying. What an idiot. Not the faintest hint of an understanding of money. Perfection, a real loser's loser. All you losers, out there in cold and sleet of low finance, shivering and miserable, come shelter with papa Ginroku. He'll take you in.

"Tabako," he says, and watches his wife scramble for Kents and lighter.

The lighter is *kako-ii*—or, as the Americans say, really neat. Clear plastic cube, and inside some sort of solar battery which you can see. Pick up the lighter, the heat from your hand tells it to turn itself on, fire up its little electric element. Because the lighter has some kind of tiny brain, works better than most peoples', and it knows what to do: heat up. Takes about two seconds, then you just stick your Kent or your Mild Seven or your Marlboro in the hole. Never needs cleaning, fixing, adjusting. Never needs fuel. Never needs anything. Ginroku thinks of his old Zippo and laughs. They called that one automatic too, but he was forever fooling around with the flints or trying to find the screw, or the spring when it jumped out. Zippo always ran out of fluid just when he wanted a smoke. It was a sort of stupid hobby. But this little plastic cube—the only gadget of his wife's that he likes—well, once you have it, you *have* it.

Zero maintenance, just like his little army of borrowers. If he wanted to, if he wasn't having so much fun, Ginroku could retire right now. His money out on the streets brings in over a million a week. Every week, automatically, ten thousand American. If he does happen to have trouble with a slow-pay, then he calls on his moonlighting yakuza soldier, who is very good at collecting. Only Ginroku doesn't have to pay him—just knock a few points off the goon's own vig! Yes, the soldier is his too. Ginroku even has a tame policeman, a whore-cop, who throws his paycheck away on the horses and drinks up the rest. It doesn't matter how hard he squeezes those poor little Soapland massage-girls, he always needs more cash. The cop is in so far he'll never see daylight again. Good! One day he could come in handy. Even cops might have their uses. Ginroku puffs to get his Kent going, laughs out loud.

His mild wife, maybe thinking the TV moron made a good joke, raises her hand to her mouth and titters. She isn't really insane, just lives inside the tube most of the time, and Ginroku still kind of likes her, especially when she's not saying anything. Every time she catches a cold she gets laryngitis too, and that's a point in her favor. She cooks, dusts, irons, all that, and he doesn't have to pay her. Just throw her a gadget once in a while. Well, why not? She's human, she has needs. Plus when they were poor she never complained. She never wears anything but her ratty old housecoat. Maybe she thinks they're still poor. If so, good.

She titters again and glances shyly across, sharing the moment with him.

"Isn't Tomori funny?"

"Hai," says Ginroku, puffing, nodding, caressing his belly. *"Honto-ni."*

People think his stomach is funny too, laugh at him, say he's fat. Well, fuck them. He *is* fat, and glad of it. Whenever he catches sight of himself in a mirror, he'll stick his stomach out a little farther and think, Not bad. For a skinny little kid that ate bread cut with sawdust and dried grass for two years after the War and wrestled in the dust with the other ragged little motherless fatherless kids for Hershey Bars and Bit O' Honeys. Scattered from the Jeeps and personnel carriers by the huge, black, laughing G.I.s. Wrigley's Spearmint! Yes! He remembers—he'll always remember—the green and white wrapper, the wonderful smell. No, not bad for a kid that nearly died from TB. Yes, Ginroku is damned pleased with himself, and rightly so.

The only thing he worries about is, well, the yakuza. No, worry is the wrong word. Concern, that's it. Ginroku is just a little bit concerned about their attitude toward him. Do they like him? He hopes so. But maybe they don't like him. Maybe they're mad at him for taking away so much of their loan sharking business. But that's crazy, because he certainly couldn't account for more than the tiniest percent of a percent of their total take. They probably don't know he's even alive. So, no, Ginroku doesn't worry about the yakuza. Besides, even if they don't like him, so what? This isn't the old days, when they'd throw you in the bay. Or Taoka! He'd gouge out your eyes, just to get your attention. But Taoka's dead. Inagawa too. They're all dead.

Or too old to care, like Teshima.

"*Anata,* look! They are selling those vacuum cleaners with spots on them and little feelers! Oh, are they not adorable? Pink. They look like cute little *tentomushi*—like ladybugs. Oh, I wish—"

189

"Mizowari," he says, holding up his empty glass, watching her jump for it.

No, Ginroku doesn't worry about the yakuza. They're too busy these days trying to get Nobel peace prizes and hiring PR geniuses to polish up their image. When times were tough, the yakuza were tough. But face it, that was years ago. They're nothing to worry about now. Ginroku grunts and reaches up for the full glass. It takes her forever to fix a drink, and that's another point in her favor. Anyway, what would they do? Complain to the police? Ginroku laughs again, and once more his wife turns to him with her sweet vacant smile.

"Anata," she says, gently, "you really shouldn't laugh about nasal hygiene. It is a very useful appliance. See? You simply insert it in your nose, then *bzzzz,* like that, and all those ugly little hairs are gone. Isn't that wonderful?"

"Better get one."

"*'Why let excess nasal hair ruin your life?'*—oh, Anata, why indeed?"

"Better get two, one for each nostril."

"Oh, Ginroku, you are so funny! Just like Tamori—"

"Now be quiet."

No, Ginroku doesn't worry about the yakuza, that's for sure. There's no reason to worry, so he doesn't. Not a bit. He takes a sip of his *mizowari*—Cutty Sark, it's all he ever drinks—then lies back, puffing on the Kent, feeling those mechanical fingers really dig into his back muscles, and not even thinking about the yakuza.

TV. There's the newsman—yapyapyap—serious-looking head but nothing inside it. Sometimes his wife talks to this newsman, What's-His-Face Ozawa. (Well, why not? That's her privilege. Ginroku himself often talks to the smart little cigarette lighter, question-and-answer stuff in the middle of the night when he can't sleep for thinking about one thing and another—gangsters, mostly.) Ginroku'll walk in, there she'll be, glued to the tube and telling the guy about their autostatic towel-rack heaters and variable-speed bio-torsionized ultrasonic toothbrushes and their programmable washing machine with fuzzy/neuro control and their rheostatic-onboard-computerized rice cooker. And Ozawa would tell her all that day's good reasons to stay barricaded inside their wonderful space-age home with the doors and windows double-locked and the alarm system on and the little closed-circuit minicam, concealed behind the cherry *bonsai*, swinging back and forth, back and forth, at the gate.

Oh, yes, in the best parts of Tokyo. Even here, in Numabukuro.

Excellent reasons to stay home, do a little flower-arranging. Reasons like *dorobo* knocking off liquor stores and blasting everyone in sight, like monster *chikan* cruising the neighborhoods and the playgrounds looking for more little girls to kidnap and rip apart, like *aka* and *ouyoku* and riot cops pounding each other into the concrete. Like, well, gangsters chewing up people who get in their way. *Yakuza.*

Tokyo, the safest major city in the world.

TV news. Ginroku snorts. There isn't much of it, once you blew off the hype. Anyway, and as far as he's concerned, the big news tonight and every night is that Sawada Ginroku has beat all the odds, is a winner, has been a winner since he quit seeing obstacles as obstacles, since he quit being afraid of success.

Since, as a matter-of-fact, he joined the *Soka Gakkai* thirty years ago. There's a real religion, one that has its priorities straight. They used to call themselves "a machine for making happiness." Well, as the Americans put it so well, that's right on the money. Life is competition, happiness is the only conceivable goal, wealth is how you know you're there. Simple. Ginroku has to give himself credit. Five hundred-plus *shin-shukyo* in town but he unerringly selected the only real one. Loonies all over the place, doing their weird little dances, standing around in their stupid hats, but Ginroku didn't give them a second look. For him it's *Soka Gakkai,* first, last and always. Sure, it costs a lot. It costs big money to get in and to stay in. But Ginroku pays gladly, because he's successful. And, as they often pointed out, he's successful because he pays and keeps on paying. His worldly blessings are the fruit of his continuing membership in a group which emphasizes the importance of such blessings. Well, Ginroku can't argue with that. Fair is fair. Besides, all the fees and donations really keep out the losers and suckers.

So now it's never either-or for Ginroku, always both-and. Plus whatever perks and bennies he can squeeze in for himself. Oh yes, these days Ginroku takes every deal to the limit. He'll pry the gold right out of your teeth. Why? Simple. Because he's learned to be his own best friend, because he's found the *Soka Gakkai* path to love and self-respect. He grabs a generous double handful of the swelling flesh at his abdomen and kneads it. He crosses his arms and tucks a hand under each armpit, squeezing his breasts together and giving himself a fierce little hug.

"—accident this afternoon," says the talking-head, a cute one for a change, but the same old shit, somebody fell off of something. Well, they're always doing that. *"Dead are Professor Yamamoto Koichiro and his wife Hatsumi. He of an apparent heart attack—"*

Blahblahblah.

"—screams, confusion. The baby was caught by an English teacher, who was injured when they hit the far bank of the drainage channel. There was some broken glass."

Well, shio ga nai, *tough luck.* No skin off Ginroku's ass.

"—whose camera club had been photographing autumn flowers by the riverbank—"

Now a picture of the kid falling and a gaijin leaping up to grab her.

Ah, *tsumaranai,* who cares about some kid and some foreigner? Who could possibly be interested in...

Everyone!

Sawada Ginroku, leaping like a gaffed billfish.

KID DOOMED, FALLING, *GAIJIN* COMING UP TO SAVE HER!

Sawada Ginroku, yelping, launching his bulk from the recliner as though bayoneted in his vast buttocks, spilling his drink, sending the ashtray pinwheeling and spraying butts across the room, Ginroku tripping, scrambling to his feet, slipping, sliding, caroming off the near wall, his mounded flesh all rippling and shim-sham-shimmying this way and that, his wife with her hands to her mouth and mewing as objects about her crash and thud, Ginroku snarling *shizuka-ni* shut up shut up as he dives for the cellular phone on the end-table and starts punching in the numbers.

KID FALLING, *GAIJIN* COMING UP!

Banzai. Banzai. Banzai.

What a shirt.

Friday, 11:02 P.M.

Thick dark, chill winds, the moon cloud-choked. Bright fall days, but the nights are cooler now, longer. Hard, cold, early-morning showers rattle and rake across the Kanto Plain, precursors of a bad winter, months of shivering numbness. But only if you're outside. Inside is warm, safe, perfect for love.

Miyajima Yoshinori watches rapt as steel talons rip and gouge, transform the girl from shrieks and spastic tremors to blood-slicked stillness and perfection. As always, and even as he feels the old arousal thick in his throat, his tears well at this perfect ending, that zoom to her beautiful unblinking eye, the organ chord swelling to solemnize this triumph of peace and love. The girl is free. Of course, he knows that she is an actress, that her death is not "real." But what *is* really real? The older and wiser Yoshinori grows, the less dogmatic he becomes about the nature of reality. One thing he *is* sure of: he *prefers* stronger, more significant realities than those of everyday. He prefers his world transformed by movies and the media into something truer, more immediate, more universal, more meaningful. That's it: the suffocating so-called real world of stones and flesh—cardboard, two dimensional, gray—is meaningless.

So Yoshinori scorns it, can't bear living in it, lives instead in a world of art. He has over a thousand videos in his personal library, and he must have seen each one at least fifty times, snuggled in this tiny room full of plush dolls and dead black modules—VTRs and CD players, directional speakers—stacked ceiling-to-floor on either side of a giant *terebi* screen. All this equipment is state-of-the-art Sony and occupies the entire wall opposite his door. The dolls are of course mostly Sanrio: Patti & Jimmy, Goropikodon, Little Twin Stars, Tabithadean, Tiny Poem, and the rest. True, he has a Paddington Bear. And all Seven Dwarfs are perched 'way up on his *tansu* (which is bursting as always with *furifuri-fuafua!*—frills and laces and wonderful soft things for dress-up). Also, there's a Dumbo on the fridge, and, on the space heater, a Pooh. But no other characters are as cute as Sanrio's. These are literally all over the place. And didn't they enchant those babies whom love has freed, especially Mai-*chan* and Yoko-*chan?*

Cutest—and dearest—of all is Hello Kitty, though Yoshinori's Kitty is nearly as big as he is. Short and delicately built, at thirty he still has a teensy bit of puppy fat around his tummy and twin dimples in his rosy, chubby cheeks. Chin and cheeks were depilated years ago. Yoshinori never has to worry about whiskers. His eyes are large and clear, the lashes long, the brows patiently shaped. His nose and mouth are dainty. He wears his hair long and full to frame his round, smooth, teen-ager's face. He often thinks, gazing into the mirror, that he looks like some Sanrio character himself.

Which may have been the start of the problem. Such red cheeks and babyish features. Well, it didn't take them long at school to start calling him *"Akachan"*—but did they think he could help how he looked? Or that his mother permed his hair? Or that his policeman father beat him where it didn't show? Father roaring or sneering. Mother whining, icy. Both usually drunk. Both hating him. Yoshinori understands now that classmates and parents had, more or less consciously, wanted to kill him, harass him to suicide.

No love anywhere, of course, and school was preferable to home, but school was the place of *ijime*, isolation and harassment. Vicious. Even now he can't even think *"ijime"* without a shudder. Hundreds of Japanese schoolchildren (as opposed to the few he has himself lovingly freed) destroy themselves every year.

They destroy their bodies after the heartless *ijime* has destroyed their spirits. Their crime? Shyness, perhaps; a slight timidity; a tendency toward sympathy and compassion. Or some tiny difference—voice, gait, dress, appearance—which draws their classmates the way fresh blood draws a school of piranhas.

Psychological murder, unrelenting years of it. So why didn't Yoshinori die? Well, he almost did—one illness after another, each worse than the last. Nausea, night sweats, terrible weakness, pain. But finally all confusion was burned away by the fevers because one morning as Yoshinori woke he opened his eyes upon his Secret.

Not just *a* secret, like other children had, but *the* Secret: *he is two persons.* There are two Yoshinoris. One is his body, a sort of robot. The other is the real Yoshinori, who rides around in the robot's head, the way Force Ranger and his comrades ride in the cockpit-head of their gigantic war-stalker. (True, Force Ranger is just a *manga* character, but the analogy holds.) Yoshinori made this discovery in grade three. Afterward, his true self always curled safely away, he directed "Yoshinori" through the school playground, nearly immune to taunts and sneers. It was like Novocain at the dentist's. The blows could be felt only as a sort of dull drumming pressure that came and went, not as pain. Therefore nobody, not even the psychologists who came later, could really hurt him. The grief and terror diminished. In their place bloomed a huge cool rage.

Yoshinori, riding safe behind and in "Yoshinori," would scrutinize his tormentors. He noticed that there were active and passive ones. The former took a positive delight in torturing him; the latter simply went along. Of the former there were three leaders: Masao, Senri, and Hiroshi. Yoshinori kept special daybooks for these three. The daybooks comprised pages of detail about what they did to "Yoshinori" each school morning and afternoon: pictures, diagrams, names of witnesses, quotes from participants and spectators, exact times. Everything logged in. This was the sort of thing his policeman father did, his father's subjects being adult criminals.

Yoshinori also kept a daybook on his father, and, till her death, his mother.

Every evening, from the fourth grade on, Yoshinori wrote for several hours, trying to include everything pertinent, making his case, sticking faithfully to matters of fact. But then, at the end, and as his reward for all this slogging crime reportage, a plunge into poetry: the just retribution. His fictive punishments, bloody from the outset, became increasingly so. Yoshinori truly exercised his imagination. His literary vengeances grew ever more protracted. And graphic. And plausible. These punishments became his art form. Sometimes, rereading what he'd done to "Masao," "Senri," and "Hiroshi," he shuddered.

But with delight.

This writing was his real education. Three or four hours every school night for nine years. Teaching himself, learning from himself, cutting, pasting, throwing copy out, and starting fresh. All this became much easier when, at age twelve, he wheedled a Macintosh out of his parents. He rewrote the journals from grades four through seven and made copies. (The original disks he hid in his father's carton of old but unopened books pertaining to the sergeants' exam; the copies he tucked in the bottom of his mother's ironing basket. When either of his parents paid an infrequent visit to his room, they were loud and slow enough on the stairs always to find him playing a computer game or writing a school "essay.") By the end of junior high school he had developed a nice tight style, had become a cool and competent narrator. By the end of high school he could block in a scene, sketch character, work up a dialogue. He had learned about economy, what to leave out. He could handle tone, point of view, all of that. Often, he was able to snap a whole page into focus with an unexpected but perfect word.

University? *Ie, kekko desu*—no thanks. He had counted twelve years of school days and hours and minutes, and he was through with that forever. Yoshinori got a job, one very much to his liking: he began as an office boy at a publishing company which specialized in *manga*—big ones, phone book thick. He worked for the group which created *High School Jumping,* a continuing saga of revenge: against overbearing school authorities, rival cliques and athletic teams, marauding motorcyclists, interplanetary aliens, playground bullies and lunch money thieves— against anyone or anything. The *Jumping* crew was therefore always scrounging for iniquity/vengeance scenarios. Imagine then their joy at learning that Yoshinori had an apparently inexhaustible fund of these. Years passed, raises and promotions continued, he became an office star. He got his own byline. And *Jumping* became the top-selling teen *manga*— although, or because, it was also the most brutal and sadistic.

Yoshinori's plots were widely admired in the trade and copied by other, lesser, *manga* writers. Here is a story line, for example, an early and famous one, dating from the period just after his mother's death, when he still lived at home:

Several scenes of grade- then highschool persecution of the hero by three thuglike classmates. The bullying becomes increasingly hellish. Finally the hero, battered, regains consciousness in an empty locker room at night, trousers around his ankles—what have they done to him this time?—face in a pool of sticky blood. In the act of raising himself from the floor, he nearly faints; the pain hits him all at once, and something snaps in his mind: he has been transformed by his agony. A huge black scabrous rat scuttles from one of the shower stalls and tries to bite him, but the hero's too fast: he grabs it, chokes it, slams it on the cement floor, raises the dazed and bleeding creature to his mouth and rips off its head with his teeth!

He is no longer victim but executioner.

Thenceforward he observes the three bullies closely, notes their daily routines, their little quirks, their habits of speech, their brand preferences of food, drink, tobacco. The hero smilingly records all these data, knowing somehow that, when the time is ripe, a perfect revenge will suggest itself. And it does. The hero buys three cheese-sausage-natto pizzas, one per week, from three separate Loma Pizza shops and buries them deep in the family freezer. He prints up three handbills at the school print shop:

DO YOU FEEL COKE?
DO YOU LOVE PIZZA?
OMEDETTO GOZAIMASU!
CONGRATULATIONS!
YOU'VE WON A FREE PIZZA AND COKE!
AND DOES YOUR PIZZA CONTAIN A FAMOUS
"GOLDEN COUPON"?
(IF SO, YOUR DELIVERY BOY WILL PUT YOUR
NAME DOWN
FOR THE GRAND PRIZE!)
WELL, THERE'S ONLY ONE WAY TO FIND
OUT!
DOZO!

That evening the hero, wearing the cold-sufferer's gauze mouth-and-nose-cover, takes the train several stops toward the city. He steals one of six delivery scooters parked in front of the Loma Pizza shop across the street from the train station. With his long wig flowing from beneath the green Loma helmet, his mirror sunglasses, his gauze mask, his jeans and *orange-purple T-rrific T-shirt—Rockmonster, fangs bared and looking like he's going to eat the mike—our hero could be anyone. He is so blazingly conspicuous as to be almost invisible. Only we see him leave. Nobody else notices when he pulls up to his own apartment block, climbs the stairs, knocks on his own steel door. No one home; parents out drinking as of course he knew they would be. He lets himself in, pops the three frozen pizzas into the microwave after dusting them liberally with rat poison, then sets off, pizzas in the back, piping hot, Cokes on the floor, frosty cold. He is whistling a happy tune.*

A cat tries to scamper across the road; he swerves, gets it with the front wheel; laughs.

First enemy. Rings the bell; bows, coughs; presents pizza, cokes, handbill; watches as family devours wedge after wedge in search of the coupon then suddenly pitch to the floor, convulse, die; takes his Polaroid from the knapsack: clickclickclick.

Second enemy.

Third.

Daringly he returns the delivery scooter, which nobody has missed, catches the late train home, pastes in the death pix at the end of the three enemy log books, puts the books under his pillow, douses the light and climbs into bed just before his parents open the door to check on him; he feigns sleep; his parents close the door, and his mother comments that he must be having a nice dream because he is smiling so sweetly.

The End

The very day Yoshinori's story hit the stands, elements of his fictional atrocity were played out in real life: "someone" stole a Phirry Pizza scooter (later recovered from the large pond in Shinjuku Gyoen), and three families were found dead of arsenic poisoning, having eaten adulterated pizza. R.I.P., Masao, Senri, and Hiroshi. Nobody, and certainly not the police, made the connection between himself as author of the story and author of the deaths. Yoshinori clipped the headlines and pasted them in his log books, which he now kept with the computer disks in a safe deposit box. Also in the box, an eight millimeter film cassette; the real-death hero had used, not a Polaroid, but a new Sony videocam. That cassette became the nucleus of Yoshinori's erotic library.

But there the matter did not end. One week later, two families in Sapporo perished the same way, and, three days after that, a Shizuoka family. Yoshinori didn't doubt that these copycat murders were also bully-executions and thus an unexpected bonus. Laughing uproariously, he clipped these headlines too, and the outraged editorials, and the government warnings, and the letters from concerned citizens. Nor did he omit the profound public expressions of regret by his company, nor their frequent and vehement denials that a harmless fantasy in their magazine could have been the catalyst for four such tragedies, nor their even more frequent and emotional, if illogical, apologies. (Expressions of corporate joy at the huge increases in *Jumping* sales, were, by contrast, entirely private.) The affair finally simmered down, of course, but by the time it did Yoshinori had another scrapbook bulging with possible story ideas and darkly humorous data.

A star was born.

One night, he was at his little desk, eating a small cheese-and-sausage pizza and working on this new scrapbook, when his father cornered him. Invaded Yoshinori's room which was himself. His thick father. Thick-witted, thick-waisted, thick-fingered, thick-lipped, fleshy-eared, yellow-tusked, bristly-haired, hot, rank, sweaty. Still in uniform, very drunk even for him, the old man stood in the doorway, swaying, legs planted wide, eyes moving over the plush Sanrio dolls, looking as though he might vomit.

"Yachin!" said his father extending his right hand, palm up. "Rent!"

"No," said Yoshinori, adjusting Kitty's ear-ribbon.

"Rent!" His father rubbed his thumb and fingers together in Yoshinori's face, grabbed the door frame with his left hand for support.

"No," said Yoshinori. "You pay me." He stuck out his own hand.

"I'll *pay* you," his father growled, going for his truncheon.

"Guess what, Kitty?" Yoshinori gave Kitty's ear a little love-nip and scrunched up his nose at her. "Your best friend Yoshinori is a murderer. He poisoned all those nice people."

"What?" A strangled whisper.

"Murderer! Me! And you're a policeman! Arrest me!"

"What?" Easing the truncheon back in its holding-ring.

"What are you whispering for?" asked Yoshinori.

"Don't want." His father blinked rapidly. "Wake your mother."

"*Wake* her? Not likely. You *killed* her, pushed her down the stairs."

"Liar!"

"She didn't fall. You were drunk. Two months ago. I can prove it."

"Liar!"

Hilarious. As the whole neighborhood knew, in life she'd been routinely roused with fists and boots whenever the old man wanted a midnight snack, or a hot *ofuro,* or sometimes just for the fun of it. And true, the old man had been drunk that night. True also, the mother had been dead for two months. And true finally, she'd been pushed down the stairs. But not by the old man. Yoshinori himself had killed her, to stop her whining and for practice.

Yoshinori grabbed Kitty and rolled on the floor laughing gaily. His father's face grew redder, his eyes bulged, the vein at his right temple became a purple rope. He clung to either side of the door frame and bent forward, breathing heavily through his hairy nose. Whiskey fumes filled the room. Yoshinori gagged. He closed his watering eyes and pressed his face against Kitty's clean-smelling plush. The old man hung forward, flexing his knees like a swimmer about to jump the gun, raging on in his ragged whisper.

"*Liar!*"

"Pizza?" Yoshinori held out a wedge.

The old man sagged further into the room, chin jutting, lips skinned back.

"Why doesn't the big *otosan* want any pizza? It's with everything—except rat poison, of course." Yoshinori crooned to Kitty, in that teasing flirty way his father hated, speaking into her ribbon ear. "Well, maybe he's thinking it might not be too good for his career. Murderer, with a mass murderer for a son, and so forth. Maybe never get to be a sergeant." Yoshinori giggled and nuzzled Kitty's cheek, then put his ear to her mouth-area. "What's that? What did Kitty say? Oh, that's right! There might be some embarrassing log-books too. Years and years and years of wife beatings. And son-beatings. Can't forget those. Dates, times, rooms of the house, snapshots of the cuts and bruises, doctors' receipts, quotes from neighbors. Tape recordings too, Kitty." Kitty seemed to bend her ear closer. "This fierce *otosan* came home late and drunk, and he talked a lot. Gambling debts, loan sharks, oh dear. Shaking down the poor little whores. He robbed them, then he made them do things. That's right, Kitty, all of this could make him look pretty bad. People might say, father or son—who's the monster?"

Blinking rapidly, the old man sagged in the doorway. His jaw hung slack. From his glistening lower lip a bright line of saliva lengthened to the carpet.

"Oh, Kitty! We both saw it. Two eye-witness accounts of that so-called fall down the stairs—and so soon after that big insurance policy!—plus a tape of the last argument. Which ends with a horrible *scream,* Kitty. Well, what is the Chief going to say? And the judge? And the jury?"

The old man pitched forward, retching, onto the floor.

That was ten years ago. Yoshinori moved out, hasn't seen him since then, never went back. Except for once. His father never came here, to the Yurakucho apartment—probably has no idea where it is— although he transfers the rent money to Yoshinori's account, faithfully, every month. Blackmailing the old man, shaking down the shakedown king. Maybe the old pig was feeling safe by now—you keep my secret, I'll keep yours—was probably up to his old tricks again at Soapland and the racetrack. Yoshinori wouldn't be surprised. Certainly the old man could have no idea what's coming. Yoshinori isn't

211

completely sure either. But he is sure it will be the very best part.

Yoshinori laughs, strokes Kitty, strokes himself. The video is over, and he has his usual cute little erection to deal with. He hits the rewind button then clicks to the news.

"*—report screams, confusion. The baby was caught by an English teacher, who was injured when they hit the far bank of the drainage channel. There was some broken glass.*"

And suddenly there she is! *The one he's been looking for. His* true *love.*

"*—caught, just on time, by F.S. Donnell-sensei,*" *says the girl.*

"*Donner,*" *says a big man, holding him up.* "*F.X. Donner.*"

"*Professor Donner,*" *says the girl.* "*Of...?*"

"*Kanagawa,*" *says the big man.*

Falling, falling, terrified—the poor baby!

Yoshinori will save her. From the foreigner, from all terror, from life itself.

Yoshinori will *free* her. He grabs an old NTT bill, starts to write, breaks the pencil-lead, throws pencil and paper against the wall, then remembers: the Ten O'Clock News is always taped now, automatically, ever since he began freeing the children. He laughs nervously at his foolish panic and hits the playback button, writes, gets it all down this time. There's the picture again: runner's hands reaching up from the right, baby falling, looking down and to her left, little ponytail with the ribbon streaming straight up… Now they zoom in on her face, *that six million people have seen,* and her terror fills the screen. Trembling, Yoshinori hits the stop button and stares helplessly at the angelic mouth and eyes so wide, so full of death, and he can't help it, he's never been so thrilled, so excited, so—oh!

Yoshinori ejaculates in great shuddering spasms, all over Kitty.

Friday, 11:02 P.M.

Captain Yoshida Makoto has an extremely demanding job which requires every bit of his skill: he must listen to Associate Chief Ishimura Yuuki for at least three hours on an average workday. He has no choice in the matter. Both men are fifty-two, but "Paperwork" Ishimura looks ten years older. Actually, however, he is younger than Yoshida by some months and was in the class behind Yoshida's at the police academy. Yoshida is therefore Ishimura's *sempai*, to whom respect and deference are due; Ishimura is therefore Yoshida's *kohai*, from whom respect and deference are due. Also, affection and gratitude. It is the classic relationship, and it might have worked for them, were it not for two difficulties.

The first being that Ishimura is Yoshida's immediate superior. Thus in their case the sacred relationship has been stood on its head. Yearly, monthly, sometimes even weekly, the police mandarins feel their power wax or wane. Influence is never constant. The myriad shifting-interlocking-overlapping spheres of authority and accountability are delineated-refined-updated in the procedural memos which issue in a steady stream from Ishimura's offices.

What it comes down to, however, is that Yoshida has for several years been, and is now, more or less in charge of metro Tokyo—generally responsible, especially when things go wrong, as they very often do—and Ishimura is in charge of Yoshida.

And of the budget. Ishimura leapfrogged Yoshida early on, having caught the eye of a very influential person in Finance and Accounting. Pinched, gray, sparse-haired, and abstemious even in his twenties, Ishimura still drinks only canned oolong-*cha*, room temperature, and smokes only Merit Lights—three per day, three puffs per cigarette. Between puffs, the cigarette languishes in Ishimura's large, circular bronze ashtray, on the far corner of his large steel desk, ignored. After each cigarette, Ishimura washes his hands, brushes his teeth, and uses a tiny aerosol of Gold Spot mouth freshener which he is never without. Yoshida has witnessed this ritual more times than he can count. Or cares to.

And perhaps that is the root of his problem: Yoshida Makoto has little interest in counting. Not a numbers man, he relishes the qualities of things, people, situations—their quintessential inwardnesses. He wants to know, What? Why? Not, How much? Yoshida is no quantifier.

Ishimura, of course, is. Reality speaks little to him unless translated into charts, graphs, diagrams, columns of figures. These are Ishimura's meat. No one in the world can gaze at such numerical data and extract the message faster than Ishimura. And the message is always the same: *we*—meaning you, Yoshida—*are wasting money.* Yoshida is willing to grant that. *Hai, hai,* he should be more vigilant, true. He grants also that Paperwork is vigilant, even visionary: a brilliant police accountant under whose hands the billions have surged and burgeoned. Early on, entire divisions came under his control. His work in Payroll, for example—superb. Pensions, same thing. More money for everyone—and that, as the Americans say, is the bottom line.

But Ishimura then extended his influence beyond the bottom line and into general administration: if he could balance the books so beautifully, could he not infuse the rest of the force with his cool analytical certitude and elegance? Could he not make the whole Force more efficient? All the waste, clutter, loose ends, open files, dead ends, false leads, indeterminables, indecipherables, imponderables—all the infuriating *maybes* through which they all, of high degree and low, had daily to wade and flounder: couldn't he do something about *these?* Ishimura didn't see why not, and neither did his superiors. Young/old Ishimura won their praise and gratitude, won a flurry of first-rank official commendations. Further, did they not, at a numbingly expensive testimonial dinner, and with no small ceremony, present him with the handsome bronze ashtray which now adorns his desk? They did, as Yoshida well knows. Yes, Ishimura won their trust; Yoshida, by contrast, won citations only for bravery and skill.

Captain Yoshida's motto is, *Every contact leaves a trace.* A print, a hair, a glimpse, a tiny stain, a hint of blood or semen, a few sloughed epidermal cells, the faintest ghost of a scent: *some trace.* Walk across the room, he knows, and subatomic particles are leaking both ways and nonstop through the soles of your shoes. The thought excites him. Here is evidence galore, if only it could be understood. Well, quarks and neutrinos are beyond him for the moment, but he has electron microscopes and special binocular infrareds and much other hugely expensive, state of the art equipment (that Ishimura has secured for him, that Yoshida could never—again, granted—have wangled on his own). Yes, Yoshida, still a detective at heart, is often right down there at the molecular level of sleuthing: *Every contact leaves a trace.*

Associate Chief Ishimura's motto is, or would be if articulated, *Every contact resulting in official notification necessitates a decision consequent, concerning a rational course of action, selected from among the full range of viable options, which decision must be cost-effective, and that cost-effectiveness must be documented with and on the prescribed forms in quadruplicate, properly initialed, distributed, and filed.*

Captain Yoshida is light years ahead of Ishimura at the detection and apprehension of criminals, but Associate Chief Ishimura—who has, entirely on his own initiative, conceived and designed no fewer than twenty-six *additional* forms in the past decade—has always been much better at police work.

Still, perhaps their inverted *kohai/sempai* relationship is not so serious.

The other difficulty, however, is that they hate each other.

Yoshida holds the receiver to his ear, thinks of a dumptruck slowly emptying itself of a load of sand, grunts politely at intervals, tries to listen, keeps one eye on the tiny Sanyo television that he uses for a paperweight, and riffles through the mess in his In tray. *"Hai,"* he says, *"hai, hai, hai,"* bobbing his neat head courteously in the Japanese manner although the two men are in different buildings, different wards. Yoshida looks to be in his mid-forties. He works out at the police gym, now, works off his frustrations instead of going to the Kado every night and trying to drown them. When he can't sleep he runs till he's tired, if it takes half the night: no more uppers and downers for him. He takes vitamin and mineral supplements, eats brown rice and stir-fried vegetables, sometimes even yogurt, which isn't too disgusting if you dollop on the *shoyu.* He is clear-eyed and solid, a stayer. He still goes to the hospital, signs himself into the *ningen doku,* the "human dry-dock": his annual two days of tests and bed rest. Twelve years ago, he and Kumiko went together and got a double dose of bad news: his liver, her lungs. His was correctable—quit drinking— hers was not. Lung cancer, but she never smoked. *He* did. She was a passive smoker, as the Americans say. She got her disease from him. At the cemetery, Yoshida ground out his final cigarette on the back of his hand, slowly. Now Yoshida is alone, except for his niece, Miyuki. He's lonely; who isn't?

He is medium everything: medium height, weight, build. He is medium-handsome, and his full head of hair, still black, is medium-length. His nose and chin are strong, but not remarkably. There is nothing physically notable about him, nothing at all, and he rejoices in this ordinariness. It renders him nearly invisible. He can walk through a room or down an alley and hardly be seen, much less remembered. He is tougher than he looks, however, and much smarter. Like Associate Chief Ishimura, he wears silver-rimmed eyeglasses, but Yoshida Makoto wears them only to read.

He is reading now: notes, memos, action reports: arson, rape, beatings and extortion, kidnapping, murder. He tries to confine himself mostly to the big one, to homicide, but has found that impossible. Violent crimes overlap; violent criminals are often generalists. So he tries to keep up, riffling and skimming, hearing without listening to Associate Chief Ishimura.

Yoshida Makoto raises his head, peels off his spectacles, gazes through the window-wall of his office and out upon the vista of his support people, row upon row, at metal desks only fractionally smaller than his own, riffling and shuffling papers of their own—

white, pink, yellow, blue: an endless pastel shimmer, like some strange borealis at desk-height—initialing them just as he does, stamping them and counter-stamping them, punching holes in them, inserting them in the appropriate ring binders, reshelving the ring binders with one hand even as the other moves toward the next mound of paper. They are fast.

Some of them are really fast, able to process paper in a twinkling, to churn through a whole drift of the stuff before lunch and do it again after lunch, only more and better. Zero mistakes. Yoshida thinks of these men as the Snowplows. He knows that several Snowplows have caught the eye of Paperwork Ishimura, knows that one or more of them may eventually be promoted right over his own head, realizes that someday he may find himself subordinated to one of them, and have to work around him as Yoshida now has to work around Paperwork. Snowplows: pale, dandruff-dusted, birdlike beings with pursed lips, hunched shoulders, wrists white and delicate to the point of translucency. Shuffling around inside their ill-fitting uniforms, their slippers going paff, paff on the tiles. To the *ocha* machine, the toilet, the file cabinets, and back to their desks. Slumping nerveless on their special doughnut cushions, never tiring or slowing in their mild labors, generating months and years of overtime. Monks at their prayer wheels. What is the current percentage of Snowplows on the Force? Whatever, it is very high. Yoshida sighs.

"Hai," he says, nodding, listening to the Emperor of Snowplows.

Who nonetheless needs Yoshida. Who—What's this? What new craziness?

Yoshida focuses on the two inch TV screen. A jumping *gaijin?* What in—

Paperwork has paused, ominously.

"Hai!" Yoshida grunts, contritely. *"Hai! Sumimasen!"*

He refocuses on the rasp in his ear, entertaining lurid fantasies: Ishimura somehow obliged always to wear his massy ashtray as a hat, Ishimura's head squeezed between stage and cover of his giant Fuji copier, Ishimura's mouth and throat distended with a fat wad of memos, Ishimura crushed and suffocated beneath all the tons of needless paperwork for which he is responsible, Ishimura slowly being fed into his own shredder…

Violent thoughts? Time for the formula. Think it three times, believe it:

Ishimura needs him.

Ishimura needs him.
Ishimura needs him.

Needs him as a budgetary bargaining chip, a selling point: our specialist.

Our man to catch the brutes, the lunatics, the monsters.

Friday, 11:02 P.M.

In the slam! Himself of all people! Uchiyama Masaaki—and for *what?*

For *nothing.* For being attacked by a fucking foreign monster. Who should be in jail right now himself. But that's how things work, isn't it? In this world, where the guilty are rewarded and the innocent are punished. Uchiyama should be used to it by now, but he'll never be used to it. He'll never quit fighting for justice. Fighting to the death.

But, oh, *eeyadah,* he feels bad. His throat is raw from screaming at the cops, trying to explain the situation, what really happened, who he is and who he works for and why the cops better watch out or they'll be dead fucking meat. Because they're playing with dynamite. Uchiyama takes deep breaths, his forehead pressed against the cool bars. His vow: very soon they will all find out the full meaning of the word trouble.

A dozen times, very patiently, he told them the true facts. Do you think they listened? Do you think they could grasp the situation with their stupid brains? No. They never even looked up from their stupid forms they kept filling out. *Where was he born? Where did he go to school? Why isn't he still working at his*

father's fish store? NONE OF YOUR FUCKING
BUSINESS, which he just about told them. *Was this
his first drunk driving offense?* Drunk! They actually
thought he was drunk! And the stupid breath machine
said he *was* drunk! They believed a machine, but they
wouldn't believe him. They preferred a machine to a
human being. Uchiyama hates machines, but not the
keisatsu, oh no. They'll trust a *thing* rather than a
person. That's the way their minds work, if you can
even call them minds.

Drunk! Uchiyama's lip curls. He was nowhere
near drunk. He drank more than that every time he got
behind the wheel of that fucking S-Cargo, which he
hates more than any machine on the planet Earth. He
has to drink, to calm his nerves, or he'd get so uptight
he really would have an accident. Uchiyama drinks for
safety. He told them that. Every individual is different,
he told them—which is a proven fact of science! Could
they understand that? Did they even *try?* Do they ever
even try to understand *anything?* Uchiyama snickers
bitterly, lights another Dean, leaves it smoldering in
the corner of his mouth, ignores it. He holds a bar in
each powerful fist—he is much stronger than he looks,
as they will soon learn, although he doesn't want to

hurt them so much as just *GET THEIR* FUCKING STUPID ATTENTION.

That's all. So he could tell them a few basic facts about reality.

Straight ahead, for scenery, a scuffed and muddy wall. A meter to the left a doorway opens to the office area of the *koban,* the little police station. Masaaki can see a cop there at his desk, squatting like a toad. Masaaki looks at the cop's bulging neck and back, watches him watch the *terebi.* TV, another machine. Tamori, another clown. A fat clown making money watching a thin clown making money.

This is justice?

"Drunk… driving." He speaks the words almost tenderly, works his face into a queasy smile, shakes his head in wonderment, winces, stands motionless. Caught, trapped, nothing to do, nothing to read. No *manga.* Cop has a whole stack under his desk there, but Masaaki refuses to beg. Ah, but he'd give anything for a bright thick *manga* hot off the presses, about twenty new full-length adventures in it. Gangs, bikers in the schoolyard, aliens. Or even an old *manga,* one he already knows by heart, if he could only hold it and turn the pages, keep his mind alive. Just anything— *Sailor Moon, Big Comic for Lady*—any *manga* at all.

No *manga*.

Floor. Ceiling. Three walls. Bars.

And, on top of everything else, he's sick. Some kind of flu or cold. Headache, nausea, aches and shakes. Little bastards at Araddin, whatever disease there is, they get it at their schools, and then of course they run right over and give it to Masaaki. Sneezing, not covering their mouths when they cough. That will do it. Or maybe the foreign monster gave it to him. *Hi there, have a nice day*—the guy breathing all over him, little bits of *gaijin* spit probably hitting him in the face. Each tiny piece of spit? It can have ten billion germs in it, maybe more. Well, Uchiyama Masaaki is a fighter, but how can you fight foreign germs? He snorts. You can't fight germs, you can't even see them, probably they're too small to see. Germs can really waste you, though. Takeshi once said the littlest ones are the worst. So no wonder Masaaki puked his guts out, anybody would, but naturally they blamed him for that too. Cleaning bill for the patrol car. Did they say, What's wrong, friend? You got the Hong Kong flu or some bad germ like that? Should we get you a doctor? Should we call up the newspapers so everybody can find out how you battled the foreign maniac even though you were also battling some kind of terrible foreign sickness at the same time? Masaaki snorts again, tastes the coppery thirst, thick on his tongue and at the back of his throat.

Maybe it's AIDS.

No! AIDS is for faggots, *douseiaisha,* and he's no fucking *douseiaisha.* Besides, you can't get AIDS from yourself, which is a proven fact, or even from a muscle *manga.* Uchiyama lights another Dean and thinks again of Takeshi, who is probably doing the same thing. Smoking a Dean, standing there at the counter of the Convenience Mart where they always stood, and thinking of him too, and wondering, Where's Masaaki-*kun* tonight? Takeshi would be really surprised if he knew, and worried too. Takeshi cares for him, one human being for another, which is what it all comes down to in basic reality. Takeshi understands about life, and he's no *douseiaisha* either, for sure. He's as macho as they come. So no little *furifuri fuafua* cuties for him, or Uchiyama either. They simply have no time for airhead teenyboppers, which is why they're both headed for the top. Which is why they're both tough, both ruthless, both true soldiers in the fight against— AGAINST THE GODDAMN FUCKING BASTARDS OF THE WORLD! Who keep you down, and bleed you white, and never give you a fucking chance!

Like old Mogi, who is going to be unhappy about the S-Cargo.

Fucking *terebi*, can't hear himself think. Not a bad life, be a cop, sit on your fat ass, watch TV all night and get paid for it from the taxpayers' money. Some guys have it all. Except when they have it all, what do they want? More. To make absolutely sure there's nothing left over for guys like Uchiyama, who just happen do the real work of the world. Disgustedly, he pushes himself off the bars, walks three steps to the sink, checks himself out in the tiny rectangle of mirror. He doesn't look as bad as he feels, but he does look bad. Eyes all red with purple bags under them. Face very pale and sort of greenish, zits hanging out there like strawberries. He breathes on the mirror to fog it, so he won't have to look, and accidentally catches a whiff of his own breath. His stomach churns, ties itself in knots, tries to climb up his throat.

Steadying himself against the sink, he feels the sweet saliva gush into his mouth but wills himself not to vomit again. Every time Masaaki vomited the cop shouted, "Get it all in the bowl, punk." Well, he's no punk. He's as good a man as any cop. Uchiyama stands tall, letting the saliva dribble from between his lips and into the sink. He takes a last slobbery drag on his Dean, drops it in the toilet, hears its split-second fizzle. He stands contemplating the cigarette butt. It floats, filter up, bobbing, releasing a dark thread of tar into the clear water. The paper has instantly become semitransparent. He can see the individual shreds of tobacco, see the tiny bumps they make, pressing outward. The butt holds together, though, except for the ashes, which don't float. These filter down to speckle the pure white bottom of the bowl. Good. Masaaki likes that. It's a lot like life.

Uchiyama Masaaki stands swaying above the toilet bowl. Hesitating. The fact of the matter is, he'd really like to take a shit. It would make him feel a whole lot better. But no privacy. Fatass cop sitting at his desk watching the tube, almost close enough to touch. All he'd have to do is turn his head slightly right during a commercial or something, and he would see Uchiyama actually on the pot. Uchiyama would feel like a fool. How can you give a guy The Look when you're in the middle of a shit? You can't. Nobody can, it's a fact of life. On the other hand, however, his bowels are about to burst.

FUCK IT! Uchiyama unhooks his thick brass Harley-Davidson belt buckle, unzips his real Levis, hesitates, then just as quickly zips them up. He stands, twitching, fingers on zipper, listening: TV, cop laughter, the gurgle of his own poor guts. FUCK IT! Uchiyama unzips once more, and jams the Levis down to his knees before he can change his mind again. He then executes a skillful backward pounce onto the toilet. There he sits, scarlet-faced from exertion and embarrassment, doubled over and looking at the scuffed and pointy black toes of his boots. Just then keys rattle, the cell door clangs open, a pair of glowing Florsheims walks in, and the door clangs shut with more key-rattling.

"Konban-wa, good evening."

Uchiyama cranes upward, his gaze moving from the shoes to the neatly pressed blue pinstriped trousers, to the bulging vest, to the deep wine-colored silk tie, to the carefully shaven chin and jowls of Mr. Mogi. His boss. Rather, his boss's boss. Mr. Mogi, *kai-cho* of Araddin Pachinko, king of the whole place, and a heartless old skinflint. Thirty-five at least, and looks it. All those endless months of faithful service by Uchiyama? Maybe Mr. Mogi would notice him, say good morning, maybe not. If he did, then Uchiyama should be thrilled. Rumor has it, however, that the old bastard knows important men in the organization, is on a first-name basis with one of Teshima's actual *kobun*. But that *kobun* got killed, didn't he? Or maybe it was someone else. Uchiyama isn't sure. One thing he is sure of, however, is that Mogi-*san* is not a sympathetic person. In fact, he is known for his cold, ironic manner, his *hiniku*. Several times in the past, Uchiyama Masaaki has been badly stung by the lash of Mr. Mogi's cruel sarcasm.

"No, no," says Mr. Mogi. "Don't get up."

See? Typical! A typical Mogi remark! No concern for human feelings, none at all. But Uchiyama dares not reply. He reaches back smartly and flushes the toilet then sits stiffly at attention, staring straight ahead.

"The good news first, Masaaki-*kun*. We're not going to kill you. Even though it took me several hours to find you. Do you know where you are—which jail, I mean? Mitaka, for some reason. Now the bad news. You're fired, and if you ever show your zits at Araddin again, I will shoot them off."

"But—"

"*Shizuka-ni!* I heard about the monster. I'm not interested in the monster. I'm interested in the S-

Cargo. It's all smashed up on the right side from where you rolled it. Well, that's not so bad. A little body work, paint on a few more Snoopy dogs, it could be all right. If that was the only problem. *Which it isn't.*" Mr. Mogi's face twists in disgust. "The truck *stinks.* What did you do in there?"

"Nothing, just—"

"*Shizuka-ni!* Puke, piss, booze! Into the upholstery, the carpet."

Uchiyama swallows hard, feels his cheeks on fire, stares straight ahead.

"Do you know there's vomit in the ash tray? The cab smells like a public *benjo.* Do you think that smell will ever come out? The whole cab is fermenting. Sitting in the sun all day, all the windows closed, and then I walked up and opened the door. *Sugoi!* Right there I decided, we don't want it back. So that's the rest of the bad news, Masaaki-*kun.* You just bought the S-Cargo."

Uchiyama feels his bowels open again. He reaches back, flushes, snaps his hand back down crisply to his side, stares straight ahead, eyes bulging: Bought the S-Cargo? The vehicle which in all the world he most hates? How could he buy it? He has no money, thank God. *Buy the S-Cargo?* Never! Never! Never! Never!

233

"We figure it's worth *go-ju man*."

A half million yen! For that piece of shit? Never! Never! Never! Never!

"How you get the money is your business, of course. Maybe you can get it from your friend who financed that nice green ring. Or some other source. But get it. Then send it by *genkin-kakitome*. You have a week. And then you may do as you wish. If you'd like some advice, however, here is what you should probably do. Get in your stinking van and drive, and don't stop driving until you get to salt water, and then stay there, wherever it is, some fishing village maybe, and grow a beard, and forget you ever even heard of the Teshima group. Because if you knew who is annoyed with you, if I were to tell you the man's name, you'd"—a smile flickers on Mr. Mogi's lips and is gone—"well, you'd shit."

"I can't even get out of here!" Uchiyama sobs. "I can't pay my bail!"

"Of course you can't. Nobody expected you to. I took care of it."

"When can I leave?"

"When you're sober. Tomorrow, maybe."

"Mr. Mogi, please—"

234

"No, no, Masaaki-*kun,* don't trouble yourself. I'll find my way out."

"Please, don't, I didn't mean, it wasn't me!"

"At ease, *bakayaro.* And *sayonara"*

The door clangs. Uchiyama sags, tasting tears.

THIS IS JUSTICE? THIS IS HIS REWARD FOR YEARS OF FAITHFUL SERVICE AND LAW-ABIDINGNESS? Uchiyama, really raging now, paces his cell like some dangerous panther, feeling destiny or something tingle through his wiry frame, slamming his right fist into his left palm, again and again, bruising the palm with his skull ring. Slam, slam, slam, he doesn't care, he's beyond pain. Well, he thinks, grimly, this is it, finally it happened. Trouble.

And he is ready for it, as they will all learn to their very great sorrow.

Slam, slam, slam.

"Hey, punk!" The cop. "Look, another maniac."

Uchiyama jerks his head away, contemptuous.

"Another foreign monster. But don't worry, punk. You're safe here."

Uchiyama peers disdainfully at the tube, squints in disbelief, and then finds himself shaking the bars, shouting move aside, turn it up, because it isn't *another* fucking foreigner, no, no, no, *it is the same the fucking very same one.*

All bloody and fucked-over—good! Does it hurt, *gaijin?* I hope so!

Justice!

Him, him, him, him. Hearing the newsgirl. Watching him, him, him.

"Dead are Professor Yamamoto Koichiro and his wife Hatsumi. He of an apparent heart attack, she of a stab wound inflicted by a katana. *They are survived by their infant daughter, who fell or was thrown over the railing. Eyewitnesses report screams, confusion. The baby was caught by an English teacher, who was injured when they hit the far bank of the drainage channel. There was some broken glass."*

Good. That's good about the glass. What's his fucking name?

*"—caught, just on time, by F.S. Donnell-*sensei,*"* says the girl.

"Donner," says a big man, holding him up. "F.X. Donner."

Fucking F. X.-fucking Donner.

"Professor Donner," says the girl. "Of...?"

"Kanagawa," says the big man. *"Works at that women's college. I forget the name. Nice place, trees, maybe somewhere around Mitaka?"*

"Edo Joshi Dai?" the girl asks. *"In Kichijyoji?"*

That's it, all right, and full of rotten rich bitches, as Uchiyama well knows.

"—so it looks like Mr. Donner is a hero. This is— HERO!

"—Kobayashi Miyuki, taking you back—"

HERO! THAT FUCKING FOREIGN PIECE OF SHIT!

This... is *justice?*

No. This is the last straw, the very last one, he can not and will not tolerate any more, because now he has reached the absolute maximum limit of his patience. The fucking bastards attacked Hiroshima and tried to blast the shit out of the entire Japanese air force at Pearl Harbor, plus they hurt the Emperor's feelings. So what happens? They give this useless cocksucking Donner a job. A *good* job. So what happens then? He attacks Uchiyama who is doing his own job as best he can so he can go on paying taxes so the Education Department can go on wasting them on places like Joshi Dai. All right, maybe Uchiyama tried to teach the bitch a quick lesson about life in the real world. So what? Whose business is that? Not the *gaijin's*, that's for sure. But what finally happens? Uchiyama gets thrown in jail, gets fired from his job which he had been doing faithfully and to the best of his ability, gets stuck with that stinking, fucking, hell-wagon of an S-Cargo—MAIDO ARIGATO GOZAIMASU!—and the cause of it all is not a criminal but a "hero"!

Uchiyama looks at the ceiling, raises his arms imploringly.

This is fairness?

Uchiyama can't help it. He grabs the bars, tries to tear them from the concrete, roars, howls like an animal, like Rambo, feels the rage galloping through him like some huge bull tiger.

"Hey, punk! Shut up."

All right, all right, he'll be quiet for now, he'll wait, bide his time.

But whose fault is all this?

Donner. He will pay. Oh, will he pay. He'll pay for the attack and the humiliation. He'll pay for this terrible jail experience. He'll pay for the fucking S-Cargo. To his last yen and drop of blood. *Hai, mochiron,* they all think they can take advantage of Uchiyama, shit all over him every chance they get. They think he'll take anything and everything, and forever. Starting with Mr. F.X. Donner of Kanagawa, who will *pay*—Uchiyama slams fist into palm, feeling the skull ring sting all the way up to his left shoulder—and *pay* (slam) and *pay*.

He is going to eat Donner alive.

Uchiyama smiles for the first time in a long time, a thin, terrible smile. In the future, when he's a full soldier, or maybe even a *kobun*, they'll all talk about this night as the turning point. They'll say, that's when the bastards finally pushed Uchiyama too far, and by the time they saw their mistake with their stupid brains, and begged for mercy with their knees, well, it was just too late. Left palm throbbing, jaw muscles jumping, breath whistling through flared nostrils, Uchiyama raises his right fist, contemplates the skull ring. Sure, it does look a little green around the teeth, and the eyes are a little scratched and maybe not real rubies after all, and probably Mr. Donner is used to lots nicer jewelry from all the money he makes out of Uchiyama's taxes, but it's Uchiyama's only ring, and he's still paying for it to that fat greedy inhuman pig Sawada, who has more money than he'll ever know what to do with, so naturally he bleeds Uchiyama white as a *daikon* for every possible yen, and—and Uchiyama's ring will have to do. Because it will be the last thing Donner ever sees. Before his lights go out. For good.

Friday, 11:02 P.M.

Hai, very well then, one final sake, but that really will be it for the evening. Kawakami Yukio sips, clicks the *remocon* again, waits for the old black-and-white to warm up and the news to come on. Yukio is himself already warmed up, a human furnace, so to speak, of well-being and positiveness. He still hurts. His abdominals, his privates, and especially his nose. He'll hurt for some time to come. He accepts this fact with a soldier's equanimity. He not only accepts but welcomes the pain, welcomes it like the tingling sting of his lash. He understands pain, knows what a friend it can be, likes it. But in moderation. Tonight, earlier, *taihen deshita,* that was excessive.

And serious. Perhaps he won't be quite so handsome in the future. Well, did he ever care much about that? There might be scars too, but so what? He rather hopes there are a few. So that he might one day say to his disciples, See that big one? And that long, jagged one in my eyebrow? Want to hear how I got them? And they would very much want to hear. Their eyes would shine with frank adoration as he sketched out for them in his modest, unassuming way the events

241

of this historic night. The night he set about saving Japan.

Still pain, but the pain is now, thanks to the sake, thanks to his own resilient mind and body, well within the realm of the bearable. One big bottle of Iichiko is empty, and he's made good progress on a second. So what? Is there any harm in it, any danger? Yukio laughs easily. Pure Japanese spring water, pure Japanese rice. No foreign poisons. No foreign profit, either. Pure sake. Of, by, and for Japan. Yukio has tried whiskey a few times, even something called aquavit. Both of them, he knows, mean "water of life." But that is a very bad joke, because they make you feel like death.

Brandy? Worse. Even those fancy French wines, which go down like fruit juice, can give you a terrible headache. Champagne, ugh. Foreign garbage for foreign garbage. Yamamoto is—*was, had been*—a big fan of champagne, Yukio is sure. And cognac. And just about anything that cost ten times too much and was imported. Guinness stout, which tasted like some asphalt road and puffed you right up like a *sembe* biscuit. Yamamoto probably drank anything at all, just as long as it was alcohol, and too expensive, and the profits and jobs went to people outside Japan.

Yamamoto the liberal intellectual. Yamamoto the internationalist. Yamamoto the traitor drunk.

Ex-drunk. Yukio permits himself a bleak little smile and one final cup of steaming wholesomeness, reaching back for the flask where it sits in the saucepan of simmering water on the *gasurenji*. Sake is all the medicine Yukio ever allows himself, all he ever needs, and it has certainly done its good work tonight. As on many a previous night. As in ages past, for countless other samurai, wounded and battle-weary.

A picture now, some newsgirl looking sick, sound coming up.

"—Yamamoto Koichiro and his wife Kazumi. He of an apparent heart attack, she of a stab wound inflicted by a katana—"

No!

"—who fell or was thrown over the railing. Eyewitnesses report screams, confusion."

Yukio snorts. Confusion, he can believe that. But the katana? How?

"—baby was caught by an English teacher, who was injured when they hit the far bank of the drainage channel. There was some broken glass."

Well, *shyo ga nai* for the stupid English teacher.

"—caught, just on time, by F.S. Donnell-sensei," says the girl.

"Donner," says a big man, holding him up. "F.X. Donner."

Donner. Another foreigner, of course.

"Professor Donner," says the girl. "Of...?"

"Kanagawa," says the big man.

Who looks Japanese but sounds American. Foreigners, thick as traitors. Where are the patriots? A tiny club, in these degenerate days. Ah, but that was unfortunate about the mother—not so much that she was killed, but the way she was killed, because it does look as though he just rode up behind a defenseless woman and cut her down, which wasn't the case at all. Leave it to the media to twist things around. Also, the police must have both pieces of the sword and his helmet. With his name in it. There can't be that many Kawakami Yukios, even in Tokyo. So he'd better make that call right away, report the theft, remove himself from suspicion. He'll do it, right after the news. He's not at all rattled, but he thinks that maybe he'll have one for the road, as the Americans say, although he certainly isn't going anywhere tonight. No need to heat another flask. He'll drink right from the bottle the way they used to do because that was the test of a good sake. *Komatta-na*, a dead woman, which of course they won't believe was a complete accident. But they should try riding a motorcycle one-handed at high speed over such terrain—bumps, cracks, clumps of dog excrement—and wielding a sword at the same time, if they thought it was so easy.

Yukio snorts. It isn't like the movies. And the baby, that's worse. They'll all say, O the poor thing, *kowai so desu ne?* And miss the point entirely. The fact is, he didn't even see the kid—not that they'll care about facts. And his motorcycle. Expensive, lovingly maintained, and now wasted—necessarily, because of the damage and because of his alibi. Yukio sighs, takes a swig, mourning the bike, the helmet. But then he brightens. He still has his leathers. Tooth-marks at the crotch and vomit all over the front, but salvageable. And, much more importantly, his mission is accomplished, after all. Yamamoto is history, a footnote to one of his own bloated, foreign language footnotes. Kaputt, as they say in Deutscheland. Where that disgusting Yamamoto dog came from. That feces factory, grotesquely long, and, now, flat. Yipyipyip… splat.

Yukio smiles, nods. All right, the operation from start to finish was a bit messier than expected, and now there are some loose ends. But is that not the very nature of military operations? As Napoleon or Bismarck or one of them said, nothing ever goes as planned. Loose ends, evidence in fact—but all circumstantial, is it not? And no witnesses. Or at least no live ones.

"Police are looking for an injured man in his 30s with a short haircut, possibly suffering from some psychiatric disorder, who left the scene on a motorcycle—"

Psychiatric disorder! How ironic. Yukio's mouth curls contemptuously around the mouth of the bottle. Well, if he's crazy then he's in good company. Ieasu, Tojo, Mishima, Sasahara. In his county's history, and leaving out of course the ignoble present, there have been plenty of men who could stomach a little blood. And nobody accused them of craziness—or at least nobody who valued his life... But that's good, isn't it? They're looking for a lunatic—wonderful! They won't give Yukio a second glance. Ha! Quick thinking at Noborito, in the heat of battle, to feign insanity. And he did so instantly, his mind outpacing awareness of its own processes. Yukio shakes his head in awe at his own unsuspected powers. Instinctively, he stood on the bike's pegs and rode off howling like an animal.

Genius. And he'd have done the same thing even if the mongrel hadn't been chewing on his testicles.

"—which witnesses described as possibly damaged. Elsewhere in the news, fire has destroyed the Yotsuya headquarters of the ultra-right, paramilitary Shining Mist organization. Officials have been unable to identify the bodies of a man and a woman, discovered in the wreckage and charred beyond—"

Bodies? Oh, no! Who? A woman? Disaster!

"—smoke inhalation. Police suspect arson by certain radical left-wing—"

Oh, thanks to the gods that he planted the hell-bitch's helmet. That was another master stroke, all right, and would save the situation. And his life. But they should call this show Bad News.

"—elements, but Lt. Yoshida Makoto stated that he is not ruling out revenge or some similar motive, by, as he said, 'some disaffected or unstable member or members of the Shining Mist group itself.'"

Yoshida! Don't be an idiot! What about the writing, the helmet?

"Meanwhile, in nearby Ichigaya, campus violence flared again at Kosei Daigaku. Tanaka Hatsue, 29, is

247

being held pending bond for resisting arrest and two counts of assault."

Assault is right! Better to call it attempted murder. What a little *kappa*. Look at that. Three uniforms wrestling her out of a *patocaa* and toward the door of the police station. Handcuffed, locked in a baton choke-hold, she's still kicking, twisting this way and that, trying to bite, obviously deranged. Would look better in color. Weird whore-makeup all over her face. *Sugoi*—no question, a totally credible arsonist. Yukio tips the bottle back in celebration.

But the good sake fails to muffle a small nagging inner voice that has been asking the same irritating question for some time now, namely, *When could she have done it?*

Any time! Yukio's soldier-self replies.

Not so, says the nattering fault-finder, *Because probably she was on campus all day, with hundreds of people who saw her there, and she didn't lose her helmet until she attacked us, and she didn't go anywhere after that except to jail, so those are a few of the problems that we have in that area.*

Yukio pulls manfully at the Iichiko, striving to block all negative thoughts.

Furthermore, she got a good look. She can identify us. Maybe the two policemen can too, the ones who pulled her off us. And sooner or later the police at Noborito, Ichigaya, and Yotsuya will put one and one and one together, and come knocking on the door. Probably sooner. Which would be good in a way, because it will be a race between the police and Shining Mist.

Three centimeters, two, one, bottle's empty, good work. No fear now.

No? Can we imagine the Leader's face?

Too easily! Heart hammering, eyes bulging, Yukio clutches the armrests—

Then start packing.

Hai! Dekimasu!—and bunches his massive arm *and shoulder muscles*—

One minute.

Hai! Ippun dake shika—and catapults himself from the chair. But the dynamics of this athlete's lunge are such that the mighty surge of his forward momentum causes him to stumble against his *terebi*—the hateful occasion of this current crisis anyway—which crashes to the floor, and, BROMP, the exploding tube sends him reeling back the other way windmilling his arms in a frantic effort to maintain his balance but accidentally tangling his feet in the regulation boxer's skipping rope which had been placed atop the terebi but has of course fallen with it, so as a consequence he trips and skids forward again, nimbly, while endeavoring with all his strength to yank his feet free from the offending coils and at the same time remain upright, and in doing so unfortunately treads on one of the discarded bottles which rolls treacherously from underfoot, landing him flat on his back, stunned, the breath knocked from his powerful lungs. A minute passes, two, three. Yukio is paralyzed. But the vicious doom-laden whispering hisses unceasingly, sears his brain with burning urgencies, causes him to draw on hitherto unsuspected reserves, goads him into rolling over, pushing himself to his hands and knees, pulling himself upright once more with the aid of the doorknob.

BAMBAMBAMBAMBAM on the door! Hearing, feeling the thunder!

It's the police, the Leader, everyone!

"Do aerobics some other time! We are trying to sleep, *bakamono!*"

Not the Leader, nobody, the idiot downstairs neighbor, thank the gods.

Pack.

Hai. Photograph of the Emperor, snatched from the wall and onto the tablecloth. Photograph of Yukio with the Leader, Yukio's Shining Mist Order of Maximum Merit—only three of these in the entire world—socks, underwear, dental floss, a box of Mr. Ito butter cookies, his motorcycle leathers of course both jacket and pants, his big jar of multivitamins, a nearly empty bottle of Bravas aftershave, a stupid High School Jumping *manga* which he hasn't quite finished, all of this onto the tablecloth—

Go.

Hai. Ite ikimasu. He'll race out the door, down the stairs, jump onto his motorcycle—he hasn't got a motorcycle! So money, he needs money, money for the train or bus... picks his wallet from the floor and throws it on the tablecloth, that was quick thinking... is there even a drop left in either of those bottles?

Move.

The newsgirl called him, Yukio, a lunatic and the foreigner a hero!

Run.

Hai. Hashite imasu. Yukio gathering the four corners of the tablecloth, swinging this bundle over his shoulder, charging out the door and down the outside stairs, tripping three-quarters of the way down and

251

rolling the rest of the way and strewing the contents of his tablecloth-bundle behind him, but too psyched-up to care or feel the pain, scrambling back up for the precious leathers at least and sprinting now, all-out—where to?

Away, anywhere, for your life.

Strategic withdrawal, yes, gaining speed, sprinting now as best he can all doubled over and clutching himself, clutching his Yamamoto-reeking leathers, across the parking lot, around the corner, down a block, away from his apartment, away from Mist headquarters, away, away. If Yukio keeps straight on, he'll eventually get to the sushi-ya where he works—worked—and he knows how to get in without a key, so he could hide there.

That's the second place they'll look.

Brave Yukio, not slowing, in fact gaining speed, but sobbing now with exertion and pain, and wondering, Did he remember to turn off the *gasurenji* and lock the door?

Train station, crowds, safety, slow down now, walk over to the Kiosk.

Gaijin! Fat tourists, skinny missionaries, noisy international high schoolers waiting for the train. Red hair, blonde hair, blue eyes, braces, unisex, all talking and laughing at once, screeching and gabbling, the center of their own little universe. Do they even know what country they're in? How Yukio hates them! Because of such and their evil influence he'll have to leave Japan, and go to some foreign country, and live there in horrible exile, and—and be a *gaijin* himself!

Get one of those gauze cold masks to cover your smashed nose.

Yukio doesn't even have a passport.

Now put the mask on.

Nor any money.

Pay for the mask. Go over and buy a ticket.

With what? Yukio has no money!

Quit sniveling. We must have a few coins left. Check your leathers.

One hundred twenty yen, after the mask that's all Yukio has in this world—

Buy the cheapest ticket. Give them some story at the other end. Do it.

No friends, no family, no money, exiled forever—

Here's a kyuko, *westbound.*

And Yukio has an unreasoning terror of airplanes!

This is a train. Get on it.

And where will Yukio get a foreign passport and foreign money?

Now just stand there.

Passport, money, where—FROM THE FOREIGN HERO HIMSELF!

And hold the strap.

Donner!

And quit crying.

Donner—of course!

Quit crying and laughing.

How perfect! How brilliant! How perfectly brilliant!

And howling.

Once again, Yukio has snatched victory from the jaws of defeat!

Everyone's looking. *They think we're a* gaijin. *They think we're* insane.

Friday, 11:06 p.m.

Donner raises the remote selector, shuts down the television, watches the central pinpoint of brightness linger for a second before the screen goes blank. The room lights are off, but the door is open, and light pools in from the hall, reflected by the pale green walls and gleaming floor. The wing is much quieter now, nurses chirping softly by on rubber soles, occasionally stopping to look in on him and the baby. No question, it was quite a day. He lies thinking about the girl from the TV station, Kobayashi Miyuki. Good-looking, or would be if she weren't quite so strung out. Hell of a job she has. Donner likes her teeth, those pronounced upper canines that many Japanese women seem to have. *Doracuras* they call them, "Draculas." Cute. She's maybe twenty-five, nice eyes, lovely musical voice. Called him a hero.

Which is really funny. Donner's many things but no hero. He's a hothead, as Buddy often points out. And a coward, as he sometimes has the nerve to point out to himself. Given time to think things through, would he have gone charging across the road like some crazed rhino into that weird little truck? Would he have risked his neck leaping for some kid? Never, not even pre-Nam. And certainly not now, mid-forties, the prudent present. He raises his right hand, lifts his chin slightly, whispers, "Never again."

Solemn vow. And yet, and yet. He is—he has to admit it—still elated. Having performed such desperate deeds and survived, he's glad. Especially about the baby. Donner's hands-on experience with infants is nonexistent. He is beginning to feel, however, that this tiny child may be in some way special.

He turns his head to look at her. She lies curled in the crook of his left arm. They raised the barred gate on the bed's left side, so she couldn't fall. Probably not necessary, because, even in sleep, she clings to his pajamas. Each tiny fist clamped to a moist bunch of fabric. Well, that's kind of endearing, isn't it? No wonder Ruriko is already crazy about the kid. So maybe they'd keep up some kind of contact after they find the relatives. Ruriko could send her little birthday presents. Puzzles, educational games. Maybe a little kimono for *shichi-go-san.* Those are red letter days for little girls, he knows. They'd take pictures of her at the temple. Donner is a terrible photographer, but Ruriko has the knack when sober.

In fact, the child—her name is Hanako they said, "Flower Girl," a pretty name—might want to spend the occasional week-end at their place. That would be okay with Donner. Make some popcorn, Ruriko could experiment with sobriety, they could all watch a Disney video. No sex or violence, because children are impressionable. Or what's that funny one? Ampanman, some kind of superhero with a dumpling for a head. Edible. They could even go on little overnighters. To Hakone or Atami, for example, lots to do down there. Beautiful scenery. Or out to the islands, take the ferry from Hamamatsucho, have a picnic. Sunshine. Fresh air, which Ruriko could try putting in her lungs. And a jolly little excursionist to take along. That's probably a big part of Ruriko's problem. No kids. Well, maybe they could do things with little Hanako.

And for her. The first thing of course would be to start a little bank account, get her to make those regular deposits. Children need love, that goes without saying, but sooner or later they also need to learn about the world. That means knowing how to handle money. The size of the account, of the deposits, these are secondary, Donner knows. The important thing is to establish the *habits* of thrift and planning.

Donner knows all about planning. He has a big poster-board in his study, tucked behind the bookshelves. On one side of the poster-board is a

257

chart: "Life Plan"; on the other side, "Ten Year Plan."
He never showed these to Ruriko or Buddy, because he
knows what they'd do: laugh. And he knows what
they'd call him: neurotic. Well, maybe a little neurosis
is healthy. It's better than disbelief in the future. It's
better than being so laid-back and well-adjusted as
never to worry about, for example, cirrhosis of the
liver or cancer of the lung. So let 'em laugh. Donner's
the one with a plan.

The goal of the Ten Year Plan is to bring out a
book-length collection of his journalism and maybe
make a little extra money. He has about thirty pieces so
far, feature articles in one magazine or another and
dating back as far as five years. Donner was somewhat
hotter back then.

Recently, things have been a little slow, although
he just did the first draft of a spoof, "The
Ironsalaryman Triathlon." It's pretty funny. Dig it, the
contestants are typical Tokyo commuters, gormless
and wasted, real Night of the Living Dead types. They
have to ride to the station on their rusty little *eki* bikes,
then take the ferry, then transfer to the train, back and
forth, no running allowed, and they have to consume
the usual epic quantities of noodles and beer and
methamphetamines, and of course chain-smoke on the

platforms, and they get disqualified if they go over the allowance that they get from their wives. Maybe a sidebar, "Cracking Down on the Drug Abstainers," plus a few profiles on the major white and black hats ("Yamamoto-*obaasan*, having won more major events than any other contestant, living or dead, literally walked away with last year's Ironsalaryman trophy, the famous "Slumpie," in 4:52:26 @ ¥2,820"). And so forth. Good stuff.

And that's not all. Donner is roughing out another put-on piece, this one about Compulsive Clowns Anonymous. Frowning thick-bodied middle-management types sitting around a big table in the church basement, space heater hissing. Suits, Kiwanis and Jaycees pins with maybe the odd Mason, heavy frames on the glasses, strands of hair slicked across pink crowns. Smoking, sipping cold coffee from brown-beaded Styrofoam cups. Americans and Japanese, East meets West, brought together by their common demon. They admit it, tell each other at length how their affliction, their infantile neurosis, brought them to the very brink of personal and professional ruin ("My family was ashamed of me, never knowing when I might launch into my cretinous merganser imitation, my co-workers refused to be seen

259

with me, clients shunned me"). Yes, brought them to the brink and would have destroyed them were it not for the intervention of a Higher Power. But, unlike their AA counterparts, the CCA men scowl and sweat. They are under terrible pressure not to start some kind of awful chain reaction by, for example, some almost unintentional pun or perhaps a not quite inadvertent burst of flatulence, because then the situation might well careen right out of control: Whoopee Cushions, one-eared elephants, and squirting lapel flowers would once again be the order of the day, and their doom would be sealed. Donner chuckles. CCA, more good stuff. Donner's full of ideas like that, and the magazine editors have pretty well quit returning his calls.

But, anyway, that's his Ten Year goal: a Donner reader.

His Life Plan goal is happiness.

Intermediate goals? Right on the study door. Donner always has one of those Itoh-ya fifteen month planning calendars—useful, because the Japanese academic year always spills over into January and sometimes February—with his various teaching and committee dates, his journalistic deadlines. All color-coded and annotated. Plus birthdays, anniversaries, various license and card expiration dates, you name it.

Donner often meditates on his calendar, drawing comfort from this soothing and orderly projection of his life, all the bright-hued days and weeks and months, arranged in rows, lined up in such a way that they might be negotiated safely and with minimum fuss. No surprises, no emergencies. A big block of time, predissected, neutralized. Harmless as a butterfly collection. Where, in all that regularity and pastel cheer, is there room for black death?

Nowhere. Looking at his calendar, Donner feels in control. He feels a momentary easing of whatever it is that keeps his belly muscles knotted. He sometimes feels almost, well, good. But not nearly as good as he feels right now. Is it the drugs? Not entirely. He looks again at the baby. How lovely she is, how exquisite in repose. What is she, two? A very cute age. Her little face is the face of a doll. Smooth and rounded, a pale tawny gold suffused with rose. Eyebrows perfectly arched as though painted on with a single-hair brush. Hair still in a vertical ponytail and tied with the same pink ribbon. Long dark lashes, tiny nose, mouth like a rosebud. Amazing flesh!

Donner pictures the bones beneath. Living bone is not white, as he well knows. Rather it is translucent and perfused with innumerable tiny blood vessels.

261

Over the skull—jaw, cheek, eye socket—and attached with such delicacy and economy, are the layers of muscle, fat, skin, which permit expression. Her face can show the workings of her spirit as a clear pond marks the passage of each subtlest breeze, as she herself, the totality of this child, might be the flesh-expression of some over-spirit. Cells, tissues, organs of face and body, bathed in pure blood, accomplishing in concert their infinitely complex chemistries, in silence and soft breathing. Precious flesh, flowering up from some ground of being. Get right down to the molecular level, you'd really see something: dazzling galaxies of atom-configurations washing past, perhaps to the sound of crystalline harp-chords.

Molecular music, well, that's pretty fanciful. Chalk it up to the painkillers. But the notion does tickle at Donner's oldest questions: why is there something— why is there *everything*—and not nothing? And why, in among the rocks and mud, is there such a wondrous phenomenon as life? And why, rising above the viruses and slime molds, is there such a stunning life-form as humanity? Yes, all right, natural selection, but not only that. Survival of the fittest, yes, but something more. And not mindless chance. Watching the baby in the dim, silent room, Donner the skeptic is less inclined than ever to take his science on faith.

Watching, he becomes aware of her body heat. The fires of life. Radiant flesh, moist and mysterious. Water vapor, saliva, the faint ammonia tang of urine. A dew of perspiration, distilling itself at her temples, welling from her closed palms. From those secret lines of destiny and force. Beauty bone-deep, profound as being.

Then he has a sudden rush of feeling, a gut-insight into the miraculousness of everyday. *If there were only one child,* how awed we would be, how we all would worship her. And if this particular child had died today, all perfection and potential, what an inconceivable tragedy. Killed or otherwise destroyed, as numberless children are daily. Numberless daily tragedies, incalculable daily waste. All the tiny unfortunates who were once Hanakos, must have been, before whatever happened happened. All of them. Janey, Buddy, Ritsuko, even himself. Even… Thuong.

Donner leans a little closer and sniffs her hair. It has a sunny, wheaty smell. Donner never smelled a child before, never watched one sleep. Where are you, little one? With your mother someplace far away and safe?

It's pretty God damn sad, any way you look at it.

A *sword?*

Donner would very much like to get his hands on that scumbag.

Without releasing his pajamas, the child brings her left thumb to her mouth, begins to suck. Soon her fist is glistening, and there is a small saliva patch on the pajamas. The dampness is cool on his chest. He pulls the thin flannel sheet a little higher around her shoulders. He can feel her breath very faintly against his right hand, can see the sheet's rise and fall. One of Donner's favorite words, the gentle breeze of respiration: "susurrus."

It is a calming word, and sometimes Donner closes his eyes and says it over and over, till the meaning refines out of it and his pulse and breath slow—after, for example, one of his and Ruriko's screaming near-fistfights about nothing, hairs in the sink, microtrivia. Which are of course not reasons but merely *occasions* for domestic brawling, while the real reason is always the same: Ruriko sees the world as basically friendly, whereas Donner knows that it is not. Ruriko frequently says and apparently believes that everything will be okay. Mindless optimism and alcohol, Donner tells her. Read the papers, read a little history and learn about very large matters repeatedly turning out extremely un-okay. Then Ruriko: Read! *Kekko desu,* no thanks, Donner, look where your reading has gotten you, every cloud with a CFC lining, *ki no doku,* you are a poison to my spirit. And so forth, several times a week. Well, Donner recognizes the need to be continually on guard against everyone and everything, whereas Ruriko recognizes no such need. Their difference is as simple as that. And as irreconcilable.

Donner might phone home on a sunny day, politely inquire if she's done the washing, hung the *futon* and blankets out to air. Well, no she hasn't, and she isn't going to. Nor is she going to vacuum, clean the kitchen, shop for groceries. It's too nice a day. What then does she intend to do—go for a walk, perhaps, or work in the garden? No, she intends no such sunshiny puttering. She is no sweaty jock, no domestic servant. She is an artist. She intends to continue with her poem, though he of course has and can have no slightest inkling of the difficulties involved. Poem! Sitting curled on the sofa all day, curtains drawn, doodling around at a haiku, hitting the rum and Coke harder and harder as the hours pass, finally crumpling all the false starts and throwing them tearfully at the wall, then passing out.

Poetry. Art.

Make hay while the sun shines. How often has he pointed that out to her? *A steady application of effort*—can't she see the wisdom there? True enough, she is not his servant, but neither is he hers, and he feels like a fool, putting in twelve and fourteen hour days—the train commute is a job in itself—then coming home to several more hours of housework. Which he always does because the clutter and filth make his flesh creep, while Ruriko lies on the sofa, forearm up shielding her eyes. At such times she offers suggestions for improving his character.

He is, she says, devoid of joy. Vacuuming violently around her, Donner agrees, but notes that the world is a fairly joyless place. He is also, she says, a sick perfectionist and absolutely no fun. Right again. Fun! Who needs it? Donner, compulsive clown though he is, never has any so-called normal fun, has never wanted to, has always been too anxious about everything to enjoy anything—except of course with the aid of alcohol, and now he doesn't drink. She shouldn't either, because she's a God damned alcoholic. Well, so is he! Granted! But at least he's doing something about it, at least he's not a slobbering God damn drunk—you heard me—and, anyway, fun isn't the point.

No? Then what, she wants to know, *is?*

The point to life is happiness: health, wealth, privilege, and time. Fuck fun. Love? Yes, love too, he supposes. But mostly the point, as he sees it, the essential point of everything, is just rewards for well-considered actions. So Donner passes his days in fear that he might lose some advantage, miss some edge or angle or some tiniest perquisite to which he might be entitled, and thus remain forever flawed and unfulfilled. So every day he does his frantic best.

He fights for minuscule tax breaks, seeks out marginally higher returns on investments, shifts little fund-clumps all over the world, keeps them chasing the highest possible interest rates in a dozen currencies which seem to destabilize upon purchase. Sometimes he sits and looks at his statements, is somberly cheered by the zeroes. He seldom achieves any return better than normal bank interest, but that never discourages him. Real estate, securities, commodities, same thing. Not knowing his ass from a hole in the ground, guessing wrong as often as not. Eggs in a dozen caskets. Slumps and fluctuations make him panicky, apt to call his broker and, for example, get himself the hell out of deutschemarks and into hog bellies, or vice-versa, while it's still possible to do that, before all the

267

doors clang shut with Donner on the outside of everything, again and forever. All by himself. And still so far from home.

Like his bonegully dreams—or, worse, The Dream. The one he's had since age five. In it, he leaves kindergarten on a sunny afternoon, sure of his directions. Birds are singing. He walks along, relishing the familiarity of houses and hedges and cracks in the sidewalk. The crumbling viaduct, the Youngs' old green Pontiac with the pitted chrome Indian on the hood. Garter snakes criss-crossing the uphill gravel path before it became a sidewalk again. Grasshopper noises and hot prairie smells. Talc-like dust. The Wallers' gleaming Cadillac which cost five thousand dollars and had on its trunk a shield with multicolored bits of glass which are to Frankie Donner almost painfully beautiful in the sun, and fire in him a feeling of some dim bloodwarm absolute, some wonderful memory of a memory.

Quickly, however, night begins to fall, and just as quickly the landmarks become fewer. Then, walking faster and finally stopping to look around terrified, he realizes that somehow he is in a strange neighborhood, that he is lost. He weeps with panic and an icy sense of loss. He has to get home, has to. So he retraces his steps, back toward the old brick school. As he does so, all the familiar details reappear and the sky lightens. Once again, sunshine and birdsong. He feels hot waves of relief that nearly buckle his knees. But when he tries again, oh so carefully, the same thing happens. Strange houses at odd angles to the street. Clouds. The sun smothers and chokes, the known shivers away in waves, mirage-like. Over and over, as it grows later and later, as he becomes more and more desperate, he hurries back and forth.

Finally, his mother drives up in his father's Studebaker. She gestures to him: get in. He hangs back, afraid. His mother can't drive, so why is she driving? Why isn't his father driving? Where is his father? His mother's smile is bad. She gestures again, impatiently. He opens the door and climbs up beside his brother, onto the scratchy gray upholstery of the front seat. Then his mother is screaming and flailing and turning the steering wheel this way and that and shouting, "Brake! Brake!" And suddenly Donner is also outside the car, on the hood by the little silver bullet with its propeller, and watching the wild faces of his mother and his brother and himself as they are slammed back and forth, as the Studebaker jounces over the last few ruts and green hummocks then

269

pitches over the rounded edge and down the raw crumbled-earth face of a cliff.

They never hit bottom. As a child, when he woke he lay panting, gripping the edges of the mattress to keep from getting sucked through it and back into the dream. There were, he almost knew, small and very evil foxlike creatures with tiny red eyes in his closet and under his bed, so he pulled the sheet to his chin and made sure that his toes were covered, although of course he still wasn't safe. He never cried out loud. Once he tried to tell his mother about the dream, but she was angry at him again that day, sitting at the vanity and doing her makeup, and not looking at him because he was bad, and he felt the familiar iron cold spread from his stomach down and out, until he backed into a corner and slowly crouched there, his arms around his head. He couldn't look up. Her footsteps crossed and recrossed the room, loudly. He didn't know how to tell her, what to tell her, how to get her back.

So later, when he was supposed to be napping, he took a pin and scratched her name on the headboard of her bed, MOM but that didn't help—in fact it earned him a spanking, one of the really bad ones, which was only right. She didn't understand, wouldn't, and she kept leaving although of course she was right there in the house. But she *was* leaving, everything was colder, and he had to do desperate things to hold her back, things which made her more icily angry still, because he *was* bad, and every day there was yet another thick frosted pane between them, until he could barely hear or see her, and he was lost, then, utterly alone.

She hated him. He no longer existed for her. Which he knew without knowing that he knew it, but couldn't believe and at the same time live. So Frankie kept hoping that if he could just do something stupendous and smart, some blazing astonishing act, then the barrier would shatter and his mother would really notice him. She would look at him when she spoke to him. She would come back to him, and say gentle words of praise, and hold him. And he would no longer have to hold himself, have to press his elbows against the cold dark place that wasn't there. He'd stop shivering, he wouldn't be sick all the time, and they could be together—they could they could they could— because he would find his way back.

Forty years later, a spark of that same impossible hope perhaps remains. These days, Donner tracks through large books on history and philosophy. He learns things, makes notes. Every morning, he plunges into the financial pages of the *Japan Times,* that thicket, that jungle, seeking some faint trail, becoming lost almost immediately of course, but looking, feverishly searching, for the prime, the all-important fact that would, properly applied, change everything, take him far away from what there is, and into some luminous was and should be. Searching, more and more urgently. For his big chance, for the opportunity which comes but once. Before it's too late.

But too late for what? Absurd, absurd. As Ruriko rightly notes, he doesn't give a damn about abstract knowledge. Even less about money. He never uses it for anything except to make more, never spends it because he has everything he wants, or says he does, certainly never has any fun with it, so, really, what is he so excited about?

What indeed? In his more tranquil moments Donner has to admit that she is mostly right. The shopping trips, for example. She'd buy things, he wouldn't. Wandering through Isetan, Sogo, Takashimaya, Seibu, Mitsukoshi—all the great *depaatos*—surveying their infinitude of goods, which he could well afford, but never making one single purchase: his idea of a good time.

"Oh," she'd say, "this is just what you've been looking for."

"No," he'd say, "it isn't. Can't justify that right now."

Or, "Oh, Donner, these are Italian, on sale."

"Mine are still okay. Maybe next year."

Now and then he'd drift by the same item several times, finally pick it up, examine it closely, nod, ask her opinion, nod again, judiciously, and take it over to the cash register, Ruriko all smiles, maybe giving him a surreptitious hug. But then, just before he handed it over to the clerk, Donner would frown, scrutinize it again, sigh, shake his head, and take it back. The first few times, Ruriko didn't realize he was clowning around. Then he began selecting increasingly bizarre items—grotesque apparel and huge clanking gilt accessories from the teen corners. Then he'd run right through his Shrewd Shopper routine: pursing his lips, cocking his head to one side, holding the thing at arm's length above his head, peering at the seams, checking the label, squinting at the price tag then reeling back in apparent shock with his eyebrows jigging all over his forehead. Putting on a little show. Aisle theater. Once, at their neighborhood Seiyu, he actually donned a garish pink and purple T-shirt featuring some leather-clad, chain-draped, green-faced hairy degenerate gobbling an orange microphone. Raised his eyes, cocked his head at Ruriko: Not bad, eh? Another time, at Halc-Odakyu, he tried on a New Age jacket. Double-breasted, the shoulders enormously padded, the fabric brick red, the giant buttons chartreuse.

"Well," he said, emerging from the curtained cubicle, beaming, "what do you think?" But then at the counter, after the long wait, Second Thoughts: turning sadly away from the cashier, showing Ruriko and everyone his plucky little smile and telling her sincerely, "I—I guess I don't really *need* it."

That was their last shopping trip together.

"Do you know what you are, Donner?"

"Yen save is yen earn. Flankrin."

"Do you?"

Donner knows. He is a pain in the ass. Once or twice he even admitted it, tried to explain himself, to himself and her. The mainspring of his nature is not, he believes, simple greed or miserliness. Rather, it is a gut-abhorrence of waste, a loathing of the missed opportunity.

For example, Donner always sifts through their garbage, retrieving eggshells, rinds, peels, leavings—anything biodegradable—to put on his garden compost heap. Certainly the smell is extreme, but on sunny days he likes to stand for a moment and watch the heap, decomposing itself to rich humus, nourishment for future generations of tomatoes. And all gratis, there is the beauty. The little bugs in there are working for him. The all have "Donner Enterprises" stitched on their little jackets. You take a bunch of useless organic crud, a liability because otherwise you have pay someone to haul it away, and you turn it into an asset. A tiny one, to be sure, but an asset nonetheless. Manure is especially good. He began taking a trowel and plastic bag along on their walks, alert for animal droppings—free nutrients, was the point—until Ruriko objected. Donner countered that *all* Japanese carry a trowel and plastic bag when they walk their dogs.

"When in Tokyo, Ruriko. A turd in the hand. It's the custom."

"It's customary first to have a dog, *bakayaro.* "

Was that an opening, or was that an opening? Donner went for it, dug up an old leash someplace. Next time out, he wrapped it around his left hand, began issuing gruff commands—"steady, Blue, heel! Heel, sir!"—whistling, now and then throwing a stick into the bushes alongside the river—"Fetch, boy!"— or, whenever they met one of their neighbors, shading his eyes with his hand and scanning the area. *"Doko ni iru?* Where'd he go?" Rueful grin and headshake. "Crazy hound!" Or exclaiming softly over path-side excreta like some avid mushroomer—"Oh, Ruriko look at that one. We're in luck today. What a beauty. Alsatian, do you think? Borzoi?" and so forth— scooping them into the bag. Free fertilizer, was the way Donner saw it, free entertainment. Have a few laughs, keep the compost heap stoked. Cash outlay, zero. But Ruriko didn't see it that way, wasn't amused, perhaps because she knew that he was only half-kidding, that he did take a greater interest in the heap than he took in most persons—*including herself*—that he did muse often on its self-sufficient mystery, its sunwarm secret heart. Ruriko is very bright, give her that.

At any rate, that was their last walk together.

Well, too bad. No more shopping trips, no more walks, no more life together, really. Now polarized, diametrically opposed on everything. One man's flesh. He loved (so she hated) their big and admittedly rather expensive Chofu solar panel on the roof. Every day, trillions of photons, *free* photons, hitting it, generating heat, raising the temperature of the water in the tank. Even in winter. How sweet it is for Donner, to go for a bitter snowy run, up along the ridge of hills considered mountains by locals, then down and back along the river. Then the payoff: shower down, and ease himself into the *furo* full of free hot water. Even now, Ruriko would sometimes join him in the tub, but still he can't get her to see that his gratification comes not so much from saving a few yen as from exploiting, rather than wasting, a natural force. She'd sit there and sip her sake or rum and nod yesyes, but she wouldn't get it. To her, water's water.

Which of course it is. But Donner was talking about the luminous principle of harnessed energies: sun and wind drying one's clothes, earnest bank personnel seeing to it that one's savings interest accrued, fruits and vegetables ripening in one's garden, real property appreciating, stock dividends declaring themselves on schedule, beneficent microbes and enzymes reducing the neighborhood offal and debris to fecund topsoil, book royalties however small rolling in. Wonderful. All these automatic mechanisms and many others redounding to his own increase.

"So what?" she wanted to know.

"Acting in your own interests, pursuing your own advantage."

"Who gives a shit?"

Not Ruriko, now excessively Americanized. But Donner cares deeply. Physical, mental, financial—whatever benefits there are, he wants them. That is Donner's deep instinct, reflex, need: to exploit every situation. Donner exploits himself too. He doesn't waste time. During his frequent bouts of insomnia he writes letters, pays bills, reads the first dozen or so pages of the improving works which he bulk-orders in hard cover from his several stateside book clubs. Any other leisure he turns to account. He lifts weights, runs marathons, pores over his investments, keeps elaborate records of his various approaches to perfection.

Who gives a shit, indeed? Donner, wishing often that he didn't, does. Donner the auto-cannibal, devouring himself with concerns about his every cell, tissue, gland, organ. Concerns too about the global environment and economy. About crime. About the manners and morals of the young. About another giant asteroid slamming into Earth and sending them all on the way of the dinosaurs. About the universe, or at least the Milky Way, and every God damned thing in it. For all of which he feels personally responsible. None of which he can trust. Only his ceaseless vigilance can maintain the exquisite balance of the status quo. Donner is sick and he knows it. But sicker than existence itself?

"Me," Donner told her. "I do. I give a shit."

"Why?"

Why? What a question. Donner was momentarily speechless. Why? Well, to combat—whatever there is to combat. Everything bad. Mental sluggishness, penury, disease, criminal assault, spiritual stagnation, degeneracy. The enemies within and without. Everything you don't want to happen to you. You have to fight. You have to strengthen, cushion, protect yourself against all possible vicissitudes of earthly life. And ultimately, he supposed, against death.

"Don't you see?"

She snickered, broke the house rule against lighting a cigarette without first turning on the exhaust fan. Open your eyes, he wanted to tell her. Look around, watch the news. Yes, and see the kinds of horror visited daily upon billions of humans all over the planet. Realize that our general operating principle is and must be, in all areas of life, Never let down your guard. Because the universe is our adversary. Brute matter: earthquakes, tidal waves, volcanic eruptions, lightning, tornadoes, floods, droughts, avalanches. Deadly plants and animals, the list is endless.

Microbial pathogens enough to fill huge encyclopedias and mutating into more virulent strains every second of every minute, as the cells of one's own body could and did spontaneously opt for cancer or necrosis. Worst of all, one's fellow humans. Given half a chance, they'll cheat, lie, draft, enslave, betray, rob, rape, beat, and, generally, eat you alive.

"Donner," she said, "you worry too much."

"Sure, I worry! But too much? I don't think so. Maybe not enough."

All things considered, probably not nearly enough. Donner lay down with a soundless sob of relief each night, each morning rose reluctantly and with dread. And rightly so, he felt. Doesn't every thinking person?

"In fact," she said, yawning, stubbing out the smoke, "you're hysterical."

Hysterical! *Hysterical?* Well, maybe so. Most of his waking hours he *does* tiptoe and hold his breath, at least mentally. His life *is* a defensive operation, a holding action, a protracted exercise in damage control, necessarily doomed and futile. He *has* developed a near-phobia about chance and change. He *doesn't* love life, or even like it, so much as he loathes and fears the very idea of death, the ultimate missed opportunity, the supreme and final waste.

But is this his morbid neuroses or everyone else's obtuseness?

"Donner, Donner, what are you so afraid of?"

"Nothing."

Everything! Donner is afraid of everything, always has been. "What do you want with that stupid rum and Coke?" he asked by way of counterattack, as she sat curled on the sofa, working on one of her "poems," knocking back the poison all afternoon. "Why don't you try some of this tiger's milk instead?"

But she turned her head away, looking nauseous. Donner's tiger's milk is based on an Adelle Davis recipe. It has everything you need. Yogurt, carrot juice, blackstrap molasses, rose hips for organic C, brewer's yeast, fishmeal, peanut butter, bananas, cod-liver oil, prunes, wheat germ, kelp, plenty of lecithin, desiccated organ meats, and a pinch of malt and cinnamon for extra flavor—plus he soups it up with every known vitamin and mineral for optimal nutrition. Donner belts back three big glasses every day, getting a sort of rush from the B complex. It is potent stuff. Sure, it takes a little getting used to, but Ruriko—alcohol and sugar, sugar and alcohol—doesn't know what she's missing. Donner just throws everything into the blender and hits the button, then knocks back the tiger's milk, all frosty and frothy. Really, it tastes quite distinctive.

Ruriko won't even stay in the same room with him while he drinks it, and Buddy once said, "Hey, even in the camp, we were putting down the bugs and slugs? I wouldn't have touched that stuff. Unless you maybe went down to the blood bank and spiked it with a fresh pint of type A." Buddy's humor, primitive; Donner's used to it. But even Janey—total fitness, black belt— same story, though of course more politely, some foolishness about her allergy. Well, that's their problem isn't it? Donner's just trying to help, looking after their basic interests. Their lives are their business, however. You can lead a person to tiger's milk, but.

Tiger's milk, Donner believes in it, but it never made him feel this good. The anesthetic is wearing off, but so is the pain. He doesn't have any really bad cuts or bruises, and the bump on his head is just a bump. But that is negative good, as it were, and Donner feels better than he should, than he ordinarily would. This feeling has to do with finding his way out of himself— and twice in one day!

Here in the peaceful room, the baby dreaming in the crook of his arm, nobody pushing him or threatening him or getting his back up about anything,

Donner's prepared to entertain some second thoughts about his life. He's willing to consider that his life may be far from perfect, far even from okay. Looked at from just a slightly different viewpoint than his usual one it appears grim indeed. Setting goals, accomplishing same, setting new ones, rationalizing away all dissatisfactions and itches and urges, until finally he has come to expect very little of existence. Which is of course exactly what he's been getting.

Because he thinks his life is Life?

Yahoo. Slamming into that van, like doing a fat line of cocaine while coming up through a cloud bank and into pure brilliance. Same thing at the bridge, reality suddenly opening to him. Ecstasy. Two violent reminders of Something. That most of the time we use only a fraction of our capabilities? That we are somehow more immense, more thrillingly significant than we usually seem? Live in a rainy country, you forget the sun is up there. Live too carefully, and you forget you're alive at all. The truth is, Donner's still tingling. Call it a nervous reaction, but he's resonating from his brush with Whatever, taking deep delighted breaths, relishing each one, enjoying the coolness in his nostrils and throat. When was the last time he did that?

283

Never.

The baby squirms suddenly, whimpers in her sleep. Can two-year-olds have nightmares? Yes, Donner believes so, thinking back. There, there, little one, we'll get things sorted out, find your people, and everything is going to be all right. And it would be. He hasn't been afraid at all today, hasn't had time. A day like this, it sort of shakes you up and turns you inside out and clarifies everything. Reminds you what's important and what isn't, what's an emergency and what isn't. Tomorrow, when the painkillers wear off completely, he might feel like Thuong's men worked him over. So what? He'll write it up, sell it to the mags, turn a profit on the cuts and bruises. *Tokyo This Month,* they'll go for it, their asshole Cockney features man with his "we run only items which are *inherently newsworthy.*" Well, here you go, Grub Street. Donner, thinking tough, exulting in his unwonted ballsiness.

The baby whimpers again. There, there. Trust Uncle Donner.

No, it really isn't just the drugs. He's calmer than he has been in a long time, more optimistic, more positive about life. Well, he has a lot to live for. Ruriko, for example, who still has her moments. Drunk or sober, she can be very sweet, and, face it, drunk or sober, a terrific piece. No love, but that's all right. So he has Ruriko. He has his small but discerning readership. He has charming and appreciative students, affable colleagues, numerous acquaintances. No real friends except Buddy and Janey, but he does have Buddy and Janey. That's two, more than lots of people have. So count your blessings. Plenty of people who wish him well, more or less. Nobody that wishes him ill—nobody that he knows of.

The child quits sucking her thumb and reaches out blindly, her hand making no contact for a second. She utters a small cry and jerks awake. Then her left hand comes to rest on Donner's chest again, but more to the left, and this time closes not on pajama but on Thuong's tooth.

There, there. There, there.

A third small friend, and—so far as he is aware—not an enemy in the world.

Donner smiles. The baby whimpers, snuggles against him. He slowly turns his head, breathes her scent again, brushes her brow with his lips. A kiss, why not? Nobody will ever know, and this is yielding-to-impulse day. Dream-wisps begin to flicker and evanesce, and he gets the idea that she is really or also little Frankie Donner, and he hugs her tightly, and perhaps she hugs him just as tightly, and Frankie feels a bloodwarm wash of pure relief and joy, and they sleep.

Saturday, 10:53 A.M.

Baby's due any second, Planman's bringing her, it's all arranged, finally, after about twelve calls back and forth all morning, and Ruriko Donner is, despite a bad case of nerves, limiting herself absolutely to three rum and Cokes beforehand. True, the first two were triples, and this one is perhaps closer to a quadruple, if there is such a thing, but she simply must remain calm for everyone's sake, and if that means alcohol, well, so be it. That's Ruriko: she does what she has to do. And, really, she'd do anything at all for that baby. Anything.

She loves that baby so much that she, Ruriko Donner, has almost ceased to exist apart from this molten adoration working through her. It is religious, Zen-like. The perfection of her love is such that Ruriko herself is no longer loving. *Love is loving.*

Ruriko is momentarily overcome with the poignancy of this insight, and her vision is blurred by tears. This feeling that has her by the throat—should she try to compress it into the white-hot diamond of a *haiku?* Could she do it? Ruriko doesn't think so. The feeling is huge and diverse, like some giant wave of flame, breaking over her and tumbling her along in a rage of tenderness and hunger. Maternal hunger so long denied because of the ice-hearted, tight-assed clown she so foolishly married. Oh, Daddy was right about him. Neurotic? She snickers, shakes her head. The mere thought of Donner drives her from the couch to make another drink, which is not really *another* drink but rather an extension of the current one, because the ice cubes are the same, so all she needs to do is just freshen it a little bit, which does require her to open another bottle of Bacardi, but there's still plenty left in the Coke bottle, so it's all right.

Where the hell is Planman?

If he stopped off somewhere with Buddy she will kill him.

The bell!

She snatches at the interphone, fumbles it to the floor, picks it up, shouts, *"Hai! Donata deshoka?* Yes, yes, who is it?"—and then thinks, Of course, he's got both hands full, can't get his keys out, and she races down the stairs, holding tightly to the railing. Halfway down she realizes she's still holding her drink. He'll make some cruel remark, she knows him too well. What to do? Rush back upstairs? Try to carry the baby *and* the drink?

Boldly, Ruriko drains her glass and sets it on the window-ledge.

"Yubin desu!" And a pounding on the door.

The post office? Some special delivery? Where's *Donner?*

Upset, confused, hurt, Ruriko unlocks the door and opens it.

The Great Healer looks at the woman in the doorway: drunk before *hiruma.* Nice neighborhood, quiet money, everything clean, late-model sedans, well-tended shrubs and fruit trees. Rose, grape, kiwi arbors. *Sentaku-mono*—shirts, pillow-cases, thick good quality towels—precision-hung and drying in the sun. Substantial two-story houses. And so-called rational human beings living in them. Sparks of the Divine, specks of the All. How can they so degrade themselves? Well, this one's swinishness will work to his advantage.

"Ohaiyo gozaimasu, good morning. Package for Mr. Donner."

"Ohaiyo gozaimasu. Orimasen, he is not here."

"Well, perhaps you could sign for it. *Oku-san, desu ne?"*

"Yes, I am his wife."

"Ja, onegaishimasu, this way, please." The Healer is not surprised. He expected that Donner would still

be in the hospital. So, simply take the woman and then take Donner when he comes for her. "It is in the car."

"Car?" The woman asks, looking hesitant. "Don't you have a truck? Don't you have a uniform? You must be *arubaito.*"

"*Eh, so desu,*" the Healer tells her. "That is right. I am just part-time."

"Maybe it's baby clothes."

"I think so. The package is light, but it is bulky. Could you help?"

"Of course. Clothes from some well-wisher, for my baby."

"Probably so. Right this way."

"Someone who saw the News last night. Many must have seen it."

"Many did."

How simple to abduct a stupid person. Open the door, push her in, tap her on the head. Not too hard— yet. The Healer chose not to delegate this mission. He desires and will get full satisfaction. He has not bothered with a disguise. He is realistic. He knows that, in the interests of justice—*not* vengeance—both the woman and her husband will have to pay the full penalty, as did the lawyer and his family. But it was of course *not* the Healer's decision nor is it his ultimate responsibility. Now as always the Great Healer is but an instrument of the All. It is the source of his humility and his power. The slanderer must die, and by the Healer's own hand. Thus it has been decreed.

At the wheel of his modest and seemly white Nissan, the Healer glances over at the woman slumped beside him, then looks up to see an ugly little pink truck approaching, weaving slightly, in the middle of the narrow road.

Another drunk? Obviously so. More evidence, if any more were needed that this present age is indeed *mappo*, bleak centuries leached of hope, eons of degeneracy and loss, from which the Healer is to redeem creation. It is his Mission to bring all scattered particularities back to Unity, to accomplish in a spiritual fashion a sort of reverse Big Bang. Was ever any human person so cosmically challenged, so worthy of veneration? He thinks not. Even the Buddha restricted his concern to sentient beings, whereas the Healer is responsible for—and *to*—the All. And yet. Here is an irony, by no means lost on the Healer: descending of necessity from the sublime to vile specifics, he has encountered this repulsive and vulgar sound truck, this *sendenkaa*, obstructing him, thwarting the Mission.

The Healer honks. The *sendenkaa* wobbles over to let him pass. Araddin Pachinko. How the Healer loathes and despises pachinko. Lights, little balls bouncing around, *pachinpachinpachin,* constant hysterical yapyapyap from the speakers, mirrors everywhere. Gangsters in the background, harvesting the money (for which the Healer could think of a thousand better uses). Rank after rank of cigarette-smoking fools sitting at their machines, leaning forward, rapt, as though transported by some religious ecstasy at a temple. That is it: pachinko parlors are parody temples, shrines of the damned. In which the faithless faithful strive to win perhaps a set of hand towels or a carton of Mild Sevens. Instead of bliss eternal, the Voidless Void, the All.

The Healer snorts. Loathes? Despises? The words are too mild. He tries to keep some of the contempt from his face as he maneuvers his automobile around the hideous little scraped and battered truck. Who would willingly drive such a vehicle? It is a garish advertisement to the world: I, the tank-brained operator of this vehicular nightmare, am a gross *namakuji* and proud of it. Up close now, so close their rearview mirrors graze in passing, close enough to *smell*—a garbage dump! An open grave! Cloying putrefaction wafts to his nostrils on a soft gust from the west—the Healer concentrates on his driving while hastily jabbing the button to roll up his windows. Normally ascetic, disdaining creature comforts, the Healer concedes that there are times when air conditioning is not merely desirable but necessary. This is one of those times. The Healer feels his stomach churn, from the corner of his eye sees the woman stir, hears her moan.

What words are there for the *sendenkaa* driver? A beast, some sort of reptile in quasi-human form. The vile operator of this stinking pink symbol of corruption glowers at him as they pass. Glowers at *him*, the Healer! Why? Oh, ironies on ironies. The lizard-boy is in a hurry, is irritated with the *Healer* for obstructing *him!* The Healer simply must scrutinize this creature. Ah, perfection: the quintessential child of darkness— must the Healer bring even this unto the All?—gaunt, wasted, greasy, purple bags under his eyes, terrible skin. Sucking on a cigarette. A degenerate boy, in all likelihood a sexual pervert. A punk, as they are called. A worldling.

Seen! Stared at! By some fat fucking bearded clown—who can identify him!—with a... woman? Passed out? Taking a nap? Or maybe giving him a

293

blowjob. Uchiyama wouldn't be surprised, not these days. He's seen too much, knows too much about rich-bitch neighborhoods. Have to be houses, apartments aren't good enough. Roses, faggotty little *mikan* trees all wrapped in twine and propped up with bamboo, probably little *koi* ponds in there too. Lifestyle people. Don't work. Who's going to hire somebody like that beard? Act like animals and think it's their right. Everyone else has to look the other way and pay taxes so that these *bakamono* can to do exactly as they please, drive a nice car, money to burn. (Meanwhile, of course, what about society?) This one looks like he wants to spit on Uchiyama—for not being weird enough, probably, for being too normal. But Uchiyama Masaaki doesn't care. They've pushed him far beyond caring about things like that. He feels his stomach heave, thinks he might vomit again as he's been doing all morning, leans out the window for a breath of fresh air. Did he hate this little truck in the past? Yes, but, as he now realizes, not with the all-devouring hatred which he now feels toward it. Now that it owns him. Uchiyama gags.

He switched off the tape deck—*MAIDO ARIGATO GOZAIMASU!*—and he'll never have to listen to that again. But he'll probably never get rid of the *MAIDO*

ARIGATO GOZAIMASU! MAIDO ARIGATO GOZAIMASU! constantly inside his skull. He still hears it, a kind of hell-echo that isn't really there except that it is. It will drive him crazy in time, he knows. The only way to silence the voice is with alcohol, and he has no alcohol. And no money. And he's not ready to suck the vodka from the still-damp carpet. Uchiyama Masaaki has his pride.

Oh, how it stinks. Old Mogi was right about that, anyway, the *bakayaro.* Who will kill him if he doesn't find the money to buy it. His S-Cargo now. The irony makes him writhe. Uchiyama can't even pay off his skull ring because of that lardassed old bloodsucker. So how is he supposed to pay off a half-million yen car? Which is worth maybe fifty thousand in a typhoon with the windows open. Well, as he decided last night, that fateful night when the terrible decision was made, the *gaijin* is the cause of the problem, so, one way or another, the *gaijin* will have to be the solution. Donner ruined Uchiyama's career, got him fired, destroyed his life. Donner will pay.

Oh, yes. Though precisely how is not yet clear. Uchiyama has no detailed plan. His strength is his ability to think fast, to use a crisis situation as it develops. Takeshi once told him in so many words that

295

he, Uchiyama, was quite resourceful. Which is true. Even now, sick as he is. He climbs shakily from the cab, pauses to tuck his *Drunky Brains Gig* T-shirt neatly into his very tight Edwins, then heads for the house, seeing everything without seeming to, scanning the address-numbers, noting the mothers and children going about their mindless business, registering a smirky conceited little *burikko* with too much makeup at the wheel of her stupid looking pink Carol that she probably thinks is oh-so-cute, rubbing his skull ring with the thumb and forefinger of his left hand, trembling, ill, but ready for trouble and itching for action, more or less.

Just his luck, a witness. Forget about the witness! *But what if Donner's asleep or busy or something?* Good! Wake him up, interrupt him! Forget about politeness. Uchiyama has always been too considerate. Forget about consideration and everything else but justice. They started it, he will finish it. This is it, the real thing, not some stupid movie. This is a fight to the finish, when they'll all learn something about Uchiyama Masaaki. This is revenge, for… everything.

Too bad Takeshi can't see him now, can't put his arm around Uchiyama's powerful shoulder and give him a brusque, manly hug—understating their deep affection, an affection all the stronger for being unvoiced—and maybe a punch in the biceps for encouragement. Well, Takeshi would find out, all in good time. Meanwhile, Uchiyama wants alcohol—which is medicine, really—and money and revenge, in that order. And he will have them. Uchiyama Masaaki smiles his terrible smile and lights another Dean. He jabs Donner's doorbell button, hard. Come on, *bakayaro,* wake up. He knocks then hammers on Donner's fancy door. He pauses, listens for footsteps. Ear to the door, he cups his hands over his face, exhales through his mouth, inhales through his nose: breath check.

The halitosis is terrible, worse than the S-Cargo with the windows up, worse than anything. Uchiyama's breath is so bad that his stomach knots up, and his knees start to tremble, and he feels the sweat break out along his forehead and temples. *Where are his Kiss Mints?*

To hell with the Kiss Mints!

Whose problem is the bad breath? Donner's!

And to hell with Donner. Uchiyama will breathe on him purposely. That will be revenge, phase one. He pounds on the door again, and again. Angered, he draws back his fist and punches the door, not full force—but look: hard enough to leave a dimple. Probably aluminum. Uchiyama snorts. If he were a *dorobo,* if he really wanted to get in there and steal things, all he'd need would be a can opener. A dimple right there at shoulder height. A dimple from his skull ring. Still queasy but smiling now, he looks at the ring. No damage, solid gold for sure. *"Sugu,"* he tells it, in a choked whisper. "Soon you'll get your chance, my friend. Be patient for a few more seconds." The scratched ruby eyes seem to gleam, and the green fleshless grin seems to widen. "Very soon."

Bingbongbingbongbingbong.

BAMBAMBAMBAMBAM.

Uchiyama leans on the bell with his right forefinger, pounds on the door with his left fist. Too bad for them if they don't like it. Uchiyama doesn't give a shit about their feelings or anything else. What are they doing, screwing in the middle of the day? Uchiyama begins pounding with both fists, then grabs the fancy handle, yanks it, rattles it. Nobody home, door locked. Well, he tried. It looks like Donner is a very lucky man. Uchiyama presses the thumb-lever on the handle and yanks—and nearly falls over backward as the door swings wide.

"*Gomen-kudasai, moshi-moshi…* excuse me… hello?"

Saturday, 11:06 A.M.

Home again, the day cool and overcast and breezy and... where's Ruriko? Donner's place: brick driveway (no car in it because Ruriko smashed up their little Juna two years ago and Donner told her, That's it, no more), little thriving apple and pear trees in the grave-sized plot to the right, kiwi vine behind the trees and snaking up the two balcony supports, almost to the blue-tiled roof. (Third year, plenty of vine, still no fruit, the kiwi's days are numbered.) Home: the boxy little tan stucco up-and-down duplex with its tiny living area and its titanic mortgage. A dead leaf blows against the windshield on Donner's side then scrapes across to the driver's side. The driver, a buxom social worker of some sort in a meter maid-style uniform, turns off the heater, kills the engine, unhooks her seatbelt. The baby is in back, sleeping in a little porta-crib. Yes, Donner's home, all right, but faintly out of synch with this place, familiar and unfamiliar, shimmering with a febrile strangeness in the fleeting patches of watery sunlight. Donner massages his temples with his fingertips. He shivers. He feels— what? Weird. Subtly stunned.

Just the painkillers, probably.

How long was he gone? Forty hours, give or take. Seems like days. But, yes, he caught the 6:15 bus yesterday, as always. First leg of his daily pilgrimage: bus to Hashimoto *eki*, fast train on the Keio line to Meidaimae, transfer to the slow Inokashira line north to Kichijyoji, bus from there to the university. Two hours. Round trip, four. Figure it out: twenty hours a week, just commuting. Then all his work on top of that, as Donner often pointed out to Ruriko. While she sits around in the living room all day, sniveling and feeling sorry for herself and driveling out her "poems" and pickling her liver. *Oh, Donner, you're such a cold superior unfeeling... bastard FOR YOUR information I'll have you know this is my... first one all day MY VERY VERY FIRST.*

Sure. No dinner, no housework, ashtray full of butts, Bacardi and Coke empties, the whole place sweetly stinking. *Amado* locked, windows closed, bugs no doubt having a field day in all the spilled and scattered crud, in the funky bedding. If she didn't air out the *futon* then those *dani* would breed like lightning and bite the hell out of him next time he lay down on it. How often has he pointed that out? And she would laugh. *That's you Donner, that's... PERFECT, Donner priorities, Donner sensibilities.*

301

Donner! Robot! PLANMAN! Ruriko frowning, squinting, barely able to sit up, getting down yet another quote-unquote poem. *Hic.*

Art.

Silly bitch. Where the hell is she?

Social worker helping him out of the car, handing him the baby.

Ouch. Stiff, precast concrete. A rough forty hours. In that time he taught his classes, suffered one of his worst Namwarps in recent years, tipped over an ugly little truck like the one they just passed. (He's never seen one before, but now they're all over the place, it seems. This one was parked on the bridge, sign of the times, maybe a *chain* of those stupid pachinko places.) And after work Donner went for a run with Buddy, usually no challenge, but this time every muscle howling from the truck episode and suddenly the baby arcing down. Then that high-pitched mother-scream like a round of incoming. Awful echoes, Quang Tri all over again. Tumble, flash, then a bad coalescence of all those slowly interleaving luminous shapes of dread, the world drifting in and out. The hospital, with its soft lights and textures, its sharp smells, its crisp functionaries. Twelve stitches, they said. He can feel them, right hip and lats. Cannibal teeth.

Do not *go, Mr. Donner, we must* to *do tests some more,* etcetera.

But there's nothing seriously wrong with him. Hospitals are not for scrapes and bruises, not for Donner. He hates and fears hospitals. And not without reason—never mind Buddy's You're a hypochondriac routine. For hypochondriac read rational. That new killer streptococcus is currently raging out of control through Japanese hospitals. Incurable. You die, or, if you're lucky, you linger for thirty or forty years. No thanks. *Everyone* should wear a gauze mask in a hospital, but do they? He didn't even suggest it to Buddy. Mr. Immunity. Does he think his upper-arm strength will protect him from that one? Does he think the bug is interested in how much he can bench-press? Does he think tough guys don't develop malignancies or myocardial infarctions?

Does Buddy think *at all?* There's the question. Full Colonel, tough in some ways, brave, good administrator, so forth—sure, Donner will give him that. Credit where credit is due. Plus Buddy sort of saved Donner's life way back when, or at least kept him from going totally insane. *But where is Buddy's common sense?* Can he not look in the mirror and see a statistic? Coming on fifty, way overweight, smokes, drinks. Classic. Not if but when. And it pisses Donner right off, because when Buddy finally blows his heart out through his ribcage, then—tough to face, tougher to put into words—the best part of Donner will die too. He'll be alone. Then what should he do? *Make new friends?* God damn Buddy and his You worry too much. Optimism, confidence: mindless—as dangerous as Ruriko's rum. And Ruriko, why isn't she charging out and snatching the baby, cooing and gurgling, running through her mom routine? Maybe having one for the stairs.

Ah, Hanako, the baby. So warm and moistly pungent in his arms at this moment. An unusual situation, surely. No relatives to claim her, no health care types able to pry her loose from Donner's neck, no real precedent for any of this. And what does Donner think about it?

He doesn't know. On the one hand, the baby might divert Ruriko for a few days, get her off Donner's back, till some permanent arrangement. She might even cut back on the sauce. But of course when the time comes she won't want to let go of the kid. To put it mildly. She'll hang onto the kid like the kid hangs onto Donner. So things will be worse than before. Probably. But who knows? Maybe it will work out, somehow. Week-end visits, she'll have to settle for that. No choice. Gush, gush, ethyl tears in the mascara, fumes all over the kid. Poor kid, maybe get some tiny gas mask. Anyhow, Donner has no options. What will be. He's wiped out. Let's get inside. He holds the door open with his free hand.

"*Ja, dozo, agatte kudasai,* please enter my house."

"*Hai. O sakki ni.*" The social worker—fortyish, stout, with a scarlet birthmark blazed across her left ear and down her throat, and a cool bleachy smell in her clothes—crosses the threshold and starts up the stairs with her large carryall. It is rectangular, white vinyl, and full of kid gear: diapers, training pants, salves, powders, special soaps and shampoos, cotton swabs, flannel sheets, fruit juices in tiny cans, a triangular pink fever thermometer, chewable vitamins in cartoon character shapes, tiny sweaters and jumpers and tights, pink canvas Hello Kitty sneakers, brush, comb, ribbons, dozens of minuscule pastel handkerchiefs, and a new teddy bear to replace the blood-sodden old one. In the side pocket are several brightly illustrated childcare pamphlets. All compliments of the Sagamihara ward office; she and Donner picked up the carryall on their way over. "*Ooish!*" says the woman, lifting the bag clear of the stairs. *"Omoi desu.* It is heavy."

Standing, both slightly out of breath, in the living room. Two bedrooms directly ahead, their sliding doors shut. Tiny kitchen-alcove to the left. Behind them the door to his study, an L-shaped closet full of books. To their right, beige drapes drawn across the sliding glass doors to the balcony. Stereo system in its black cabinet. Opposite the kitchen, in the angle made by the far wall and the balcony doors, Ruriko's black leather-and-chrome couch, her chrome-and-smoked glass coffee table. (What the hell makes them hers?) Three tan leather cushions and a fake Afghan rug on the carefully waxed veneer parquetry floor. On the white walls, too-large Mexican oils and oil-acrylics by Eugenia Curto and Manuel D'Rugama: mestizo faces, so eloquent and reposeful, so beautifully what they are. Donner is faintly embarrassed by the feelings these paintings evoke in him. Why does he love them? Because they seem reflections of the god within? Something like that. Because they seem to shadow forth the shape and play of essence.

That sunny market scene, for example, which never fails to boost Donner's spirits a notch or two, even in the rainy season. Even during typhoons, that make the whole house heel-to and thrum, its walls the thinnest drumskins. San Cristobal de las Casas: earth tones and textures: dust like talc, adobe, serapes, and placid peasants bathed in clarity. Simple scenes, glowing. Well, why isn't he still in Mexico? Stupid question. No money there, no goals, no planning beyond *manana*. In Mexico scorpions and black widows whisper in the walls, mad dogs and federal police prowl the night streets, killer amoebas lurk in everything—the food, the water, the stinking air. Never mind the standard gut-monsters; some of the more exotic ones go right for your vital organs. And there exists one very special amoeba whose ideal niche is behind your contact lenses and whose ideal food is, first, your corneas, and then your optic nerves, and then, at long last and exquisitely, your frontal lobes. (Of course, if you act quickly you can foil the demons simply by having your eyeballs removed.) Finally, in Mexico there is that dank and clammy, death-loving Aztec-Catholicism suffused like some slow poisonous stench through every thought and impulse, every dream. That's why Donner no longer lives there. Excellent reasons. But still, there's not much magic in Japan. He'd never admit it to Ruriko, but he misses the magic. His San Cristobal fruit-seller, his enigmatic Puebla beauty, his

Tarahumara flute-dancer: aren't they sorcerers of a sort, light years from the here and now?

Which is this woman and this baby and no Ruriko.

"Koko ni iru," says Donner. "Here we are."

"Okusan wa...?" The woman looks around.

Good question. Donner has no idea where the fuck his wife is.

"Kaimono ni, tabun. Akachan no mono, to omoimasu."

Probably out shopping for baby things—well, it could be true. Though for all he knows she's passed out in the *ofuro* again, like that time during her sherry phase: two (count 'em) empty bottles of Sandeman on the edge of the tub, red sweaty face framed in bubbles, snore like a chain saw. (The Sandeman courtesy of Buddy, from the Class Six on base. A nice gesture, but Donner had to tell him, Desist.) Donner is nervous. Any kind of drunk and disorderly now, and the woman will just get on the phone, and that will be that. Wasted time. Also, in all likelihood, a scene. Donner pictures some kind of gruesome tug of war with the kid, Ruriko yanking and blubbering away, the baby screaming, the social worker grimly determined not to leave a baby with a drunk. Afterwards, of course, it will all somehow have been Donner's fault, and he will hear about it and hear about it. The sooner this lady leaves the better.

"*Ano, neh, matanai de kudasai.* Please, no need to wait."

"*Ie, daijobu desu.*"

"*Honto ni. Matanai.*"

"*Daijobu, daijobu.*"

No need, no need—ach! She's lowered herself onto Ruriko's couch, wrinkling her nose at the stale-liquor puff of air from the cushions, eyeing the dozens of sticky interlocking Coke rings on the glass coffee table. *Mr. Donner must understand that she should speak to the woman of the house, to whoever will be caring for the child.* Ah, but Mrs. Donner might be gone for some time—you could leave her a note. *No, no. That would not be proper.* Really, leave the note, and she can call you later. *Very well, then, for you must know today is one very busy one, regrettably.* I understand. Will you drink some coffee? *No thank you, but where is your toilet?* Back the way we came, at the head of the stairs—without, Donner hopes, Ruriko passed out in there, sprawled in a welter of puke.

Finally, finally. The sound of rushing water, taps being worked. *Sayonara* to the social worker. Donner bowing, his arms full of whimpering damp infant. At his feet the baby's bag. Beside it his gym bag crammed with socks, Adidas, and filthy, torn, bloody sweats— which the nurse wanted to throw away! Beside the gym bag his briefcase with all his plastic (he has nightmares too about losing this case, with its ID cards, credit cards, keys, checkbooks; and then, after losing the case losing himself: more or less ceasing to exist). His briefcase and his suit, rescued the night before, from the trunk of Buddy's car. Here's Donner, back in that suit, his favorite Korea Tailor three-piece—Italian wool, six fittings, worth maybe a thousand 1994 dollars, although naturally Donner got it for a fraction of that, a lifetime suit—now ripped at the seams and soiled, jacket pockets bulging with pills for himself, antibiotics and painkillers.

"Hey! I'm home!"

Not in the *ofuro.* Not in this bedroom. Not in that one. Not out on the balcony. Therefore not home. No note. Could she have actually forgotten? The thing about Ruriko is, she's home, always. Except on Saturday mornings—well, this *is* Saturday morning— when she goes downtown to Do Sport. But surely she wouldn't have gone today? Do Sport, that's a laugh, cost him half a million to join. So she really makes the most of it. Aerobics, for maybe thirty seconds, then a

310

quick steambath and massage, then hang around the bar all afternoon in her designer sweats—another fifty thousand for each of those outfits—plus the headband and the Reeboks with the big squashy laces. Perrier and vodka, lime. Come home ripped as any salaryman on the last train home, stagger in flecked with puke and weeping because some guy groped her. Probably the other way around. Oh yes, Ruriko is a real problem. All his.

Like this baby. Easy, easy, Sweetheart.

In ancient China, any man who saved a woman's life was henceforth responsible for her. Interesting custom. Well, it would make you stop and think. Except that, had Donner stopped and thought for even a nanosecond, they'd probably both be dead right now. She certainly would be. Could Donner have leaped so prodigiously, propelled by will instead of pure adrenalin? Probably not. He'd have been like the coyote, trying to make it across in two leaps.

Sshh, Sweetheart, shh. Don't cry. Did she pick up on his thoughts?

Coffee. That's what Donner's thinking now. He couldn't drink the stuff at the hospital. Hospital coffee isn't coffee at all. Donner remembers the Malaysians' *kopi kasang*: rich, thick, potent, luscious—even if they do put butter in it. And back-country Honduran, a sort of viscous black cocaine, steaming aromatic mugs of magic. Donner can't have those fabulous brews now, but he can have actual coffee, the real thing, hot and double strength, to wash down a fistful of his new drugs. By then Ruriko will be home, and he can turn the baby over to her (maybe!) long enough to soak away the rest of his aches in a steaming *ofuro.* Then he'll come up with some kind of a plan. He always does. *Planman!* Ruriko's ultimate insult.

Donner takes it as a compliment.

Donner is Planman, a Clark Kentish Marvel Comicoid superhero resembling perhaps Bob MacNamara in those early, upbeat Viet days: patent leather hair, rimless glasses, neat two-piece (plain, cuffs, one pleat), and redolent of Ipana, Dial, Old Spice. Planman, with the ability to pop impeccably up in the midst of severe disorder and non-purposiveness. Planman, able to motivate the inert. Coffee-klatchers, for example, Danish-crumbs on their chins, their voices tinny with discontent, their mornings hemorrhaging away. Tabloid-readers and soap-watchers. Couch potatoes and pallid pub creatures, mouth-breathers and bottom-feeders: Planman's fellow Americans. Believers in debt-consolidation.

Believers in progress and in themselves as Exhibit A. Believers in belief, in faith without works. Whiners and blamers and time-servers. Slobs all, all to his mill the grisly grist. Whipping out pad, pencil, and calculator from the secret pockets of his gray flannel cape, standing with his Florscheims planted wide, Planman takes charge: polite but pointed questions about ends and means, goals and schedules, accountability and responsibility, commitment. Soon rationality is pervasive, objectives are in sight, that which was perceived as impossible is now perceived as not merely possible but rather inevitable. Stern endeavor is now a kind of high, hard, karmic delight. Venting fierce barks of joy into their two-way wrist radios telling their brokers buy this sell that, caught up in their new life-adventure, their self-esteem soaring, the quondam losers discover fathomless wellsprings of determination and talent. Suddenly, in their heady rush of winning, they look around, thinking to thank the one responsible—but where is he? Gone! Whither? Off to save some other tacky, unfocused group, no doubt. Gee, what a guy. But look! He left this behind. What is it? Why, it's a box of Daytimers! And a card. Quick, take it out of the envelope. What does it say?

313

ALWAYS REMEMBER:

ONE SIMPLY CANNOT OVERESTIMATE THE

IMPORTANCE OF

A STEADY APPLICATION OF EFFORT

TOWARD SOME

PREVIOUSLY DECIDED-UPON OBJECTIVE.

Golly, Planman, thanks. Thanks for unfucking things. We'll remember!

Snickering, filing the episode away. Maybe write it up, send it off to *Spy*. Gotham rascals, but you never know, they might go for it. Donner remembers Politeness Man in the *National Lampoon* when it was funny. Kenney and O'Rourke. Worth a try, nothing to lose. At least he could use it later on Ruriko.

Donner is Planman now as, prioritized lists forming in his mind's eye, he replaces the baby in her portacrib and sets about making coffee. Into the mill he puts the standard five heaping scoops and then, perhaps in honor of the occasion, he adds a sixth. He cranks on the grinder as always in three twenty-second bursts: a full minute of pulverization, the noise of which always rouses Ruriko to vein-bulging, saliva-spraying fury: *Donner! Read the directions! Five scoops, no more! Ten seconds, no more!* Donner

314

chuckles. If she's anywhere near, that should fetch her. Then she could change the kid's diaper. (Though Donner will give it a try if he absolutely has to.) He snuffs the nascent coffee-perfume, imagines himself actually *in* the little jets of water now gleefully perking through the freshly ground beans. Coffee. Hot, thick, sparking with alkaloids.

Donner hits more buttons, brings the place to life: lights, space heater, television—and there she is, the newsgirl. What's her name? Kobayashi something. Miyuki, that's it. He really likes her teeth. She's a sweetie, all right. Looks better in the flesh. Or maybe she's not feeling well? More on the latest kidnapping—that could do it, make a person look sick, talking to the parents. *What are your feelings about your daughter? Are you worried about her welfare? What are your feelings about the kidnapper?* Yow. She has to ask, but Jesus. NHK, talk about ham-fisted. Anyway, no bottle of ashes on the doorstep, yet. No nothing. Police investigating. Is that a slight tremor in Miyuki's voice? Fade.

Now their own story, yesterday's stuff. Cut over to Noborito, the riverbank, up to the railing: old footage, voice-over: mother dead, stabbed; father dead, heart attack; reports by witnesses—maniac on foot, on a

315

bicycle, on a motorcycle—roller skates, anyone? Pogo stick?—two maniacs, three. Cops proceeding systematically. Donner snorts. He believes the systematically part.

Pour the brew. Hit it. Ahh.

"Child," he tells her. "The police are in warm pursuit."

Tokyo cops: the most systematic in the world and the most decorative. Bustling about, frowning, they do look good on the tube. Shut the fucker down. Donner raises the remote-control device. No, wait. We're somewhere else, and it's a newsboy this time, interviewing some lardass in a T-shirt. Interviewing is the wrong word, because the lardass has grabbed the mike and is elbowing the kid aside. What's on the T-shirt? It almost looks like… *it is!*

Donner snaps alert, nearly spilling coffee. The baby whimpers sleepily.

"Kid, that's us. He's wearing our picture."

Donner scaling stomach from the left, baby tumbling down right breast.

Magenta, tangerine, acid yellow. Who told him he could do that?

"During three hours!" crows the fat man, grinning ferociously. "Just three, and here is result. Shot of century, like Zapruder. Everyone could become part of this event. Everyone could wear this history."

"*Arigato,* Sawada-san." The newsboy reaches for the mike.

"Five thousand yen only!"

"*Go sen yen desuka? Chotto takai, desu ne?*"

"Five thousand? Expensive?" Scowl. "We are talking concerning art."

"And how much for Hanako-*chan?*" Good question, pal.

"How much for who?" The fat man, Sawada, scowl deepening.

"Her." Forefinger jabbing tit. "Baby orphan, Hanako."

"Not decided," the fat man growls. "Not yet. Not decided yet."

Fuck you, sack of pus.

Who told him he could do that?

Click.

Fade, silence.

Coffee. Painkillers. Warmth.

"Hanako? Sweetie? Would you like some apple juice?"

A beautiful child, no question. Big deep eyes, tiny mouth, round rosy cheeks. But confused, unhappy, clutching Donner but still looking around. For her mother? And remembering? And softly weeping. Well, it's pretty God damn sad. There, there. Ah, good, falling asleep again. Apple juice can wait. Put her in the portacrib, move that into the spare bedroom. Extra blanket. Surprisingly, Donner seems to have a way with infants, or at least this one. Is two years still infancy? Late infancy, early childhood. Was Donner ever that young?

He tries to remember. Five? Sure, that was kindergarten. Sweet Miss Rogers, songs in a circle, a brown and yellow bath mat during nap time. She brought back a coconut from Hawaii and gave them each a little piece stuck on a toothpick. Four? Yes, that was when they lived in Brookfield, and his father used to take them to the zoo. A huge place, exciting, with big bright wooden signs carved in the shapes of animals. The pachyderm house with its echoes and smells. He never tired of the zoo. Or of his father, a gentle humorous man who loved him. His mother didn't—why does he keep coming back to her? On good days, she'd tolerate Donner, but when she looked at him her face twisted. The bad days didn't bear thinking about. Three years? Two? One? Lost love, agony.

Learning the pain and danger of love.

Learning to keep everyone at arm's-length, always.

Door opening downstairs. About time, bitch. Stumbling on the stairs. No surprise there. Looks like Donner is the official diaper-changer this morning. And drunk-minder. He sighs, turns his head toward the door as it opens, gets ready with, Well, how's the new mother?—which will be lost on her anyway, opens his mouth to speak… then simply gapes.

"Who the fuck are you?"

Who indeed? Kawakami Yukio strides boldly into the decadent living room, striving to conceal his limp, ignoring the pain of his many wounds, intent upon his quarry. The foreigner, same one. Yes, it is he, Donner. The *hero.* Coffee in one hand, TV *remocon* in the other. Who am I? A better question might be, who are you? Who are you to push yourself into another's business, in another's country? To steal another's glory, to make good appear bad and bad good? But Kawakami Yukio is silent. He glides forward, eyes glittering with hate, in the relaxed but rock-solid combat-stance of the black belt. In a second, his fists will speak for him.

Lunatic. Limping. Face cut, bruised. Nose like some organ meat. Leathers, boots. Donner's coffee jumps at the man's head, the remote control device stabs at the man's eyes then bounces off the rug. Donner's left hand then both hands find the crazyman's throat. And squeeze. Nothing fancy, just squeeze and keep on squeezing. They crash to the floor, Donner on top. The man's fingers rake Donner's face. Donner rears back and slams his head into the man's nose and mouth. Again. Once more. And then really digsdigsdigs with his thumbs as the man's mouth opens, tongue protrudes, eyes bulge and redden, body starts to vibrate. Nearly there, good. Deeper with the thumbs. Shake him, shake the life right out of this cocksucker. Nearly insane himself, Donner lifts the crazyman's head and smashes it to the floor, smashes it again, and once more—just as Donner's own head explodes in a blaze of light.

Standing, swaying slightly over the foreigner, Uchiyama Masaaki smiles his terrible smile of vengeance and raises the half-empty Bacardi bottle for a killing stroke. Then his smile becomes more terrible still as he sees the blood welling from the old *gaijin's* scalp and realizes that there is no need. One blow, a lightning-flash, and suddenly justice returns to the world with the foreigner's departure. But what's this? Movement! Uchiyama gives a grunt of astonishment. The foreigner's victim is alive!

"Donata desu ka?" Uchiyama asks. "Who are you?"

"Ka," says the battered man, gagging and gasping, rubbing his throat.

"Have a drink." Uchiyama lifts him to a half-sitting position, holds the rum bottle to his lips, watches as the bruised and bloody but handsome young man tips it up for long three beats. Uchiyama takes the bottle and matches him swallow for swallow, still cradling the fellow with his strong right arm.

"Ka," says the young man again, then coughs. "Kawakami Yukio *desu.*"

"Uchiyama Masaaki *desu.*"

They drink.

"Hajimemashite."

"Yoroshiku."

They drink.

"You—you saved my life," gasps Yukio. "Where did you come from?"

"I was hiding in the *oshire*, in among the *futon.*"

"Clever. Were you there long?"

"I had this." Masaaki holds up the rum, smiles. "You are *ouyoku?*"

"Yes," says Yukio. "And you are *yakuza?*"

"Yes. We are brothers."

They drink.

"Why are you here?" asks Yukio.

"Vengeance. This old *gaijin* destroyed my career. And you?"

"Also vengeance. He has disgraced me."

"To vengeance, then," says Masaaki.

They drink, finishing the rum.

"Let's steal him," says Yukio, "and see who will pay to get him back."

"But he's dead," says Masaaki, feeling for a pulse. "And bald."

They laugh.

"Yes, dead," says Yukio. "But who else knows that?"

They laugh harder.

"I'll take his feet, you take… his hair."

They laugh uncontrollably, and, lifting the foreigner, Masaaki gripping his feet and Yukio his upper arms, grunting with the effort, they stumble, slip on the rug, lose their balance and land all together in a hilarious heap. Masaaki cups his hands around the foreigner's ear.

"Moshi moshi! Are you hurt?"

"His name," says Yukio, shaking with laughter, "is Donner."

"Was," says Masaaki. *"Was* Donner."

Hanako, Hanako, Hanako. Miyajima Yoshinori can think only Hanako.

He has loved her for thirteen hours, ever since last night's news. His love will free her, as it freed Mai-*chan* and Yoko-*chan* and the others. Their earthly sorrows and sufferings are now ashes. Yoshinori feels a pang of guilt; he should be at work. He's never been absent before, never even late. Right now, his team is putting the latest *High School Jumping* to bed, getting it ready for the printer. This is the crucial time, when so many things can and often do go wrong. The team will have to work twice as hard with him not there. They are depending on him, and he is letting them down. Oh well, he'll be there as soon as he possibly can. This is the kind of opportunity that will never come again. Hanako—so famous, so real—are you in there?

Yoshinori found Donner's house easily. He is parked just around the corner but with a clear view of Donner's front door. His is the cutest possible car: a hot pink Mazda Carol with blue ladybugs appliquéed to hood, trunk, and doors. When you see Carol you just want to give her a hug. Carol-*chan,* with all her plush bunnies and puppies in the rear window. Also, Hello Kitty is with him, of course. She is cleaned off and in the passenger's seat. Yoshinori has seen a limping motorcyclist enter the house. Yoshinori has waited. He has several times checked himself in the rear-view mirror—rosy cheeks, dimples, long perfect hair—wrinkling his little button nose at his reflection, thinking, Yoshi-*kun,* you are cute, cuter, cutest.

But finally he says aloud, "Kitty-*chan,* what are they doing in there?"

Suddenly the door bumps open. A punk—where did *he* come from?—walks unsteadily out, down the street, and around the opposite corner. Yoshinori waits. Five minutes later a banged-up old S-Cargo pulls up, then backs around the corner and up Donner's drive, the punk driving. The S-Cargo is not cute at all. It's pale pink and covered with Snoopies dressed like Arabs, but that just makes it more pathetic. It's a wreck. Yoshinori wouldn't be caught dead in something like that. He pities the punk, who gets out of the little truck, opens its rear doors, and re-enters the house. Now, punk and biker emerge, staggering and almost falling under the weight of a rolled rug, which they heave into the back of the truck.

"Kitty-*chan,* was that Donner in there? Is he dead?"

Yoshinori watches them drive away.

"Dead or alive, Kitty, he's gone."

Yoshinori waits some more.

Finally he drives boldly up. At the door he rings, waits, knocks, waits.

"Pizza!" he shouts. "Pizza!"

Nothing. He looks around then timidly opens the door, peeks inside.

"Pizza!"

No vacuum cleaner, footsteps, running water. Nothing. He enters. The downstairs suite is locked. Yoshinori climbs the stairs, tiptoes into the upstairs suite. Where is Hanako? He searches, looking in one bedroom… now the other bedroom…

Ah. Yoshinori is overcome with tenderness. He stands looking down at the sleeping baby. Then, gently, gently he lifts the portacrib by its straps. And what is this? An open bag of baby supplies. Take that too. Slowly and carefully, both arms full, he leaves the way he came. Carol's back seat is just big enough. Turning onto the Machida-kaido he selects a tape of his favorite children's songs, from the television program *Okaasan to Issho*—Together With Mom—and pushes it into the deck. Then the two jolly chums listen to those bouncy tunes turned very low, so as not to wake the baby. Yoshi does the introductions.

"Kitty-*chan*, this is Hanako-*chan*—in the flesh."

Saturday, 11:19 A.M.

Uchiyama Masaaki's bladder is about to burst. Now that the excitement of the kill—the kill!—is easing, he has to find a place to relieve himself. He turns left, off the Machida-kaido, and guns his S-Cargo along a side street. The sky has closed in. The morning's chill mist has become a drizzle. He clicks on the wipers.

"Doko eh iku?" mumbles Yukio, cupping his flattened nose.

"What?" Masaaki downshifts, deftly whips the little pink truck around a stopped taxi, leans on the horn, guns the engine and gears up. Every move perfectly coordinated, seemingly effortless: Donner's rum. Masaaki is now equal to any task. He thinks back to his earlier nervousness, and smiles. Coolly, he sticks a Dean in the corner of his mouth, punches the lighter. He flicks a glance to the outboard mirror: nobody tailing them. He runs a professional eye over the gauges: fuel at empty—*uh-oh*—needle on the left peg. He looks over at Kawakami Yukio, this muscular crewcut young man who would easily be as good-looking as Takeshi, were it not for the injured nose and the crude brush-cut. Well, couldn't Masaaki educate

327

him a little about hair styles? Peroxide streaks, punch-perm curls. Over the collar at least. It would make a world of difference, a little sophistication. Well, maybe later Masaaki would counsel him. "What?" asks Masaaki again. "What did you say?"

"I said, *doko doko,* where are we going?"

"Piss." Masaaki touches the lighter's glowing coil to his Dean.

"Good. And then?"

"No idea." Masaaki drags the smoke deep, exhales a rich jet from his nostrils—the Dean is still in place, still in the corner of his mouth, where it will remain till it's only a filter. It's his last Dean. He gears down for the light. They are at a T-intersection and facing a high chain link fence. Just inside is a narrow blacktop road, paralleling the fence. Beyond the road is a vast expanse of open ground, weed-covered, the weeds roughly mown perhaps in mid-summer and now layered palely atop the still-green shoots. In the distance: row upon row of olive drab jeeps and trucks and personnel carriers, and, behind these, dun-colored warehouses, hulking, smudged-looking in the rain and fog.

"Camp," says Yukio. "*Beigun.* Sagamihara Depot."

"This place, American army? How do you know that?"

"I *know*. Shining Mist knows. Medical supplies, all kinds of storage."

"Shining Mist is your group?"

"Was my group. I resigned."

"Is your group famous?"

"Very famous, very secret. Mishima Yukio was once a member."

"Who?" Masaaki squints. "This place is big," he says.

"It's huge. But nothing like Yokota or Kadena."

"Let's piss on their fence." Masaaki laughs, looks over at Yukio, who is once again doubled over and cupping his nose in both hands. "Your nose is bleeding." Yukio groans, curses. Masaaki grows serious. "By the way, Yuk-*kun*, do you have any money?"

"No." Yukio begins rolling up his window. "It's raining."

"Don't do that! Forget the rain. The stink in here is terrible."

"I'm getting wet. Anyway, I can't smell anything."

"You can't? What's wrong with your nose?— Sorry, I mean, what's wrong with your sense of

329

smell?… Well, anyway, we need gas. Does he"—Masaaki jerks his head back toward the old foreigner—"have money?"

"Not in his pockets. Maybe in his briefcase. But we left it behind."

"Well, we'll just have to go back," says Masaaki. "But first a piss."

One second before their light turns green—Masaaki always keeps an eye on the cross-street's signals—he swoops the S-Cargo right, then around a parked trailer truck. When he pulls to a stop the tires, he knows, are no more than a centimeter from the left curb. It's a gift, car sense. Some have it, most don't. Automatically, he yanks up on the parking brake lever. Much as he hates the S-Cargo, he has always been more or less careful with it. And now it is his, his only possession, except for his skull ring—neither of which are paid for! Oh, he can never go home. They'll be waiting for him. Waiting for their money. And his balls.

He leaves the engine running, the heater on. The two friends climb out of the S-Cargo and walk over to the fence, fumbling with their zippers. Gratefully they relieve themselves, directing their streams skillfully through the links and onto the base itself.

"Hey!" A big American soldier prowls up in combat gear: helmet, fatigues, trousers bloused into the tops of his rain-beaded black boots, poncho shifting for a glimpse of his service Colt, holstered. The soldier has a German shepherd on a leash. He gives the friends a hard look, eyes icy blue. Masaaki feels a chill jolt of panic. And another as he remembers they have a corpse in the S-Cargo! But then he realizes that the sentry can do nothing. He is on one side of the fence, they are on the other. And they are breaking no law. For Yukio's benefit Masaaki salutes.

"Good-o moningu, GI! Howah you? Nice doggie!" Masaaki raises his arc in an effort to reach the shepherd. "Dog pissed once upon a time my shoes!" Stony-faced, the soldier watches them. "GI! GI! We are top gun!" They laugh, their streams of urine wobbling. The sentry notices Masaaki's modest-sized penis and smirks before twitching the dog's leash and striding away. Masaaki looks down. He feels and sees his member shrivel further in the icy rain, notices that Yukio's, by contrast, is smooth and very large. Eyeing it, Masaaki growls, "I would guess the women like that!"

"No," says Yukio, shaking off and zipping up. "No women."

"None? Why not?"

"Because women understand… *nothing.*"

Exactly!

"Nothing important," says Masaaki.

"Nothing at all."

"About," says Masaaki, heavily, "*life.*"

Exactly! Masaaki is obviously intelligent, Yukio now realizes—certainly no ordinary punk *chinpirra*. He is much smarter than he looks. And, in his own way, attractive. True, his skin is troubled, and he smokes cigarettes, and he wears that huge skull ring which has to be brass and bottle glass. True also he doesn't have much of a chin, but, Yukio ruefully admits, he himself no longer has much of a nose. And, most importantly, Yukio owes his life to this fearless young man.

"By the way, Masaak-*kun*, what did you kill the foreigner with?"

"This." Masaaki smiles and holds up his right fist.

"One punch?"

"It was enough."

"*Sugoi.* That's power." Smarter than he looks, and much stronger.

"This," says Masaaki, pointing to his ring, "was the last thing he ever saw."

"That's quite a ring."

"It's more than a ring. It's my friend, *Shi-san.*"

"Mr. Death. Good name."

"Good name for a good friend. Like it?"

"Well, sure."

"Really, do you?" Masaaki shakes off and zips up. "Then it's yours." He removes the ring and, looking away, thrusts it at Yukio. "It's your ring now," he says gruffly. "Take it."

"No, really, I couldn't."

"Take it. Remember this day of justice."

"Well, thank you." Yukio tries the ring on each of his thick, blunt fingers. It is too small. Finally he works it onto his left little finger.

"Wear it always, for my sake."

"I will." He can always twist the skull around so it doesn't show. Anyway, Yukio will have time later to educate Masaaki a little bit, introduce him to some of the basics, so he won't be a complete *gyangu.* "Now, where are we going?"

"Your place?"

"Not possible." Yukio shudders. "Yours?"

"Only if you are interested in suicide. Did you ever hear of Mr. Mogi?"

"Who Mogi?" Yukio is getting hungry.

"Mogi Mogi! *The* Mogi! A very important and dangerous man."

"Who is he?"

"My ex-boss. A friend of Teshima-*sama's* number-one *kobun.*"

"Who Teshima?"

"Teshima Tadao! Teshima *Oyabun!* The legend!"

"Ah." Yukio could almost smile at that. If he were in the mood he might tell Masaaki about a true legend: Nakatani Taro, Yukio's Leader. Yes, all right, former Leader—but Yukio knows, deep down, that things will work out, somehow, someday, despite his enemies' inevitable slanders. Probably they are going on about Yukio right now: he broke our sword, he torched our hall. Yap, yap. Well, their historic *katana* is broken, true. And their headquarters is a charred ruin. *But:* warriors make mistakes because warriors take action, and Yukio is a warrior who, with the best intentions, has made a few honest mistakes. Microphone men, by contrast, never make mistakes because they never do anything—except perhaps show off for their girlfriends.

Microphone men, ladies' men, wordbags. The Leader knows, must know, the difference between Yukio and the microphone men. Because he *is* the Leader. The stories they tell about him in the War. If all the Emperor's officers had been like the Leader, then the Pacific would now be Japanese, and Japan would not now be crawling with foreigners and degraded foreigner-lovers, and Yukio would not have had to take such drastic action yesterday. For which, in a year or two or ten, when they meet again, the Leader will discipline him, severely. Oh, yes, no question. Like a stern but loving father obliged to correct a favorite son. And won't Yukio accept that correction! Double it! Triple it! Whatever it is—fines, demotion, privation, mutilation—Yukio will run to it with open arms. And afterward the Leader will say, in so many words, unable completely to extinguish the twinkle in his eye, You took your chances like a man, and you took your punishment like a man, and I am proud of you. We understand each other, Yukio. The rest of them can have their soft women and their soft lives. We have each other—and Japan!

Yes, thinks Yukio. He feels the cold rain on his face, and two hot tears.

335

"And that's the joke. Isn't it funny?" Masaaki snickers mirthlessly. "I say, that's the big joke."

"What is?" Yukio asks politely.

"I'm the one. That's the reason why I'm always so bitter and cynical, because Teshima-*sama* is probably looking for someone just like me, but Mogi-*san* has probably been steering him away from me, afraid for his own job. So yesterday when that old shit of a foreigner attacked *me*, and the cops threw *me* in jail, well, that was Mogi-*san's* big chance, wasn't it?" Masaaki laughs bitterly. "Fired! But that's the way it is, right? *Shio ga nai.*" Masaaki spits. "That's life."

"I'm sorry."

"Forget it," Masaaki tells him harshly. "Let's go."

"Yes—but where?"

"I don't know. But let's get out of the rain. Let's just go."

"Okay. Back for the foreigner's money, and then..."

"And then gas up, and then dump him—in Mr. Mogi's trunk!"

"Or somewhere, and then just drive. Far away. The ends of the earth."

"Yes! Okinawa. Or even Hokkaido. Change our names, get new jobs."

"That's it. Just disappear. Become invisible."

"And then sell that pink piece of shit."

"Sell it?" Yukio laughs. "Who would buy it?"

"Someone! It's a little banged up, but really, you know, it's a pretty good little machine. I mean mechanically. It corners well, it has plenty of acceleration at stoplights, the brakes are first-rate. I changed the oil myself, and I always drove it right. You know, kept the revs up. I actually have a kind of soft spot in my heart for this little S-Cargo, but I guess I could be talked into parting with it. Maybe one of your old group would like to buy it now, and we could take the Shinkansen or fly to Okinawa. The S-Cargo is a very practical vehicle, you know. There's lots of room in the back."

"Right now," says Yukio, patiently, "the back is full of dead foreigner."

Saturday, 11:35 a.m.

Lock... the *doors.* Donner depresses both locking buttons.

Climb... into... the *driver's seat.* Donner drags himself forward.

Feels like something broken in his head, but no drifting in and out this time. No, he just snapped awake. Maybe it was the stink, like smelling salts. He sees a punk and the maniac in leathers, taking a leak over there by the fence. He sees a big sentry striding away. One of Buddy's men! What should Donner do? Honk? Scream at him to call Buddy? Donner dithers.

But the cobwebs clear, and Donner's plan this time is starkly simple: *go.*

Seatbelt... fastened. Parking brake... off. Engine... start.

Screeeeeeeeeee.

Idiot, cretin, sub-moron! It's running! Uh oh, their faces. Quick now.

Clutch in. Shift lever... first? Feels like first. Ease out that clutch.

Lurch, stall.

Not first! Fucking fourth! And now it's flooded.

And here are the maniacs. The punk—yesterday's punk, is that possible?—leaping around embracing the truck, scrabbling at the doors and windows. And, oh, Jesus, the one in leathers, moving up with a big rock, over his head. But the punk drags him away, that's good. Now start, you stinking piece of shit! *Rrrrrrr.* Got to give it a minute more. Punk screaming. Has the other one backed against the fence. Try it again. Catch, catch, catch—catches! Rev it, speed shift—first?—pop the clutch—first it is! Lay rubber, nearly hit that *yaki-imo* cart, tough shit, swerve out, punch it.

Police station?

No, *Buddy! Get around the camp to the gate. Get to Buddy.*

Red light, run it. Now left. Shit, look at the traffic. Lunch time. Have to inch along just ahead of the clowns... go, go, go—okay! Clear stretch, run through the gears, clowns way behind now, Jesus, do they look stupid. Ha.

Tracks ahead. No train no train no train.

Train! Wouldn't you know.

Wait it out, here come the clowns, specks getting bigger

End of train. Go up, gates. Up, up, up...

Another train! Southbound. Fucking Yokohama line.

Wait it out, end of train, gates up. Creep across the tracks, a left, a right on this sidewalk masquerading as a two lane road. Oozing up to the light, which is green… green green green—amber! Old lady, old lady in the car ahead—go through the yellow!

Red!

Fuck, that did it. Here they are, the assholes, actually on the truck, on the roof, screaming, pounding. Hand reaching down… key!

Punk has a spare! Reaching down with it, jabbing at the keyhole.

Green.

Around the corner swing wide around the old bitch, cut in front of a horrified young mom and her baby carriage, tighten the arc, tighten it. Maniacs on the roof, thing is lurching and bucking like hell. Wide blank faces turning.

Shake those fuckers off! Swerve, pop the clutch, jam on the brakes.

Hah! Punk somersaults onto the hood. Great!

Sirens! Flashing lights! Cops up ahead and closing fast! Thank God.

Cops racing by. Not even a glance at the S-Cargo.

Donner punches it, gears up. Punk hanging by the wipers. Next light: green, green, green, green...

Green.

Sagamihara Station a blur on the left, gear up to fourth, engine hiccups.

Corner light: red, red, green, green, green...

Green.

Left around the corner on two wheels, punch it again, very close now.

Only have to cross the tracks again, pass the little hospital, make it to the guard at the gate, hundred yards at most. Guard's phone... Buddy.

Engine coughs, catches, coughs, dies.

Into neutral. *Rrrrr.* No gas. Rolling to a stop, fifty yards from the tracks.

Punk at the driver's door now, stabbing at it with his key. Other moron at the passenger's door, shaking the whole truck so the punk can't get his key in the lock. But in a few seconds they'll get their act together, and he *will* get it in, and *they* will get in, and...

Fuck this. Punk with his nose practically in the keyhole, concentrating. Right hand on the door lever, Donner leans left... *timing, timing...* waits, and, as the locking button pops up he jerks back on the door lever and wrenches his upper body right, slamming into the door with his shoulder, catching the punk between his beady little imbecile eyes with the door-edge and knocking him on his ass. Listen to him screech! Donner swings the door wide and jumps—and nearly strangles himself on the seatbelt! Cursing, he undoes the belt and jumps again, feels his suit jacket catch and rip on something, hits the blacktop and rolls, hears the footfalls, scrambles to his feet and sprints, hears the footfalls hears the harsh breathing, sprints, feints left ducks right, catches a glimpse of leathers, hears the ragged breaths growing louder, closing.

MAIDO ARIGATO GOZAIMASU! MAIDO ARIGATO GOZAIMASU!

What the fuck is that? Donner is sprinting all-out now, faster than yesterday, if anything, but he can feel heat off the maniac in leathers, and the only thing he can see is those railroad tracks. No train, no train, no train.

Train!

Donner flying past how many stopped cars trucks cars, watching the barriers come down on either side of the tracks. The barriers, he notices, are bamboo poles, covered with yellow and black plastic, and strung with little red lights. Down, down, fully down and bouncing a bit at the bottom of their arcs. Lights, bells. Here comes the train. Oh, Jesus, the maniac has outflanked him, to the right. He'll be across the tracks before Donner. The son of a bitch was limping this morning. Why isn't he limping now? He's across! Donner jumps, stops, veers right, rolls under an Army flatbed, and scrambles up clinging to one of its metal posts. The post wobbles in its square socket like a dead molar.

MAIDO ARIGATO GOZAIMASU! MAIDO ARIGATO GOZAIMASU!

Train, an express this time. Maniac on the other side, punk streaming blood dashing up from behind, punching a barrier light, looking wildly around.

Train past, barriers rising, lights and bells off, truck moving.

Maniacs in the way, waving their arms and screaming at each other. Truck driver leans on the horn, they look over, and Donner ducks but not fast enough. They must have seen him anyway, or seen his knuckles on the post, because here they come, one around the front of the truck—*hoonnnkkk,* again—and one around the back. Donner says a prayer and jumps for the big truck's passenger door handle, swarms into the cab, locks the door, behind him, and turns to face the olive drab driver—a woman! Pale lipstick, mascara, blonde hair pinned up, fatigue cap perched on top. Young, thin, face pale, dark eyes wide and burning.

"It's all right! I'm a friend of Colonel Nakamura!"

"Yeah right."

"I am!"

"You are a fuckin' bozo."

"Go! Go! To the guard!"

"You got it."

She guns the engine, shifts, roars up to the Japanese guard in his neat blue uniform chatting up some girls at the checkpoint. Donner checks the rearview: maniacs running back and forth, undecided. The driver cranks down her window, motions the guard around to her side.

MAIDO ARIGATO GOZAIMASU! MAIDO ARIGATO GOZAIMASU!

"Gimme your piece," she tells him. "Call the MPs."

"Nan desuka?" The guard's eyes bulge. He hands her his sidearm.

"We got us a asshole supreme."

She works a round into the chamber of the guard's Colt, levels it at Donner.

"Make a move, dickhead. Make my day."

344

"At least let me use the phone!" That face, that voice... Tifni? Yes, it *is.* It *is* Tifni, Tifni... Grozniak, that's it. Ex-student. What luck. "Tifni!"

"What?"

"Tifni, it's me. Frank Donner. Basics of Elementary English Comp?"

"Three credit hours, Mary Land College, Asian Division, Camp Zama, term two, 23 October to 18 December, 1989, Education Center, Room 3-B, Mondays and Wednesdays, 16:45 to 19:25 hours. You was moonlightin', tryin' to pick up some extra cash from the military."

"Tifni, you remember!"

"Sure do. I reckonized ya, underneath all that blood an' shit."

"Great. So here's the situation. It's an emergency. I have to—"

"I also remember ya gimme a fuckin' D... *minus.*"

Saturday, 11:45 a.m.

Wouldn't you know it? Lunchtime, and a staff meeting coming up at one. What Buddy needs, more hysterical bullshit from Donner. Buddy puts down the phone, scrawls a note for Sgt. Waldren. Well, it won't be the first staff meeting he ever missed. In fact, he's not displeased. You've been to one, you've been to all of them. *What if Mrs. Vanzandt (that yappy bitch!) gets in for another term as mayor? What if she doesn't? What if that ultralooney gets in? How about sterner sanctions for trash privilege abusers and non-sorters? What are we going to do about biting at the day care center?* (Nothing! Little fucking cannibals, give 'em ketchup and piccalilli, problem will solve itself. Ha.) *Who will draw up more stringent procedural guidelines for Halloween trick or treat?*

This is an agenda for a senior warrior?

Depot Camp. Committees and subcommittees and sub-subcommittees. Grievances and action lines. Boredom you could stick a bayonet into. The end result of all his military training and experience. Buddy is a colonel in a bird colonel's slot—to be brutally honest, any half-assed major could handle it—and how this situation has come about he hasn't a clue. Enemies

346

in high places, enemies in low places. Some Pentagon honcho decided he's too fat, bad image? Could be. Buddy's got those burly, blocky G.I. Joe good looks with a little slant to the eyes. G.I. Joe, Dell Comics are good comics. G.I. Joe didn't do low-impact aerobics and suck on a bottle of Perrier and eat tofu 'n sprouts with ginger that Janey keeps almost shoving down his throat and making him listen to inspirational self-help tapes on his Walkman. G.I. Joe would say fuck that. G.I. Joe was a real guy with guts and a gut. *Cigar in the corner of his mouth, one sleeve ripped away, bloody compress. Catches the potato masher in mid-air, flips it back,* whuddd, wrenches the .50 caliber off their burning personnel carrier, lays down arcs of fire, laughs, *C'mon an' get us, ya Kraut bastards!*

What G.I. Joe did was the job, period. Like Buddy. But, peacetime, everyone's your enemy. Except maybe Donner, who's too stupid. Halfway to the door, Buddy does an about face and marches back to his desk. Command decision: he will at least bring along his sandwich. What the hell, it's a hero.

Saturday, 12:03 p.m.

Teshima *Oyabun* has a trick. He has of course many tricks, but his favorite is remaining impassive under all circumstances. Whenever he might be tempted to betray an emotion, he instead vividly pictures himself expressing that emotion. Joy, rage, frustration, grief—he lets the little mental Teshima do it. Under extreme circumstances the mental Teshima is permitted to laugh uproariously, bellow, kick furniture, weep, turn cartwheels of joy. Meanwhile, the real Teshima remains unreadable, his body and his facial muscles in control absolutely. It is a good trick, and, he does not doubt, the source of much of his power.

Teshima learned it from his own *oyabun*, Moriuchi Tadamasa of revered memory, who, in the evenings, would smoke and strum on his *shamisen* and tell his men about the books he had read. In this way young Teshima learned of other times and places. Apparently the world was round, immense, and more wonderful and terrible than Teshima could have imagined. Tokyo was only part of it. *Japan* was only part of it. The vast distances, the awesome phenomena, the sweep and power of the ages. Thinking of such things made his mind feel as though it were rushing out into space. In fact, men had found gigantic bones and fiery diamonds deep in the earth. Teshima had seen the photographs. There were also drawings, incredibly ancient, of strange animals in strange caves. And for five thousand years, all over this globe, humans had been writing things down. Events, ideas, luminous hymns to the Authors of Being.

One night, after all the smuggled and stolen goods had been carefully locked away in the warehouse across the street, and the guard posted in the corner window of their second floor dormitory, Moriuchi-*sama* told the story of an old-time Roman soldier and his *daimyo*. The *daimyo* summoned the soldier to the palace and asked him, "Are you brave?" By way of reply the soldier stuck his fist in the *hibachi* until his forearm was burned to ashes.

"Sugoi!" said the men, said young Teshima. "Very brave!"

"Brave, yes. But also very stupid," said Moriuchi-*oyabun*. "A simple yes or no… *desu ne?…* would that not have sufficed?"

That became one of their best jokes. Moriuchi-*sama* would say, "Are you brave?" By way of an answer, Teshima or one of the others would put some little steaks or skewered chicken livers on the *hibachi*.

349

Then Moriuchi-*sama* would exclaim, *"Yoku dekimashita!* Well done! You are brave enough to consort with gangsters and smart enough to keep both hands for stealing."

Yes, it was funny. And yes, the Roman-*jin* had been stupid. There had been another story, however, this one about the old-time Mexico-*jin*, the Aztecs, who sought to increase their courage in various brutal ways. They would grasp venomous insects in their bare hands. They might start with honeybees, then work their way to hornets and finally to scorpions. An Aztec warrior could reach down and pick up an adult scorpion, and suffer the sting—which is like the blow of a sledgehammer—without flinching.

This practice made a lot of sense to young Teshima. Life was pain. One couldn't carry around a knapsack full of painkilling drugs all the time, so the thing to do was toughen up. Therefore he began the same long series of trials on himself, inoculating himself with and against pain, until he could casually grasp anything at all that had mandibles or a stinger. Could and did. In later years, when he no longer lived with Moriuchi-*sama* and the brothers, when he lived with dear Hanako, that is how he would dispose of noxious insects in their rooms. Spiders, wasps, *kamikirimushi*—he didn't care. The more painful the better. They kept him in condition. She would shriek with dismay and excitement. She would scold him, kiss the welt or swelling, and they would laugh. It was part of their private mythology, from which they both drew comfort: Teshima was above pain. Cuts, burns, scrapes. All such, he simply refused to acknowledge.

Once, at work, unloading a big crate of Wrigley's hot from the PX at Sagamihara Depot, far to the west, he lost his grip. (Well, chewing gum is extremely heavy.) One second later, he stood regarding a wooden splinter like a small dagger blade, deep in the meat of his left palm. Looking down, he saw the corner of the crate resting on the mangled laces of his right Florsheim. *There is no pain, he told himself. None.* And, in a way, there was not. DiGiralamo gaped at him. Sgt. Joseph Di Giralamo: hairy-handed, pigeon-chested, thick-hipped, uniform always perfect with knifelike trouser-creases, dark brown palm-waved pompadour, whiskers so thick and dark it seemed there was not room for them all on his thin face, pencil-line mustache, red wet lips always pouting around a Pall Mall. Joe was Mr. Larceny from Jersey, wherever that was. He was tough enough, but that morning the color drained from his face, and he said, "Oh Jesus Tod your

351

foot," and sat down suddenly with his head between his knees.

Teshima lifted the crate from his foot, swung into the saddle of his Harley-Davidson, kick-started it (well, he felt that, all right) and revved the engine for a few seconds while he jerked the splinter from his palm with his teeth. The tiny Teshima in his mind's eye was howling, but the real Teshima sat looking thoughtful. He put on his sunglasses and adjusted the springy metal ear pieces. "Joe," he said, "I'm going to find a doctor. Do you need anything?"

DiGiralamo looked up and just shook his head. Teshima roared off into the baking Kanda afternoon, swerving and skidding through the rubble, powering through the turns. He stopped six times on the way to the doctor's, taking orders, buying, selling, haggling, figuring the percentages as closely as he ever did. Business as usual, except for the trail of ruby drops in the dust. He took an order for the Wrigley's on his second-last stop. The doctor, who was as far into the black market as most cared to go, cleaned up his hand and set the bones in his foot for a carton of Old Gold straights. He was a good doctor, and might prove his worth again and again. Teshima, who knew when to be generous, threw in three pairs of nylons and a Zippo.

He was back at work by five, his foot in a walking cast. Then, as they often did after a major diversion of resources, they worked through the night—loading, unloading, sorting, storing, recording, and getting the word out to potential buyers. Teshima never faltered, never groaned. Always after that, Joe called him Mr. Stoneface.

So when—feeling good after his morning walk and looking forward to lunch, seated in the living room with his *kobun*—he sees, on the television, a pig-faced man wearing a T shirt imprinted with the image of yesterday's falling baby and leaping foreigner, and when he comes to understand that the swinish man is selling or attempting to sell these T shirts bearing the image of his great grand-daughter, in an effort to profit from her yesterday's tragedy, Teshima Tadao does not betray his feelings by so much as the flicker of an eyelid.

"—thousand yen only!" crows the fat man on the tube, grinning, sweating.

"And how much for Hanako-*chan?*" asks the newsboy.

"How much for who?" The fat man scowls.

"Her." Forefinger jabbing the fat man's breast. "The orphan. Hanako."

353

"Not decided," the fat man growls. "Not yet. Not decided yet."

Click.

"Sawada," breathes Teshima. "Sawada Ginroku." Teshima makes a V of his first two fingers, waits for the cigarette, waits for the light. "He looks *dzurui*, sneaky. There is something familiar about him."

"So desu ka?" asks Morinaga Eiji, his *Ichiban.* "Really?"

"Yes. Something. Who is he? Find out."

"Hai. So shimasu. Right away."

"After lunch is soon enough."

"After lunch, then. What is your thinking, *sensei?"*

"Perhaps he touches our interests? In some small way."

"Wakarimashita. I understand. A sneaky fat T-shirt man."

"A thousand yen," says Tetsuo, his *Niban.* "For a T-shirt."

"Takai, desu ne?" Akio, his *Sanban,* asks. "Isn't that expensive?"

They laugh, rise from their chairs, move toward the dining room.

"Truly it is a lot of money," says Morinaga Eiji. "Too much."

"It *is,* " says Teshima, "outrageous."

Saturday, 12:03 p.m.

Tanaka Hatsue doesn't mind jail. In fact, she is enjoying herself, here, in Sugamo, the very citadel of the enemy. She loves taunting the big sluggish police matron assigned to her. The television, of course, is a nonstop lie and a convenient source from which to draw her jibes.

"Look, Tomita-*san*. That fat capitalist pig is going to keep all his precious T-shirt money for himself. Isn't it obvious? And he won't give one yen to the little girl. The thought of sharing never crossed his mind. What do you think about that? What would you like to do to him? Do you want to know what I would like to do to him?"

The matron sighs and shakes her large head.

"Just what I did to that right-winger. Oh! You should have seen him. He was so pretty before he attacked me, but then—*sugoi!* Nose all over his face, guts rammed into his backbone, testicles flattened like little *daifuku*. What does that feel like, did you ever wonder—a *kendo* staff in the balls? We women are lucky, in a way, don't you think? I mean, that's one thing we'll never have to worry about. Maybe the only thing. Because in other ways we're not so lucky, are we? For example, they threw me in here because *he* attacked *me*. Not verbally but with his fists. Because I am a woman and a communist, whereas he is a man and a fascist. Well, don't you think that is a nice piece of justice?"

"Soon one's lunch must be finished."

"Lunch," says Hatsue, sweetly, pushing the tray to the floor, "is garbage."

"Soon the cafeteria must be cleared."

"It is slop for pigs. They should send it to the T-shirt pig. I will have sushi, or nothing. By the way, Tomita-*san*, who do you think is paying your salary? I will tell you. Ten million gentlemen just like him, except most of them are worse, greedier and more ruthless by far. How does that make you feel? Proud? Happy? Like a productive member of a just society? Or maybe like some blowfly in a corpse?"

"Now rings the bell. It is obligatory to—"

"Let us talk about yearly incomes. Do you know how much civil service employees make in relation to other sectors? Let me assure you, it is pathetic. Do you know how much women make in relation to men? For the same work? It is worse than pathetic, it is criminal. Nurses, for example. Policewomen. Matrons."

"Also, the regulations stipulate that at this time the television—"

"No! Wait!"

There on the screen, a girl's dream come true: weird-suited firemen knee-deep in steaming muck, charred beams at odd angles, our wonderful news lady, Miss *Bijin* Prettygirl, a little pale but giving us all the terrible news that some bad arsonist has destroyed… *yes…* the Yotsuya headquarters of those very same right-wingers! Oh, oh, oh, oh. *So* good. Her plan, she's been urging it for years, but always her people have lacked the courage, preferring to wage war with placards and bullhorns. But they finally did it, and she will get credit for the plan. And she will move up, to divisional level at least. For the first time in a very long while Hatsue feels some pride in her comrades. *And what's this?*

"Wait! Please!"

The set is off, but no matter. Tanaka Hatsue has seen them: *bodies.*

Actually, she has seen only two flaccid black body-bags being slid one after another into the ambulance. Ah, but that is enough. She can easily picture them, twisted and charred, in their bags.—Maybe one of the cadavers is him! Her man, her nazi. Tenderized by her

358

and then cooked to a turn. *Let it be so.* She tingles, can hardly breathe. She feels that languorous thick lust at the back of her throat. Oh, ecstasy.

"*Banzai!*"

"*Shizuka ni!* Shouting is prohibited by the rules absolutely."

"*Banzai! Banzai! Banzai!*"

Roast pork.

Saturday, 12:03 p.m.

A thousand yen! A thousand yen! Sawada Ginroku is enraged.

"Oh, *Anata*," giggles his wife. "On the *terebi!* You are famous."

Ginroku heaves himself half out of his massage-recliner chair and punches her squarely in the face.

A thousand yen. One thousand. Ginroku is sick with fury. How could they do such a thing? Have they no standards, no principles of conduct? In the interview he said *go sen,* five thousand, very clearly— but the TV bastards cut the *go* and everything before that! And most of the middle part too! Result? He is presented as some kind of orphan-robber. He feels like telling them all, Listen, I *paid* for that negative, for the whole roll, big money, it's mine. Ginroku also worked hard on it. He does all his own enlarging, retouching, double-exposing—whatever it takes—and not to save a few yen. Or not for that reason only. No, he does his own photographic work because he's the best at that kind of doctoring. He can take any kind of shot at all and give it impact. And with a dynamite shot like The Catch, well, when it comes out of Ginroku's darkroom, and you see it on a T, it will make your heart beat like a trip hammer.

But no, now they're all saying, Oh that poor baby and that bad greedy man.

Gross, gross, gross injustice. Ginroku's eyes prickle with tears of rage. Oh, yes, a real image problem, and he is going to sue the station for that. But, even worse, *now he must actually sell the shirts for one thousand yen.* True, that is approximately 900 yen over cost, amortizing the machinery and even using a somewhat inflated figure for overhead, and thus represents a thousand percent markup. But so what? This shirt might well be The Shirt, the classic, the acme of his career. Isn't he entitled to a bit extra for his imagination, initiative, drive, skill? And for those hours of frantic and exhausting work? Yes. And he will get it, too, because already he is evolving a plan.

"*Biru...* Beer! Quit sniveling and get me a Kirin."

He will do what he has never done before. He will advertise. On the television. The same station which betrayed him. And he will beat them on the price, and he will find out who was responsible for the outrage and try to have that person fired. He will buy ten second slots, maybe twenty of them, prime time. Cost

361

of doing business. He can still use the tax write-off even though most of his shirt business—and all of his lending—is cash and doesn't show on any ledger.

Ginroku accepts his beer with a grunt.

"Tabako."

He smiles sardonically and nods as his wife hands him the Kents and his little automatic lighter. Yes, he is calming. And the calmer he gets, the better he is thinking. And the better he thinks the more certain he becomes that he will find a way to turn this treachery into a triumph. He is not the king for nothing. For example, the commercial will make it very clear that it's a thousand yen, yes, *but for the first one hundred customers only.* That will be a start. Who will wear the shirt? Ginroku himself? Possible. But how about that little faggot they're all so creamy about this week? Senri Oki, is that his name? Or better yet, an American. Michael J. Penn. Yes, that brash little dream-boy. Michael J. Penn, in a form-fitted Hanako T, will look right into the camera, cocky, grinning that famous grin, but with an underlying touch of deep sincerity, genuine concern, and he will say . .

"Anata, I really wish you wouldn't hit me."

"Shut up!"

Michael J. Penn will fix those baby blue eyes on ten million people, and he will say… he will say… *See you at the concert.*

Brilliant. See you at the concert. The Help Hanako Benefit Concert.

Banzai.

Penn he'll get for free. It's a benefit, after all. Plus huge free publicity for him. He's always flogging some stupid movie. Plus Ginroku will put Penn's face on the back of the shirt, maybe raffle off—*auction* off—a dozen autographed shirts. Proceeds to Hanako, more or less.

Musicians? That's the easy part. Ginroku must have fifteen or twenty little burnouts and has-beens jumping counters for him. *Boys, this is a benefit, the object is not to make money, the object is to help a tragic little baby, so I was just wondering, well, if you could, you know, donate your time and your splendid talent for a worthy cause?* Hah! What wouldn't they give to get back up on a stage again? Wear those leather jockstraps, wiggle their asses, lip-synch some hysterical shit form New York, slightly modified, listen to all the screaming little *burikko?* Ho! If they had any money, the little has-beens would pay *him!* So he'd only need one headliner. Or not even that. Just hang a guitar on Penn.

Where? Nakano Sun Plaza? Too little. Tokyo Dome, that's the place. Three performances, fill it three times, maybe thirty thousand admissions. Starting at *ichi man* yen—it's a benefit, after all—but okay, maybe twenty percent off if you're wearing The Shirt. So ten thousand yen times thirty thousand could gross 300 million. Then sell it to the networks, sell the ad slots—Coke, Honda, JAL, pimple cream—they'd all go for it. It could be the Japanese Woodstock of the 90s. Fifty years from now the losers will still be saying to each other, Oh wow, *sugoi*, were you at Help Hanako? A hundred million in shirt sales might turn out to be the least of it. *Okane ga kakarimasu,* the money will add up, oh yes. To what? A billion?

It is possible.

One billion yen? Is Sawada Ginroku about to double his net worth by picking up the telephone right now and making three or four calls? He is rippling, tingling. He feels a wild giggle fizzing against the back of his teeth.

"Oh, *Anata*, there was some kind of a fire."

And that *dzurui* little bastard at the TV station?

"And oh, *Anata*, here is that new *obosan* they call the Healer. Takeshita-*sensei*. He says, 'Where is our faith in faith?' Oh, *Anata*, maybe we should join Zenbu-kyo. Many are joining, and they are happy. We have only to write to that address, and enclose ten thousand yen, and he will send us his wonderful books, and then we will be able to throw off our golden fetters. Takeshita-*sama* says, 'Wealth is damnation.'"

What *would* he do about that sneaky little TV bastard? Well, maybe that would be revenge enough: no job for him and a tidal wave of yen for Ginroku— who would be sure the little bastard found out. Send him a glossy big *nengajo* every New Year's: Thanks, asshole.

"Oh, *Anata*, look at that. An Egg-Mighty special egg-slicer."

Thanks, asshole—and there's a shot of Ginroku in the back of his stretch Caddy, champagne, six or eight naked *burikko*. Every year, different limo, different bimbos. And send him special T-shirts, no message, just a photorepro of a big, hairy, puckery orifice.

"It slices eggs many ways from Quick & Enjoy Cooking."

Ginroku laughs out loud, grabs the phone.

"Seriously, *Anata*, I wish we had such a slicer—or, or look at that! An electric razor with a tiny computer which is able to monitor every single whisker on your face."

Ginroku is laughing so hard he can hardly punch in the numbers.

Saturday, 12:03 p.m.

First they had to pry some yen out of this fat stupid cop at the Sagamihara station *koban.* Just a few thousand, which he pretty well had to lend them. But he would hardly even look at the two friends, just kept staring out the window with his bulgy eyes and yawning. Smoking one cigarette after another and not offering one to Masaaki, even though he was dying for a smoke. They weren't his brand, Deans, but they were almost as good: Sometime M.I.A.S.S. Masaaki badly needed a Sometime or a Dean.

What a *bakamono* cop. Every time he yawned he grew about twelve more chins. Yawning and blinking, oily sweat on his face, elbows on his desk and big sweat patches under his arms, body like some bloated sack of grease. His uniform was about six sizes too small, stretched as tight as the skin on a *shamisen.* Maybe he was afraid to move, afraid all his buttons would go popping off and bouncing around like bullets. Masaaki imagined this lardass chasing a real criminal, actually running, all purple in the face, maybe blowing his whistle, trying to get his pistol out of the holster without shooting off his *chinchin.*

This cop was just like the one last night in Mitaka. They're all the same, and that's why Masaaki hates them all. No respect for anyone, terrible attitude, not interested in anything except maybe lunch. And cheap. This one, sitting there like a huge sweaty pink frog, soaking up the friends' taxes. You'd have thought they were trying to borrow a trillion yen, from him personally. He didn't care about their problems, that was obvious, although the friends gave him a very good story: they were stuck because someone, probably a communist or some other kind of radical foreigner, had siphoned the gas from their tank.

Well, *it could have happened.* Easily. And how could the cop know for certain that it hadn't? But he just snickered. Why was Yukio all banged up? Where did they live? Where did they work? Why weren't they *at* work? How much alcohol had they been drinking? When? And so on and so forth, smoking, farting out little squeaky farts, grunting out the questions. The friends had to really kiss his fat ass, and for what? One thousand yen!

Oh, thank you officer and we will pay it right back. Grunt.

They gassed up the little truck, which was really starting to reek in the noon sun. And they ripped up the ticket on the windshield because the stinking thing was *illegally parked.* A ticket! Because they had been pleading with the stupid-brained cop for enough money to buy a little gas to move the thing so as *not* to get a ticket! Masaaki could almost laugh: here was more of society's so-called justice. Takeshi had once said to him, "Oh, you are so cynical." Takeshi, in his little store, how innocent.

Well, they finally got the fuck out of there.

But then. The hard decision to pawn Masaaki's— now Yukio's—ring. That hurt. They had to eat, though, didn't they? Except for the S-Cargo that ring was their only object of value. And Yukio was unselfish enough, and realistic enough, to understand that was their only course. In fact he was the one who suggested selling it. Masaaki was touched. He could tell how badly Yukio felt about that and tried to console him: "Don't worry, Yuk-*kun*, we can pawn it, then come right back for it as soon as we get Donner's briefcase." Except of course Donner by then was probably back at his house already, locked in and trembling at his close brush with death, maybe gulping down tranquilizers, and Norshin for his headache, and telephoning every fat-ass cop in Kanagawa *ken*. But why point that out to Yukio? Why depress him even further? The thing to do was find a pawn shop.

So they asked around about the nearest one, the nearest *shichi-ya*—it turned out there was one in Fuchinobe, just south, two stations down toward Yokohama—and they drove over there, finding it eventually, a big old paintless wooden place, sagging between a Convenience Mart and a Chinese medicine store, sooty, tin-roofed, with barred, shuttered windows and flaking, gold-colored *"SHI CHI YA"* in *kanji*, 質 屋 on a black sign above the door. The door was iron, and rusty. It creaked when they shoved it open.

And that's when the humiliation really started.

"How much for this ring?" Yukio held it for the old woman to see.

She ignored them, stared right through them. She was alone in her cruddy store, which was cold and dark and more like an indoor junkyard or some kind of tomb, with ancestor's kimono and plates and *kotatsu* and coat hangers and picture frames and trays of tarnished silverplate tableware, and big piles of magazines and *manga* comics and thick albums full of dead brown photographs, all jumbled up in heaps and smeared with cobwebs. Masaaki looked around, feeling depressed, queasy. He saw the moldering carpets, twenty or thirty of them, rolled in the corners, slumped and lifeless. And the smell. Masaaki hated it. Like the furnace room of his grade school but stronger. A smell you couldn't get away from. Mildew. Dry rot. Some kind of bad fungus, growing in the dark and poisoning everything. Or something worse—the smell of some fear that you haven't really thought about yet. And on top of the smell a sickening sweet incense.

He glanced at the rows of old military uniforms hung on pipes running the length of the walls to left and right. What color were the uniforms? Masaaki had no idea. The dust on them was thick as snow. In front of them and also covered in dust, an ancient acid-green adding machine, a gross bulbous thing with a spool of paper and a crank handle, sat on a glass display case. A tangled mass of old green medals took up the first shelf of this case, which was mostly displaying dead bugs. On the floor were balls of lint the size of small cats.

"Look," said Yukio, pointing to the left of the display case. *"Katana."*

Masaaki looked. Rusty old swords, maybe twelve or fifteen, were stuck point-down in a blue ceramic umbrella stand. *Katana* and old German sabers. Masaaki nodded, shrugged. What you needed in the

371

real world was not some big clunky sword but a switchblade or a gravity knife. And a *gun.* Who would want a dumb old *katana?* Or any of this shit? Masaaki glanced around at the price tags, all curled and discolored, and shrugged again. Everything cheap as mud, but who would be stupid enough to buy it?

Anyway, they had come to sell—or pawn—not buy.

The old woman was maybe in some kind of trance. The friends didn't seem to exist for her. She sat on a kitchen chair, between the display case and a kerosene heater, all bent over and huddled up in her scarf. Masaaki tried not to think about her underwear. Like some old skin of a cicada when it climbs out and flies away or whatever it does—that's what she reminded him of. *Ugly*, all wrinkled up, no teeth, scraggly hair in a bun, maybe ninety-five or a hundred, ratty kimono, not even shoes, *tabi* and *geta* on her feet, which didn't touch the floor. Not a sound except a kettle hissing on the scabby old heater. She just sat there, gumming a cigarette and sipping *cha*. Watching a junky old black and white TV that was balanced on a stack of rotting brown newspapers. The sound was off. It was some kind of kid show, everyone grinning and jumping around like morons. Masaaki didn't like the old woman's eyes. They were like Mr. Mogi's—very black and bright and… sarcastic.

Yukio stuck the skull ring right under her nose.

"Moshi moshi! How much?"

No response.

"Hey! How much for the ring?"

"How much?" She blinked, snickered. Her voice was like sandpaper.

"Yes! How much?"

"A hundred yen to take it away."

"What the hell do you mean by that?" Masaaki shouted.

"I mean the ring is *gomi*, it is garbage."

"It's gold, you old bitch! And rubies! It cost plenty."

"Ah, maybe so. Perhaps it cost a great deal. However, that would depend upon the purchaser, would it not? On his or her intelligence." Her laughter sounded like crumpling up an empty cigarette pack, but louder. She pulled a handkerchief out of her sleeve and blew her nose, still laughing. "You see, there is sometimes a considerable difference between purchase price and value. Perhaps your ring cost a hundred million yen. Or more. But that is not what it is worth. It is worth nothing. Because it is trash."

"Then how much for these motorcycle trousers and jacket?" asked Yukio.

She laughed, dabbing at her eyes with the handkerchief.

"Hey, old whore, if you don't like the leathers and you don't like the ring, then maybe we'll just keep them—and take your money anyway," said Masaaki, boldly. "All of it."

"Robbery? You'd rob a helpless old woman?" But instead of trembling and screaming, she began to laugh more loudly, coughing, spilling her tea, nearly falling out of her stupid chair. "Well, go ahead, I'm insured, I certainly can't stop you. Will you go so far as to bind my feet and hands? Will you be so brazen as that? If you do not, I will be able to telephone the police! Also, I will feel cheated, and I *will* phone the police."

The friends were undecided. They'd come this far, threatened her with robbery—which the cops would believe, more so-called justice, never mind that it would be their two words against hers—so, well, why the hell *not* rob the old bitch? Masaaki slapped his open hand on the display case, raising a small cloud of dust. Unflinchingly he looked her in the eye.

"Show us your cash box!"

"Here it is!" She opened her kimono and pulled out a moldy drawstring bag, stained and faded, which Masaaki didn't even want to look at, never mind touch. It was contaminated, the whole place was contaminated. "Take it!" Sullen, disgusted, the friends stuck their hands in their pockets, looked away. "No? What's wrong? You have changed your minds? Please do not, I am so bored. I would have something to talk about. I would be on the News."

She emptied the bag on the counter top. A soft damp wad of bills, a clattering of coins. "You boys haven't been killing baby girls, have you? Are either of you the monster? No, I didn't think so. Well, all right, then." She counted the money swiftly and deftly. "Eighteen thousand four hundred eighty-six yen—oh, and fifty sen."

"Sen?" Masaaki asked. "What the hell is a sen?"

"The hundredth part of a yen."

"Keep it, *obaasan.*"

"No, please, it's yours. Never before was I robbed. It is so exciting."

Masaaki spat right on the floor, narrowly missing a cockroach.

"What is wrong with your nose?" she asked Yukio.

"None of your business," Yukio told her bluntly.

"That's right," said Masaaki. "Mind your own business."

"Would you boys like a cigarette?" she asked. "Sometime Slims?"

"All right," said Masaaki, taking one and ripping off the filter, sticking it in the corner of his mouth and lighting it, not even bothering to say *domo,* just grunting. His lips were curled in a sneer. Sometimes, all right. But Sometime *Slims?* What a *wagamama* of a smoke. The girls at that women's college probably smoked Slims, when they went out to drink foreign champagne with their foreign professors. After tennis, of course. Masaaki thought of the girl yesterday, screaming and pissing herself in the middle of the road. His sneer widened into the hard smile his enemies knew only too well.

"Take two," the old woman said. "Take the whole pack."

Masaaki did, contemptuously.

"Oh, this is wonderful." The old woman's eyes were even brighter, and she had a faint pink spot on each sunken cheek. "You boys are young, and you don't look as though you have much imagination, so you probably can't think what it is to be old. My son and even my grandchildren are grown and gone away.

They never visit, seldom even call. My granddaughter is a communist. My husband has been dead forty-five years. Now there is nothing but watching the *terebi*. Well, yes, sometimes when my arthritis is not so bad, I can go out. I ride the trains. Even as far as Shinjuku station."

Masaaki noticed that her cigarette was half-soaked with saliva.

"Shinjuku. Yes, I remember when it was just a flat expanse of smoking concrete rubble and twisted girders. Nothing growing, nothing alive. Everything gritty with brick dust and glass powder, and the people moving through this place like ghosts. The smoke would sting your nostrils, it was bad, Shinjuku itself was hell. After the war, after the terrible carpet bombing."

Masaaki shrugged, glanced at Yukio. Carpets?

The old woman shook her head, then suddenly blinked and looked up.

"But now! It is transformed. Trees and parks and gleaming automobile-cars and giant buildings rising into the clouds. Young people, some of them big as foreigners, flesh on their bones, wearing good clothes, laughing, shopping, going to their jobs, going out to eat a good lunch. So much color and activity, so much life. Worthless Shinjuku now costing a hundred million, two hundred million, per *tsubo*. Shinjuku station, completely new, truly it is enormous. Studio Alta, with its huge *terebi* screen, is just across the street. One may watch the screen and pay no money. That is good, for an old widow-woman.

"But mostly I love Shinjuku *eki* because so many insane persons are there, especially at *higashi guchi,* the east exit. It is so funny. Always there are the big pink *gaijin*, wandering around lost. WHERE... IS... KINOKUNIYA... BOOK... STORE? WHERE... IS... A... BATHROOM? WHERE... IS... SHINJUKU... *EKI?* WHERE... AM... I? They are Americans, mostly—how could such people have won the Pacific War? It is still incredible to me. They can barely manage their own body functions. Anyway, I love them. Also there is the young man in the dress and makeup and wig of many colors who walks around carrying his parasol and his pretty dolls. I like him too. He is *subarashii,* wonderful."

"Wonderful," said Yukio, disgustedly, looking again at the *katana.*

"*Douseiaisha,*" said Masaaki, harshly. "Transvest. Faggot."

"But the most fun are the *shinko-shukyo* people, all those lovely new religions. There are those who shuffle around in a dance, while singing through their noses. They are excellent to observe. There are the colorful Krishna people with their drums. And there are the ones who catch the sunbeams in their hands. I like them very much. My favorites however are those who wear hats in the shape of *sai*, the rhinoceros. Oh, if you could see them, all so solemn, so very sincere, but in those hats! They are the believers in Zenbu-kyo. I sit in the sun and laugh at them, and sometimes they come over and say harsh things to me, threaten me with violence. Then I simply can not stop laughing. I feel so good. At such times I can almost forget that I am old.

The old woman shook her head and chortled.

"*Almost* forget." She puffed on her cigarette, released the smoke in a long sigh. "You boys too, you will be old. Believe it or not. And you will be so amazed. You will say to yourselves, When did this happen? How *could* such a thing happen? How could it happen *to me?*"

She paused, dropped her disintegrating cigarette into a tuna fish can half-filled with water and six or eight more slimy butts. Masaaki looked away. She lit another cigarette.

"Do you see this lighter? It is a true Zippo, of gold entirely. It belonged to my husband, Tomekichi. He and I and all our friends, we were ready to face the Americans with sushi knives and stones and kendo sticks. We would have defended the home islands, fought to the death. I tell you, we were not afraid. In fact, we were *sukoshi* disappointed at the surrender. We would have died for the Emperor, died laughing. What had we to lose? Tokyo was mostly gone, the destruction extending even out this far. But my husband, what nerve he had, he came back two days after the armistice, and found our little property under the rubble. He pounded in four wooden stakes and strung up a perimeter of ropes. And do you know, we camped there! Right in the middle of where our house used to be. For twenty-six months. And he defended our land, fought for it more than once, against usurpers. There were many such, because of course all the old deeds and titles were destroyed, burnt up in the firestorms. One such greedy man was killed. I do not say my husband killed him. I say only that the man became dead.

"During the night I heard my husband leave our tent, to urinate, or so I thought. In the morning a body was found in a ditch nearby with the flesh of its throat hacked open. It was the corpse of our would-be land thief. Tomekichi said, '*Ah, zannen desu ne?* Isn't it a shame?' And that is all he ever did say, but we had no more troubles of that kind. This happened just across the street and around the corner, where there is now a fine new apartment block. Which is mine. This side of the street is mostly mine as well, and do you know why? Because my husband expanded our holdings. He did this at night also. Quite simply he moved our stakes and ropes, meter by meter. He moved them outward!"

She laughed. Masaaki reached towards the warm, wadded banknotes then drew back his hand. They lay slowly uncurling like something barely alive. He looked away, then down. He spat directly onto the cockroach, which was on its back, waving its legs feebly in the air. Sick, probably dying. And no wonder, in such a place. But *shio ga nai* for the roach. Masaaki had problems of his own. Hunger. Unemployment. Poverty. The S-Cargo. Mr. Mogi and his merciless crony, an actual *kobun* of Teshima-*sama*, and therefore nothing more or less than an angel of death. Masaaki nudged the roach with the toe of his shoe. It was just a stupid bug, knew nothing of life, but maybe for that reason it was lucky. It didn't know life so it couldn't fear death. Masaaki nodded, deep in thought. The more you knew about life, the more you realized we were all stupid bugs, more or less, just waiting to die.

"There was a man, Tomekichi. He feared no one and nothing. Do you know, at this time we had a cat, Mac Arthur-*chan*, a big tom. We fed him bits of fish, and we petted him. He would catch mice in our tent. One December day—it was bright, and there was snow—a hulking man came up to our tent. Tomekichi was out on some errand. Mac Arthur was sunning himself in front, licking his paws. The visitor was a gangster. Short haircut, insolent, boorish. He was vulgar, a very low-ranking yakuza, not a soldier, probably not even a *chinpirra* because he was too old. His clothes were bad, smelly, and he had brown stains on his teeth. Everything about him was sloppy and loose. His left eye was sightless, just a blank milky blue. He grabbed Mac Arthur. I said, 'What are you doing?'—although of course I knew—'What is your purpose with our cat?' The man said, 'What do you think, foolish woman?' And he snapped Mac Arthur's neck and tossed him in a big sack. I began to cry. The man laughed and said, 'Cheer up, your cat will soon be quite melodious. His tune will be much improved.' That was his joke. The stupid *gyangu* was going to cut up Mac Arthur and sell his skin and tendons to the makers of *shamisen*. But, you know, that did not happen, because that man died too. And this one I am sure my husband did not kill."

"How do you know that?" asked Yukio.

"Yes," said Masaaki with a sneer. "How do you know he didn't?"

"Because *I* did," said the old woman.

The friends stared at her.

"I told him, 'Well, I should thank you, sir, because that cat ate everything and left nothing for my husband and me.' And he said, 'Is your husband here?' And I said, 'No, he is away.' And the man said, 'Then why don't you invite me into your tent and thank me properly?' 'Please,' I said, *'agatte kudasai,* come in.' I let him kiss me and fondle me."

The friends shuddered. Masaaki lit another Sometime.

"He became excited. I said, 'Would you like something special?' And I gave him some black market Seagram's. He drank it—how shall I say… he drank it *feverishly*. He tipped up the bottle and pulled on it in a greedy fashion. He looked ecstatic, like an infant at the breast, or some filthy saint in prayer. Then I took the little *hocho*—I had been chopping vegetables—and I drove the point through his blind eye."

Masaaki took a long drag on his cigarette.

"Deep into his brain. Tomekichi came back and saw the corpse and said, 'Woman! Who is this? What has happened?' I told him, and he was angry, for he had been terribly fond of Mac Arthur. He said, 'We will wait for darkness. And in the mean time let us bury our dear pet.' So we dug a grave and buried Mac Arthur and the two other cats who had also been in the sack. As he shoveled back the earth my husband was trembling with rage. 'These good animals,' he said, 'will have their revenge.' He returned to the tent and removed the dead man's liver, kidneys, and heart, mincing them finely with the *hocho*. The smell was very strong. Then he skinned the dead man's tattooed back. I asked no questions. Later, we dragged the corpse around the corner to a lot the people were using as a refuse dump. This dump was infested with rats, and packs of wild dogs roved through the area. We knew that soon the yakuza's bones would be picked clean.

"Then my husband and I looked in all the alleys and bombed-out cellars until we found another good cat, enticing him home with a can of King Oscar sardines. This one had a shredded ear, and he was smaller than Mac Arthur, so we called him Truman. He was strong and very fierce, but my husband understood cats and quickly tamed him with love, stroking his fur and hand-feeding him bits of the yakuza's heart.

"Next day Truman ate kidneys for breakfast. My husband petted him saying, 'Ah, Trum-*kun*, you are a good animal, aren't you? Maybe cheap gangsters are good for something after all." Then he took the skin from the dead man's back and left. One evening a week or so later, when all the interior organs had been consumed and Truman was eating mostly Chicken of the Sea tuna fish, my husband returned with a new *shamisen* which had, yes, a tattooed dragon on the tightly stretched skin. I said, 'Husband, have you acted wisely? The craftsmen now know of this matter, and probably many another besides. Word may reach back to Big Motorcycle himself, Tadao-*san*.' But Tomekichi just laughed and said, 'Big Motorcycle is going to run out of gas. Tonight. And soon you will see some real money.'"

The old woman sighed.

"Well, he was a fearless and a formidable man, but he should never have challenged Big Motorcycle. Tomekichi left that night, and I never saw him again.

In the spring Tadao-*san* came to see me, roaring up to the front of the tent. He presented me with two Southern Comfort bottles, clean and neatly wrapped in fresh newspaper. The bottles contained ashes. I didn't have to ask him whose. 'Because of your dead gang member?' I asked. 'Revenge?' Big Motorcycle actually smiled. Usually he neither smiles or frowns. 'No of course not,' he said. 'I would have killed him myself, sooner or later. He was worthless and stupid. He stole from me, trifling amounts, and he drank the money away. At one time he had some small honor, a few grains of intelligence, but he had become untrustworthy, a drunkard. I knew him for many years. I inherited him from Moriuchi-*sama*.' 'Did you know that I, not my husband killed him?' I asked. 'I stabbed him in the eye.' 'Really,' said Big Motorcycle, and his eyebrows went up slightly. He was very surprised.

"'Well,' he said, 'Good for you. But, whoever killed him, that was not the problem. The problem was, your husband tried to kill *me*. He had a good business himself, but he wanted mine too. I can understand his wish to expand, but not at my expense, you see. I had no choice.' Tadao always spoke softly, and the truth. Well, how could I hate him? But how I mourned Tomekichi, how I wept. Big Motorcycle would come by for tea once or twice a month, always with some little *omiage*—cigarettes, usually, or money. Guilt, perhaps, or gentlemanly concern. Anyway, our association ripened into friendship. He helped me secure new titles to my land. He gave me advice about my husband's black market operations, which were now mine. Over the years he helped me become rich."

Masaaki looked around the dump and snorted. "Rich!"

"Truly. It is astonishing how much this my land is worth today. You would have to rob many old women to make up such a sum. You would need to steal perhaps a million yen a day for ten years. You should take me and hold me for ransom—except that nobody would pay to get me back. Especially my grand-daughter. *Wasabi*, I call her, horseradish. She hates me, hates my wealth. Do you wish to hear my excellent joke?" The old woman cackled. "'When I die it is all hers!' I told her that, told her how much, and she screamed at me. 'I'll never touch your stinking money, *Obaasan*, you bloodsucking old monster. Or if I do I'll buy some Cruise missiles and blow up your precious Emperor!'" The old woman cackled again. "Oh, she is piss and vinegar, as the Americans say. So like her grandfather. She even has Tomekichi's nose. Such a good girl."

"Wealth!" said Masaaki.

"If you are so rich," asked Yukio, "Why are you in this shithole?"

"Memories, dear boys. Of much better days, of my own little black market. Right here is where I struck our tent and erected this commercial building. And there was commerce indeed, most of it illegal, but so much the better. Here I dealt with men from Yokosuka and the new bases. And of course the Depot Camp, which was in those days much bigger and busier, the treasure of America piling up there. Piling up, trickling away. Do you know the history of this area? Long before the Americans it was the preserve of the Imperial cavalry. Did you know that? Even now that intersection at the far corner is called *Bamba*, The Place of the Horse. Our soldiers tested their tanks behind there in the early days of the war, roaring back and forth along the spine of *Oyama*, Little Mountain. Did you realize that? Isn't that interesting?"

Masaaki spat, again on the roach, which was now barely twitching.

"But then the Americans. Some of them were decent lovers, and all of them were brilliant thieves.

We got on well, I say. Too bad about Tojo, Anami, Suzuki, and the rest. They were yesterday. I was making money. Here I bought and sold Crisco and VanCamp's and Dole and Hormel and Philip Morris and Spam and Pillsbury and Coca Cola. Yes, and Old Granddad and even sometimes Jack Daniels. The sun shone through those windows in the morning, shone like fire on row upon row of goods. Mine.

"Quality merchandise. Nylons, Campbell's soups of the numerous varieties—yes, and true Levis, and bomber jackets. Of pogey bait we had all kinds: Mars Bars and Hersheys and Tootsie Rolls and Bit O' Honeys and Good 'n Plentys. Wristwatches by Longines and Hamilton, twenty-three jewels, genuine pigskin bands. I had them. I had items from the Spaulding company—strange balls and swollen leather gloves—which I did not then even know the use of. No matter. Others knew, and were willing to pay. I had the Sluggers from Louisville, huge clubs of dark wood. I had everything. Cases, truckloads. And at a time, please remember, when others less cunning and fortunate were starving. Starving and rotting by the tens of thousands. Unfortunates, who lived in the train stations. Who fought for a place to curl up on a square of cardboard on the stairs. That was life, after the war, always on the razor's edge. Huge opportunities, huge risks.

"Do you know the drug cocaine? Its effects? To be alive and drawing breath in the sunlight then was like cocaine. Life was thrilling.

"Let me tell you that right here at this counter Big Motorcycle and I once contracted to purchase an entire *planeload* of White Owls, Chesterfields, Nunn-Bush shoes, Schwinn bicycles having three gears, King Oscar sardines, Case and Keen Kutter and Camillus pocket knives, and Carnation milk. Of Nescafe alone there were twenty crates. It was a cash transaction. *Genkin*, do you understand? Nearly all we had. But I sold everything inside a month, quadrupling our money. I lived a dozen lives in those years. Every second something new, dangerous, thrilling, satisfying. Then as now, my husband's ashes were in the *butsudan* over there." She jerked her head to the shelf on her left, toward a small but elaborate cherrywood cabinet—dustless, freshly oiled, glowing. "Then as now, incense burned before it. Several sticks. Sandalwood, the best, for Tomekichi."

Masaaki shivered. Ashes. Incense. *Tsumaranai.* Fuck that.

"Often, I could feel his presence. During some major negotiation, I would sense him nearby, offering comfort and encouragement. In fact, sometimes now I can see all of them—the G.I.s and the *geisha* and priests from the shrines and the skinny *jinrikisha* men and the fat policemen—all my old customers. I see them thronging the aisles, jostling each other, laughing, shouting to me high spiritedly—do I have this or that, why are my goods so shoddy, why so dear?

"Of course, they are long dead, most of them, so therefore I am insane. They are ghosts, vapors, the product of a senile brain. But they are often more real to me than the ones of today. Even dead, they have more vitality. I see them as they were, but lit from within, beings of light. Let me tell you that I knew real soldiers and real gangsters. True men, not a couple of play-acting *douseiaisha* too cowardly to rob an old woman of the cash in her till." She took a deep drag on her cigarette, then dropped it in the tuna can. "By the way, do you boys have AIDS?"

Tsumaranai! Masaaki ground the roach into the old woman's linoleum.

She paused to light another Sometime Slim.

"I dislike these. They are tasteless. My former brand was Kools."

"Import them," Masaaki told her. "You are so wealthy."

"You do not believe me, and I do not care. But here is the golden Zippo, why do you not snatch it from me? Here on my wrist is Tomekichi's golden Rolex, which has not lost more than a second or two in forty-five years. Why do you not take it? And hidden in a secret place about my body—perhaps in some crevice or other?—are three large diamonds and six rubies. *Real* rubies. Why do you not look for them?" She laughed. "Or how about a handgun for your robberies? You cannot buy such a thing anywhere in Japan, but you can buy—or steal—one from me. Colt .45s, right here, at least a hundred, in concealment."

"Nickle-plated?" Masaaki asked. "Pearl-handled?"

"No. Regulation bluing, walnut grips."

"Good condition?"

"From the factory. Still in the cosmoline, the oiled paper."

"Ammunition?"

"Regulation too, though very old, half a century or more."

"How much?"

"One million yen! Each! Unless you ransack my poor store and discover them and steal them, first binding my hands and feet and ripping the telephone cord from the wall." She laughed. "Big Motorcycle still purchases a Colt now and then, nobody else. He comes in for tea. He brings incense for the *butsudan*, and we pray. It is good. Sometimes I say to him, 'Big Motorcycle, maybe someday I will avenge Tomekichi and drive a butcher knife into your eye.' He never smiles, but he looks at me fondly and says, 'Yes, I believe you might. It is part of your charm. Ah, Kikuno, weren't those the days?'"

"Uso!" said Masaaki. *"Hyaku pahcento!* One hundred percent bullshit."

"Show us something," said Yukio. "Real proof."

"Show us the fucking Colts. Right now."

"Show us the jewels."

"No. Those you must find for yourselves."

"Then show us—show us the fucking *shamisen.*"

"The *shamisen?"* The old woman frowned. "You do not want to see it, believe me. It is a grisly object." She shuddered. "I do not wish to touch it, or even think of it. Human flesh. Human skin." She shuddered once more. She huddled more deeply into her moth-eaten shawl. "It is horrible."

"Show us!"

"Truly, I do not even know if I could find it, now, in such disorder."

"Show us now!"

"Well, if you insist." The old woman slumped in her chair. "And to get rid of you, perhaps I must." She leaned over and lifted a grimy instrument, like a square banjo, from behind the counter. "Here it is—catch!" And she threw it with surprising force at Masaaki, who shouted in alarm and twisted aside, tripping and falling in a heap on the floor, one hand in the slimy mess of smashed cockroach. The instrument fell clattering beside him.

"What?" he roared, doubling his fist and shaking it at her.

"You wanted the *shamisen*," she said, cackling. "There it is."

"Turn it over," said Yukio. "Pick it up."

Masaaki did.

The friends held their breath and looked.

The cracked and yellowed skin beneath the three strings was blank.

"No tattoo!" he shouted.

"No tattoo, no dragon," said Yukio. "Fake."

"It's a fucking fake!" shouted Masaaki. "You lied!"

"Perhaps!" she laughed, gaily, rocking back and forth. "Perhaps I did."

"Liar!" Raging, Masaaki scrambled up and faced her. He grabbed the bills, scattering the coins. Seldom had he been so angry. "You're a liar!"

"Perhaps I am. But if you will wait a minute I will prepare a box lunch for you boys. Would you not like that? Steaming *gohan* and slices of fresh salmon? Maybe some of that new Hello Kitty fishcake? I will give you scarves, genuine Burberry, to wrap around your throats. The nights are now cold, and you should dress warmly."

The friends stormed out, Masaaki with the money, Yukio with a *katana*.

"Wait!" she called to them, when they reached the doorway. "Here is something for you to consider. Perhaps I lied to you about the *shamisen*, but perhaps not. There may actually be such an instrument. Perhaps, one golden day when the cherry trees were blooming and I had just taken title to that fine apartment block across the way, I gave the *shamisen* to Big Motorcycle."

"*Bakayaro* bitch!"

"In friendship, for his help and encouragement."

"*Uso!* Filthy liar! Lunatic old corpse of a whore!"

395

"But, whether I did or not, you will never know." Cackling. Hag.

"Really, we should have killed her," says Masaaki, slurping noodles, intent upon a tattered *manga* on the counter by his bowl.

Yukio nods, drains his Kirin, orders yet another. "How is your *soba?*"

"All right. But, you know, I am hungry for fish."

"Me too, as a matter of fact," says Yukio. *"Shiake."*

"Salmon, yes, and fresh," says Masaaki. He half-turns on his stool toward Yukio. "I did the buying, you know, at my father's *sakana-ya.* Three days a week, four in the morning, all the way to Tsukiji."

"Yes, I sometimes went there too," says Yukio, "for the *sushi-ya.*"

"Are you a good sushi chef?"

"Not bad. I am good with the knife. Skillful and fast."

"And a *katana*?" Masaaki asks. "Are you fast with a *katana* too?"

"Sushi," says Yukio. "Fresh salmon or *maguro.* Good strong *shoyu.*"

"Is that why you took it from the old woman?"

396

"Strong soy sauce, rice all steaming, freshly ground *wasabi.*"

"Why did you want that *katana?*"

"Let's have another beer, Masaaki."

"Our money is almost gone."

"True. So what? *Oyaji-san! Kirin o futatsu tsuika shiteh.*"

"We'll go back for her gold and jewels."

"Drink your beer, Masaaki."

"And kill her."

"Drink up."

Yukio sighs. They will not go back to the *shichi-ya.* He knows that. They will certainly not go back to their homes. When night comes they will sleep in some train station, or in the stinking little truck, without blankets. And tomorrow they will—what? Yukio has no idea, wishes that he were truly drunk, like last night, able to blot out everything. Why *did* he steal the old woman's *katana?* It is a mediocre one, no legendary blade like *Mitsumasa.* Yukio is as far as ever from his true goals. And as far as ever, and in just as much danger, from Shining Mist. The microphone men he is of course not even slightly worried about. They would hold a series of fiery meetings, pass a series of bloodcurdling resolutions and denunciations. And then go home to snuggle up with their warm, pliant girlfriends. Yukio almost smiles. The microphone men, a swarm of gnats.

Ah, but the Leader, the Leader.

Well, the friends are safe enough for now in the smoky little *soba-ya.* Two tables, five stools at the counter, the old counterman dribbling sweat and cigarette ash into the lunchtime noodles as he serves them, red plastic beer crates stacked by the door, windows steamed, linoleum tile floor tracked with mud, fat *manga* strewn around, tiny television crackling away up in the corner niche. Yes, for the time being safe. Masaaki gropes for another *manga,* his nose still buried in the first. And consider the other positive aspects. Yamamoto is still dead. And the wife, too bad about her, but *c'est la guerre* as the Leader says. And Yukio still has his freedom and his life. Didn't he outwit the police? And that crazy, vicious little student communist! She couldn't have burned headquarters, true—bad tactics on Yukio's part, granted—but she *is* in prison, the murdering hell-bitch.

So, two of the enemy, neutralized in a single day. And the dog, don't forget the loathsome Yamamoto sausage-dog. *Yiiiiiii... splat.* Yukio will drink to that.

He tips his bottle up, wishing it were *sake*, watching the *terebi.*

News at Noon, blah, blah. Same as last night, same girl, same footage: fat Yamamoto-mounds under their shrouds, blood on the railing, a pool of it on the sidewalk, Donner all smashed up and looking stupid, saying *gaa* and holding onto that baby. Pan to the broken Mitsumasa, a sight which stabs Yukio afresh. Oh, if only, if only. Interview with new witnesses, the disgusting and effeminate college students—all right, one is effeminate and the other, the foolish girl, is unfeminine—who were, it seems, able to focus briefly on something outside their own decadent flesh: motorcycle, motorcycle leathers, crew cut, yapyap. Not good. No camera, at least. But they use the word *ouyoku,* right-winger. And the word murderer.

From the corner of his eye Yukio sees Masaaki regarding him intently.

"Yukio, did you, was that—"

"Shh. Read your *manga. "*

Pan to some fat cretin in a T-shirt.

"Sawada!" exclaims Masaaki, "That bloodsucker!"

"Quiet, Masaaki. Please."

Now the fire.

"Yukio, that ring is *yours,* nobody else's. Always remember that."

"*Shizuka ni!* Quiet!"

Smoke, firemen and hoses, headquarters now nothing but ashes and a few blackened uprights, *zannen,* but, well, it was rented, nothing theirs but folding chairs and sound equipment. Some banners in the Leader's office, his camp bed, maybe a little money in the safe, their ledgers, their charter. Odds and ends, knickknacks, souvenirs. That's all. It's unfortunate, certainly. It could, however, be a great deal worse. *But what's this now?* Yukio swallows beer the wrong way, coughs, gasps, feels Masaaki pound him on the back, keeps his eyes on the screen. *Yes.* Body bags, two of them. Ambulance. No, no, no. Yukio puts down his beer, buries his face in his hands. He has killed two comrades!... Two idiots! Two shit-brained microphone men! What were the stupid bastards doing at headquarters in the middle of the night? How could Yukio have known? He couldn't have, no one—not Fujiwara, not Napoleon—could have anticipated such a possibility. Yukio is guiltless, guiltless.

Ah, but tell that to the Leader.

Yukio groans, feels Masaaki shaking him, hears the word terrorist.

"Yukio," Masaaki whispers hoarsely, "was that your headquarters?"

Yukio groans again, nods.

"Don't worry, Yuk-*kun*, they'll get him. The bastard who did that."

Yukio groans once more, nodding slowly.

The friends are silent, each with his own thoughts, while the lunch crowd departs, and a chill settles on the *soba-ya*, drafts from the sliding door opening and closing. If only Yukio could have disemboweled himself on the bridge. *Seppuku*, that was the honorable way out. Well, maybe he still could do it. He now has another *katana*. Could he cut his guts out with such a long blade? Could he cut his guts out at all? Yukio shudders. The old woman's *katana*. The old woman. She would be delighted, certainly. Yukio's intestines spilling hot to the floor, slick pink and glistening.

"Let's not go back there, Masaaki. Forget the jewels. I hate that place."

"Boku mo, I do too."

"She was lying about the jewels," Yukio tells him.

"She was lying about everything."

"She was, that's right."

"Big Motorcycle." Masaaki snickers, lights his last Sometime Slim.

"Big Motorcycle," says Yukio. "Real soldiers, real gangsters."

"Real *men*. She called us—called us *douseiaisha*," says Masaaki, softly.

"She did, that's right."

"That rotten old bitch!" Masaaki hisses. "*Douseiaisha!*"

Yukio puts his hand on his friend's forearm, squeezes, then feels Masaaki's hand, its slight tremor, as it covers his own, lightly at first, then very tightly. "That's right, Masaak-*kun*." Yukio's throat is feeling thick, constricted. Side by side on their stools, the friends look down at the counter, "that's exactly right."

Saturday, 12:03 p.m.

Captain Yoshida's phone rings. He lifts the receiver, reluctantly.

Yes: Paperwork. Last thing Friday night, almost the first thing today.

Paperwork Ishimura, *Who needs Yoshida as much as Yoshida needs him.*

To look good, to make the numbers work.

Remember that. Repeat it. Believe it.

Ishimura complaining, urging him on to greater feats of caution.

Ishimura's voice, an even spill of sand: *some recent difficulties and irregularities. Two of Yoshida's men damaged their patokaa last night: bumper, grill, left front fender. Is Captain Yoshida aware of that regrettable and altogether preventable accident?* He is now. *Is Captain Yoshida familiar with the principles by which departmental vehicles are amortized?* Regrettably, he is not. *Ishimura Yuuki is not surprised at this ignorance; is the Captain at least aware of the circumstances pertaining to this accident?* He is. *Would the Captain be so kind as to indicate the nature of these circumstances at this time, in anticipation of the official report?* He would. Briefly, the two constables were answering a call for reinforcements from the riot detail at Kosei University, Ichigaya campus. A small fracas, the communist demonstrators becoming unruly, a prudent call, therefore. An officer injured. *The nature of the injury?* A bitten ear. *Or ear-lobe?* Yes, perhaps the lobe, although that is of course part and parcel of the ear itself, and thus it is proper, when speaking of an injured ear-lobe, to speak of an injured ear. *Is the Captain quibbling?* The Captain hopes not. *Does Captain Yoshida understand about group medical insurance premiums and the necessity of keeping these to a minimum by curtailing all unnecessary claims?* He does. *As, for example, this present claim. Did not the armed and armored and fully supported officer weigh over eighty kilos and the lone female assailant weigh less than half that?* He did, she did, yes. *Then how could such a ridiculous thing have happened?* It is being studied. *Was it not negligence?* That is one possibility. *Was it not negligence, pure and simple?* That is perhaps even a probability. *Is it not a certainty?*

Yoshida coughs.

Is it not?

Yoshida coughs.

And, finally, would not Captain Yoshida, mulishly declining to make such an obvious and just concession, grant at least that his various officers have had a more than usually expensive night? Would he not grant that clear fact? Would he not grant it? Would he not?

Yoshida scowls and jerks his head left then right. But then he sighs again.

"Hai, hai," he says. *"Tabun so deshita."*

Maybe they have. Maybe so, *bakayaro.* Yes, yes, nod, nod, riffle, riffle.

He is riffling through the horrors.

Murder on the bridge, the jumping *gaijin.* Saw that last night. No arrests.

Riffle.

Homicide arson at the right-wingers'. Old stuff. No arrests.

Riffle.

Chubby missing lawyer and his chubby missing family. Still smiling on the posters, still missing. Still dead, as Yoshida is ninety-nine point nine percent sure. He is also that sure the religious lunatics are responsible. Yoshida has been researching those *shin-shukyo* people for months. He could wrap up the case in an hour. Beat the living *unchi* out of their Great Healer, and Yoshida'd have that missing family, the evidence, the cadavers. *And no job, and a substantial prison term for himself,* once the lawsuits started to fly, and Ishimura decided that Yoshida was expendable. So, nothing new with the lawyer.

Yakuza doing this and that, mostly to each other. Certainly nothing new.

Riffle.

Here: the monster, the spoor of the beast. Every contact leaves a trace, and the trace is a butchered baby girl, her flesh all flayed away and burned to ashes with her bones and then later, sometime, when everyone is least suspecting it, hand-delivered to the parents like some hellish *oseibo* present: a little token of good wishes arising from our happy association over the past year. It is an outdated flyer, the one in his hand: "This little girl is two years old. Her name is Nakamura Izumi. Have you seen this little girl?" Yoshida did, last night on his way home—saw, touched, sifted, marveled. Izumi returned last night in her whiskey bottle.

Yoshida pictures the monster: gross, crude, shambling, moist.

Pictures him easily, having observed him, knowing who he is.

Knows who must be the monster and who cannot be. Yoshida's problem is that these two individuals are the same man. Who left, it is true, prints, traces. The fingerprints match, you see, but the times and places do not. The monster was nowhere around in the midst of the horror. Could two persons have exactly the same prints? The man has a son, living on his own. Lieutenant Kamijo checked the kid out. Nothing. The son is a little *otaku-zoku,* a stay-at-home couch potato. Goes to work, comes back, that's it. Well, is there some long-lost twin brother? No. And even if there were, identical twins, adults, do not have identical prints. There is always a difference, *always.* Some little flaw or wrinkle. Some little something. So: must be and can't be, a real problem

Yoshida's other problem is that this man is a cop.

What to do? Twenty-four hour surveillance, naturally. Several top-to-bottom searches of the home: skin magazines, closet full of empty whiskey bottles, shoebox full of crumpled shakedown money—in other words, nothing. He didn't need Ishimura to tell him about surveiling and searching. But then what? Arrest the man and hold him? For how long? And on what charges? Slapping around a Soapland whore? Unnecessary roughness to the winos and stinking *furoshiya* who foul the train stations with their presence? No, no. The man is a pig, but that is legal. As his lawyer would point out.

Or rather his team of lawyers. How long would it be before the lawsuits hit? They would be big, a jackpot for the monster. He'd make enough to retire. And how long after the first lawsuit before the headlines hit? Ishimura, six months ago: *"Amari yokunai,* this is not good at all, Captain! What will such headlines do to next year's budget?" Paperwork wailing, taking a fourth puff on his cigarette, and blinking his chewed-caramel eyes rapidly for fully half a minute.

But, as Yoshida argued then and a hundred times since, the alternative is worse: leave The Officer at large, let him continue, keep trying to catch him in the act, keep hoping that the lid will stay on while knowing that it won't. Knowing that when the miso boils over it will look like incompetence and negligence and complicity in about equal amounts:

GHOUL COP!

YOUR TAX YEN AT WORK!

FORCE LOOKS OTHER WAY!

They would all be fired, remain unemployable, soon have to fight with the *furoshiya* for space to curl up in the parks and stations. If Option A was a bomb, Option B was a timed thermonuclear device. Their Department would look like Hiroshima. Yet, of course, Option B was the one Ishimura chose—though to give him credit he did change his mind about twelve times a day.

"*Ie, zannen,* nothing new about The Officer," he tells Paperwork. "Home all night... absolutely didn't leave, couldn't have left... *hai, wakarimashita,* I do understand. Prints on the urn, but Officer in the house... no, *dekinakatta,* not possible... in the house, all night, sleeping in front of the television—no, not a dummy—he was breathing, snoring. The team went in and took his pulse. The Officer was *there,* drunk, passed out even before the video finished... a rental video... 'Soapland Slasher,' I believe... yes, oh yes, very suggestive indeed. But entirely legal."

Riffle.

Another flyer, curled and yellowing: "Have you seen Narui Megumi?"

Yes, her too. Rest in peace, Megumi-*chan.*

"*Hai, hai, shitsurei-shimasu,* good-bye... sir."

Associate Chief Ishimura Yuuki replaces the telephone receiver with an inward grimace. Captain

Yoshida, how pathetic, how limited in every way, with his gumshoe's world view, his complaints, his excuses. His, well, obtuseness is not too strong a word. Ishimura looks at his watch. They are still recessed; it is not, however, time for his cigarette. Not for another nine minutes and thirty-five seconds. Ishimura accepts that. He is neither pleased nor displeased by this datum on his dial. The time of day at a particular place on the earth's surface, that is to say the City of Tokyo, is a matter of fact. Not opinion, not belief, not "hunch." Fact. Not what we wish; what is. An adult human does not waste time butting his head against matters of fact—though of course Yoshida is another story:

"Captain Yoshida, an organism needs blood; an organization needs funds."

"But Associate Chief, with respect, that is insufficient."

"It is insufficient. But it is also primary. No funding, no Force."

Ishimura puts it to him that way, often, in terms that a child could grasp, but always the man wants to argue. Ishimura by contrast never argues. Everyone knows this. He never makes recommendations if he can help it, never uses the words "should" and "therefore." He even avoids the use of sentence connectors and semicolons. He lays out the facts. He deals them out like cards—*snap, snap, snap, fact, fact, fact*—in short, crisp declaratives. These facts speak for themselves. Others, whose job it is, might draw conclusions from these facts. Or perhaps not. That is their concern. It is not his. He will not insult their intelligence. He will not interpret, assess, opine. He *will not.*

Pressed for his view, he retaliates, pounces: "Sir, that is not for me to say," or, "Ah, *shitsurei*, opinion is not my proper sphere." Pressed further, by a person of consequence, he sometimes employs a conditional: If X billion yen are diverted to Y, then a rational decision-maker who keeps his options open might reasonably expect Z. But he much prefers to counter such pressure with facts. Real quanta, communicated with perfect objectivity in his best sandpapery monotone. At the crucial second round of talks last year, for example, with the Governor of Tokyo's man—a hard inner-circler, the one they call "Katana" because of what he can do to a budget proposal:

"Ishimura-*san*, what about Homicide? Why augmented funding again?"

411

"For fiscal previous, Homicide's budget was enhanced by 12.38%. During that period the number of solved major crimes rose by 14.97%."

"So, augmented funding for Homicide?"

"Those are the figures."

"*Jya,* all right, augmented. To what extent?"

"Output over input is a confirmed 2.59 plus or minus a hundredth."

"It is, isn't it? *Jya,* very well, then, substantially augmented. "

And so forth. Ishimura at point.

Ishimura's Chief beamed at him across the big teak table. Beamed.

Now, this year, at the same table, his Chief is beaming still.

Ishimura Yuuki will himself be Chief, someday.

Someday soon. As they resume, the men in tailored suits and the men in tailored uniforms, Ishimura permits himself a tiny inward smile. Yes, he is the money-bringer, the diverter, the favorer, the witholder. Even down at the precinct level they all owe him, are obliged to him variously and significantly. One might reasonably suppose that, the Force having been enriched by X trillion yen over the past five years, and Ishimura Yuuki being perceived as largely responsible for this enrichment, then, when the present Chief retires…

Perfect.

If only it weren't for the Beast! The Chief is beaming at him, true, but less radiantly than last year. At that time Ishimura welcomed the killings—no, of course he did not welcome the *killings.* Only a psychopath could welcome the killings. They were and are horrible. Hideous is not too strong a word. Ishimura Yuuki most emphatically did *not* welcome the killings. He did, however, welcome the opportunity which they presented to ameliorate their budgetary stance: more men, vehicles, electronic devices. More everything. Such amelioration was in everyone's interest, really, given the nature of police work.

But now, here, despite all the smiles, there is something in the air: a general feeling that, by this time, perhaps all these revenue expansions and diversions might—even *should?*—have resulted in the apprehension of the Beast. If only they knew. This monster is one of our own, The Officer. Or might be. Or perhaps could not be, as Yoshida pointed out so often. The Chief knows, but he is the only one. The Chief says patience; Ishimura agrees. What happened in Russia? A comparable situation, the facts speak for themselves. The Russians rushed to judgment and executed the wrong man for that serial killer-cannibal Chikatilo, or whatever his name. They lacked certainty. What they wanted obscured what was. Well, that is about what you expect from Russians

But in this matter Ishimura himself lacks certainty! Months oozing by, and he still lacks the true hard good facts. He wishes it were otherwise. He hopes... *no.* He does not hope. He does not deal in wishes. Ishimura permits himself a small inward frown. Captain Yoshida will apprehend the Beast, the Monster, The Officer, as they call him. And the apprehension will be effected in an expeditious manner. Or it will be much the worse for Captain Yoshida. Who is perhaps less indispensable than he realizes. Who is far from being the only glorified gumshoe on the Force, the only plodder promoted and promoted on the escalator far beyond his level of competence. It is the Peter Principle. And it is a fact.

Anyway, it is almost time for Ishimura's cigarette. Another fact.

Saturday, 12:08 p.m.

Donner's phone is ringing.

Why then does he not answer it?

Seated at his desk, in his leather chair, which is his and his alone, which was in fact custom-made to accommodate the amplitude of his person, Zenbu-kyo's Great Healer, Takeshita Satoshi, holds the receiver to one ear and listens exasperated to the intermittent buzz, never taking his eyes from the woman. Who is demented. Writhing and bucking like an epileptic, jerking the cords at her wrists and ankles, chewing at her sodden gag, grunting and growling and slobbering. Truly, she is altogether in and of *mappo*, this epoch of degeneracy.

The Healer itches to hit her again, very much harder—and *now,* not later on. For she has rolled across the study and gouged one of the doors of his fine teak display case with her shoe buckle—a long, deep gouge—and then driven the pointed heel of that same shoe into the genital area of Tedzuka-*san*, who was endeavoring only to restrain her. Confusion, consternation. And when she rolled back the other way, colliding with his desk, the Zenbu-kyo Rhinoceros Buddha, porcelain and priceless, toppled to the carpet. Fortunately, the sacred figurine was not broken; unfortunately, it rolled across, and was thus contaminated by, a pool of her fluids—tears, mucous nasal discharge, alcohol drool. Ruriko Donner, a moist beast, fit consort for a *gaijin.* A Japanese animal mated to an American animal.

Both slated for extinction.

The Healer listens to the ringing, with his free hand flips through his well-thumbed back issue of *Tokyo This Month* to Donner's vile article. Like a cut tongue returning to a broken tooth, the Healer has read and reread this piece, "Oh, Come Now, All Ye Faithful." The tone of it, the cheerful contempt for new religions generally and Zenbu-kyo in particular, thickens his throat with rage.

And he is alive to each putrid nuance of phrasing. Oh yes, the Healer's English is excellent. He worked in Manhattan, after all, at Drexel-Burnham, that den of greed-vipers. Hustling junk bonds with the best of them, with Millken himself. (The bonds were of course *not junk,* as he never tired of pointing out, but rather diamonds in the rough, thrilling growth opportunities for those with sufficient means and nerve.) Worked at Drexel, learned what he could, took a lateral over to Random House, discovered that publishing is no different from investment. You crunched the numbers, you crunched the words, the bottom line was the bottom line. Principles? The Healer has to smile. Principles in a whole city full of money-mad degenerates? Principles in *gigoku*, hell? The Healer labored there in darkness, patiently, keeping his eyes open, until he saw the Light. The Light, yes—refracted through Mr. Hubbard's flawed prism, granted, but light nonetheless: the way to acquire the means to achieve his goal. His goal, his divine Task. The Healer labored and learned. So he understands American irony, knows that the article is, to that pitiless race, funny. He hasn't missed the slimiest subtlety. He knows lengthy passages of it by heart, the most sarcastic ones, the most cutting, the cruelest.

Why is everyone laughing at them?

This article.

And why are so many puling, weak-minded, backsliding brethren casting aside their Rhinoceros hats, withholding their contributions, deserting the fold, even seeking legal redress?

This article, and the dozens it has spawned.

And why are book sales slumping so drastically? *Teachings of the Sun, Lessons of the Moon Goddess, Spiritual Guidance of the Stars, True Secrets of*

Uranus—previously million-sellers, big, big titles. Now? Ingloriously neglected all over the city, all over the country. Ignored, remaindered. Why?

This article.

And what therefore is Donner's death-warrant?

This same damnable article.

Death warrant, yes. If the Islamists can do it, can defend with the supreme sanction their murky and distorted perception of the All, how much stronger is the mandate for those of the true faith to do the same. Are infidels to be more zealous than the righteous? No! But alas how often they *are* more zealous, these days.

Yes, oh yes, this age of *mappo*, these eons of ashes and unbelief.

The Healer feels a muscle jumping in his cheek, hears the ringing of Donner's phone, watches the woman warily as she squeals and squirms beneath the weight of Tedzuka-*san* and his son, sees her saliva in a golden pool of sunlight: droplets flashing like diamonds, bright threads gleaming, glistening, crisscrossing his carpet. Celestial blue, pure wool one hundred percent his.

Saturday, 12:09 p.m.

Kobayashi Miyuki did not cry this time. Dry-eyed, her voice rough, she interviewed the parents of Nakamura Izumi. Miyuki caught them—late twenties, thin, hunched against the wind—just outside their second-floor Ebisu apartment, on the open-air walkway. Crows, raucous and huge, filled the golden gingko opposite. Lining their street, trees and bushes muffled the horns and diesels on the expressway two blocks south. The mother and father were taking small, careful steps. They were on their way to the cemetery, with Izumi's ashes in an urn, which was at least an improvement on the whiskey bottle.

"It is an *ai no tsubo,*" said her father. "A love urn."

It was round, glowing, crafted from some rich, whiskey-colored wood. It had a drawer below the ash compartment. Izumi's father opened the drawer to reveal a plush Cookie Monster.

"Izumi-*chan's* favorite toy," said Miyuki, not making it a question, and the father nodded, closing the drawer carefully. Would they talk to her, answer a few questions? Yes, they would; how could it hurt? (In fact, the parents of all four girls had said the same thing, in almost the same words: how could it hurt?) So

419

Miyuki did fairly well, with only a quaver or two toward the end, when she had to ask, "How do you feel about your daughter's murder?" And the father just shook his head, squinting up at the clouds, as though trying to pick out something beyond them. Then he blinked, cradled the urn more closely in his left arm, made a dismissive gesture with his right hand.

"He can't hurt her." The father was brusque. "Not anymore."

The mother's face crumpled. She said, "Oh, Izumi!" in a low reproachful voice, as if she had caught the child in some bad mischief. The mother turned and pressed her face against their steel door, robin's egg blue, with its little white sign,

209—Nakamura: Senri, Sanae, Izumi.

How do you feel about your daughter's murder? What a question!

What studio imbecile thinks of them? Miyuki has a fairly good idea.

And the other one, *What are your feelings about her killer?* Stupid!

Back in the van, let's go.

In the old days, she knows, a killer was released to the victim's relatives. Frankly, Miyuki sees nothing wrong with that. She would like to... to do... something. Something decisive, final. *Something*—to make certain that he never does again what he did to those four babies. Miyuki's fists are doubled and trembling in front of her. Her face is hot. She is breathing raggedly, almost snarling. She looks up, sees her eyes in the rear-view mirror, and gasps. Really, sometimes Miyuki frightens herself.

But, oh, the beast. She dreams about him. She is at the wheel of her van. The killer is running along the highway, trying to escape, looking back over his shoulder terrified. His face is contorted and rippling. He is hideous. Miyuki's cameraman Hiroji is trying to eat his *bento*, stabbing at the rice with his chopsticks, and screaming, Slow down, slow down, slowww dowwnnn. A policeman blows his whistle at her, soundlessly, then loses his mustache to become Miyuki's seventh-grade teacher, Nogizaka-*sensei*— furious, cheeks distended, rouge and lipstick vivid as a clown's. The van closes in, the killer is trapped against a blank brick wall, and then they realize just how huge the killer is: the bumper crushes only his ankles. He falls, roaring, onto the van, which collapses under his

421

weight. Miyuki and Hiroji are crushed together in the dark, hardly able to breathe, the roof bearing down on them. There is the groaning, almost musical sound of sheet metal crumpling and shearing. The noise is deafening, terribly painful, as though the bones of their skulls were crumpling and shearing as well. The roof is creaking and bulging just inches from their eyes. Suddenly, two filthy fangs punch through.

Same dream, three or four times a week, for the past year.

Miyuki is crying now, her forehead on the steering wheel, while Hiroji takes longer than usual stowing things in back, giving her some time. The truth is, this past year has been… really too much for Miyuki. She sometimes wishes she were back at her first company, where she'd have to deal with a few flabby middle-aged men who couldn't keep their hands to themselves. Soft little tofu hands, no butcher knives in them.

She has been finding gray hairs lately, three more this week.

Miyuki has pills. They do no good.

Promise: when she gets home, an iced vodka, a triple. Then another.

In the meantime, she will call the foreigner from yesterday, Donner. She will ask how he is feeling.

"How y'all doing?" She will ask him that, jokingly. (Miyuki has been to Houston.) She will inquire about his cuts and bruises. And then she will ask him about the baby, Hanako. Is she eating well? Is she sleeping better? Does she laugh and splash even a little bit in the *ofuro?* What about a bubble bath? How is Mrs. Donner getting along with her? Have they located any relatives? Are the neighbors coming around to help? Do they have any plans for Sunday? If not, or even if so, maybe Miyuki could drop by with a present for Hanako—it's nothing, really, just a little something, a rag doll, from Toys R Us on Route 16. (What a place—huge, like everything American, endless vistas of toys, but very nice too, and the prices were quite reasonable; she had bought the doll on impulse two years ago, when she did her *Toyzowus* feature.) Just a little Raggedy Ann—for you, Hana-*chan.*

Maybe the baby will grin shyly and cuddle it— maybe even give Miyuki a soft little hug of thanks. Wouldn't that be nice? Feel her tiny arms, smell her clean, soapy infant smell. A little dimpled smile, a breathy word or two of goodness.

Miyuki needs a little good news for six o'clock, needs some for herself.

Saturday, 12:10 p.m.

Hashimoto Hanako sits on her chubby ankles, on the heated carpet in the fluffy little room where everything is white or pink. She is crying. She does not know why she is crying. She is crying and looking at her cookie. The girl who is a boy gave it to her. It is chocolate. It is the kind that she likes, a sort of sandwich. Two crunchy round parts, and creamy stuff in between. Sweet. Hanako likes to take the cookies apart, then lick the creamy stuff completely away, then eat the two halves very quickly. Crunch, crunch. *Okaasan* doesn't like it when she does that. These cookies are good with milk, if the milk isn't too cold. Hanako doesn't like milk if it is too cold, and she doesn't like ice cream. She likes ice cream, but she doesn't like it. It hurts her nose. *Otosan* always says, "Hana-*chan*, we can't warm it up for you! Sorry!" Then he laughs and laughs. Sometimes he tickles her. *Otosan* is funny. Where is he? Where is *Okaasan?*

When Hanako thinks of them she feels pain, coldness, in her throat.

Hanako looks at the cookie. Now it is all wet with tears and breaking and a piece falls onto the carpet. She does not like this cookie, but she does like this kind of cookie. After their nap, *Okaasan* gives her three of them and a cup of milk. The cup is pink. It is Hanako's special one. No one else can use it. If she drops her cup, it won't break. It just bounces, which is funny. But if there is still milk in the cup when she drops it, then *Okaasan* says, "Oh, Hanako, what are you doing?" Pikkoro is on the cup. Pikkoro is a penguin. She is cute and funny. Hanako likes her. Every day, Hanako watches Pikkoro on the *terebi*. They sing songs together. They sometimes dance too. Pikkoro is on the *terebi*, and also on Hanako's cup. So the cup is very, very special.

The cup has two handles for Hanako's two hands. Hands, handles, hands, handles. *Otosan* says, "Both hands, Hana-*chan*." *Otosan* is fat. He is fatter than Pikkoro. On top of his head is red and sweaty. He is fat and funny. Where is he?

And the scratchy old man who is not funny but Hanako likes him anyway. Hanako remembers, and starts to tremble. Another piece of cookie falls on the carpet. A terrible motor noise, then bump, then falling and falling, then hurting and can't breathe, then crying so hard. But still the old man holding her. Where is he? Blue eyes, strange growly words, strange smell. Strange old man with scratchy hair on his face. Tickly

425

hair. Hanako didn't like the tickly hair, but she kind of liked it. Tickly, funny. Maybe the old man is funny too. Anyway, she likes him, and he likes her. If the scratchy old man gave Hanako a chocolate cookie, she would eat it. She would eat it the right way, without taking it apart first. And then she would say, *Domo.*

But Hanako will not eat this cookie. *No.* She won't, she won't, she won't. She hates this cookie. This cookie is from the girl who is a boy. She hates the girl who is a boy. The girl who is a boy isn't a real girl or a real boy. He isn't a person.

Miyajima Yoshinori, shortly after he joined *High School Jumping*, wrote a series of stories for that popular *manga*. The first episode concerned Doctor Fong, a mad genius, a counterfeiter, with a death's head face and mustaches like the tails of rats. Doctor Fong's ten thousand yen notes were impossible to distinguish from the real thing. He used the standard photochemical process, but with his own refinements: better paper, computer enhancing, plus some kind of sinister Mongol necromancy. First episode: *Fong, who considered himself a great artist, despised other counterfeiters, hated them, thought of them as dilettantes and bunglers. They were not worthy of the*

*name counterfeiter. Their very existence galled him—
to be classed with them, to be robbed by them. Robbed,
yes: every contemptible bank note they managed to
pass should have been one of his, for his were so
greatly superior. The injustice of it ate at him. Fong
would fly into terrible rages, deep in his subterranean
printshop/laboratory, crumpling their pitiful false
banknotes in his skeletal fist, dashing them to the floor,
trampling them.*

*Doctor Fong decided to eliminate his lowly
colleagues. He began seeking them out. This was not
difficult for a man of his genius and ruthlessness;
besides, they shared many contacts. His first victim
was Fujiwara, the Tokyo kingpin. One night, in a
Ginza side street, Fong clubbed him senseless then
pressed the man's hands against two squares of
Plexiglas labeled "left" and "right," afterward
carefully covering the finger and palm prints with two
other squares of Plexiglas, these slightly concave. He
taped the two glass sandwiches together and slid them
into close-fitting envelopes: the prints were safe.
Nothing could touch them.*

*Fong then robbed the unconscious counterfeiter,
making the attack look like a simple mugging, laughing
at the irony of it: the great Fong, filching a wallet full*

427

of crude, ugly, botched ichi man *notes. Fong would of course not wipe his boots with such garbage. It was a good joke.*

Back at the lab, Fong burned the offensive counterfeit bills, hit the switches, started up his machines, lit the Bunsen burners, set the retorts to bubbling. By an occult photochemical process, very similar to the one by which he crafted his masterly bank note plates, but using a different organic acid compound for the final etching, he was able to transfer Fujiwara's prints, perfectly, to the palms and finger pads of two surgical rubber gloves. Each tiny whorl and ridge and line. Each pore, even. The pores were real holes, permeable to perspiration and bodily oils. Fong donned the gloves, touched another pair of plates. He then spent a full hour peering into the microscope, comparing the two sets of prints. A hundred power, two hundred power, it made no difference. The prints were identical.

Two nights later, when Fujiwara had recovered and been released from hospital, Fong took his wickedly curved Triad killing blade, rolled on the special gloves, and began stalking the rest of his pitiable competition. One after the other, night after night, he killed them—all, of course, except Fujiwara.

How he hated them. How he loved driving the knife into their hearts, into their necks, twisting it, dodging away from the jet of crimson. Laughing and laughing. And managing always to leave a clear Fujiwara print or two for the police. Who dithered and fretted, worried and hesitated. But finally, when the last bungling counterfeiter had gone down before the blade, the police arrested Fujiwara, tried him— already a three-time offender—and imprisoned him for life at Sugamo.

Fong was triumphant. He had cleared the field.

He laughed until he wept, wept until he laughed once more.

One whole *manga* page was devoted to this climactic scene: Fong, arms aloft, head thrown back, his ghastly mirth echoing in giant majuscules off the walls of his underground domain.

The End.

But Yoshinori is distracted. What is wrong with little Hanako? Weep, weep, weep—a difficult child, no appreciation at all. Were she older, she would understand that her new friend is Someone, a storyteller of genius, creator of Fong.

Horrid Fong who, could he have but halted the bloodbath, would never have been caught. He couldn't, however; in the next episode, fans were not surprised to learn that Fong was once again up to his old tricks. *He had begun killing etchers and engravers at the Japan mint. Why? Because he came to hate these government workers also, to despise them for bunglers worse than the dead counterfeiters. Fong would hold a real bank note up next to one of his own and see, clearly and disgustedly, the former's relative inferiority: drab, sloppy, uninspired. Real bills were boring. Fong took them as a personal affront. He began to think of the mint workers as thick-fingered clowns trying vainly to copy him.*

Only one thing to do: break out the dread Triad blade.

As fast as he killed the mint workers, however, more were hired. He grew desperate, careless. For example, he continued to use the Fujiwara gloves. The police thus came to realize that they had somehow incarcerated the wrong man. Behind closed doors, Fujiwara was retried, pardoned, set free. Then Fujiwara the Nihon-jin began stalking Fong, the demon from the Middle Kingdom. Stalked him through seven pages and fifty-six panels, stalked him to his horrid laboratory, dueled with him hand to hand. Their battle to the death occupied five consecutive pages of *High School Jumping,* a record. *For a while the drug-crazed Mongol had the upper hand, but slowly, slowly, Fujiwara wore him down, knocked him unconscious— this punch took up a whole page all by itself: huge Fujiwara fist, deforming Celestial jaw, stupendous star-shaped shock waves—transfixed him with his own pitiless knife.*

The End.

You'd have been impressed by that one, Miss Hanako.

And much moreso, next episode: *even the opening scenes were bloody, horrific, the panels rendered with stark boldness. Undeterred by giant rats and a devilish array of booby-traps, Fujiwara dragged the Doctor's body through seven pages and sixty-one panels, up from the dank and loathsome cellar and down moonlit alleyways, throwing it at last into the Sumida river. Why? Then, gasping for breath, he telephoned police headquarters, told them of the fight, directed them to intercept the body. Why? Because... yes! Fujiwara is a detective lieutenant, who, working deep undercover,* had been framed and imprisoned, then vindicated and avenged, then finally promoted. A police hero.

But why had he thrown the body in the river?

Why, Hana-*chan?* Can you guess?

Next episode, three months later: *Fujiwara, at the wheel of a long, gleaming Rolls-Royce automobile. Why? How? Drinking champagne and smoking fat cigars. Laughing coarsely. A dire personality change, an ominous improvement in lifestyle—portending what? People whispered that Fong's devilish spirit had returned, taken over Fujiwara's body—rendering the good detective a vicious counterfeit of himself! That would be revenge indeed! Was Fujiwara in fact possessed?*

Perhaps. Anyway, perfect counterfeit yen were flooding the economy, so perfect that nobody even realized what was happening—only that there was much more money in circulation than there should have been. The Governor of Tokyo, the Prime Minister of Japan, pleaded with Fujiwara to do something. Pleaded unavailingly. Fujiwara couldn't or wouldn't— anyway, he didn't. Also, underworld figures were being butchered, and the prints were those of Doctor Fong. Had the wily Mongol returned from the dead? Impossible! The corpse was resting in the morgue cold-storage room. Did Fujiwara and others actually sight him at various locations, engaged in his grim butcheries? Or, likelier, were they lying? Or was Fujiwara indeed possessed by the Oriental, whose vengeance reached beyond the tomb? Or, finally, a much simpler explanation: has Fujiwara, tempted by infinite wealth, gone bad? For he has kept the key to the lab of Doctor Fong.

Even in death, Fong triumphed, corrupting Fujiwara, his nemesis.

Or maybe not. The fans didn't seem to like that.

Current episode, therefore; the question: *Is the intrepid policeman instead employing a cunning ruse, trying to lure the real evildoer, the Fong impersonator, out into the open? Who else has a key to the lab?* Many large-paneled pages bearing a highly ambiguous tale without words: *Fujiwara ransacking the lab for occult pharmaceuticals, ingesting these, reeling and staggering under their dire initial effects, clutching chairs and wardrobes in order to keep his feet, then, tentatively at first, tracking "Fong," catching glimpses of the hated black cloak just disappearing down vile alleyways, over moldering cemetery walls. But what is real? Are these actual sightings, or are they hallucinations brought on by the drugs? Why has*

433

Fujiwara been taking the drugs, anyway? In a brave but misguided attempt to give himself the Chinaman's own powers? Or has Fujiwara enslaved himself to these terrible potions out of foolhardiness and sheer bumbling curiosity? Is he using the drugs, or are the drugs using him? Is there a Fong impostor or not?

Clearly, either way, Fujiwara is flirting with insanity.

Final pages. *A worse question assaults then ravages his fevered brain: assuming that there is a Fong impostor, possessed of surgical gloves bearing Fong's fingerprints, then whose corpse is even now frozen in the morgue? Fong's or "Fong's"? Did Fujiwara kill the impostor, the double? Horrible possibility! And is the real fiend even now pursuing his nefarious designs, vampirizing the economic lifeblood of Japan? The economy, on whom so many "little" people—not least of whom sweet Sawako, Fujiwara's mistress—depend for the very rice in their bowls. Late one stormy night, Fujiwara, tormented by such questions almost beyond endurance, visits the morgue, lets himself into the freezer, slides open Fong's drawer, and... horrible!*

The cold room of a morgue is horrible, Hanako. Count your blessings.

Half-page panel: *the corpse grins evilly—is this merely death's rictus on a man who looked dead even when he lived and breathed? The pitiless blue lips are skinned back from the long yellow teeth, the slanted eyes are staring. Fujiwara whips out his magnifying glass. Something... what is it? There! Somehow they missed this before: on the corpse's left ear-lobe—is it a blue smudge? No. It's some kind of miniature tattoo, tiny letters...*

"FONG CLONE #426"

Fujiwara reels back from the sardonic ice-face. It's true, then: Fong succeeded in counterfeiting even himself. The real Fong is still on the loose, along with at least 425 facsimiles. Or more! Probably more. Possibly thousands. But no! Wait! Not necessarily! Why trust Fong? There could also be fewer clones than 425. In fact, there could be only one or two... or none.

Yes, there could be no clones. This thing in the drawer could be Fong himself. Because this is the sort of depraved trick Fong would play regardless, is it not? He would tattoo himself. To be certain, even in the event of defeat and death, of poisoning Fujiwara's fine spirit. Of destroying the policeman with horrors of doubt. Fujiwara, sentenced to life, never to know if he had won or lost. It is pure Fong, a stratagem of consummate villainy. Indeed, it is too hideous. Fujiwara grasps his forehead in a quarter-page panel as the realization sinks in. The policeman is astonished, paralyzed by this glimpse into the bottomless depths of his archfoe's perfidy.

Fong, the personification of evil.

Is this Fong, leering frozen in his drawer?... Or, is this Fong, in the guise of an emaciated morgue lab assistant, stealthily closing the freezer door— Fujiwara-san! Behind you!—upon our stunned and hapless detective?

To be continued.

Yoshinori chuckles. Don't worry, Hana-*chan*. I'll protect you.

Definitely to be continued. Fong and Fujiwara will duel again. Yoshinori has nearly completed the storyboard for the next episode: *the dead Fong is a clone, all right, and the real Fong has locked Fujiwara in the freezer, and Fujiwara does in fact freeze, face-to-face with the grinning corpse in the drawer. What thoughts does Fujiwara harbor in his last moments? None, as it turns out, or few, because he too is a clone. The real Fujiwara, clone-master on a par now with Fong himself, laughs triumphantly, clicks back the hammer on his police revolver, draws a bead on Fong just as that evil genius throws the locking lever on the freezer door. Fong whirls, raging, as the bullets tear through him, as one bullet, deflected, takes off the lobe of Fong's (or "Fong's") left ear...*

And so forth. Yoshinori will keep the two enemies locked in this increasingly arcane mortal combat, their various overt struggles often mere surface ripples indicating much deeper games-within-games. Fong and Fujiwara have been good to him. They have earned him a promotion, two raises, respite from the standard high school vendetta/good *chinpirra*-bad *chinpirra* scenarios, and a bigger byline. They have made Yoshinori mildly famous, and he has no intention of killing them off. He wouldn't if he could, and he can't. The fans wouldn't let him. During and between episodes he gets hundreds of letters, mostly subliterate but not all. Letters advising, pleading, demanding this or that plot-twist. These letters come to him care of *High School Jumping.* Recently, however, an even greater number of letters has been arriving, dumped twice daily on his desk, addressed to Inspector Fujiwara care of *him,* Yoshinori!

Hilarious. Everyone at work loves the letters. His coworkers joke with him, and he looks down shyly, smiling and blushing. (Of course, they all assume he's a homosexual, but they are so wrong; Yoshi likes girls, all right.) Even Mr. Matsuura, their *kai-cho,* so old and formerly so bleak, these days glowing with the tonic of big and regular *Jumping* circulation increases, occasionally grabs a fistful of the crazy correspondence and walks around between the desks and drafting tables, intoning, "Letter for Inspector Fujiwara! 'Urgent'!" And, "Letter for Doctor Fong, 'Private and Confidential!'"

Yoshinori likes the Fong letters best. Some are from unbalanced but devoted readers suggesting ingenious and brutal new anti-Fujiwara stratagems (a few of the eye-gouging best of which Yoshinori intends eventually to use, giving credit and a year's free subscription to *Jumping,* because Mr. Matsuura said that was all right and in fact a good idea). Most Fong letters are from earnest imbeciles warning the archcriminal of possible police entrapment (*"Keisatsu wa*—the cops, man, watch out for them fuckers they'll try to get ya like they got me I was just driving along in my van minding my own business doing my job and this lardass cop pulls me over, You're drunk he says I'm not I tell him you're full of shit but he gives me the fucking ticket anyway because he said I was drunk which was absolute bullshit because I can drink a lot more than that and not even feel it or show it in any way and then my boss found out and raised hell and nearly fired me, that's justice from the cops Fong so watch your ass, PS, Kill Fujiwara!!!"). And several dozen Fong letters were weirdly scrawled orders for pairs of the special fingerprint gloves.

Fans! Lunatics or morons. Or both. Whatever, Yoshinori loves them.

Fingerprint gloves—possible? Yoshinori doubts it. Otherwise they would be at the top of every criminal's shopping list. Which, so far as he knows, they aren't. So it is simply a case of meager intellects befuddled, unable to distinguish illusion from reality. Yoshinori never confuses the two. *But he knows that reality itself is part of the illusion.* He knows that the true reality is enclosed within the seemingly real, just as schoolboy Yoshinori rode around safe in the head of "Yoshinori," his flesh robot.

Yoshinori still inhabits "Yoshinori," but knows the day will come when he may cut himself free, may do for himself what he has done for the babies, out of love for them. Love, yes, though to a superficial observer it might not seem so. Love is, however, the reality of existence. The rest is hell, love's absence. And its presence? Where *is* love? Love lurks beneath flesh, below bone, past pain. When you seek after the heart of love, you have to use a knife. That's life, and the life beyond life: love must free love. Yoshinori glances again at Hanako, at the tears glistening on her round rosy cheeks. Hanako and her cookie. He smiles at her, a smile full of love.

Others are confused; Yoshinori is not. He deals in illusion, inhabits reality. He never even considered trying to make fingerprint gloves. No, his method was much more straightforward: he lifted the prints, over a period of weeks, from his father's fingers—his father of course passed out from alcohol.

Yoshinori got the idea when he pushed his mother down the stairs, breaking her neck but then having to kneel on her chest—what a look she gave him!—until she finally quit breathing. Wearing mittens, he simply took her wide black vinyl belt from her closet, jammed his father's limp hands one after the other on the front of it, slid it around the corpse's abdomen, took a photograph, removed the belt, carefully rolled it and placed it in a plastic Sanwa grocery bag, and hid the bag with his current logbooks. First the belt, then everything else he could think of that would take prints: matchbooks, gum wrappers, crumpled cigarette packs, coins, little packs of Kleenex, little leaflets with

whores' phone numbers, telephone cards, bus tickets—
any and all of the old man's debris which wouldn't be
missed. Oh, certainly, he also plucked hairs; scraped
dandruff and dead skin; collected tiny bottles full
blood (pricking the old man's finger-ends, milking
them), saliva, sweat, and semen (Yoshinori found,
under the seat of the squad car, a used condom,
knotted; he simply slid it into an ancient container of
orange juice concentrate and jammed the container
against the rear of their frost-clotted refrigerator
freezer). In all, quite a collection.

So, when he moved out, much of his father moved
with him. Yoshinori packed it all very carefully—
everything that wasn't already in the safe deposit
box—and took it along. Cartons and cartons of
evidence (for something; he didn't yet know what,
hadn't thought that far ahead), of logbooks, albums,
typescripts—his life's work. Sayonara, home sweet
home.

"And guess what, Hanako? I never went back."

Except for once, years later, in the spring. About
four a.m. he pulled the Carol into the old man's drive,
cut the engine, set the brake, and opened the rear deck.
Then he rummaged around in the carport trash till he
found what he wanted: sealed beneath a pile of

441

magazines and *shinbun* a carton of six empties, Old Parr. Squat, brown, bulbous bottles. Dustless, pristine. It had occurred to Yoshinori that, since his father had no further use for them, they might be recycled as crematory urns.

Saturday, 12:11 P.M.

"Hello?" On the tenth ring.

"Ah, Mr. Donner, you are home."

"Yes." Donner, out of breath from the stairs. "Who's this?"

"Perhaps you would care to exchange a few words with your wife?"

"Yes! Who *is* this? Who—who's speaking?"

"Donner, you idiot! Who the fuck do you think?"

"Ruriko! Where are you?"

"Here! Obviously. Somewhere. I don't know where. They've got me."

"Got you? Who?" Donner and Buddy, head-to-head, sharing the phone.

"Got me! Stole me away! These fucking weirdos. The guy hit me, and the next thing I know I'm tied up in this room with a God damn huge gag in my mouth. One of the weirdos made a grab for me and just about said good-bye to his dick. And all the while I'm thinking, What in the fuck is going on? What kind of Donner bullshit is this? And I'm thinking, Where was fucking Donner when I needed him—*did you stop off for a drink, you bastard?*"

"No, of course not, I don't—"

"And most of all I'm thinking, How's the baby?...
Hello? I said—"

Buddy, dashing from room to room, returning,
eyebrows up.

"I heard you. The baby is gone. The baby is not
here."

"You lost her? Donner, you moron!"

"I didn't lose her!

"Donner!"

"I said she's not here! I didn't say I lost her!"

"Donner! I'll kill you!"

"Somebody tried! He jumped me—pow! Out cold,
get the picture?"

"*Who* jumped you?"

"Right here! How do I know who? Assholes. And
by the time I finally—"

"You left her alone and you lost her! Oh, Donner,
you are the—"

"She's there! Whoever's got you has got the baby.
Think for a change."

"Donner, you cretin, she wasn't home then!"

"They *waited*, you stupid bitch! Must have. How
else—"

"What an asshole you are."

"Ruriko, I never hit you before, but—"

"Well, Mr. Donner, are you satisfied that was your wife?"

"Yes! Now who in the fuck—"

"Then here is what you will do. Listen carefully." Buddy and Donner head-to-head again, both still puffing and gasping like plow horses, Buddy scribbling in his little red spiral notebook. "Do you have a personal vehicle? No, according to your wife. So call for a taxi. Call no one else. Take the taxi to Hashimoto *eki*, Yokohama line. Board the 12:57 train northbound to Hachioji. If you are early, wait. You must be on the 12:57. Then change trains at Hachioji. Change again at Nishi-Kokubunji, the express for Mito. Stay on that train until someone takes your elbow and says, *'Oriru*, time to get off.' That's all. Now go. Oh, one thing more. Certain individuals will be on all those trains, watching you, to ensure that you come alone. If you do not, if some foolish confederate is detected, then no one will take your elbow and say, 'Time to get off.' You will ride to the end of the line, waiting for that to happen. But nothing whatever will happen, except to your wife."

"Don't hurt the baby!"

"Mr. Donner, do you understand your instructions?"

"Yes, I understand the instructions. What I *don't* understand is—."

"Please follow them. This call has lasted ninety seconds, much too short a time for you to have set up a trace, even had you been prepared to do so. Your only hope is to do exactly as you have been instructed. Exactly, without the slightest deviation. Hang up now and call for a taxi. Do not deviate, Mr. Donner, if you wish ever again to see your wife alive."

The Great Healer replaces his telephone receiver. Baby? Frowning, he glances up. "Tedzuka-*san*," he says. "For your patience, *domo arigato. N*ow you may kill her."

"Oh, Jesus, Buddy. What if they kill her? What are we going to do?"

"Fuck the cab for starters. My car's outside. Sweats are still in the trunk. Nikes are still in the trunk. You drive. I'll kind of hunker down in the back and change out of my uniform. Change into the sweats. Got blood on 'em, but maybe it won't be too obvious. I can limp, make it look like I fell or something, scraped a knee. We get to the station, I roll out, you go park the car someplace. Lock all my stuff back up in the trunk. You got a baseball cap or something, cover the GI haircut? Then presto, I'm just another slope jogger, right?"

"Here's Ruriko's from Do Sport."

"Pink, Jesus. But adjustable. Now let's get the hell out. Careful on the stairs, you dumb shit. Lock the door. I'll get my stuff out of the trunk. Get in the car, here's the keys, hit it, time is fleeting by, drive the car. Where was I? Okay, we get up to the platform separately, understand. Big crowd coming back from lunch, no problem. But you get on toward the front of the train, I'll get on toward the back. Maybe buy a *manga*, bury my nose in the fucking thing, but really I'm watching all the time, right? Because they might grab you *anytime,* not just after the second transfer— Donner, hello, are you following this?

"But after the second transfer I'm closing the distance. Casually, you know? Moving up. Till we're in the same car. Maybe I flop down in a seat, start snoring. But I'm watching you, watching that elbow— Donner, slow down! There's time! That was a cop back there. So if and when our boy makes his move, I'm on him. He grabs your elbow, I grab his. And I don't let go. What do you think? No, that's wrong, that's stupid, don't say it. Try again. Our boy makes his move—picture it. What happens? His people are waiting on the platform, whatever platform it is. I wake up just in time, get off just as the door shuts, scope out the situation, follow, jog, puff around, nobody'll look twice. So, the enemy. They'll probably march you over to some vehicle and cram you in there, unless they've got a helicopter, which they don't, or why fuck around with trains at all?

"Donner, it'll work, quit shaking your head. I hate it when you do that, you're so fucking negative. Grasp this: they're counting on time, whoever they are, they're thinking time is on their side, like you have no time to call anybody, no time to lay out any kind of decent military contingency plan, so you're running scared, you basically have to hustle your ass and do just like they told you. So they gotcha. But they're wrong, in a way we've got them. Little do they know. So really the advantage is with us. Don't panic, quit chewing on your God damned lips. They're not gonna kill her, guaranteed. They want something, they want to talk, they've got Ruriko for a lever. They want ink, they want airtime. For whatever. Save the whales, nuke the Emperor, doesn't matter. The bottom line is, they get ready to stuff you in the car, I swoop down and clean their clocks."

"Got a piece?"

"No piece, it's in my desk, but I got this tire iron."

"That'll have to do it, then."

"I can roll it up in a newspaper. Or a racing form."

"Got one for me?"

"No. But it's all right. I'll clean their clocks."

"I wish I knew what's going on. I wish I understood the situation."

"That's two of us. Welcome to the military. Welcome back."

"Some assholes with a noseful. Want to make a statement."

"That's it. Gotta be something like that. Saw you on the television."

"Saw me on the television, crawled out of the fucking woodwork."

"Yep, same old shit. But I'll clean their fucking clocks, Donner."

"I hope so. If they don't have about fifty guys."

"They won't, get serious. If they tried this shit with Janey—Jesus! They'd be dead already, unless they used a Tomahawk on her or something. Or a Cruise with the big warhead. The slaughter would be terrible. She would've already cleaned their clocks."

"Punched their tickets."

"Stamped their passports."

"Here we are, Bud. Get ready to hop. Jesus, orange sweats. Perfect for surveillance. Why orange? You look like a harvest moon."

"On sale. Janey got 'em, gotta wear 'em. But orange is good, right? Orange is reverse psychology, the gaudier the better. I'm the last one they're looking for. Use your lobes, Donner. Think like the enemy, put yourself right into his sick head. And bank on it. I'll clean their clocks but good. I'll eat 'em alive."

"Mash your shoes down at the heel. Don't tie 'em. Wear 'em like slippers."

"What is that, more authentic? Fuck that. These are new."

"Oh, Jesus, Buddy, I hope she's okay."

"Don't worry, she's a tough bitch. Us Japs are tough."

"Tough? Buddy! She's only *two!"*

Saturday, 2:06 P.M.

Buddy Nakamura, straphanging, still thinking on his feet, now literally. Feeling okay but looking not much like a senior officer in the Army of the United States. That of course being part the plan. Fast strategic thinking, a Nakamura specialty. And so far, so good. So far being the Niiza area, eastbound. Buddy is pretending to read his stupid *manga*, but don't worry: out of the corner of his eye he's watching Donner—at the opposite end of the same car—like a hawk.

Then the train stops, and here's this large herd of American diplobrats stampeding into their car, mashing Buddy against the far door. Highschoolers. Maybe up from that dump in Yamamochimai. Yap, yap, shriek, shriek, all at the same time, stoned on teen wonderfulness. Blonde curls, blue eyes, perfect rosy milky skin. Designer everything. Perfect teeth, or braces—or maybe braces *on* the perfect teeth, for that little added charge of grooving around with a twelve thousand dollar mouth. Perfect bodies, not an ounce of fat. Shit for brains. Typical of today's youth. The world is theirs, nobody else really exists in it, nobody else can speak English. And of course right away they start in with their witty remarks.

"Good Christ, lookit the size of this one. Does he stink, or what?"

"Big fat guy and his big fat comic. Biff, pow. Micromind."

"Hey, Darcy, quit pushin' me into him! Maybe he's a sumo."

"Use your eyes, dweeb. No greasy fag hairdo."

"Love the hat. Love the whole outfit, orange and pink."

"Real athlete, this guy. Just about ready for the Olympics."

"Marathon man. Got it under three and a half days."

"Great tits."

"Super gut."

"Wonder who ties his shoes?"

"Oo, gross abdomen. When was the last time he saw his dick?"

A *girl* says that! And they're all collapsing into each other and pissing themselves and yodeling, and Buddy thinks, Oh, Jesus, if they were only recruits.

Then they start whispering *dare ya dare ya,* and Buddy stiffens, tenses his whole body, because he knows what's next. He's braced for it: some daring alpha-asshole is going to get up his nerve—or *her* nerve!—and squirm through all the packed flesh and look him innocently in the eye and say, *Excuse me, sir, when was the last time you saw your dick?* And Buddy will have to smile apologetically and say, *Ah, so sorry, but I don-to speaking Eengureesh.*

Can he do it?

The back of Buddy's neck is hot, it's baking. His ears are on fire. A drop of sweat is hanging on his nose. His fingers are digging into the squashy fat comic, his eyes are riveted to the page. Sweat drips onto the bad *manga* punk, who is really an extraterrestrial, as he sneeringly draws a bead on the good punk, pow zap. Any second now: *Excuse me, sir, when was the last time*—and will Buddy be able to restrain himself from wasting the little bastard?

They're all crammed up against him so he can hardly breathe. He feels like saying to them, Back off. He feels like saying, Why aren't you little cocksuckers in school in the middle of the day? Are you playing hooky? He wouldn't put it past them. They felt like doing something, they did it. They felt like saying something, they said it. But not in Buddy's day, no sir. In Buddy's day it was different. Young people had some fucking respect. He feels like asking them, Hey, is that what me and Donner fought the Viet Nam war

453

for, and rotted in that fucking prison compound, and nearly got wasted by that fucking monster Thuong? To amuse a bunch of spoiled little rat-bastards like you? So you could grow up in the lap of luxury and then have a wonderful time with all your TOTALLY UNCALLED-FOR REMARKS OF A HIGHLY PERSONAL NATURE?

Buddy feels like saying those things and quite a bit more. But he doesn't. He's got the old Nakamura control, another trademark. He puts the tip of his tongue between his teeth and bites down, doesn't say word one. Because, of course, if he did, there would go his cover, wouldn't it?

For whoever is watching. And he has to assume someone is.

When? *Excuse me sir...* Fortunately, a change of topic:

"So we're in the lab, and we throw our frogs against the wall."

"Oo gross, Courtney."

"Alaric and them. Me too. We're fucking around with the scalpels and basically shredding the frogs anyway, so finally we're all like, fuck it, and splat."

"Yuck city, Courtney."

"Hey, dork, that's biology. You don't like it, take *world literature.* So then we scooped 'em back on the trays, looked okay to me, just like the manual. But Gorsic seen us."

"Gorsic, ho."

"Yeah, poor old fuck, knocks down like forty a year if he's lucky, comes waddling on over, and he's like, 'Boys, you really shouldn't chunk your frogs against the wall like that. That's the lazy man's way. Lab is supposed to be a learning experience.' And I'm like, 'Yeah, right.' So he's like, 'Yes it is. You're supposed to dissect out every little organ, the way I showed you, just like I do.' And I'm like, 'Mr. Gorsic, what's your time worth?'"

That's really funny too, of course. Laughing, screaming, staggering around all jammed together in their perfect little teen dream-bubble. They'd fall down if there was room. Teacher's probably a veteran, they don't give a shit. Buddy's control is fraying. He's just about to initiate hostilities—and suddenly they're gone.

Train stops, door opens, diplobrats surge out, and that's it.

Relief.

Except Donner's gone too!

455

Buddy missed the contact. Where—there! Thank God. There they are, on the platform and walking briskly, the guy with his hand on Donner's elbow, just like he said. Buddy leaps for his own door, following the A.S.O.J. brats—and sprawls on his face halfway through! His legs are paralyzed! They refuse to move separately. He kicks them, there's no independence of function. And here come the doors, closing on his kidneys, *brump*, that hurt, open a ways, catch him again, *brump*, and there's Donner at the exit already and the highschoolers passing them on the stairs, running flat-out, hysterical, and it begins to come together for Buddy as the doors catch him again, *brump*, and a bell starts ringing somewhere, and he pulls his knees to his chest and rolls out and onto the platform, then works himself to a sitting position and remains thus immobile for a full ten seconds, gasping, and looking at his Nikes. At the bright green nylon shoelaces. Joined by two neat tight squareknots.

Sit there and work out the knots?

With what—his teeth?

Fuck that, Buddy's not a full colonel for nothing, he rips off the shoes and hangs them around his neck, scrambles up—there goes his change all over the platform, of course—and sprints sockfooted for the exit.

And stops short at the top of the stairs. Big line at the fare adjustment window. Buddy has to wait. He can't go through the automatic gate like the highschoolers because he has no pass, and his ticket is for the wrong fare, because how could Buddy know where Donner'd be getting off? So he'll have to make up the difference. Barge on through! No, he can't call attention to himself. Well, Donner and the nutbar have to wait too. There they are, up ahead. He doesn't take his eyes off them for a second. The guy is thin, comes about to Donner's shoulder, maybe forty-five fifty, glasses, looks like a wimp, coat draped over his right hand, holding a piece for sure.

The guy swivels around, Buddy crouches down. The guy turns back, says something to Donner. Donner nods. The guy casually fires up a cigarette, nervy bastard. The smoke curls up then drifts back toward Buddy. He catches a whiff. It smells good. Buddy wishes he had a cigarette—plus thirty seconds with each of the highschoolers and a good brick wall to throw them into. He pictures their healthy pink organs, neatly labeled—"Liver," "Pancreas," "Ovipositor"— some adhering to the wall, some sliding slowly down,

subsiding into the scarlet garbage at its base. Take a
puff, strangle a little bastard with his own shoelaces,
then splat, then another puff. Real smoking
satisfaction.

Is Buddy really that bloodthirsty? No, and probably
that's his problem.

The line inches forward, shuffle, shuffle.

Buddy's impatient, but he's also really winded, so
a little shuffling at this point is in order. That standing-
start sprint up the stairs, Jesus. He can feel his heart,
it's like someone is hitting him on the chest with a
hammer, and his lungs are full of fiery cinders—okay,
okay: Donner's right. Command decision: Buddy *will*
quit smoking, and very soon, or at least cut right down.
Relatively enormous, purple-faced and literally
steaming, Nikes around his neck, orange Buddy grabs
huge, ragged sobs of air, all the while trying to remain
inconspicuous.

Still thinking on his feet, though, still formulating...
What's he going to use for money?
It's all over the platform down there!

Go back for it? Not feasible, there's a dozen people
behind him already, more coming up the stairs. Borrow
it from someone? Also negative, he can't even
remember the word for "lend." Or "money." Give the

guy at the window some story? *Sorry, but I'm just a dumb foreigner and I lost my change and I can't speak Japanese for shit.* All true, but how will the guy understand him, and if he did understand, why should the guy believe him? Probably a cynical fucker, hears bullshit lines all day. Which anyway work only for roundeyes. And how long would it take, all this talk, and where would Donner and his new friend get to in the meantime? Donner—weird, neurotic as hell, boring beyond his years—who also however saved Buddy's life once, in the crunch. And who is counting on him right now. Buddy flashes on his own big bones, gleaming in the gullygrave.

Shuffle, shuffle. Colonel Nakamura, shuffling forward in his tube socks.

His socks! Of course! He usually keeps a couple bills—why didn't he think of this earlier?—tucked in there for emergencies. Maybe… Buddy, hopping on his left foot, bumping into the little old women ahead of him—sorry, "Gomenna-sigh," that means sorry, give them a nice smile—yanking off his right sock, feeling it… nope. Buddy, smiling, wheezing like a hippo, just as glad the highschoolers are nowhere around to see this, hopping on his right foot, yanking off the other sock, feeling it, peering into it, feeling it again along the whole length of it, shaking it upside-down… nope, nothing, nary a rustle. Colonel Nakamura, war college superstar, tactical hotshot, now standing barefoot on the cold concrete, pockets inside out, shoes around his neck, socks in his hands.

God damn it.

"Gomen-nasai." The tiny old women ahead of him, touching his wrist, pointing down, chittering like sparrows. *"Okane."*

Okane! Means money! And there it is, all wadded up like a Chiclet, right between Buddy's giant feet! He must have dropped it. A thousand yen, two thousand, maybe three, all stuck together and sweat-soaked, but whose problem is that? Not Buddy's, that's for sure, as he shoves it all under the grill with his ticket, and turns to say *domodomo* to the wonderful old ladies one more time, with a winning smile and a very polite bow.

Where's Donner?

The fare exchange bastard, no expression, a robot, diddles his machine and shoves back Buddy's receipt, a thousand yen note, some coins, and a tubesock.

Where's Donner?

Buddy dashing to the head of the stairs, looking down for any sign of Donner—where, where, where?—nearly crashing into the old ladies, who are

460

saying good-bye to each other and very elaborately, bowing like a couple of toy drinking birds, perpetual motion, chirping at each other a mile a minute, trying to out-nice each other, meanwhile of course nobody can go anywhere, the old bitches are blocking the stairway. Nobody can come up, nobody can go down. God damn them, they have to say good-bye right here, nowhere else will do, and the rest of the world can go fuck themself is the idea. And what's Buddy supposed to do? Wait till they run out of sweet things to say to each other? Push them out of the way, maybe waste them in the process more or less accidentally? Buddy edges around them, *domodomo,* big smile. "I am an American," he says, sort of bellying them out of the way as they crane their necks up at him then exchange a sour look and a nod: an American, that explains it.

Buddy bulling down the stairs scattering natives.

Buddy out on the sidewalk.

Where's Donner?

Where's Buddy? The man—only one? Why only one? Where are the others? Shouldn't there be others? The man, the contact, is poking Donner in the spine with a hard blunt object which Donner has to assume is a handgun, is shoving Donner into a car—white, of

461

course, maybe a Nissan?—in the underground lot, of a department store, he thinks. Seiyu? Seibu? One of those. Donner knows he should be making voluminous mental notes, but, to tell the truth, he's been hustled along so fast that the details are all blurred. Minami-Urawa, all right, that's the name of the town, at least. South Urawa. So, in a rough and theoretical way, Donner knows where he is.

He does not know where he's going, or with whom, or why.

He does not know where Buddy is.

Donner in the passenger seat. The man throwing handcuffs into Donner's lap, gesturing with what is indeed a handgun, a little automatic, maybe .25 caliber—Beretta? Donner with the left cuff on and the right ready to click in place, the gunman keeping the automatic leveled at Donner, easing into the driver's seat, feeling for his keys. Starting car, fastening seatbelt, locking door. All by touch, eyes never leaving Donner. Who clicks the cuffs together and pretends to fasten the right cuff. The gunman is not fooled. He switches gun hands, to his left, and lashes out—once, twice, the blows having little effect, the first catching Donner on the right cheekbone, the second on the shoulder. The gunman draws his hand back again, when suddenly everything inside the car is diamonds—diamonds or what seem to be diamonds but is of course broken glass, spraying and shimmering into the passenger compartment, sparkling on the gunman—on his shoulders, chest, thighs—shivers of glass everywhere, as Buddy raises the tire iron once more.

Buddy's bulk suddenly illuminated, turning toward a roaring light and stepping back at the same time throwing his tire iron at the rushing grill of another white sedan as Donner finds himself wrenching at the little automatic with his cuffed left hand while gouging with his right thumb up, up, up under the man's jaw, and somehow all this activity goes forward in the tiny interval before the second car crashes into their own and makes everything stop, even thought. Stop inside a huge resonating gong that shoves Donner against the dash and traps him there for several stretched seconds.

Buddy now at the wheel of a delivery van, a *takubin*, turquoise and beige, with the black momma cat carrying the kitten in her mouth, the idea being that the tender *takubin* people will move your stuff just that gently. Maybe it's true, and Buddy wishes he could've been gentler with the little *takubin* driver. Buddy's seen plenty of these vans before, never driven one, certainly never stolen one.

Buddy, wheeling the boxy little rig around corners, jamming it through the gears, breaking many other laws, he's sure, besides grand theft auto. Donner on the passenger side, down on the floor with the first villain, the older one, right on top of the guy, roaring at him, spraying him with spit, the guy flat on his back, looks like he's trying to climb up under the dash. WHERE IS SHE WHERE IS SHE, Donner really pressing the point, *DOCHIRA DOCHIRA* WHICH WAY. The guy's pants are down around his ankles, and Donner's working on him like somebody trying to start an outboard motor.

How about some music? Buddy punches the buttons, twists the knob, trying to get the Far East Network, crank it way up, drown out the screams.

"Next left!" Donner yells. "Follow the signs to the highway! Then north!"

"Left and north!" Buddy downshifts, hauls on the wheel.

"About six kilometers!"

"Six it is!"

"Watch for the sign, Shanglira love hotel."

"Love hotel it is!" Buddy gears up. "By the way! Where's F.E.N.?"

"Effie? Effie?"

"F.E.N.! Eight-ten, maybe? Or eight-ninety? Can't find it!"

Donner ignoring him, very busy with the guy, WHO'S GOT HER WHAT ARE THEY DOING TO HER, going to rip the guy's balls right off. Buddy looks back at the road, feeling not too great. All in all, he's just as glad to be driving. Really, Donner hasn't mellowed all that much.

Buddy didn't even want to boost this van. But, say they didn't show up wherever: what happens to Ruriko? Transportation, they had to have it, and this was it. Guy pulls up to the service elevator while they're still staggering around and shaking off the broken glass. He's making a delivery, whatever. Timing was good, at least from Buddy's point of view. From the driver's point of view, of course, maximum bad. Little driver, now cuffed in the back of his own van and bouncing around on his own parcels, probably wondering if he'll ever get to deliver them. Well, sure, but none of this is Buddy's fault. He's doing his best, and that's pretty good, except for that minor glitch at the station, which is history. Both cars smashed up,

465

radiators drooling, fenders mashed against the wheels. So what choice did Buddy have? None. Liberate the van, carry out the mission, keep soldiering on.

But, Jesus, what was he trying to *do,* the backup man, the kamikaze? Squash Buddy? Fat chance, Buddy's way too fast. Little extra ballast, so what? Buddy's agile, and that's a fact. Backup nearly put himself through the windshield. Some backup. Twenty year old fuckup in a rock concert T-shirt: purple-haired gutscreamer, green eyes, pink mike. Punk still out cold, tied up with his own belt and now bouncing along beside the little driver. When the punk wakes up, he better lie there very still, pretend he's still out, or he'll have to talk to Donner too. The screams are really bad now because they're almost inaudible. Guy's got no voice left, just a kind of hoarse whistling noise. Buddy looks for the love hotel sign. Where's Ruriko? He punches the buttons some more. Where's F.E.N.?

Saturday, 2:32 P.M.

Kobayashi Miyuki tries again. Perhaps she got the number wrong.

She could have, easily. She is so tired. She is weeping with tiredness.

Miyuki sighs, shudders, tries pulling herself together with a therapeutic fantasy, one of her favorites: she is Sailor Moon, the *manga* heroine whom nobody can really destroy, because of her super powers and because of *Takushido no Kamen-sama,* the Masked Boy in the Tuxedo, who always manages to be around just when Moon needs to be dragged from slavering jaws. Uncle Makoto is Miyuki's *Kamen-sama.* She is his Sailor Moon. Together they will battle against Yoma, evil in its numberless manifestations, and they will triumph, yes, won't they? Or maybe they won't…

No good, Miyuki shudders again, breaks the connection.

She tries once more. She lets it ring and ring…? Ah, *zannen.*

No answer at Donner *sensei's.*

They are probably out shopping, she hopes.

Hana-*chan*—will she like the doll?

467

Miyuki is so tired. Sleep is flickering around the edges of her awareness. The Dream is waiting. Hiroji drove back from Ebisu while Miyuki catnapped, and it was the Dream again—how long does it take in real time? Five seconds? Ten? The dream, but this time worse: at the end, she and the Monster somehow changed places, herself on top, crushing the van, and the Monster himself inside. And when the fangs punched through the metal they were hers.

Saturday, 2:48 P.M.

Off the highway, too fast down this gravel road, the old guy on the floor twitching and whispering out directions now on his own, spontaneously, Donner just translating. Buddy and Donner very alert, scanning the roadway and both sides. Buddy slowing now, turning off on a lane and winding through a stand of bamboo, sun-dappled and dusty. Cloud cover thinning. Wood smoke in the still air. Then the bad old memory ambushes him: Buddy and Donner, trussed up in the back of Thuong's truck, bouncing along to the skull gully, all those wide white grins of welcome. Buddy rams those images back down where they belong—hey, who's driving today, and who's tied up in back?—downshifts for a steep little hill, then eases around a hairpin driveway into a farmyard.

Which is cut into the base of the hill: on the right, a high, mossy, fieldstone wall. To the left, perfect little fields of gray rice straw stubble. A cat on the well-cover. No dog. No chickens, no pigs. Little family cemetery: smudged black stone, rusted railings in a square enclosing the wooden sticks like big tongue depressors and holding them upright. Tiny red shrine on concrete blocks. Old wooden farmhouse, all

469

shuttered up, no paint, tile roof. Tractor shed, tin roof. Smell of old manure, old wood in the sun. Up ahead, a big stone barn, thick little window-hatches open, wooden door opening too now, and a man coming out. Coming out fast. Tall guy, furious, squashy-looking, shaped like a pear. Wearing a robe of some kind, blue and gold. Forty, forty-five, some gray in his beard, big eyes getting huge as he sees Donner leave the cab and move on him.

Guy turns, stumbles for the door, tries to get back inside, almost makes it. Donner tackles him, gets both knees in the guy's back, gets a fistful of the guy's long hair, yanks his head around and jams the little automatic in the guy's eye—*in* his eye, right in there, the muzzle digging in a full half-inch, the guy sort of shrieking, and then Donner, WHERE IS SHE WHERE IS SHE, while Buddy sets the brake, jumps out, dashes past.

Buddy's through the door, suddenly it's dark, a smell of hay and old piss, the cool feel of packed earth on his bare feet. Stalls of some kind along the far wall, a shaft of sunlight poking in through the little window in the loft. He's peering and blinking, trying to see— and he trips, he's down, he's not hurt, he just rolls out of it, looks back, tries to make out what it was he tripped over. And it's a long sort of package, some old blue sheet wrapped around and tied with yellow nylon cord in a sort of running stitch down the length of it, from head... to toe.

"Donner, gimme your knife."

Buddy with Donner's prized Gerber single blade, working on the ropes. Donner dragging the guy in the robe through the doorway by his hair, pistol-whipping him, throwing him down beside the package, the guy saying, "Oh, Jesus, my eye!"—a kind of strange thing for a Japanese to say. Buddy now has two of the ropes off and the sheet ripped away from the... head. Which is Ruriko's, staring. Not much blood, but the face is bad, smashed, forehead caved in, mouth all twisted around from a broken jaw. Buddy and Donner kneeling there in the dirt, looking. An ant comes out of her hair and starts across her left eye.

And Donner says to the guy, "Your eye hurts? I'll fix it."

And he jabs his thumb in the guy's left eye and scoops it out, the guy is arching his back, screaming, flopping around.

Donner gets his thumb in the guy's *other* eye, gouges right on in there.

"You speak English. Where is the baby?"

Donner's got his left hand around the guy's windpipe and his right thumb past the nail in the corner of the guy's right eye. The left eye is hanging by a few shreds, and the memories come surging back, stronger, more real, the last twenty years shimmering and dreamlike, and Buddy feels the need to vomit.

"Where is the baby?"

And the guy, "What baby?"

And Donner, "The baby!" Jabbing deeper, to the first knuckle.

And the guy, "Corner!" Flailing around, pointing, splattering blood.

"Buried?" Donner's voice breaks.

"Yes!"

"How—how long?" Donner's crying now.

"About eighteen months!"

Donner looks like somebody slapped him. "Well then fuck you," he says, much quieter, and rips out the other eye.

Saturday, 2:59 P.M.

"Moshi moshi?"

"Moshi moshi—er, hello. Kobayashi-*san?* Donner *desu."*

"Ah, Donner *sensei!* I just tried to call you, maybe one-half hour since. So, you are home again. *Genki desuka?"*

"Well, actually we're not home. We're in Urawa."

"Urawa? Far up there?"

"Somewhere around Urawa. An old farm. And we're not very *genki."*

"No? What is wrong?"

"My wife has been murdered."

"Murdered! And the baby—"

"Hanako—"

"Hanako—"

"—is, well, she's gone."

"Gone!" The icy fist. "Do you mean…?"

"Gone, Jesus. Maybe kidnapped, I don't know. Anyway, not here and not home. Also here—where we are now? Some problems. My friend and I—do you remember Buddy? Colonel Nakamura? We were wondering, basically, well, what to do. In the States, we'd know, but here? We're not so sure."

"I know well. First thing, have you yet telephoned to the police?"

"Not yet. You see, that's one of the things—"

"Do not. I will telephone them for you. Where are you calling from?"

"A farm. A van in a farmyard. There's a phone in the van."

"A van?"

"Takubin. We stole it, so we could find the baby. Not really stole, just borrowed. The driver is here. He's just upset, not hurt. Well, he's hurt, but he's okay, basically. But he's the only one who is. I mean, everyone else is mostly dead, some maybe buried."

"Mr. Donner! Are you in danger right now?"

"Maybe. Buddy thinks so. He says the others might be along soon, we have to assume that. Whoever they are. So he's in the bamboo, watching the road. Buddy has the piece—the gun."

"Mr. Donner! Can you tell me how to get there?"

"Matter of fact, yes. From Minami Urawa *eki?"*

"I know it, of course. Tell me quickly. I am taping to you."

The baby! The monster! Kobayashi Miyuki does not even hang up. Merely she breaks the connection with her finger, then punches in the number she knows well—Uncle Makoto's. Thinking helicopter helicopter.

Saturday, 3:51 P.M.

"*Matte kudasai!*" Yoshida Makoto shouts. "Wait till the rotors slow!"

His niece sits, tensed forward, her hand on the door latch. They look out through the Plexiglas bubble, at the *takubin* van, the buildings, the fields. Remote. An isolated old farm. Smoke drifting, no animals, nothing moving, no one.

Ah, someone, a man, a foreigner, from the surrounding bamboo. No gun.

"Donner-*sensei!*" Miyuki opens the door, climbs to the ground, crouches and runs through the swirling dust and bits of straw. Her cameraman follows. Yoshida lifts the automatic rifle from its bracket between the front seats. He waits, still watching.

Another man, a very large *Nihon-jin.* From the opposite direction. Gun.

The man shades his eyes, looks for a long moment at the helicopter, at the Tokyo Police logo on the fuselage. The man holds the pistol by the barrel, holds it up for Yoshida to see, then pops the clip loose and holds that up too, then stuffs it in the pocket of his bright orange sweatpants. The man works the action of the pistol, sends a bright cartridge spinning to the dust.

Yoshida nods.

He climbs down, the rifle slung on his left shoulder. The rotors have stopped. He walks toward the group of three men and his niece.

"My name is Yoshida Makoto, Captain, Tokyo Metropolitan Police."

"Colonel Nakamura, U.S. Army." *Not* a Japanese. Huge hand out.

"Donner." Tall, stooped, balding, speckles of dried blood on his *megane* lenses. Left arm around Miyuki's waist. She is leaning into him, her face tight with trying not to cry. Bloody right hand shaking Yoshida's.

"Mr. Donner. I saw you last night on the television, catching that baby."

"Yes, well, that's the problem. The baby. She's missing or maybe just lost, somehow. Anyway, we don't know where she is. That's part of the problem. We called Miss Kobayashi."

"And she called me. Have you called anyone else?"

"No. We took cover and waited. For whoever."

"You didn't call the local police, or ambulance, or anything?"

"No, I just told you that. Now, this is the situation, which makes no sense. My wife was killed here, in

477

there, the barn—or maybe killed somewhere else and brought here. And she's not alone."

An old stone barn, solid, the outside in good repair.

Inside, Yoshida blinks, wrinkles his nose at the stench of blood, cloying and rich, and of rotting flesh, hideously sweet. He is familiar with both smells.

On the dirt floor, a wrapped corpse; a woman's face, battered.

"Your wife?"

"Yes. Ruriko."

Crumpled beside her, a bearded man, bloody, eyeless, breathing.

"Who?" Yoshida knows, but asks anyway.

"No idea," says the *Nihon-jin* looking man, the American colonel. The tall man, Donner, shrugs, points back toward the door. In the shadows on either side of the door, two more twisted forms. Yoshida walks over. The bodies of a young man and an older one. Yoshida crouches for a closer look. Faces battered, gashed. Necks nearly severed. "No idea who they are either," says the colonel. "Maybe they worked for the bearded one?"

The cameraman begins panning from side to side. The camera whispers. Its bluish light picks out the bodies in sharp detail—an eye, a shirt collar sticking up.

Yoshida looks away from the light, shakes his head.

"There was a… fight," says Donner.

"Fight? This one's arms are tied behind his back. And this one—"

"Yeah, well." Donner shrugs again. "That one." He gestures over to the eyeless man. "He said the baby was *buried*, you know, and I said, buried how long, and he said, *eighteen months*—I thought maybe he was trying to be funny, a joke, who knows? It cost him the other eye. Then I took that shovel off the wall and started digging. Thinking, you know—well, not really thinking anything, just throwing dirt as fast as I could, and Buddy's right where this clown is now. Buddy's got the piece, he's covering the doorway."

"Right," says Nakamura. "What's coming through next, is the question."

"I'm throwing dirt. It's loose, I'm getting down fast. Because the thing is, when people are buried, and they're not quite dead, they can live for a while."

"Right," says Nakamura. "Hours sometimes. You'd be surprised."

479

"Especially if they're unconscious and not breathing much, the oxygen lasts. So I thought, well, maybe."

"Nothing to lose," says Nakamura.

"That's it, nothing. But then I got down a couple feet, and it hit me, the smell hit me in the face, climbed right up the shovel and grabbed onto me. Eighteen months, he wasn't kidding, and, well, Jesus, it was—it was just like…"

"Like Nam," says the big one, Nakamura.

"Just like Nam," says Donner. "When everything crumbled away, and you crumble away from yourself, and there's just nothing and you're nothing, there's no reason for anything, no meaning at all, and it's the worst thing in the world. I mean the worst. I mean just nothing. Do you understand what I'm saying?"

Nakamura nods.

Yoshida, Miyuki, and Hiroji the cameraman shake their heads.

"Well, anyway, I lost it there for a minute or two, is the point. I hauled these clowns out of the van and did 'em. Did 'em with the shovel, right there. Dragged 'em in here afterward. Too bad for them."

"Except that they could have told us something," says Yoshida.

"Well, yeah, except for that."

"And the driver of the van?" says Miyuki. "You said…"

"Yes, the driver," says Yoshida. "Did you kill him too?"

"No! Little bump on the head," says Nakamura. "He's okay."

"Where *is* the driver?"

"Still in the van. Handcuffed. Don't worry about him."

Sound of a starter motor, grinding and stopping, grinding again.

Donner, pivoting toward the sound, dropping to a half-crouch.

Sound of an engine catching, sputtering and coughing, dying.

Donner in the lead, the others all stuck, jostling in the doorway.

Sound of a starter motor, grinding. Sound of an engine catching, revving.

Saturday, 3:58 P.M.

With a trembling hand, Sawada Ginroku replaces his cellular telephone. He is deeply shocked. He has just encountered real greed. Of course he assumed that Tokyo Dome would be expensive—but *that* expensive? He didn't want to *buy* it, after all—just rent it, just for one little day. But oh, the money. And all up front. No token sum down and the rest covered by their cut of the gate. Oh, no. Not possible, so sorry. Not for someone like Ginroku, an "unknown." (The T-shirt king—"unknown"!) Now, if Ginroku were a gangster, well, that might be different. Tokyo Dome, Yakuza Dome. But Ginroku isn't some hoodlum, some scummy crook. He's just a struggling businessman. Therefore, money in front for Ginroku. Or forget it.

So it looks like he'll just have to forget it, the idea of a lifetime.

Ginroku vents a long shuddering sigh.

Why didn't he call the Dome-heads, *first?* Why did he save them for *last?* Everyone else is in place, more or less, Penn's agent sounding tough but definitely interested, the musicians of course on board whether they realize it or not, things clicking into place, faxes starting to come stuttering in, his machines all this time barfing out T-shirts by the thousands, the whole deal starting to steam and hum. But then stopped dead by the Dome. Four hours, wasted. Two, three hundred thousand yen for the phone bill, wasted. Ginroku's genius, wasted.

Eeeeyahdah! And it felt so right! It could have worked!

"Mizowari!" he barks and watches his mild wife scramble for the Cutty.

His commercial too. It could have been great, a classic. Wonderful concept: Penn, sure, but also some *burikko*, a Tokyo girl, maybe what's her name, Ginroku's favorite punch. There they are, zoom: both wearing The Shirt. They're sort of nuzzling each other: East meets West. Then angle on her from the back— hair up, gorgeous ass—and him from the front, maybe a little bulge there. The front of the shirt is of course the famous picture of the falling baby and what's his name the foreigner, with "Help Hanako" in panic-pink kid-scrawl along the foreigner's outstretched arm and "Photo By Hashikura Taiyo," in script below the picture. Dynamite front. The back is great too: in computer block printing, on the left,

```
H        O
A        F
N        F
A        I
K        C
O        I
         A
S        L
H
O        S
T        T
         A
         T
         S
```

On the right, in a column, the place, date, time, light intensity, camera and model, shutter speed, film and developing techniques, lens—everything, specified and quantified to the nth degree. Techno-Truth.

That's good enough by itself, but there's more: the *burikko* bites Penn on the ear and whispers something. He laughs and says, *Sure... after the concert.* Then a warm, caring voice-over: *The Help Hanako Concert. See you there.* Penn and the bimbo turn to the camera, smile, turn back for another quick nuzzle. Fade.

Thirty seconds. A great concept.

Super-great, because both of them would be working for free.

Super-super-great, because, as Ginroku just now realizes, he could easily take a still from the video— it's his, right?—and turn it into yet another million-selling shirt! Or two stills, or three! A galaxy of breath-taking possibilities! A whole Hanako industry, right there, waiting! Waiting for some Napoleon of commerce. Waiting for him, Ginroku.

God damn it!

He grabs the whiskey and water from his wife, drains it savagely.

"Anata, why are you crying?"

"Shut up!"

Manfully, he bats the tears from his cheeks, too down even to punch her.

True, he still has the Asshole concept, a potential minor gold mine. He just whipped down his trousers and sat on the copier, faxed it over to what's her name for a workup on the drawing board and from there right to the machines. A near-record in terms of speed. Therefore tomorrow, and for the next few months, certain individuals will go into a buying frenzy—THE PERFECT GIFT FOR THE PERFECT ASSHOLE—all of them crazy to present each other with high quality, pre-shrunk enlargements of Ginroku's anus. The hemorrhoids for color and a highlight on the big one, makes it really stand out, a nice touch, yes—but what's the bottom line here? A few million yen. Hardly a consolation for losing the Hanako concept. Which is, as the Americans say, no go. No commercial, no concert, no billion yen.

"Oh, *Anata*, look."

No moment of greatness. No fame. For the King, poverty and obscurity.

"Look, *Anata,* the *terebi*. There you are again."

Ginroku looks. He blinks away the tears. No, it can't be. It is!

Ginroku is half out of his chair, eyes bulging. No! Yes! It's the *same interview!* They're running it *again!* And after he called them and screamed at them and threatened legal action and called them a slimy bunch of rotten syph-sucking sons of a rat-assed little *burakumin* monkey-whore, and he got cut off, so he called again and screamed some more! And they're still running it! WHY?

"—thousand yen only!" says the smiling and handsome tube-Ginroku.

"FIVE thousand! FIVE thousand! FIVE FIVE FIVE!" he roars tubeside.

"And how much for Hanako-chan?" asks the obnoxious newskid.

"How much for who?" Tube-Ginroku's winning smile fades; he frowns.

"Her." Faggot newskid jabbing Ginroku's tit. "The orphan. Hanako."

"Not decided. Not yet. Not decided yet."

Ginroku hurls his automatic cigarette lighter at the tube, full force.

The lighter bounces off, hits the carpet, skitters.

Ginroku falls back into the chair, his jowls gusting with impotent fury.

"... just a few minutes ago. Severely injured and in custody, Takeshita Satoshi, 48, detained last year by Captain Yoshida Makoto of the Tokyo Metropolitan Police in connection with the disappearance of the lawyer Iidzuka Masanori and his wife and infant son... Zenbu-kyo... searching the area... dead are tentatively identified as Donner Ruriko, 45, Tedzuka Keiichiro, 50, and his son Masao, 21... arrest by Captain Yoshida, who has also stated that two year old Hashimoto Hanako, rescued yesterday, is today reported missing and feared kidnapped."

Kidnapped!

No! That's the last straw. No concert, no commercial, and now no kid!

Why, God?

Stop. Wait. Calm down. Think. Kidnapped? That's good not bad. That's more reason than ever to have a concert. Not, *Help* Hanako. *Save* Hanako. Not a billion yen. Two billion, maybe three. The rescue of the century. Save Hanako. Save her, buy the T-shirt, go to the concert, buy the video, buy the LP laser disc, buy the Hana-*chan* doll that screams if you drop it, buy every single spin-off that Ginroku can dream up in the next year. Buy it all, everything, the whole package.

"Oh, *Anata,* how can the Healer also be a killer?"

Forget the commercial? Forget the concert? *Chigau!* FUCK NO!

"Oh, *Anata,* poor little Hanako. Has he got her, the monster?"

But the money—how to get it without stripping the flesh from his bones?

"Oh, *Anata,* look! I can now redesign my kitchen using virtual reality."

How? How to do it? Who? Who will furnish that that up-front money? Who will get him the Dome for one glorious day? Ginroku sits, hearing and seeing nothing. Then he smiles, a widening smile. Not a cocky grin, no. Rather, an expression of open-mouthed astonishment, of rapture, of humble thankfulness at this latest glimpse of the awesome dimensions of his own genius: who will pay the nut on Tokyo Dome? The Dome-heads themselves! Or at least the *terebi* bastards! Everyone but Ginroku.

Saturday, 4:02 P.M.

Him again! The T-shirt pig, peddling his filthy garments, profiteering, capitalizing on the tragedy, in obvious cooperation with the venal broadcasting station. Oh, Hanako. Teshima Tadao regards the television with such concentrated loathing that his three *kobun* begin to blink, fidget, edge away. Teshima *oyabun* permits his tiny mental Tadao to spit at the disgusting creature on the screen.

"—*thousand yen only!*" *crows the fat man, grinning, perspiring.*

"*And how much for Hanako-chan?*" *asks the newsboy.*

"*How much for who?*" *The fat man scowls.*

"*Her.*" *Forefinger jabbing the fat man's breast.* "*The orphan. Hanako.*"

"*Not decided,*" *the fat man growls.* "*Not yet. Not decided yet.*"

"*I* have decided," says Teshima, evenly, "that Mr. Sawada Ginroku may be worth a minute of our time. Did you check him out?"

"Yes, *oyabun*, you were right. He is making loans in competition with us."

"Bring him in."

490

"Tiny loans. He is a tiny fish."

"Tiny, of course. But he stinks. Bring him in."

"Hai, so shimasu."

Teshima Oyabun returns his attention to the screen.

"... just a few minutes ago. Severely injured and in custody, Takeshita Satoshi, 48, detained last year by Captain Yoshida Makoto of the Tokyo Metropolitan Police in connection with the disappearance of the lawyer Iidzuka Masanori and his wife and infant son... Zenbu-kyo... searching the area... dead are tentatively identified as Donner Ruriko, 45, Tedzuka Keiichiro, 50, and his son Masao, 21... arrest by Captain Yoshida, who has also stated that two year old Hashimoto Hanako, rescued yesterday, is today reported missing and feared kidnapped."

Kidnapped!

Teshima grips the armrests of his chair. His grand-daughter killed, his great-grand-daughter orphaned—and now kidnapped?

"Donner? Was that the wife of the man we are following?"

"Hai, oyabun," says Morinaga Eiji, *ichiban kobun.*

"And the lawyer Iidzuka, didn't you say..."

"Hai, Oyabun. He was my *kohai.* At University of Tokyo."

"What is going on?"

"Oyabun, wakarimasen, gomen-nasai."

491

"Well, find out."

Saturday, 5:01 P.M.

The Great Healer is in mid-miracle. Yes, his sacred eyes have been torn out by the foreigner, Donner, the Principle of Evil. But the Healer himself is the Principle of Good, and Evil cannot long triumph over Good. As proof of that, the Healer is even now in the act of healing himself. He is restoring his own eyesight. He is growing new eyeballs.

It is purely a matter of will. Since regaining consciousness he has felt the power, the grace, course through his being. How long has he lain here? His only indication of time's passage has been the murmuring of the hospital staff—it must be a hospital, it smells and sounds like one—and the sharp little nips from the injections. Then, after each bite of the needle, a sort of warmth and clarity infuse the darkness. The darkness no longer seeks to devour him; rather, he drifts along in its bosom, in no hurry to be born. An hour, two? No matter. He can feel the new organs of sight beginning to form as buds along his optic nerves. The sensation is of a mounting pressure in the front part of his face. A lesser man might misinterpret this sensation as pain.

The Healer knows better. It is the will of the All focused upon the First Servant's flesh. For what is

493

flesh, but a reflection of the God within? Therefore, when the hospital functionaries remove his bandages, they will behold two perfect eyes, clear, and like twin sapphires flashing with the fire of this indwelling Deity. They will fall on their knees and beg forgiveness, and there will be no prosecution, no problems at all for him or Tedzuka-*san* or his son or any of the remaining faithful. Those fallen away from Zenbu-kyo will return, penitent, shedding tears, proffering gold and jewels, hoping somehow to make amends.

Yes, the fiery light blazing from his new eyes will kindle the world. Zenbu-kyo will rage like wildfire around the globe so that soon humanity will be one. One heart, one mind. Humanity will bury him in diamonds and emeralds, will beg him for pearls in return. Pearls from his lips. He will give them the Lotus Sutra. He will smile and hold up the flower. And humanity will grasp, however haltingly and imperfectly, the shining fact of this century, this millennium: the Healer's Buddha-hood. So when he commands them, they will obey. And he will then lay upon them the holy mandate to rip Donner's eyes from his skull and his flesh from his bones.

And, in a twinkling, this mandate will be accomplished. There will be nothing left of that demon loosed from the iron confines of *gigoku*—nothing but a stain. Then will justice roll down in ever-during waves from the heavens, drenching the earth with perfection, readying it for the Great Epoch of Faith. Yes, then will it be so. Soon.

Right now, however, he wishes they'd hurry up with his shot.

Captain Yoshida walks in, past the police guards at the door, refolding the wallet containing his badge and replacing it in his pocket. He stops and looks around. Private corner room with two windows, gleaming green tile on the floor, white screen around the bed, music piped in. Bathroom door ajar. On the bedside table, a small bunch of red chrysanthemums in a chipped blue vase. On the bed, like a waxen effigy, Takeshita in a huge white bandage. The bandage is like a gauze turban or space helmet. Only his nose and mouth are showing. An intravenous tube squirms down from the suspended bottle and into his arm. His chest rises slightly, slightly falls. Is he asleep?

"Takeshita Satoshi *sama, desu ka?*"

495

"Hai." A whisper. "You are late with my injection."

"I am sorry, Healer," says Yoshida. "For you, the purest morphine."

"Well, now that you have it, please inject me. Are you Zenbu-kyo?"

"I am thinking to apply for membership, Great Healer," says Yoshida. "But I am unworthy. My faith is weak. I need a sign, though my heart is already with those of the true faith. I have read your wonderful books. As a doctor, I have pondered them deeply."

"You have done well to read them. Which ones have you read?"

"Teachings of the Sun, Lessons of the Moon Goddess."

"Spiritual Guidance of the Stars?"

"Yes, that one. Also *The Path of Elvis."*

"All right, your heart is indeed with us. You may ask your questions."

"Myself and the others wish to know of the horror at Urawa. How could you have let that happen? Who were those buried ones? Were they enemies of the faith, as I believe? What did the police do to you? And what about the foreign devil, the one they call—"

"Donner," says Takeshita, his voice louder, stronger. "Devil indeed."

"What of this devil?"

"He haunts me, writes lies about me, comes out to my retreat and—"

"It is yours, then, the old farm?"

"Donner, the perfect man of *mappo*. Do you know *mappo?* It is this age, it is now, these degenerate times. The previous epoch, and the one to come, they were and will be times of faith, strength, regeneration, joy. But this one? It is the hell of the righteous, the heaven of the materialist, the hedonist. Of all those who glory in their golden chains, their silken bindings of the flesh. Such a one I saw this morning, a boy like a lizard, driving a van like a huge pink snail. A nightmare vision, yet real. He is the man of the future."

"Where was this?"

"Near the home of the devil. Do you promise to tell no one?"

"Of course, Healer."

"I went there to abduct Donner's wife, and I did abduct her."

"The better to ensnare Donner himself. Clever. What else did you see?"

"Nothing. Women hanging out their washing, airing their *futon*. Two little boys playing badminton in the communal drive. A pretty girl driving past the house of the devil."

"Pretty girl?"

"Yes, pretty. Why are you asking so many questions?"

"We are preparing a vengeance, Healer. The select faithful and myself."

"A vengeance?"

"It is all I can say at this time. There may be listeners, if you know what I mean. Police. Here in this room. Electronic devices, perhaps. We must assume that there are. But I think that when I speak of vengeance you can know my meaning. You are the Healer."

"I am the Healer and I do know it."

"Then you also know that we must have all possible particulars, even the seemingly trivial and irrelevant. Because then the pattern will emerge, and the sinful will be revealed."

"The pattern, yes. All right, the girl was perhaps twenty. She wore a soft pink fluffy sweater. Her face was lovely, plump and rosy, and her hair was down to her shoulders. I remember her well. As our cars squeezed past each other she gave me a shy little smile. I smiled back. We were two exiles from a better age."

"What kind of car was she driving?"

"A little one, appropriate for a young lady. Pink, but a darker shade than the lizard boy's. A small, rounded *minikaa*. It looked like a *tentomushi* or some little animal—oh, and on the seat beside her there was an animal—a very large, white, plush cat."

"A cat?"

"What they call Hello Kitty, I believe. A *kyarakuta*."

"A character, I see." Yoshida leans close. "Healer, before this special morphine, it is advisable to sip some pure water, which will assist in dispersion of the active substances." With his handkerchief Yoshida lifts the glass to the blind man's lips, helps him to sip—"Please hold it yourself too, Healer, so there is no spillage"—notices a white-gowned figure, waiting in the doorway. "Ah, good. Now my assistant will administer the injection. And remember, trust no one. Speak to no one. Ours is not an age of trust."

"Indeed not. Rather, of degeneracy and betrayal."

"Truly," says Yoshida, pocketing the water glass. "I will return. My code name, do you wish to know it?"

"No. I will give you one, and it shall be yours. It is The Avenger."

"Healer! That is it! How did you know?" The wan, swaddled figure on the bed smiles slightly. "Truly, truly, you are the Healer. For now, good-bye."

Yoshida beckons to the doctor, nods to the guards.

Elevator, roof, helicopter.

The pilot, waiting.

"NHK, again," Yoshida tells him. *"Mo ichi do."*

Saturday, 5:37 P.M.

Kobayashi Miyuki in the grimy little studio—stage facing the lights and cameras, cords and wires taped down and snaking around all over the floor, blue striped background, four black chairs around a low, brick red table, artificial *kiku,* chrysanthemums, in the big orange vase. It is a plastic place. But on screen it looks good, warm and bright. Miyuki has taped the interview, and now she is waiting for her Uncle Makoto. He is on his way back from the hospital in Akabane. He telephoned her from the helicopter. He should be soon to here.

Miyuki is disappointed. The point for television interviews is talk, but when people just shake their heads and shrug and stare at the floor, well, the viewers are likely to switch channels, understandably. She still grasps little of what happened at Urawa. Probably Yoshida Makoto comprehends more. She will tape a final ninety seconds with him. As for Mr. Donner, *shyo ga nai,* this is after all television. She could hardly expect him to admit blinding one man and butchering two others—whose hands were bound behind their backs. Mr. Donner must, he said, talk to his lawyer. She asked, Did he think the police would

501

arrest him? Mr. Donner shrugged: he did not know, did not wish to speculate. She asked, who killed his wife, why, who were the buried bodies, what were the possible reasons? Shrug, shrug, shrug. And especially he did not want to talk about the baby, Hanako. He was still dazed, that was it. And the huge orange colonel, who is Japanese but not Japanese. Not so very talkative either. He just wanted to go home and shower and change clothes. Both of them still sitting there, covered with splotches of dried blood, hands on their knees, looking down at the floor, lost, gone.

The little *takubin* driver by contrast extremely vocal: "Give me back my van. Give me it." Whatever she said to him, always that. "Give me back my van." In the corner, the driver trembling, watching Mr. Donner, obviously terrified of him, will not say why. What did he hear or see? "Give me back my van."

Miyuki sighs.

Captain Yoshida knocks then walks into the studio.

"Give me back my van."

"It is outside," Yoshida tells him. "Take it. Go."

The *takubin* man scurries for the door.

Signal to Hiroji: get ready, try with Uncle Makoto.

"Captain Yoshida, what can you tell us about Urawa?"

"Very little. It appears the farm was a retreat of Zenbu-kyo sect. Six bodies were found in the barn, three recently killed and three buried, decomposed. Of the unburied corpses, one was identified as the wife of Professor Donner."

"From Kanagawa. Why was she there, in Urawa?"

"We do not know. The other two were members of Zenbu-kyo. The three buried corpses have been tentatively identified as those of the lawyer Iidzuka Masanori and his family, missing since last year. The prime suspect, Takeshita Satoshi, is in custody. He is seriously injured and has made no statement. That is all we know."

"Who injured him?" Well, she had to ask.

"That aspect is being studied."

"Who killed the two members of his organization?"

"That question too is now under review. There are various possibilities. Perhaps they attacked each other. Tests are being done. Dental records are being checked. That is all I can tell you. Conjecture is at this point premature. Those are the only facts, and facts are what we must go by. Hard data."

"What of the missing little girl, Hanako?"

"Nothing."

And that is all: a second miserable interview.

503

But then the interphone: come up to the *kai-cho's* office.

And his office: smaller than she would have expected, in a corner of the building, very little furniture, many plants: bamboo and fig in glazed tubs on the floor by the windows, vines trailing from hanging pots in three corners. On his desk, in a shallow iron-gray planter, a gorgeous *bonsai*, a tiny mountain pine, all knobbed and gnarled. A hundred years old, *tabun*. All the plants seem healthy, well-tended, their leaves dustless and glossy. The air feels cool and moist. It has a loamy smell, no hint of tobacco smoke. This is Miyuki's first time here. Like his room, the *kai-cho* is small. He is old but bustling with energy, his thick silvery hair parted in the middle and stubble-short on the back and sides. The amber frames of his glasses look like real tortoise shell. His shirt collar—plain, no buttons or tabs—and his tie are, even at this hour, still perfect.

"*Kai-cho,*" she says, bowing low, "you are working late."

"And you, Miyuki-*san.* Our guests?"

"Professor Donner, Colonel Nakamura."

"Gentlemen."

"And you know Captain Yoshida."

"*Eh, hisashi-buri desu ne,* Captain?"

"Yes, it's been a while. Three years or so. *Genki desu ka, Kai-cho?*"

"*Hai, okagesama desu,* I'm fine. What is it? The killings in Urawa?"

"That is right. Miyuki-san was taping an interview."

"Well, look at this. It came ten minutes ago."

The *kai-cho* gestures down at his desk-top. On it are a large Mach-10 courier envelope, opened, a smaller business-size envelope, also opened, a letter hand-scrawled in blocky *hiragana* script, a photograph, and a ribbon.

Yoshida picks up the letter by one corner, holds it between fingernail and thumbnail, reads it aloud:

We have Hanako. You can save her. Put ten million yen in a bag. Where and how you get this money is your problem. Put the bag in one of the coin lockers near the Be Me exit of Machida eki. It does not matter which locker because the keys are numbered. Put the key on top of the lockers, far back, out of sight. Leave the area. Tell no one. The area is of course being watched. You have until 8:00 tonight, no later. Carry out these instructions perfectly or the baby will die.

505

And your television station will have killed her. And the world will know.

"Motorcycle courier?" Miyuki feels the sick rage thick in her throat.

"I called the company," says the *kai-cho*. "Spoke with the courier just now, caught him between deliveries. The man who gave him the envelope was a policeman, so he says. But anyone may rent a police costume. And the courier could also be the kidnapper, of course. Here is the sender's stamp, 'Suzuki'—but you can buy one of those *hanko* anywhere."

"The ribbon too," says Yoshida. "And the photograph is no good either. It's faked, crudely. She is holding today's *Yomiuri Shinbun,* but the arms and hands are wrong. You see? Really, she is holding something else. Maybe something rounder. Or much thicker."

"Maybe my neck."

"Yes, maybe Donner *sensei's* neck! That is how she looked, yesterday."

"So?" asks the huge colonel. "What does it add up to?"

"Not much," says Yoshida. "A crank. The city is full of them. They see something on television, and they react irrationally. But predictably."

"Try to get in on the act?" says the colonel.

"*So desu.* It is a big invisible club composed of fools entirely. I must deal with such individuals on a continual basis. But there are some questions. Where did the picture come from? Who took it? The picture is suggestive, but it proves only that this particular fool is not much of a dark-room man."

"Or woman?"

"No, *Kai-cho,* these individuals are nearly always men. And this one is crazy, perhaps—incompetent certainly. But, *zan-nen,* the picture does not prove that he *does not* have her. Absence of evidence is not evidence of absence. So we must follow it up. This letter, the motorcycle courier, the possible policeman. Lieutenant Kamijo can handle all that—if there is anything to handle, which I doubt. I will send him over with some plainclothes people. Of course I do not have to tell all of you to stay away from there, but I will say it anyway. Stay away from Machida *eki.* Now I must leave. I have to go talk with the Associate Chief."

"About the baby?" asks Miyuki.

"About the budget."

"Captain, ten million is a lot of *genkin.* Two hours is not much time."

507

"Not cash money, *Kai-cho.* Do you have a paper-cutter? Chop up some scrap the size and shape of *ichi-man* banknotes. This sort of thing has happened before. Bundle them up with wrapping paper and thick rubber bands. Put real bills on the top and bottom. Write down the numbers. Before our hoaxer can check them, the Lieutenant will have him. Or should have him. Kamijo is all right, I suppose. Anyway, he just did the *omiai* dinner with Ishimura-*san's* daughter—"

"Honto ni?" Miyuki is surprised; she has met Ishimura's daughter, who is older even than Miyuki—mid-thirties, stale Christmas cake for sure—and extremely, well, plain.

"Yes, really. And that affects the general situation. Ishimura-*san* says I am keeping Kamijo-*san* down. Says I do not use him on interesting assignments, do not give him a chance to show what he can do. Well, perhaps he has a point. So why should I not? This whole business of the letter is really amateurish. That is my... what do the Americans say?

"Gut reaction?" says the colonel with the giant stomach.

"It is my gut reaction. Depend on it, this kidnapper is no kidnapper."

"Really?" asks Miyuki.

"What is he then?"

"A *bakayaro*, Mr. Donner. What you call a moron."

Saturday, 6:58 P.M.

Sawada Ginroku, a genius, another Ieasu or Mac Arthur for bold and brilliant scheming, sits by the window in this smoky little *cafe-baa,* watching the muffled multitudes surge to and from Machida station. Gray evening, gray lives. Wage-slaves: salarymen and office ladies. He smiles. At his feet is a large, flat black, lozenge-shaped Aiwa stereo tape deck and radio—a ghetto-blaster, as the Americans call them. The room is warm, but Ginroku is wearing his genuine London Fog raincoat, purchased on a recent trip to Los Angeles. He purchased also a matching coat for his wife, but she never wore it, because she never goes outside. Too frightened—of the predators, of everything. So he gave that coat to his *ichiban ouaki,* a fabulous piece with a very difficult name, one of those red-hot little Thais. Why let the coat go to waste? Plus a real Burberry scarf. She was thrilled. Tokyo is heaven for her. What is there in Bangkok? Sit around in a giant whorehouse and wear a big number. Earn enough for a bowl of *cha-han,* maybe. If she is permitted to service Japanese company men on a sex tour. What kind of life is that? Much better to sell the T-shirts. Maybe Ginroku will pay her a visit when tonight's business is done. Like everyone else, she is always glad to see him.

In the inside pocket of Ginroku's coat is a black garter belt for her, from the PX at Yokota Base, and a filmy black brassiere with two holes. Yokota, yes, he has connections even as far west as Fussa. In his left pocket is a string of big firecrackers. In his right pocket is a child's mask, Mickey Mouse, rolled beneath an XL Asshole T-shirt for Miyajima.

Baka Miyajima, red-eyed and sullen, sits across the tiny table from him. Miyajima: big, thick, sweaty, almost too stupid to breathe. Face blotched and puffy, thin bristly hair tousled, fat arms folded across fat chest, uniform creased and greasy. Ginroku's personal law enforcement officer.

"Wish I had a drink," says Miyajima. "A big one."

"Later." Then, whispering, "You handed off to the courier."

"Hai. Just before I went off duty."

"You were not at the *koban.* "

"Not at the *koban.* Give me credit for some brains. I flagged him down."

"You threw away the Suzuki *hanko.* "

"Hai, hai, hai, hai, hai!"

"Good. Now repeat what I told you."

511

"Ahh. Enough of that bullshit. *Wakarimashita*, I *got* it."

"Then repeat it. And keep your voice down."

Miyajima sighs. "I hear the big commotion. I run up. I say—"

"Run up where?"

"To the coin lockers. And I say—"

"To who? Who's there?"

"Probably some plainclothes guy. I say, *Get that money out of there.*"

"Good. And?"

"*And—and put it someplace safe. The lieutenant says so.*"

"Right. The lieutenant, that's important. Or should it be captain?"

"Lieutenant's good enough."

"Okay, lieutenant. He opens the locker. Then?"

"I grab the bag. Pull my gun, hit him in the head. Whistle."

"Uniforms come pounding up, and you say…?

"Arrest this man."

"*This is the kidnapper, arrest him!* Say it good and loud."

"THIS IS THE—"

"Not *here*, shithead. Whisper, please."

"Hey, Sawada, what if there's more than one?"

"Hit them all. Blow the whistle on them all. *A kidnapping ring.*"

"Then you come by, and I hand off the package to you."

"Excellent. Then we walk not run in opposite directions."

"But not before I get my reward."

"You get it later. And we'll talk about it later."

"We'll talk about it now. A hundred thousand yen. Cash."

"All right, thirty thousand."

"Seventy-five."

"All right, fifty. But of course not cash. Subtracted from your debt. However, here, this is for you, a present, *dozo,* a small token of my esteem. It will brighten your day. Don't open it till you get home."

"Sawada, you bastard. Do you think I want another fucking T-shirt? This is serious. I could get in a lot of trouble for this, what do you care? In fact, I'm in a lot of trouble already. Months now, cops around my place, *aru,* every night. Six of them, eight. Kamijo's men. Watching."

"Why?"

"They think I destroyed my wife."

513

"Well, did you?"

"I don't think so. I think she just fell down the stairs. But I also think maybe some little bastard tipped them off it was me. So now they follow me all day, on my beat. Then, I get home, I'm surrounded. Plainclothes, uniforms. It's a war of nerves. I know they're there, they know I know. They want me to break down and confess. Well, fuck them, I never will. *I never killed her.*"

"Calm down, asshole."

"I'm calm, I'm calm. But, every night, cops. My place is sealed up tight. A *gokiburri* couldn't get in our out."

"How did *you* get out? You're even bigger than a cockroach physically."

"*Yasashikatta*, it was surprisingly easy." Officer Miyajima snickers. "Cops are so fucking dumb. They're all wandering around in the dark, bumping into each other and talking to each other on their walkie-talkies, so I just turn off my lights, wait a few minutes, the spotlight moves off my back door, and I slip out with *my* walkie-talkie. I hold it close to my face, send some fake hand signals. I'm in uniform. Who's going to notice one more cop when there's already a *kyu-nin* of them stumbling around in the yard? One is perched in the tree like a giant *karasu*. The tree is nearly destroyed. I should sue them."

"How do you get back in?"

"Should be even easier. Far as Kamijo's concerned I'm already in there, right? Most of his people are asleep at this point, snoring away in their cars. I've watched them. So is he asleep. The ones who aren't are looking *toward* the house, of course, never the other way. So I just march right in, maybe growl a few orders into the walkie-talkie, which is turned off. I could go in with a parade, probably, it would be okay. I'm going to do this a lot, now I know how easy it is. Sneak out, go get drunk, get laid. Blow off steam. Stay sane."

"*Dzurui desho,* very devious and intelligent."

"What?"

"I said you're pretty smart."

"Yeah, I am. Don't know why I never made sergeant. Well, I do know why. I just never had time to take the exam, always too busy. But how tough can it be when some of these *namekuji* can pass it?" Miyajima sighs, leans forward on his elbows. "They're getting on my nerves, though. Them waiting, me waiting. Stress. I'm going crazy. Murder—how can they prove it? Well, they can't, they don't have a case, or I'd already be in Sugamo. But they will harass me forever. I'm sure the neighbors think I'm public enemy number one. I'm innocent, but I'm in a terrible predicament."

"You'll be in a worse one unless you do exactly what I tell you."

"Ah, Sawada, you son of a Soapland whore, don't I always? Say, can we at least go and fuck some of your *burikko* afterwards?"

"Not tonight. Maybe next week. In the meantime, remember how much you owe me. Keep in mind your situation. Carry out your mission without fail."

"Carry out my mission. You're such a bastard. You have too much shit around your asshole, no offense. Hey, maybe I go to the gangsters, tell them about your money-lending activities. Will they like that? *Tabun amari, neh?* What will happen? Maybe they're grateful, my debt gets canceled, and you get destroyed."

"Maybe so." Ginroku gives him the famous smile. "But probably not. Here is a likelier scenario. You do that, and at least one gangster who also belongs to me will be at your place within the hour. A huge one. He is the one with the gravity knife, the one they call

Major Surgery. He won't fool around with a walkie-talkie. You will be *sashimi.* "

"Ah, Sawada, can't you take a joke?"

"No."

"I'm kidding."

"I'm not."

"Ah, shit, couldn't we have just one drink? My nerves are destroyed."

"Okay, one." Ginroku looks out over all the smoking heads bent over all the little marble-topped tables. He signals for the skinny little waitress. She scurries over holding her tray like a shield. To protect her nonexistent tits? Ginroku chuckles. *"Mizowari, futatsu, "* he tells her. "Cutty Sark."

"No Cutty for me," says Miyajima. "I want Old Parr. A triple."

Saturday, 7:12 P.M.

Dead flesh stinks, even chilled nearly to freezing, and the formalin-reek makes it worse. Captain Yoshida Makoto is breathing in sips through his mouth, standing in the cold room of the police morgue, Shinjuku. Just standing, letting his thoughts move around freely, in this place of scraps and husks.

He has no immediate concerns. His meeting with the Associate Chief is not until eight. And he already called Lieutenant Kamijo, reached him as the Lieutenant was on the way over to Miyajima's, told him about the ransom note, directed him to detach some of his men from the Officer detail. *No uniforms. Go with them to Machida, surveil the coin lockers by the BeMe exit. Watch for what? Yoshida couldn't say. Some kind of* dzurui *foolishness. But it could be dangerous foolishness too. So stay alert. Hai, so shimasu.* Kamijo. Well, at least the man was brisk and respectful, seemed to understand that he was working for Yoshida, and not the other way around—yet.

Yoshida still has nearly an hour—and what better place than a morgue to prepare oneself for a meeting with Paperwork Ishimura? Yoshida needs the time to think, to sort things out. But how he hates the morgue, especially this room. That may be his only point of agreement with Ishimura, who loathes it so much that he visited it only once, as a recruit. Well, it is a vile place: long, narrow, windowless sealed-concrete walls and floor, brilliant fluorescents high up, two facing banks of outsized file cabinets. One tragedy per cabinet.

Yoshida peers at the labels, pulls out a drawer—"TEDZUKA KEIICHI"—to reveal the senior Tedzuka, deep shovel-gashes in his face and cranium. Who did this? Donner. Why? Because of his wife, presumably. And because of the baby, so he said. The baby, whom Donner has known for approximately twenty-four hours. Does that make any sort of sense? Perhaps. Maybe some kind of supernormal life-and-death bonding. However: Tedzuka's arms were tied when he was killed, just as the wife's were tied. So who is the worse criminal?

Yoshida peers, pulls out another drawer: "TEDZUKA KONO." The son. Similar wounds, the boy with his jaw nearly hacked away. Who did this? Again, Donner. Why? Same possible reasons, and just went berserk with the shovel. Maybe so. But maybe not. Perhaps Mr. Donner just likes to kill people.

A third drawer: "DONNER RURIKO." The wife. No gashes, bludgeon marks. Who did this? Tedzuka-*tachi*, perhaps, or Takeshita, the Healer. Or both. Or neither. Maybe Donner and the big man killed them all, faked the kidnapping. How? Hit her, drive around, find some rhino hat *bakayaro,* torture them for directions to the Zenbu-kyo hideaway, knowing there would be one somewhere. Donner reads the papers, he's lived here for years, he knows what's going on. Then, at the farm, kill them all. Make it look like a cult slaying. The buried corpses would just be a piece of luck, more red herrings, very ripe. It is possible.

But not likely. Donner *is* a killer, however. In his essence. That is certain. Yoshida has encountered several such. Maybe Donner does not like to kill, but he does not dislike it all that much, either. Yoshida would bet on that. Does Donner drink? He is a Celt. Donner, on fire with whiskey and every other raging thing in his twisted Irish spirit: the thought sends a small electric trickle of anxiety through Yoshida. Donner-*sensei*: stooped, balding, half moon reading-*megane*, chalkdust on his fingers, eyebrow dandruff. A typical professor—bumbling, harmless, a kind of joke. Perhaps he often searches all over for his hat which he is wearing. But watch out for him, be careful around

Donner. That is what Yoshida's instincts say. Because Donner is a natural.

Still, did Donner and the big pseudo-*Nihonjin* kill them all? Probably not. But was Ruriko's life insured? And if so by whom? Donner? Yoshida would like to quit thinking about Donner.

Yoshida peers and pulls: "ISHIDA KAZUO." Massive head wound, skull smashed in. The lawyer, they are almost sure. But how different from his picture on the posters. Death, the supreme caricaturist, exaggerating the lawyer's corpulence with bloat, widening the grin with rot and adding a leer. Still, it is remarkably well-preserved for a year and a half, the barn so dry and cool, the soil of the floor so sandy.

Yoshida peers and pulls: "ISHIDA MUTSUMI." Massive head wound, skull smashed in. The wife, hand still raised in supplication, mouth still open in a scream—*please don't hurt my baby!*—body twisted with the rigors of death, leaking putrefaction.

Yoshida peers and pulls: "ISHIDA SHIN." No wounds. Strangled? Buried alive—just thrown in with the parents? One year old, a tiny baby boy.

Enough.

Yoshida Makoto closes the file drawers, walks out of the cold room, hangs the blanket-cloak on its peg to the left of the steel door. He is now in the main room, with its gurneys, its big freestanding lights on tripods, its pale green steel and glass instrument cabinets against the walls, its three big stainless tables, and its three deep floor-gutters leading to the barred drain near the far wall. The smell of formalin is worse in here. No, not worse. Stronger. Well, stronger is worse, and Yoshida is leaving, but first a quick call to the lab. He picks up the wall phone by the exit, hits the numbers. Koyanagi should still be around, even on a Saturday.

"*Moshi moshi. Koyanagi-san? Yoshida desu. Konbanwa.*"

"*Hai, konbanwa. Nan desuka?* What is it, Captain?"

"Prints. Do we have a match?"

"On the photograph, nothing. It is wiped. On the letter, a partial, and on the flap of the small envelope, a nearly complete thumb. Not on file."

"The glass from the hospital?"

"Four clear, complete. Not on file."

"Those are the Urawa lunatic. And he is not the Beast?"

"Definitely not. But the matchbook? Soapland? Two smudged, one clear but partial—maybe eighty percent. Right index."

"Him The Officer?"

"Hai."

"No question?"

"None."

Yoshida breaks the connection, punches in the numbers for NHK. Miyuki? Donner? A *recording: NHK's hours are—*

Four baby girls dead, five and six in the jaws of the beast.

Yoshida hangs it up.

All that, and now Ishimura.

Saturday, 8:00 P.M.

Miyajima Yoshinori is looking good. His long lustrous hair is freshly washed with Kanebo baby ultramild—two soft sudsings, then the conditioner, and finally the hair pack followed by a long body-temperature rinse. Yoshinori uses only Kanebo, and he is scrupulous about shampooing every other day. Yoshinori's father is going bald, and what little hair remains is just filthy, greasy hog-bristles, and the reason is simple neglect. So Yoshi is careful, even with the hair drier. He never uses the hot setting, or even "warm." "Cool" takes more time, but so what? Yoshi's not going anywhere.

At least not tonight, not with Hanako, so incredibly beautiful, right here. She is a difficult child, however, and Yoshi may free her sooner than planned, if she continues to weep and run away from him and burrow into corners. He tries to calm her with loving caresses, but she just gets more hysterical. And louder. Yoshinori has neighbors, after all, above and below and on either side, and they know he lives alone. True, the soundproofing is good. True also, his fluffy rugs and stuffed bunnies must absorb a lot of noise. But

Yoshi still has to be careful. Late at night there is nothing louder than a live baby.

"Hana-*chan*, want to come and smell my hair?"

Wails, trembles, crouches lower behind his big wonderful Hello Kitty.

Yoshi sighs. He sets the brush and mirror on the floor. He fluffs out his skirt so that it covers the cushion on which he is kneeling. He adjusts the pleats until they are all equally expanded. His skirt is the lovely flower, he is the beautiful stamen—or is it pistil?

"*Oide, oide.* Come on, Han-*chan*. *Onee-san desu,* I'm your big sister."

He is wearing this big-sister dress for Hanako, but she doesn't like it. Or acts like she doesn't, which is the same thing—except possibly ruder and more hurtful. Well, there is nothing wrong with the dress. It is a very good one. Yoshi got it at a *chukohin-ya* last month, in Shimbashi, on the way home from work. He pawed through the tables of second-hand clothes for twenty minutes before he found it, his prize. Only 800 yen for a schoolgirl's sailor uniform: dress, belt, blouse, kneesocks. A little drycleaning, and the outfit simply sparkled. Like new, perfect fit—except for the shoes, which were too small, but he already had some black pumps that would do very nicely thank you. His dress even came with the little gold-enamel insignia. Ochanomizu senior high, an excellent school.

Yoshi has already worn his outfit to the club twice, and everyone loved it. He'd be sitting there demurely with his cocoa, and other boys would come up in their pinafores and jumpers, and tell Yoshi how nice he looked. They'd say, *"Sumimasen,* I forgot to study my home economics. May I please look at your notes?" Sometimes they would offer to buy him a soda or a shake, and once he said, shyly, "All right, if it's strawberry." And the boy—who was really about thirty-five—opened his tiny patent leather purse and took out an even tinier coin purse and said, "Is strawberry your favorite?" And Yoshi said, "Yes." And the boy said, "Why?" And Yoshi said, "Because strawberries are the cutest!" They laughed and laughed.

Yoshi is very popular at the club. Even with the boys he doesn't like so much, the really old ones, Yoshi is always nice. He smiles and wrinkles his nose at them, then looks down bashfully, blushing. The blushes are real. Everything about Yoshi is real. He has the natural, rosy glow of youth. Even at the club he wears hardly any makeup.

Why in the world should he? Why should he plaster himself with lipstick? And foundation, and eyeliner, and all the rest of that expensive *kessho-hin* junk? That's one thing that makes Yoshi so mad, one thing he feels very strongly about: the cosmetics companies advertising their products in such a way that young people are supposed to feel bad about themselves or not-quite-dressed if they aren't wearing about twelve different kinds of garbage. Yoshi sniffs contemptuously, tosses his head in disdain. Garbage is the word for it. All that *gomi* caked and troweled on, plugging up the pores and concealing the skin's natural beauty—in an effort to appear natural! Well, it just strikes Yoshinori as really perverse.

"Han-*chan, ichigo miruku!* Won't you drink your strawberry milk?"

Oh, she is a sulky, disagreeable child—but her complexion! It is not of this world! Natural beauty indeed. It is the most gorgeous he's ever seen. Petal-soft, luminous, radiant. If he could only take her to the club. He sighs again, again looks at his gorgeous big Hello Kitty, which now has two ribbons: her own red one, and Hanako's pink one peeking up from behind.

"Kitty," he says, trying to be cheerful. "Who are you hiding?"

527

Actually, Kitty has hidden four other little girls, hidden them completely, because Kitty has a secret too: she is hollow. Two years ago he paid a *refom* lady to take out most of Kitty's stuffing and line the cavity with nylon fabric and put in a zipper. So Kitty is— besides of course being her own darling self—also a big plush bag. Roomy Kitty. Most of the time Yoshi keeps a pillow in there, but not always. Sometimes Kitty holds the ashes of a little freed angel.

These days, people are always speculating about how Yoshi does the actual cremating, and there have been some elaborate theories in the editorial columns and on the talk shows. *Does the monster—they call him that—have some connection at a crematorium? Is he perhaps even an employee of some* yakiba*? Or even an owner?* Yoshinori has to laugh. Because really it is so straightforward and easy. Even kind of fun.

When it is all over, and the baby is freed, and the freeing of course preserved on videocassette—so she is both freed *and* saved—Yoshi simply places each piece—the little arms and legs hardly bigger than poultry wings and thighs—in a plastic bag. (He uses the ones from Sanwa's produce section because he shops at Sanwa, where fruits and vegetables are a little more expensive, true, but everything is always so fresh.) Then the six bagged pieces go into a regular garbage bag, and that one into a second. Three layers of plastic, no possibility of leakage.

And then into Kitty, and off to work. No one thinks twice when they see Kitty on Yoshi's desk, because she's there nearly every day anyway. Oh, the first few times there were some jokes and questions, but Yoshi just said, "Kitty is my inspiration," and Mr. Matsuura heard him say that, and Mr. Matsuura replied, jokingly, that if so he should put her on the payroll, because Yoshi's stories—Fong/Fujiwara and all the rest—were propelling *High School Jumping* far beyond their competition. Then Mr. Matsuura had an inspiration of his own. He gave plush Kittys to all the other writers and cartoonists along with their last year's Christmas bonuses.

The bonuses were the same size, of course, for each grade of seniority. But the Kittys were not. Some employees, even a few twenty-year men, got tiny ones, smaller than real kittens, and the clearly understood message was that these people, though certainly part of the team, were also fairly peripheral, and their contribution to *Jumping* relatively slight. Such miniKittys were used by their disgruntled recipients as paperweights or were impaled on pencils and pens.

Other employees, however, got larger ones—some very large indeed—and, yes, it was all a sort of joke, but in a way it was not. These more productive people would find a clean desk-corner for their Kittys, vacuum the plush when old Mr. Nakatani came around with the cleaner, and generally cherish them. The leading artists, having no desks, wired and thumbtacked their Kittys to their drafting boards. These crucial people came to be called *Oki Nekko*: the Big Cats. Now you can look over the *Jumping* workroom and see a Kittyscape and tell the key players at a glance.

Who has the biggest Kitty of all?

Yoshinori, of course. And who works late most nights? Again, Yoshinori. *"Shimpai nai, Nakatani-san,* he often says. "Don't worry, I'll take care my own trash, but not yet. I'll finish burning for you. Good night."

Then, when he is alone except for the dozing guard at the entrance, he empties Kitty, puts the bag in his wastebasket, carries it down and out back, and throws it into the incinerator. Usually, the fire is still burning strongly with the combustible waste of the whole building. Whether the fire is raging or smoldering makes no difference, however, because Yoshi throws in the remaining bags, all collected and lined up beside the incinerator by the grateful Mr. Nakatani, whose back is so painful. Soon the incinerator is roaring, its iron belly cherry-red.

Half an hour, forty-five minutes.

Then Yoshi shovels out the ash into the three big orange canisters. He is happy to be able to spare Mr. Nakatani this hard, sweaty, bent-over work. (Several times a month he finds on his desk a pretty package containing Mrs. Nakatani's delicious home-made *daifuku* or other sweets, for her "Darling Yoshi.") While shoveling he sifts for the baby's tiny bones, not much bigger than a chicken's. Some, like the fingers and toes, are burned completely away. Others he misses in the sifting. Yoshinori doesn't feel guilty about these missing bones, however; he always does the best he can, under the circumstances.

And he loves these blackened shards. Most people don't realize how erotic carbonized bones can be— pelvis, arm and leg bones, ribs, vertebrae. Life's prison-stones, life's echoes. These and her skull he crushes, for quicker cooling, but he tries to leave some teeth intact for the police. Then, wearing gloves of course, he funnels the ashes into an Old Parr bottle, wraps the bottle in a newspaper to protect his father's

531

filthy fingerprints, and puts the wrapped bottle in another plastic bag. He secures the neck of the bag with the short length of green paper-wire, three complete twists, and he is finished. Then, back she goes into Kitty.

Four times he has done this.

He looks over now at his wonderful plush friend, at her ribbon, her whiskers, her adorably blank expression. The cruel baby is still lurking behind her, whining and sniveling. Next she'll fly into a rage with one of her tantrums.

"Kitty," he says. "What's wrong with me? Hanako doesn't like me."

Hanako begins weeping more loudly, gratingly.

"Oh, Kitty!" Yoshi is on the verge of tears himself. "She *hates* me."

Hanako is hungry and thirsty. But she is sick, with a kind of trembling. She won't, won't, won't drink the strawberry milk. *No.* Even though she loves strawberry milk. Mama gives her strawberry milk in the special cup all the time. Both hands, Hanako. *Hai, Okaasan.* Then Hanako uses both hands and picks up the cup and drinks every drop and then shows her mother the empty cup. *"Motto kudasai!* More, please!" And then they laugh, because Hanako always says, *"Motto, motto!"* because that is so funny, and so they laugh, and her mother goes back to the *reisoko* and opens it up and takes out the strawberry milk again. Hanako's *reisoko* is white, and it has her crayon drawings taped all over it. Drawings of Pikkoro and Podori and Jajamaru. Then when *Otosan* comes home from work, he says, "Hana-*chan*! Did you really draw that? All by yourself? *Yoku dekimashita!* Well done!" He always says that, and he is happy and fat. And Hanako nods and smiles and feels very proud, and so their *reisoko* is nice, and it says *hmmmmmmm—click* sometimes, and she likes it because of so much *oishi* food that her mother puts in and takes out, and Hanako eats it and says *"Gochisoosama!"* and they all laugh because Hanako can't quite say it the way it should be said, but that's all right, because *Okaasan* and *Otosan* know what she means, and they all like the *reisoko* because it's nice, but the girl who is a boy has a *reisoko* that isn't nice and isn't good and Hanako saw in it when he opened it and got her strawberry milk and it's so bad that it's... At Hanako's real home the *reisoko* is very nice and kind of her friend... But this one here, it's not even white, it's pink. Hanako's isn't pink, it's white, and *Okaasan* sprays it with the *Magikku-Krean* spray

533

every day and then wipes off all the handprints and makes it so shiny. This one is shiny, too, and clean on the outside, but Hanako saw... she *hates* this girl who is a boy and she *hates* this milk. This strawberry milk is bad. It is the same kind as *Okaasan* buys, and the carton is just the same, but this strawberry milk is different and Hanako won't drink it, she *won't*. Or even touch it. Because it stinks.

Saturday, 8:01 P.M.

Kawakami Yukio and Uchiyama Masaaki are now making money honestly though very slowly. Yukio's whole body aches. His nose is broken, both his eyes are blackened. And Masaaki looks sick. The two friends are far from Fuchinobe, far from the depressing little second-hand store and the low-class *soba-ya*. They are a three minute walk from Korakuen and Tokyo Dome, outside Suidobashi train station, facing the entrance. They are standing, shivering, under the harsh station lights and in a dank and rancid slush of mulched *manga*, Lotte chocolate wrappers, newspapers, racing forms, cigarette butts, clotted tissues, losing *takarakuji* slips, boxing programs, and pigeon feathers and excrement. To their left, at the base of a green I-beam, pigeons in a circle peck at a slowly effervescing mound of beer-and-*soba* vomit.

"So, Masaak-*kun*, what do you think?" Yukio makes a sweeping gesture.

"It's all right. It's a job. But I'm starved. *Sushi o tabetai desho.*"

Good old Masaaki. He's tough, no whiner. Neither is Yukio, who has been in much worse places—quite recently. And the smell here isn't that bad. It's winey,

535

as though the sidewalk *gomi* were somehow fermenting. Anyway, it's better than the smell inside Masaak-*kun's* little pink S-Cargo. Above them are the tracks of the Chuo and Sobu lines. To their left, between them and the I-beam, an ugly old shoeshine woman—an *eta*, casteless, a kind of animal—sits cross-legged on her pallet, in the blue-white cone of a street light, impassive as the Buddha. The sullen little river sucks past, invisible from their angle, its bridge is to their right.

By the bridge is a filthy little *tacoyaki* stand—cart, propane tanks, three stools, faded red-and-white-striped awning. A tiny gasoline engine mutters to itself on the sidewalk, generating power for the lights strung around the awning. The twisted little gnome of a cook is listening to a radio talk show as, bent to his task and oblivious of his three customers, he deftly minces octopus, fills the hemispherical molds, and sets them over the hissing flames. The spicy aroma drifts over to the friends.

"Sushi," says Yukio. "Me too. Or even a little *tacoyaki.*"

The friends stand with their backs to a row of rusted bicycles jumbled against the metal railing between sidewalk and street. These bikes have been here a while. They are all grimed to nearly the same color, and their baskets and child-carriers are crammed with garbage—disposable diapers, plastic *bento* boxes, flyers, crumpled coffee cans, tiny bottles which once held Vita-C and Regain. Yukio and Masaaki huddle under the rumbling beams, passing out small packets of Kleenex.

Why Kleenex?

Why not?

The friends were hired to this labor by a gangster-type, punch-permed and burly but jovial, bursting into the *soba-ya,* just as the proprietor was starting to drop broad hints about either ordering something else or leaving. Were the two friends busy? Would they like to make some money?

"Three thousand now," said the *gyangu.* "Three later."

Six thousand yen. Not much, but what better offers had they had lately? The gangster bought them each a beer, gave Masaaki a cigarette and complimented him on his hairdo, told them a few yakuza stories. Then they followed him downtown.

It sounded easy enough: distribute these free tissues. In practice, however, it has proved difficult. So Yukio is working on his technique. The trick is to shove the packets right in their faces, so that the people almost have to bat them away. Bat, touch, grasp, take. A sort of reflex, which works only sometimes, however. The commuters, heads down and striding purposefully, some of them trotting, the occasional very late one actually sprinting, brush by in a rush, mostly ignoring the free tissues. Occasionally, the human riptide snatches a packet and bears it away. More frequently, a train groans by overhead, and the pigeons flutter briefly in the girders and shit on the two friends who are now much more than that.

Masaak-*kun* scrutinizes a packet. "Oi," he says. "Look at this!"

Yukio looks, then smiles. The packets are advertisements for Soapland whores. "Call Tomoko, a sweet blossom who knows about bees, 03-3479-0018. Call Mamiko, who could be YOUR special *gahlfurendo*, 03-3682-2092."

"What do you think? Should we call one?" asks Masaak-*kun*.

Yukio laughs. The friends blush slightly and exchange a look: *maybe a* douseiaisha's *life isn't so bad—at least it's a way to save some money.* They have been here for nearly three hours. What makes it bearable is, well, the excitement of each other. Smiling, laughing together, now and then touching.

"Free *Kureenekusu*," says Yukio, jabbing with his left.

"Dozo," says Masaaki, counterpunching, packets in both fists.

The old shoeshine woman finishes with a customer, holds up her hand for the coins. These she deposits in her clean and neatly-tied apron. Indeed, though her face is a bad potato, bulbous and warted, her clothing is perfect: kerchief, shawl, smock— overlapping layers of wool and cotton perfectly in place. She sits, solid as a turnip-half on its base, surrounded by her boxes of brushes and jars, watching her little Sony.

Yukio sidles over for a look. The bright colors on the screen contrast with this drab, dun, gritty Tokyo night. He sidles closer.

"Donner!" he shouts. "Masaak-*kun,* look! It's Donner!"

Masaaki is there in a flash, balling his fists, crushing Kleenex packets.

"Donner!" he snarls, bending over the shoeshine woman's shoulder, riveted by the hated figure on the screen.

The toadlike shoeshine woman turns slowly and regards them for a long minute from below her lidded eyes. Then she reaches out a strong brown hand and switches off her television.

"AIDS no hito desu ka?"

Are they infected with AIDS? The old pig! How dare she?

"Hey!" shouts Masaaki. "Old woman! Fuck you!"

"Douseiaisha," she grates out. *"Chirashi kubari. Kojiki."*

Incredible! Are Yukio's ears malfunctioning? Or did this old lump of nothing, this pariah, this—this *burakumin*, just call them a couple of faggot train station beggars?

"Yuk-*kun*," says Masaaki, raging, "give me the skull ring."

"No, Masaak-*kun*," says Yukio, the voice of reason. "Don't kill her."

He has his arms around Masaaki's waist and is pulling him away, when suddenly Yukio feels a blow to his face and simultaneously a terrible burning sensation, and, howling, he reaches up and scrapes away the greasy and sizzling *tacoyaki* ball which has flattened itself against his cheek.

"Leave my wife alone, *bakayaro!*"

The friends, still locked pelvis to buttocks by Yukio's powerful left arm, look up. They see the little *tacoyaki* troll brandishing his steel *taco*-turning implement. They see three round, chewing, red, sweating, drunken salaryman faces swivel to regard them. They see a lean and angular policeman, sitting bolt upright and pedaling his white bicycle slowly in their direction. Yukio's cheek will blister, he knows. It is on fire.

"Beggars?" Masaaki hisses at her. "I'll have you know my father owns the Uchiyama Sakana-ya! Owns it!" Yukio feels his friend's belly muscles rippling with rage, feels the thrills and spasms of his fury. "Which is only the best fish shop in Tamachi!"

The old shoeshine woman, staring straight ahead, blank as an iguana, produces a pack of cigarettes from beneath her apron. Deans. She shakes a cigarette free, puts it in her mouth and lights it. She inhales deeply, leaving the cigarette in her mouth.

"Let's go back," says Yukio. "Let's rob the old *shichi-ya* bitch."

"No." Suddenly Masaak-*kun* is calm. Perhaps the smell of tobacco smoke has eased his terrible anger. "No, we're almost done. Another hour, he'll be back. We collect the rest of our money and go. Another hour, that's all. Then, real sushi. And Kirin beer. And for me a pack of Deans."

"Let's just toss them in the river."

"No!" Masaaki's eyes are wide. "Don't even think about it. He is yakuza. He might be downstream, you never know. That's the sort of thing he'd notice, five hundred packages of Kleenex floating along. No, we just have to move as many as possible. One thing you have to understand, Yuk-*kun,* don't ever try to cheat one of the brotherhood. Or there will be big trouble."

The cop coasts by, gives the friends a long, mean look.

"Free *Kureenekusu,* Officer?" says Masaaki. The cop ignores him.

"Listen, Masaaki, what if the guy doesn't come back?"

"That's another thing you have to learn about the brothers. If they say they'll do something they'll do it. He'll be back. How's your cheek?"

"Hurts," says Yukio, licking the tasty octopus juice from his right hand.

"Grease burn. Stick some Kleenex on it."

"Like a bandage, you mean? Okay."

"Looks a little strange, but so what?"

"We've still got two whole cartons left."

"One more hour," says Masaak-*kun.* "We can do it. Then sushi!"

"Free *Kureenekusu*," says Yukio, jabbing with his left.

"Dozo," says Masaaki, moving like a fighter, Kleenex in both fists.

Saturday, 8:10 P.M.

Buddy is having one hell of a time. He finally gets
through to Janey on a pay phone at Machida station,
and immediately catches a real barrage—*Is it true
about Ruriko? Is it true about those wackos? Is it true
about those stiffs? IS IT TRUE ABOUT THE BABY?
How's Donner? How're you? Where've you been?
Have you been pigging out? When are you coming
home?*—and he does his best, which isn't very good,
and he's down to about three yen on the meter and no
more coins, so he shouts, Call Yoshida, and gives her
the Captain's number, and then, *Guess what big guy I
been brawlin' again*, just as the thing goes *meep*.

Buddy is finally finished bellowing on the phone—
Buddy, still in his shocking orange sweats—and
Donner is grateful for small mercies. Buddy and
Donner have more less ignored the Captain's orders,
but it's all right, they're not hurting anything. Yoshida
said stay away, but Donner couldn't. So he and Buddy
are just trying to hang out, look inconspicuous, blend
with the homebound salary men, keep an eye on the
coin lockers in the station, see if anybody tries to grab
the ransom bag—but here's this beaky old carrot-

haired cretin and his muffin-shaped blue rinse of a wife from Enid or Provo or some similar shithole. Won't go away. Standing there, blocking the view, waving their arms. The man, gawky and wry-necked, looks like he's being yanked upward, hooked by some fisher of men. The woman looks compacted. They are of course lost, asking for directions. Not asking, demanding.

"We're late!" says Carrot. "Where the heck is Machida station?"

"Here," Donner tells them, again, and very patiently. "You're in it."

"We're lost!" says Blue Rinse. "Oh, Pemberton."

"But it says Machida *eki!* And we want the Odakyu line."

"Yes," says Donner. *"Eki* means station. The Odakyu line is that way."

"Well, then, why the heck don't they just say so? *Eki!"* Carrot snorts. "What kind of a dingbat word is that? *Eki! Eki! Eki!"*

"Keep your voice down," says Buddy, walking over from the phones.

"For golly sake, why should I?" asks Carrot. "Didn't come all the way from Salt Lake to whisper. Came to shout the good news."

545

"This fat foreigner speaks English," says Blue Rinse.

"Don't see any trains, that's for darn sure," says Carrot.

"Now the both of you just fuck right off," Buddy tells them sternly.

Donner and Buddy watch with some satisfaction as the couple rear back tiptoed and bugeyed as though swiftly and deftly sodomized. The podgy old woman works her mouth like a fish low on oxygen. A hiss, a squeak. "I'll have you know my husband is a cardiologist." Deep breaths, a quavery yodel. "I'll have you know that we are missionaries."

And then they all heard it.

Mr. M. Mouse, a.k.a. Sawada Ginroku, cranks up his boombox full blast, fights the urge to cover his ears as the taped sirens and gunfire swallow every other urban sound. Swallow even the jangling of glass as he pitches the boombox through the window of Styley Boys Club, one of his chief competitors out here in Machida and also downtown. Swallow even the first detonations of two hundred firecrackers on a string which Ginroku lights and slings in after the boombox. Swallow even the shrill sounds of two little *burikko* diving behind the Styley Boys counter and shrieking so high as to be almost inaudible to the human ear.

Perfect.

Racket receding as he sprints for the corner.

Racket growing as Mr. Sawada Ginroku, puffing only slightly, Mickey Mouse mask in pocket, does an about-face at the corner, works his face into an astonished frown, and marches back the way he came, into the *eki* and toward the coin lockers. Sawada Ginroku, well-respected businessman, solid citizen out for an evening stroll, more than a little annoyed at all the hubbub, meets the first forms sprinting his way, toward the noise. Huge fat *Nihon-jin* with a bad haircut. Familiar-looking thin-haired foreigner. Solid-bodied individuals—plainclothes policemen?—pounding up.

Ginroku gives them all a very senior glower, looks, sees Miyajima.

Miyajima by the lockers, a navy blue-suited man approaching him, the suited man producing a key—to the locker? The key to the locker? Is it? Is it? Looks like it, certainly looks like a locker key. Ginroku is close now.

"Get that money out of there!" growls Miyajima.

Good, good, the asshole actually remembered.

"Who are you?" says the suit.

Not so good.

"Get it out! And—and put it someplace safe. The lieutenant says so."

"The lieutenant? I *am* the lieutenant." Bad, very bad. "And you! You're—"

Ginroku watches as Miyajima whips out his revolver—this is terrible, awful, completely wrong—and slugs the suit—the lieutenant?—slugs him hard, grabs the bag, and starts to run.

Ginroku runs after his idiot cop, gasping.

"Tomate kudasai! Stop! It's me, you idiot!"

Ginroku hears a real whistle pierce the night, hunches his plump shoulders against a possible burst of real gunfire. Worse and worse. How could Miyajima fuck things up so quickly? Oh, what Ginroku won't do to his repayment schedule. And what Ginroku's giant punchpermed yakuza won't do to Miyajima's bones.

Fast, faster than Ginroku would have believed possible, the two fleshy men fly out, around the corner, and down the cobbled lane. Pursuer and pursued, entrepreneur and mongoloid. Miyajima skids, stumbles, twists his ankle, caroms into an elderly American couple, knocking them against a giant trash dumpster by the Macdonald's, falls heavily to the pavement. As Miyajima struggles to his feet Ginroku rips the money bag from him and sprints toward the car. Maybe, maybe. Ginroku's almost there. Once behind the wheel he's as good as home.

Home, home, home. Dome, Dome, Dome.

But oh, Buddha, was that really a lieutenant?

Well, what if it was? Nobody saw Ginroku, he'll deny everything, nobody will believe shit-brained Miyajima who probably did kill his wife. Ginroku's own wife is waiting for him in good old Numabukuro. Or not even waiting, because she probably never realized he was gone, and that's what she'll tell them, and that's the actual fact, because Ginroku never left his house all evening. Who will they believe? Gutsy Ginroku, sweating, panting, still moving strongly, his torso rippling like a champion's. When the going gets tough, as the Americans say. The tough. Get. Going. And tough Ginroku is going like a bat out of hell, as the Americans also say, hugging the money, hugging it against himself, hugging himself. Well, he deserves a little hug. Because it looks like he did it! Ginroku did it! In spite of Miyajima and everything! *Banzai.*

Ginroku turns for a quick look back at Miyajima and runs into a wall.

A wall of meat. Or, rather, a large man. In fact three large men.

Gray three-piece suits, punchperms, dark glasses in the dark.

Ah, no.

A black Mercedes, smoked windows, right passenger door gaping.

No, no, no.

Iron hands on his upper arms.

Ginroku shaking his head, his whole body.

"Chigaimasu!" he shouts. "Wrong! Not me! I'm someone else!"

Saturday, 9:57 P.M.

"Hanako, almost time for bed."

The naughty girl is quieter now, and Yoshi is almost ready to forgive her. After all, she's just a baby, she doesn't understand.

Yoshinori is out of his schoolgirl costume and into his favorite nightie. Not the pale blue one figured with oodles of tough-cute Goropikadon boys in red pounding their drums. No, tonight is girls' night, so tonight it's the pink flannel—very reasonable, only twelve hundred yen on sale last year at Seiyu—with those adorable Cheery Chums bouncing all over it in magenta and purple. On his feet are huge, fuzzy, orange Persian kitten slippers—darling little eyes and noses at the toes, thrilling little whiskers—that make Yoshinori feel all scrunchy and gulpy, like he's walking home a long, long time ago on two little sunset clouds.

And, although she made such a scene and fought him screeching and clawing—four scratches across Yoshi's cheek, four droplets of Yoshi's blood!—over every single mother-of-pearl button, a tiny matching outfit on Hanako. Orange and pink, Yoshi-*kun* and Hana-*chan*. Cheery chums.

551

"Cocoa, Han-*chan!* Before we brush our teeth. Want some?"

Oh, what a face. So sulky, so pouty.

"Want to go to the *toireh* once more, and tinkle?"

Pouty, sullen, spiteful. And *bad.* But, oh, how beautiful—the most beautiful baby yet. She melts his heart. Really, television doesn't do her justice. Face like a valentine, skin like plum blossoms, lips like— like… Yoshinori is getting impatient now, and more than a little excited. He is full of love for her.

"Hear the wind, Hanako? The *tenki-yohoh* is for frost. Brrr."

Not in here, though. Glowing space heater, fluffy futon, so cozy.

"Want to see a video, Han-*chan?* It's about a little girl, just like you."

Saturday, 9:59 P.M.

Clang, clang, clang, doors shut lights out on Hatsue *"Wasabi"* Tanaka, lying on her prison-cot. She is having second thoughts, except that she isn't, not at all, she truly hopes it *was* her nazi in the body bag. He dragged himself away from her university and over to his lousy headquarters, just in time for someone—oh, that it had been herself!—someone, anyway, to throw some wonderful incendiary device in there. And roast him.

And anyway they aren't so much second thoughts as second feelings. Hatsue feels—something, she feels it, whatever it is, violently, she feels it very violently, this feeling that she feels. She shudders with the violence of it. Because he's not dead, her beautiful smashed-nose nazi, because he can't be, because that would just break her heart, because it is for Hatsue herself to kill him. Either that, or he really is dead. "Nakatani Taro?" Was that what they called him, her pig? Was—is—that his name? But was that really him in the bag? Hatsue's nazi—and his damned girlfriend in the other bag? Some damned little Filipina slut! Dripping with AIDS! If so, Hatsue will kill her—except that, of course, if so, Hatsue won't kill her, because the slimy girlfriend, if that is what she is, or rather was, and Hatsue's own dear nazi are already as dead as they can possibly be, incinerated. And Hatsue is delighted. She yanks the stupid little disinfectant-smelling pillow from beneath her head and throws it against the far wall of her cell, cursing.

She lies there, feels the thin bunk mattress which is really just a sort of pad, hears its plastic cover crackle beneath her shoulder-blades, looks at the bars without seeing them, tries to think. Does she want him dead? Yes!

No! What does she want? To smash him again, to beat him again, to give him the stick again and again and again until he screams and bleeds. To feel that impact all down along her arms and right to the center. And then cling to him. And never let go. The fucking bastard. The strutting beast. Pure ego, ruthless, laughing at the world, a menace to everyone on the planet. Just like Hatsue's father, just like her grandmother.

Who paid her bail, the old bitch. Hatsue is out in the morning.

But she'll never see him again—good! She's glad! How she hates him!

She won't cry and ruin her makeup even though she isn't wearing any.

Hatsue lies there, tasting wet salt at the corners of her mouth.

Saturday, 10:00 P.M.

There! On the *terebi*—the scratchy old man with the blue eyes that are not brown! He is talking with his sounds that Hanako likes very, very much.

"*—dental records are being checked so I have been given to understand that is all I can tell you those are the only facts and the missing little girl Hanako.*"

"Nothing new," says the girl who is a boy. "We'll tape the rest."

Click

He turns to look at her.

"Which hand, Hana-*chan?*"

He has his hands behind his back. She turns away.

"You're supposed to guess which hand."

She moves behind the huge Hello Kitty again.

"Here, Hana-*chan,* a surprise! A little Hello Kitty, all for your very own!"

Hanako sticks out her lower lip. She makes a fist and bats Kitty away. She doesn't want it. She hates it. She hates the nightie and the slippers and the fuzzy big Kitty and this fuzzy little Kitty. She hates this place. She hates the scary movies because they are so scary and bad and they scare her. Most of all she hates this girl who is a boy, who is turning the lights almost off, and lifting her into the futon, and lifting her nightie which isn't really hers, and pulling down her panties which have Pikkoro on them from *Otosan* and *Okaasan*—where are they? And where is the scratchy old man? And hurting her! Hurting her with his finger! And saying *shizuka-ni,* bad girl be quiet, and pushing the little Kitty into her mouth. And hurting her, and hurting her.

Saturday, 10:32 P.M.

Teshima *oyabun* sits erect, hands on knees, flanked by his *kobun*, on the clear-plastic-covered, floral patterned, American colonial-style *sohfah* in this "living room" of the sprawling Numabukuro house of the fat and disgusting T-shirt pig, who is slumped, facing them, on a straight-backed pine chair with organdy frills around the seat cushion. Slumped, twitching, blue-lipped and staring, in a T-shirt which bears the wide-eyed likeness of Teshima's own great-grand-daughter, falling, and the foreigner, wiry like DiGiralamo but much less hair, stretching to reach her. The baby's tiny pale heart-shaped face or this gross panderer's above it—which is more terrified? Hard to say. The shirt is arresting, he'll say that for it. And the shirt man is an intelligent coward who obviously understands his situation. He is clutching a soiled canvas bag—what is in there?—and oozing cold greasy sweat and filling the room with a faint gut stink of mortal dread.

Loan shark? Loan jellyfish.

Does Teshima really have time for this creature? Where is little Hanako? That is the question. Gone, kidnapped. He still can not believe it, does not want to.

Because the best part of himself is now in danger of crumbling away too. Infant though she is, stranger to him though she is, she has been... supporting him. Supporting him, yes. Giving just enough meaning to his old life, so that he can continue it. And connecting him with her great-grandmother.

Hanako is the link to Hanako.

Was. Was the link. And the vibrating pig before them has plastered her picture all over these vile shirts, and scattered the shirts all over Tokyo. Making money from this tragedy, perhaps for the purchase of more and greasier fast food, gaudier artificial flowers, a more gigantic television receiver. Oh, yes, Moriuchi-*sensei* told him there were men like this, the voracious self-pampering ones. Teshima is near the limit of his considerable patience. He permits his mental self to pounce on the pig and gouge his eyes out, as Taoka-*sama* used to do in real life when annoyed, as Teshima himself would very much like to do right now. But he can wait a few minutes. They are here, after all, for a purpose, however trivial. His purpose is business: dealing with competition, gathering information, and possibly turning a modest profit. And he is now as always the instrument of his purpose. He is *oyabun*.

Teshima, bland as an egg, looks around, inwardly wincing at the window-chintz, at the stupid saddle-bridle-riding crop patterned wallpaper, and at the two plastic-draped Vibraloungers positioned like guests of honor in front of the huge television screen—what could the airwaves possibly bear to merit such scale? *Tsumaranai!* And at the putrid abstract expressionist messes on the walls, and at the bile-green nylon carpeting which is of course wall-to-wall, as the Americans used to say—perhaps to distinguish it from floor-to-ceiling? And at the oh-so-rustic and authentic pine rocking chair, and at the pine coffee table, both of them out of the Ai-World catalogue and piled with slick bright lifestyle magazines. And at the bookshelves full of not books or manuscripts but videocassettes, and at the rest of the hideous plastic Western-ness enveloping and smothering them. This room is Teshima's idea of hell.

What would DiGiralamo say about it? Nothing, because his old partner is dead, dead in the penitentiary—where at least he never had to open his eyes on anything worse than steel bars and concrete. *Organdy frills on the cushion.* And Moriuchi-*sama*, his great *sempai* in the brotherhood. Long dead. Teshima permits himself a private sigh. And Kikuno, once a tigress, now too old for anything but remembering. Well, Teshima is almost that old himself. Ah, Hanako. With the ancestors, with them for so long, dead, like nearly everyone and everything true and fine. While this pig is alive.

Well, Teshima can fix that.

"*Okyaku-sama. Irrasshai.*" Addressing them, the pig's wife, emerging through the tasteful blue and white curtains in the doorway. "This foolish old woman is your servant."

The wife herself is not piggish at all. Rather, a pleasant and open-faced woman of middle years. Attractive, even in her thrifty housecoat. Hospitable, though seeming slightly dazed, perhaps with fatigue, or from having been suddenly awakened at their arrival. But no hint of complaint or reproach. In fact—unless she is an accomplished actress—actually glad to see them. Well, well. Bowing low, on her knees in the gracious old way of generous gestures, smiling, full of welcome. Courteous. Calling them honored guests in a soft, seemly voice. Mannerly. A plump, bustling *okusan.* She reminds Teshima of Hanako—but then of course nearly all smiling women do. What is such a person doing with such a person? And why is the right side of her face so bruised?

561

"*Konban-wa.*" Teshima inclines his head, wishes her a good evening.

"*Konban-wa.*" She bows again, touches her forehead to the ugly carpet. "*Kochira wa Sawada Rumiko de gozaimasu,* this poor person is Sawada Rumiko."

"*Teshima Tadao desu. Hajimemashita,* now our acquaintance has begun. And these men are my business associates."

"Teshima!" A hissing insuck of breath from the pig man.

"*Hajimemashita. Yoroshiku onegaishimasu,* it has begun with very good wishes," she says. "Do you know, I had a friend one time in Nagasaki. Her name was Teshima. Teshima Takako. She could sing."

"Ah," says the *oyabun.* "No relation, I am sure. My family are all long-dead. I was raised in an orphanage."

"I too," she says. "My parents were killed. Takako also died, but not in the War. She died of typhus. Her voice was the most beautiful you ever heard. Even speaking, it was a kind of song. Takako."

"Teshima!" The pig man again, hissing and groaning.

"Well! Enough of that! This is here and now, and you gentlemen are our guests. So! From this, your worthless servant, would you gentlemen graciously accept a cup of *o-cha?"*

Green tea. Not Coke, not scotch, not Pocari Sweat, not some sugary tropical mess festering in a big glass crammed with crushed ice and fruit, and with a little umbrella on top. How long since a woman in her home has made him a cup of real *cha?*

"Hai," he says. *"Onegaishimasu."*

She bows once more, withdraws through the curtained doorway.

Does she, Teshima wonders irrelevantly, want a job?

"Please don't kill me." The pig man, whispering. Teshima and his *kobun* sit regarding him. "This is all for you," says the man, opening the bag and dumping it out on the floor. "Money! *Issen-man.* Ten million, all yours."

Morinaga Eiji bends, retrieves a bundle, pulls the knife from his sleeve and cuts the twine. Scrap paper in his hands, now fluttering to the carpet along with two *ichi man* notes. Eiji smiles very slightly and does not replace the knife. The pig man's gaze moves back and forth between the knife and the trash on the floor. Teshima will not be obliged to rip the eyes out, because they seem ready to pop out of their own accord.

"They tricked me," says the pig man.

"Who tricked you?" asks Morinaga-*san.*

"The *terebi* bastards. They wouldn't even put up ten million."

"Ten million for what?" Morinaga-*san* becoming more lawyerly.

"The ransom."

"The ransom for whom?"

"The baby, Hanako. That was the whole idea."

Breathless, Teshima feels his own eyes protruding.

"Ah, you kidnapped the baby and then demanded a ransom," Says Morinaga-*san,* left forefinger pushing his eyeglasses back, higher on the bridge of his nose. "I see."

Teshima's shoulder and thigh muscles are tensed. He leans forward.

"Yes—no! I demanded the ransom, but I didn't kidnap the baby. You see, I bought this whole roll of film, and so I thought, well here is a once in a lifetime opportunity, which maybe you gentlemen can appreciate, and so I just fiddled with the negatives, and that was good enough to fool the *terebi* bastards— except I guess it wasn't."

Teshima feels the rush, feels his big old hands forming claws.

Now.

"Well! Here we are, gentlemen, and I hope you like it."

No.

The wife, back from her kitchen. "Fresh hot *o-cha*. It's special, from Okinawa. I use it in my *terebi* tea ceremony lessons. See how frothy. It's because Ginroku bought me an electric whisk. So it's just whisk, whisk, whisk and there you are. All the goodness of real *cha* in just a fraction of the time. And bless his heart he also bought me a big new Zojirushi so we always have boiling hot water, twenty-four hours of the day, enough for as many as one hundred guests, although we never have that many. In fact we never have any guests at all, because Ginroku does not bring any of his friends home—till tonight! So I am very happy. Mine is the best Zojirushi, and it is preprogrammable to save us money, because it knows what times of the day we will want the most hot water, and it just keeps simmering the rest of the time. My husband buys everything for me. He *is* everything *to* me. He is all I have. Is the *cha* hot enough? He loves me."

Teshima takes a deep shuddering breath, raises the cup to his lips.

"Is it all right? I can always make more. Do you like it?"

Still fighting, Teshima sips. Ah, strong and bitter.

"Umai," he grunts politely. "It is excellent."

"Oh, *ureshii,* I am so happy."

"It is very good," says Morinaga Eiji, holding the cup in his left hand.

"Delicious," says Tetsuo, the number two.

"Refreshing," says Akio, the number three.

"I'm so glad! May I refill your cups? If you would replace them on the tray… there. Believe me, there is plenty. And are you gentlemen hungry? Would you like something to nibble on?"

"Hai," breathes Teshima, pulse slowing, muscles easing.

"Wonderful. Because I have the best *daifuku,* hundreds of them, so sweet, so chewy. Regular *daifuku* and *daifuku* with a little strawberry inside. But—but oh! They are all frozen!"

"Calm yourself, dear lady," says Teshima. "The secret is to remain calm."

"There is plenty of time," says Eiji, knife under right hand on thigh.

"Oh, it will take but a very few minutes! I have in my kitchen a special microwave which is able to pre-thaw in seconds, then cook to perfection in minutes. There is no timer, no need for one, because the oven knows when the food is cooked. Ginroku bought it for me at Yodobashi Camera, which is a famous shop selling not only cameras but a wide array of labor-saving electronic wonders. Their prices are fully competitive with those one finds in Akihabara. You see the delightful Yodobashi advertisements all the time on the *terebi.* Do you like our *terebi?* It is new, new last year. Isn't it big and wonderful? Dear Ginroku bought it for me, also at Yodobashi-*ya*—and he almost let me come along to pick it out! So now we watch the Yodobashi commercial messages on the Yodobashi television itself. So it is very special. Would you gentlemen like to watch the *terebi?*"

"Hai," says Eiji. *"Onegaishimasu."*

She pushes a button on the remote control, bows, leaves.

"Where is the baby?" asks Eiji.

"Who knows?" says the pig man. "Who cares? I just wanted the money, for—for you. For you gentlemen. But they double-crossed me. You see, the truth is, I've been sort of working for you all along, as a freelancer, so to speak. Making loans, collecting, saving. So I could give it to you, your percentage. A—a present." The pig man, facing eight human eyes. "So please don't kill me."

"We won't," says Teshima.

"Oh, thank you, thank you, *maido arigato gozaimasu.*"

"You will kill yourself. *Seppuku.*"

Teshima looks at Eiji.

Eiji proffers the knife.

"No!" A breathy pig squeal.

"It is the way," says Eiji. "Jab in the navel, rip up."

Pig lips frozen in a soundless no.

As the doorway curtains part once more.

"Here we are, gentlemen! I told you I wouldn't be long. *Daifuku!* For you, sir, and for you and for you and for you. Don't they smell good? *Anata,* would you like one as well? Maybe not, dear, you're supposed to be on a diet. My husband should take better care of his health. Ah, the *terebi.* Did you gentlemen see the news?"

"No," says Eiji. "We missed it."

"Missed the news? Missed the news? Really? You are not joking? Sometimes Ginroku jokes with me, and he is just as funny as the men on the *terebi.* But perhaps it is just as well you missed the news. You are better off not knowing the latest, because it just gets worse and worse. Oh, Tokyo is terrible. They say it is the safest major city in the world, but, if that is true, I would certainly hate to live in any of the others! Gangland slayings, and a gruesome ritual murder of some nice professor and his wife in Tamagawa, and now their little orphan baby is missing, and Lieutenant Yoshida said maybe—maybe kidnapped! Another one! To come back home, ashes in a bottle! Oh, it's too much, I can't stand it."

The wife covers her face, sobs.

Teshima silently gives her his handkerchief. She dabs at her eyes.

"Thank you, you're so kind, and I am so foolish. Ginroku says so, and I know it's true, although I do my best. I *do*. Do you believe me?"

"*Hai,*" says Teshima. "Hush now. *Shimpai nai,* don't worry."

"Don't worry, don't worry, that's what Ginroku always says, stay inside, lock the door, make sure the minicam is switched on, *and don't worry,* and I try not to, but how can I help it? How can I help worrying when so many terrible things are going on right around me? There was that horrible little insurance salesman who disemboweled—yes! Disemboweled! Didn't you hear about that? Disemboweled another commuter on the train—and why? Because he was bumped, jostled. With a butcher knife. That's all, no other reason, the man bumped him. Well, what did he expect, rush hour on the Tozai line? He died. On the floor of the train, all the poor man's organs, how terrible. And! There was some firebombing attack on those people who are trying to save Japan and the Emperor. And! Some religious people were murdered even though they were religious, and that nice lawyer and his family were finally found and dug up, but it was too late."

"The lawyer?" asks Eiji "Iidzuka-*san?*"

"*Much* too late. Oh! Every day! Bombings, shootings, knifings, clubbings. And there was that convenience food poisoner extorting money from Glico and other major companies who was quite willing to sacrifice the lives of innocent people that they never could catch, and—"

"*The lawyer?*"

"What lawyer? Ah, Iidzuka-*san*, you mean. Yes, he was a lawyer, and very brilliant because he graduated from Todai, and he was killed by Takeshita-*sama*, so they say—but how could that be? How could he be a murderer if he really is the Buddha, as he says, and, if he is, he would certainly know it, wouldn't he? I mean, does that make sense? Would the Buddha go around killing people? So it can't be him—or, or maybe it is. To tell the truth, I don't really know."

"Takeshita?"

"Yes, of course. The one they call the Great Healer, the one who says we must throw off our golden fetters and live free, which I also believe. As I said to my husband, *Anata*, I said, we must do that, we should snap the chains of gold that bind us, throw off our burdens of material trash, because—"

"Where is he?"

"Right here, of course. Do you think I'd let anyone, even you gentlemen, into my home if my husband were not with you? That would be foolish indeed. We have three locks on the door because my husband is so worried about me, and also because he keeps such a huge amount of *genkin* hidden here, right there in the *kinko*, behind that big picture of the blue Western girl with three breasts and both eyes on the same side of her head like a *hirame* fish."

"Where is Takeshita?"

"Who? Oh, the Healer. The *terebi* lady said in hospital, badly injured."

"Sawada-*san*," says Teshima, "is there more tea?"

571

"Yes! A great deal more. Would you like some?"

"Please. It is so very special."

She bows through the curtains again.

"Once more," says Teshima. "Where is the baby?"

"I don't know! No idea! Please."

"Seppuku, then."

"No, no, no, no, no, no."

"It's the only honorable way."

"Honor! Fuck honor! What is it? Do you think I care about honor? Do you think I want to die like a stuck pig for honor? All I want is a little financial security for my old age—and hers! Please, who will take care of my wife? I'm—I'm all she's got."

"Yes." Teshima, a little sickened by the slobbering, more than a little impatient now, needing to be off, to continue the search. "Live then. But empty that safe."

"It's almost all I have!" Teshima, eyebrows up. "And—and it's yours!"

Pig man, shoving the picture aside, opening the *kinko,* scooping.

Money changing hands, good thick bricks of it—real this time.

In the bag, a solid evening's work.

"Now the shirt off your back."

"Hai! Dozo!"

"And the gold in your mouth. Open up, let us see-"

"More *o-cha,* gentlemen!" The wife returning, bowing, the door-curtains rippling behind her. "Plenty for everyone, and nothing but the best, because my dear husband spares no expense. Isn't that, right, *Anata? Anata,* where is your shirt? Oh, look, *Anata,* on the *terebi!* Isn't she cute? Gentlemen, it is that wonderful Fukuko good luck doll, which they are selling for only *yon man.* Forty thousand, that's not much, is it? For what you get. Because the person who buys Fukuko will certainly experience good fortune. I remember, one person has said, 'I couldn't believe all the good things that happened to me after I bought Fukuko.' Oh, *Anata,* we should purchase such a doll."

"Sawada-*san,*" says Teshima. "What happened to your face?"

She looks down, blushes.

"Oh, well, that was just a mistake."

"Yes," agrees Teshima, looking hard at the pig man.

"More tea?"

"Thank you, no. We are leaving shortly."

"Oh, so soon?"

"Zan-nen, regretfully."

573

"Well, would you gentlemen like to use our toilet first? It has a computer in it—I mean, in the seat, you can program it for any season along a full range of desired temperatures until there is one just right for you. It is as easy as pushing a button."

"Maybe some other time."

"Oh! So you'll be back."

"Very possibly," says Teshima, looking at the husband again.

"No more tea, you are sure?

"Thank you, no. But do you mind if I smoke?"

"*Dozo.* Ginroku smokes all the time. For his nerves."

"*Tabako!*" Teshima barks at the pig man, ignoring Tetsuo's unfiltered Camel and Akio's golden Zippo proffered on either side, watching the ex-loanshark snap back to life, bounce from his chair, skid kneeling to a stop in front of Teshima and holding a Kent in his left hand and in his right a Lucite cube.

"This is a lighter!" he shouts, waving the cube. "Automatic! Has a little brain, smarter than most people. Just put it in the little hole, you'll see!" Teshima puts the Kent between his lips. The pig man inserts the tobacco end in the cube. They wait. "The heat from your hand is what does it. Human warmth."

They wait. Nothing.

Sawada removes the cube, shakes it, holds it to the Kent again. They wait. Teshima sitting immobile, big hands on big knees, cigarette in his mouth. Again, nothing. Giggling, quivering, his face awash with tears and sweat and *hanamisu* from his nose, sodden Sawada once again removes the cube, peers into the hole, blows into it, tries once more, his writhing smile a sight to turn from.

They wait.

Nothing.

Saturday, 11:03 P.M.

Kawakami Yukio sniffs, wrinkles his damaged nose, takes a bite.

Bad. Yukio chews the rank stringy tuna, watches the little sushi-bearing saucers circling on their conveyor belt at eye level above the U-shaped counter, swallows, kills the taste with a sip of Kirin. Sushi-mat sushi, all they could afford. Three thousand yen—how far does that go these days? Even at some run-down little after-hours place in some stinking Suidobashi back street? Not far.

"Mazui." says Masaaki, chewing, looking up from his *manga*. "Yuck."

"Umakunai," Yukio agrees, taking another reluctant bite. "You know, maybe he got lost. Maybe he looked for us at the wrong exit."

"Maybe not," says Masaaki. "He wasn't a real yakuza, that's all."

"Well, we've got a lot of Kleenex."

"Fuck the Kleenex," says Masaaki, going back to his comic.

"How is your sushi?" asks the big red-faced chef, molding fish to rice.

576

"Fuck the sushi," Masaaki tells him, not bothering to look up.

"What's wrong with it?" asks the chef, getting redder.

"Oh, nothing much," says Masaaki, flipping a page. "Just everything."

"Stale fish for starters," Yukio says, loudly, in the hearing of the other customers, four elderly male construction guards—blue uniforms, yellow belts, torch-batons under the counter on the shelf, helmets on their knees—hunched and blinking on their stools across from the friends. "This *maguro* has been around for a long time. Maybe it was even... frozen*?*"

"*Chigaimasu!*"

"It has that thawed mushy-mealy texture."

"Not frozen!"

"So you say. But I know fresh *maguro*, and this is far from fresh. So is the *hamachi*, the *ebi*, the *taco*—"

"Bought this morning at Tsukiji! Right off the boat!"

Masaaki giggles, nose in comic.

Yukio laughs, pushes away his saucer. "Your rice is low-grade too. Thai? American? And overcooked—that's why it's so crumbly—with too much salt and not enough sugar. Your *wasabi* is right out of the tube."

577

"Ground fresh daily with my own hands!"

"If your sushi was free I wouldn't complain."

"Could you do better?"

"Easily. I am head chef at Nakamori's in Iidabashi. Probably you've heard of Nakamori's. Iidabashi sanchome."

"That's right," Masaaki snickers. "He practically runs the place. And I know a bit about fish myself."

"Well, if you two gentlemen know so much," says the chef, slamming fish to rice, "why don't you leave—and open your own sushi-ya?"

"Perhaps we will," Yukio tells him. "Would you care to invest?"

The friends are laughing and slapping the counter, when Masaaki glances up at the little television mounted near the ceiling, in the corner above the service door. He stops laughing. "Donner again," he says.

Yukio looks up. Yes, Donner. And the same girl, yap yap. Now the fire, same terrible footage, smoke, firemen and hoses, headquarters in ashes, now the two horrible body bags, the ambulance.

"Don't worry, Yuk-*kun*, they really will get him. The one who did that." Masaaki snickers, goes back to his *manga*. "I'd hate to be in that bastard's shoes."

Yukio drains his beer.

"... and this just in..." The cute soft little newsboy, yapyap, who never had to make a hard choice in his life, a natural little microphone man, soft as a girl, frowning in that flirty perky way of junior newscasters to indicate Concern—as if they gave a shit about anything outside their own perfumed flesh! *"... identified as Maria Robledos of Manila, and Nakatani Taro of this city..."*

Nakatani Taro!

No.

Just no.

Absolutely not.

Kawakami Yukio did not, did not, did not kill his Leader.

Sunday, 7:01 A.M.

Yoshinori is so mad. She wet the futon! And threw a tantrum! And *hit* him! Doubled up her fist and struck him deliberately in the mouth, when he was only trying to comfort her afterwards. Oh, it was terrible—don't parents teach their children anything these days, manners, how to behave? Yoshinori got hardly any sleep. And *now*, she's in the *furo*, sitting by the tub, won't come out. Pouting. Yoshinori hates a pouter. Well, he just won't speak to her till she says she's sorry.

Also, as soon as possible, he'll set her free. He'll enjoy that. She won't.

Yoshinori yawns and sips his warmed-over cocoa. He taped the news but he's up, so he might as well watch the latest. When was the last Sunday he was awake by seven? He can't remember. He picks up the *remocon* and moves to the *terebi*. He has an erection but it's just a weensy morning one.

Click.

He sits, arm around Big Kitty and Little Kitty on his lap.

"*... Lieutenant Kamijo is in satisfactory condition. No arrests were made following the Machida incident,* *but police have surrounded the house of Officer Miyajima Ryota, 50, in Okubo. We take you there, to Kobayashi Miyuki. Kobayashi*-san?… Hai, *Kobayashi Miyuki* desu, ohayo gozaimasu. *I am at 3-10-432 Okubo* ichome *before the house of Miyajima Ryota, a constable with Tokyo Metropolitan police. As you can see, his brother officers are everywhere. Ryota*-san *is wanted for assault with a deadly weapon and resisting arrest. Authorities also believe he may be linked to the disappearance of Yamamoto Hanako and the five other little girls. Associate Chief Ishimura himself has taken charge. He has been using the bullhorn, urging Officer Miyajima to give himself up. He has given it as factual that stronger measures will soon be in order if Officer Miyajima is not more forthcoming. Ishimura*-san *has promised us an interview shortly. Captain Yoshida Makoto is also here. The Captain has declined comment, however. Now back to central… In other news—"*

"Kitty!" He hugs her tightly, breathless, nearly weeping with joy.

Years of planning—and now success!

And look at his erection now!

Forget the schedule.

"Hanako!"

Sunday, 8:53 A.M.

Captain Yoshida Makoto—dismissed, reinstated, suspended pending a hearing, and officially reprimanded by Associate Chief Ishimura, all in the space of about twelve minutes—is, after a night of pacing and telephoning, in Okubo. Houses nearly touching, miniature gardens, housewives goggling down from their balconies, pretending to hang the wash. He has been here since 4:00. He has not slept. Neither has the Associate Chief who, after their budget meeting, and when Lieutenant Kamijo finally regained consciousness and began raving, and after people started to listen to these ravings, and after word from these people worked its way up the chain of command, arrived with Yoshida and took over the Monster case at 6:30. So Yoshida has nothing to do. He was wrong, Ishimura was right. Time to think about early retirement. He has always wanted to travel. He wishes he had a cigarette. Perhaps he will start smoking again. Why not?

His feet are wet. He is standing in a tiny open space on Officer Miyajima's sodden front lawn, itself about the size of a bathmat. The street, lane, and sidewalk are choked with gleaming police vehicles.

The house is surrounded by uniforms, nearly a hundred of them, three deep and shoulder-to-shoulder. Standard operating procedure. But Ishimura is taking no chances. Reinforcements are on the way, from Sugamo and elsewhere. Wan daylight, but big lights are still trained on all doors and windows. The house is locked, quiet, no sign of Miyajima, no sign of the baby, Hanako. Ishimura has tried the loudhailer, now it should be the ram.

But Ishimura is dithering: *if Miyajima is not home, as he almost certainly is not, and if he is somehow not guilty, although he almost certainly is, and if they are without the proper judicial warrant, as they still unfortunately are, it being Sunday morning, then the Department is clearly liable—and from hard money categories. There is no insurance coverage for such a contingency as this, can Captain Yoshida grasp that? Those are the facts. Not what we wish but what is.* Well, true enough, sir, but he might be in there and carving her up even now. *That is understood. This is not the Captain's show. Is that understood?* Well, so be it. Yoshida knows it is too late anyway, for the baby. Rain and snow have fallen during the night, but now the sky is clearing, and some of the uniformed officers have begun going over their *patocaa* with chamois and feather dusters.

Standing with Yoshida are his niece, her cameraman, and the Americans, Donner, Nakamura, and his wife. The wife's hands are bandaged. Why? Yoshida doesn't care enough to ask. What he wants is a cigarette.

"Excuse me, Mr. Donner, could I borrow a cigarette?"

"I was just about to ask you. Buddy? How about it?"

"I'm out. I mean, I don't smoke."

"Buddy doesn't smoke," says Mrs. Nakamura. "And neither do you!"

"I don't drink either, but I'd sure like a slug right now."

True enough, Mr. Donner looks terrible. Nerves, no sleep. They all look bad, standing around rumpled and sniffling, red-eyed. Yoshida himself, who seldom catches cold, feels one coming on.

"Forget it!" she says. "You want to calm down, do some aerobics."

"Aerobics, great." The colonel snickers. "Hey, Janey, your knuckles."

"Told you on the phone, Wonder Woman has been fightin' a little bit."

"Violence never solved anything."

"Bullshit, Buddy. It solved this one little rat-bastard on the train. I'm on the way home from Do Sport. I'm thinking how I don't have to carry Ruriko upstairs for a change, and I'm wondering about her and the kid. I'm standing. There's a wad of international school kids sitting. On the silver seat. And there's these old ladies are standing. They're holding onto their shopping bags and each and trying not to go down in a heap every time the trains start and stops. *Old* ladies, you know? Tiny. All bent over. So I go to the kids, 'Hey, silver seats are for senior citizens, you know, old people.' And the big one goes to me, 'Hey, bitch, we *are* old. Scheherazade is sixteen, Siobhan here is going on nineteen because she got held back, had to repeat a few grades, had a little trouble with drugs, didn't just say no.' Giggling like mad, all of them. 'Me too,' he says. 'I'm almost eighteen. The old man's giving me a Daimler for my birthday. Eighteen's pretty old. Not as old as you, though.' I'm pissed, I tell him, 'You're supposed to be ambassadors of good will for your country. So move your ass, or I'll clock you one.' That really gets him laughing. 'Hey, bitch,' he says 'my old man *is* the ambassador, so fuck you.' He's chewing on a Reese's Peanut Butter cup and laughing and spraying little bits of chocolate crud all over, so I clocked him a couple good ones in the braces. What a mess. I go, 'This hurts you more than it does me.' He's crying, holding his mouth. I tell him, 'Come back in a couple years, I'll give you one in the throat.'"

The colonel embraces her, kisses her.

"Jesus, Buddy, what are you doing? You stink. Get away from me. Let's all do a little running in place, get the old blood circulating, what do you say? One, two, one, two. Come on, Donner, sweetie, it's good for you. Freeze your ass and get cramps, it won't bring Ruriko back. Jesus, I'm sorry, I feel terrible. I just can't get over it, she's dead. Think about that. But the little baby could be anywhere, probably just lost. She'll turn up. Won't she, Captain?"

"Ah, *tabun*, maybe so." Puff, puff.

"They'll find her in somebody's garden or doghouse or something, and she'll come out rubbing her eyes and wondering what's all the commotion, you'll see. Come on, Buddy, get those knees up."

All of them, huffing clouds of steamy breath, running in place all jammed together on the mushy weeds—Miyuki, the cameraman, Donner, the colonel, and his wife—under the icy eye of Ishimura. Yoshida does not care. In fact, strangely, the exercise does seem to help. Lightens his mood, clears his mind.

"Oh," says Miyuki-*san*. "I am not dressed for this."

"Honey, so what?" says the colonel's wife. Then, to the colonel, "Up, Buddy, up! Squish, squish, squish! Jesus, you're fat, I didn't realize. Look at you in those sweats. Wow, soldier, when was the last time you saw your dick?"

"Yes," says Miyuki-*san*, "Hanako is probably just lost. This often happens. In fact, we have a special word, *maigo*. It means a wandering child."

"That's what'll happen, right, Captain?" asks the colonel's wife.

"It is certainly our hope."

"That wasn't my question."

"All right, then, I will tell you." No one running in place now, all eyes on Yoshida. "The news is very bad. In the kitchen of Mr. Donner's home. On a tumbler in the sink, three fingerprints. These are a positive match with the ones on the whiskey bottles. With those of Officer Miyajima."

"Then *get in there and kill the fucker!*"

587

The colonel's wife, swooping down on Ishimura-*san*, who has no English.

"He's here, you think?" asks Uchiyama Masaaki. "Donner?"

"So they said," grunts Kawakami Yukio. "The hero."

Yukio, his nose and eyes looking even worse than yesterday, his whole face a swollen blue-olive-magenta bruise, is slouched in the passenger seat. Maybe he's depressed about being a *douseiaisha*. But hey, it's not so bad. It's life, it's reality. Nothing is either good or bad but thinking makes it so fucked. That's Masaaki's philosophy. So don't think. Do. You're alive, you deal with the situation as it is. That's what Masaaki's old man says. *Douseiaisha?* Masaaki doesn't give a shit. In fact he always kind of knew it. And what a night they had in the back of the S-Cargo, horsing around on a bed of *manga* and Kleenexes. It was even comfortable. And a hundred times better than jerking off into some muscle *manga*—even *Powahrifutah*—which basically are not reality.

Reality is no gas, again. Had to leave the engine running all night and the heater on. Train station soba for breakfast, the early news while they're gagging down noodles: Donner. And then that other shit came on, and Yukio stormed out. He's moody. Could that interfere with their relationship? Maybe. But Yukio is really built, a genuine hard guy. And, well, Masaaki loves him.

What Masaaki really needs right now, however, is about six Deans, one after the other, because his nicotine level is almost as low as his alcohol level, which is lower even than the S-Cargo's gas level. Nevertheless, he has piloted his little pink truck safely all the way to Okubo, running on fumes, and parked it expertly—setting the brake and locking all doors—at the outer fringe of the fucking cop cars. Which make him wonder if this is really the best place in the world to kill the foreigner once and for all. Yukio with that creepy fucking *katana* wrapped up in his coat. Sure, the old bastard ruined their careers. Sure, he disgraced them. Sure, he has no business here in the first place, and Japan would be well rid of him. *Mochiron,* obviously. But the closer they get to the center of the action the more Masaaki wonders.

"Yuk-*kun*," he has to ask, finally, "is this such a good idea?"

"Is *life?*" his friend turns to him wild-eyed and snarls, "Is *life* a good idea?"

589

Well, Yukio's got him there.

"Wait," Teshima Tadao tells the driver and gestures to his *kobun.*

Associate Chief Ishimura is busy. That is a fact, understated. This case is important to him. That is another extreme understatement. The insane foreign woman is prodding the Associate Chief in the chest with her forefinger. It feels like the butt-end of a riot stick. This must and will stop. And what's this? *Zan-nen, komatta-na,* some old skinhead gangster with his cohorts, shouldering through the uniforms. Just what he needs, a bunch of yakuza hoodlums.

"You!" shouts Ishimura. *"Gyangu!* Back behind the cordons!"

Confusion compounded, when the essential situation is now so clear. Get Miyajima. Ishimura turns to his circle of aide-uniforms. "You officers, get these people back. That means everyone." Amazing, look at the woman, how brazen, how violent. "And you. Tell the riot bus personnel to deploy."

There. And now for the cunning Beast who devoured dull Yoshida.

And Kamijo, too, perhaps. *Zan-nen.*

And Kamijo's uniforms. And a whole school of other small fish.

And of course all those baby girls.

But not Ishimura, no indeed. Not the shark.

"The loudhailer, please… thank you… OFFICER. MIYAJIMA. LAST. WARNING. IF. YOU. ARE. INSIDE. COME. OUT. OR. WE. ARE. COMING. IN."

He's *not* in, of course. He's nowhere near. He's a monster, but not a stupid one. He proved that by eluding Kamijo. So really this is all a very expensive game of charades. But there is the NHK girl, there is the cameraman, the little red light. So the Associate Chief must do something, if only just for show. He is surprised and mildly pleased to discover that he has a flair for this sort of thing.

"MIYAJIMA-*SAN*. DO. YOU. HEAR. ME."

What he'd really like to do is smoke a cigarette, right now and right down to the filter. But it is not yet time, not nearly.

The huge gray riot bus slows, and Tanaka Hatsue drops lightly, and as nonchalantly as possible, from the rear bumper. Not even nine o'clock. Very good time from Sugamo. She'll remember that, next time she has to get across town in a hurry. Jump a riot bus. It was easy. Free on bail and out on the sidewalk, standing there cursing, Hatsue was suddenly enveloped in choking clouds of diesel exhaust as three armored buses lumbered out of the yard and gunned toward the freeway. She coughed, caught a glimpse of helmeted pigs grinning down through the mesh. That did it. She hopped on the last bus, didn't care where it was going, was willing to go anywhere for another chance at a riot cop—a nose, an ear, anything at all. If you can't be with the one you hate.

But now—*sugoi!* Climbing out of that ugly little pink truck. No, it can't be. It certainly looks like him from the back, however. Hatsue wants a look at his face, whatever is left of it.

Bloodlust, it's not just a word.

Sunday, 8:54 A.M.

Morinaga Eiji, *ichiban kobun* but wearing a physician's frown of concern and a stethoscope around his neck and a white smock over his suit, carrying a clipboard, brushing past the two somnolent police guards, and striding up to the sunlit figure on the bed behind the screen: the Great Killer, of friends, women, babies. Formerly. But now swathed and swaddled, a huge Q-Tip, and very much at Morinaga's mercy.

"Takeshita-sama, desu ne?" Morinaga whispers, bending close to hear.

"Hai." Soft as a breath. *"So desu."*

"The Great Healer of Zenbu-kyo, *desu ne?"*

"Hai, so desu. And you are… the Avenger?"

"Hai!"

Sunday, 8:55 A.M.

"OFFICER. MIYAJIMA. THIS. IS. YOUR. LAST."

"Bakayaro!"

There! In the upstairs window! Revolver in one hand, bottle in the other! He *is* home. He *is* a fool. Kamijo was right. Wonderful. Associate Chief Ishimura's heart gives an almost painful lurch of joy. He will have an unscheduled cigarette. Because soon he will be 'Associate' no more. And that is almost a fact.

"CHANCE. COME. OUT. WITH. YOUR. HANDS. UP."

"Bakayaro! I never killed her!"

Sunday, 8:56 A.M.

Humming high in the back of his throat, Yoshinori removes the unresisting baby's clothes. Drapes drawn tight, door double-locked and chained, Ansaphone on: *Moshi moshi, Miyajima Yoshinori de gozaimasu, I am not home right now, please leave a message, gomen-kudasai.* The lights are romantically low, and all his jolly fuzzy characters are looking down, watching from their perches. Kitty too, of course, but she's right on the floor beside them. On the video, baby Sayako's freeing, sound very low, no more than a sort of intermittent mew. In the play of light and shadows from the screen, their two nearly naked bodies—Yoshinori is down to his training bra and naughty little garterbelt—lying on the shower curtain.

Sunday, 8:57 A.M.

Uchiyama Masaaki's mighty right, minus the skull ring but still deadly, flashes in the sunlight, connects with Donner's own skull.

Buddy Nakamura, blinks, turns, jumps this weird little shit that just popped out of thin air and slugged Donner. Gonna flatten him, stamp his fucking passport.

Kawakami Yukio unsheaths his stolen *katana* and leaps for the huge *Nihon-jin* who is crushing the life from Masaaki.

Janey Nakamura sees the flash of steel, crouches, pivots, grabs the maniac's sword hand, a real maniac with shiners, before he can decapitate her husband, grabs and twists, twists hard until he grunts and drops the thing, and then she lands a good solid one to the heart, pulling back now for a throat shot.

"Kare to wa te o kiteh! Hands off!" screams Tanaka Hatsue, sprinting the last few meters then

bringing the riot baton down across the shoulders of the murdering foreign bitch. *"He's mine!"*

"FIREARM. DOWN. AND. COME. OUT. WITH."

Yoshida Makoto snaps into uncomprehending action, disentangling the sudden combatants, Yoshida joined now by three men in dark glasses. He does not know who they are, but he does know what. However, they are helping.

"IN. CLEAR. VIEW."

Teshima Oyabun, standing to one side, frowning. Two of these individuals he has seen before. The foreigner... on television, on the T-shirt, leaping. The girl... also on the television, she is a newsperson? Yes, there is a man with a camera. A *gaijin* woman—the leaper's wife? A skinny *chinpirra*—where before has he seen that rat face? Ah, yes, the shrine. Teshima waits, watches, standing erect and immobile. What is the meaning of this skirmish? What has it to do with Hanako? Is she here? Does the uniformed madman in the window have her? It is probable and has been so announced. Should Teshima shoot him, to be prudent?

Yoshida Makoto has separated these snarling individuals. He questions them, probing for motive. Wrenching the police riot baton from her sinewy little hands and returning it to its indignant owner, he learns that the tiny stick-wielding girl was trying to save the nose-damaged man from Mrs. Nakamura, who was trying to prevent the murder of her husband, the colonel, whom Yoshida of course knows. Fair enough, there is the blade, the old hoodlum bending to retrieve it. Why then did the nose-damaged man attempt this murder? Because the colonel was crushing and pummeling the nose-damaged man's *chinpirra* friend. A series of attacks and rescues. Various points of view, like that movie of the Rosho Gate. Officers holding the rescuer/attackers, restraining them.

"Finally why," Yoshida asks the *chinpirra,* "did you attack Mr. Donner?"

"IF. YOU. DO. NOT."

"You!" shouts Donner. "Punk!" And dragging the officer who has pinioned his arms Donner leaps again for the skinny boy, biting him in the neck and wrenching back and forth, an ugly sight. The officers drag them apart again, but there is a bright bloom at the corner of the screaming *chinpirra's* jaw, the blood welling and streaming.

"Animal!" he shrieks.

"You little fucking lizard!" snarls Donner, red-mouthed, raging, two more uniforms on him, his eyeglasses hanging from one ear. Well, he is insane, a real *hen-na gaijin*—and this is a respected *Eigo no sensei?* Yoshida shakes his head.

"Cannibal!" The *chinpirra,* holding his throat, pressing back against the officer for protection.

"Yesterday! Yesterday too! You jumped me yesterday too!" shouts Donner. "You and your asshole friend! And! Friday! I know you! Friday! Captain, arrest this little bastard! One of my students, Friday afternoon! Almost hit her, killed her—nice girl, sweet, wouldn't hurt a soul—scared her half to death. Drunk. Little cocksucker, little drunken cocksucker. And kidnapped me! Arrest them both. Arrest everyone."

"Young man," says the big old shaven-headed yakuza, handing the skinny boy a handkerchief. "I know you. Do you know me?"

"No." Taking the handkerchief, pressing it to his neck. Sullen.

"You were one of my *chinpirra*." The skinny boy's eyes widening. "Perhaps you used to drive a little pink truck. And your name is…" turning to a younger, even larger man at his right.

"Uchiyama Masaaki. Araddin Pachinko, Asagaya. *Sendenkaa*, handyman. DWI Friday afternoon, Kichijyoji, incarcerated, bail in the amount of *san man* paid by Associated Holdings, fired, damages to the vehicle deemed in excess of its current market value, it therefore deeded over to him, title and registration pending a lump sum payment of *go juu man.*"

"Uchiyama Masaaki. And mine is Teshima Tadao." Color draining from the skinny boy's face, knees buckling. The officer releasing his hold, the boy landing on his knees in the mud. "Do you know me now?"

"*Hai, Oyabun.*" Very faint. The boy squat-kneeling, head down, bony shoulders shaking. "Please don't torture me first." The old man raising his eyebrows, looking left and right at his companions, his companions shaking their heads and shrugging.

"All right," says the old man. "No torture. But do you think you could help us with some information? Do you think you could help us find a missing child? Would you be so kind?"

"*Hai, Oyabun, zehi onegaish'tain desu,* yes, a thousand times, and from my heart. If you will kill me quickly, mercifully."

"Please understand that our chief concern here is the baby. Yamamoto Hanako. Who fell from the bridge in Noborito Friday evening, spent the night in hospital with this *gaijin sensei*"—a polite inclination of the head towards the bloody-mouthed Donner—"then went to his home with him the following morning. Late morning. That much seems clear. But where is the baby now?

"Here," says Yoshida. "In that house, Officer Miyajima's house."

"So this Officer Miyajima took her away?"

"That is what we think. His fingerprints were found in Mr. Donner's home. And have been found on other... articles... associated with the abducted infants. Except that this officer was in his designated *koban* at the time, with his assigned partner, on duty in Shinjuku Gyoen. His partner swears to that. Other witnesses we have, certain young prostitutes. He was an hour away from the scene. At least that. Always. Even as much as ninety minutes. At the times of the abductions he is on duty. Or if not on duty then in some cafe-*baa*, drinking."

"So this Officer Miyajima did *not* take her away."

"That is what we—some of us think. Some of us thought. What *I* thought, used to think—but somehow I was wrong, he was too clever. Perhaps the man on duty was a confederate, or something, possibly impersonating him. Although you would think his partner—"

"A police captain. A captain of the police."

"Sir, *gomen-nasai,* I am sorry."

"I pay taxes. I know your Chief. I know him well." The old man, stony.

"I am so sorry. This baby, was she—"

"Is! Is! She *is* missing! And we must find her. *Is she in that house?"*

"Associate Chief Ishimura thinks so."

"The rude little sluglike person with the loudhailer?"

"That is him, yes, and he thinks so, but I didn't— don't. Somehow."

The old man turning abruptly back to the skinny boy.

"Uchiyama-*san,* what can you tell us?"

"Oyabun, I was at Donner's home—and for a very good reason! Revenge. Trouble, sir, bad trouble. The *gaijin* ruined my career, he tipped over my *sendenkaa,*

he got me jailed, he—" A sigh from the tight-lipped old man, a hard look for the boy from the associate. *"Oyabun, imashita,* I was there."

"And what did you see?"

"Housewives, children playing. Playing badminton with no net, there in the lane. One fat man with a big beard in a car, I mean not just the beard was in the car, he was, and he was driving along with this woman beside him. Her head was in his lap, like she was... sleeping. Or something."

"I saw him too," says the crew-cut man with the bruised face. "Fat, ugly, bushy beard. Decadent-looking."

"Like some kind of Buddha-type, but hairy?" asks Donner.

"Like that. But I didn't get a good look."

"I did," says Uchiyama. "Cod-roe lips, bright red. I nearly puked."

"That was what's his name," says the colonel. "And Ruriko."

"We know about him," says the old man's assistant. "Eiji knows."

"What else did you see?" asks the old man.

"Nothing, *Oyabun."*

"And you?"

"Nothing," says the crew-cut man. "Only a little *burikko* in a little pink car, some silly girl. She had a big plush toy in the passenger seat, I remember."

"Anything else?"

"Nothing."

"May I ask your name?"

"Kawakami Yukio *de gozaimasu.*"

"Can you help us understand why you were at the house of Mr. Donner? Did *you* take the little girl? Perhaps you wanted to save her from the foreigner."

"No, sir. I saw no baby."

"He didn't! It's the truth! He was with me the whole time."

"Kawakami-*san,* why were you there, at the home of the foreign *sensei?*"

"Also revenge. But now it is—I will tell you, if you will spare my friend."

"Yuk-*kun!* Don't do it! Cops!"

"Captain, ask your officers to give us a moment," says the old man.

Yoshida gives the order.

"This one too! The fucking Captain!"

"As a matter of fact," says Yoshida, "I just got demoted and fired, you see. I think Ishimura-*san* has the authority to do that. So probably I'm not a captain anymore. Perhaps not even a police officer."

"*Usoh!* Bullshit!"

"Masaaki, it doesn't matter anymore. I was there because the foreigner caught the baby. They were calling him a hero, and they were calling me... and I hated him, decided to rob him, get some money and his passport at least, so I could run away, because the woman was a mistake. I tried to kill the husband, Yamamoto the stinking socialist, and I killed the woman instead. The wife, the mother of the baby. With the sacred *katana*. And broke it. Then he died too. And then this girl beat me terribly—"

"I'm not sorry!" wails the fierce girl.

"That's right, I deserved it, I deserve it even more now, so then I took her *aka* helmet to our headquarters—"

"Our?" The old man peering sharply over his dark glasses.

"The Order of the Shining Mist, my organization, and—"

"Shining Mist? The group of Nakatani Taro? Who was burned to death?"

"*Hai*. Nakatani Taro-*sama*, who was our Great Leader, and I dropped the helmet and threw a bottle

605

filled with gasoline through the window, to make it look as though the Reds had—"

"*Ouyoku* bastard!"

"Get her off him."

"*Hai, Oyabun.*" The *kobun*, yanking and wrenching.

"So you killed Nakatani Taro?" *Oyabun, kobun,* exchanging glances. "That man was known to me."

"*Hai!* I killed him—although I had rather killed myself. And that is why I now will do so!" Kawakami diving for the *katana*, one *kobun* kicking it away, the other *kobun* kicking Kawakami in the side.

"No, Yuk-*kun*!"

"MIYAJIMA. *JIKAN. GA. TARINAIN. DESU.* YOUR. TIME."

"I want to die!" Wailing. "Please let me die!"

"Don't worry! *I'll* kill you, I'll beat you to death. I'll give you another thrashing, you bastard, you fucking beautiful nazi pig."

"IS. RUNNING. OUT."

"Ishimura-*san* is correct about that, at least." The *oyabun*, snapping his fingers for attention. "Time is running out. Let us not grieve over some dead leftist professor. We all make mistakes, and perhaps he will not be greatly missed. Still less the strutting demagogue, do not blame yourself too much for him. He was expendable. They are not worth *seppuku*. You do not kill yourself with a *katana* anyway. It is too long, you would cut your hands. You use the *tanto*, the short blade, and then your second uses the *katana* on your neck. If you are going to do it, then do it properly. But why kill yourself at all? You are young, active, impetuous. It is a pity about the woman, however. And the baby. Were it not for you and your little motorcycle... You will pay for them, Kawakami-*san,* a token payment. Your little finger, the one with the ring. To the second knuckle. Send the finger tomorrow by mail, to—Associate Chief Ishimura, something for him to ponder, food for thought. *Sokutatsu,* special express. Without fail, *inochi o kakete,* on your life. Send the finger."

"I will! Gladly!"

"Keep the ring. And now, speaking of fingers, Captain or ex-Captain Yoshida, how do you account for the prints appearing where the man was not? I am not a detective by profession, but that would seem to be our central problem."

"It is, but I don't, I... can't." Yoshida shrugs. "Account for them."

Each member of the little group searching the faces of the others.

"Oyabun," says the skinny boy, Uchiyama. "May I speak? I once read a story about a mad scientist who invented these special rubber gloves with another man's prints on them and then the mad scientist commits many crimes and then the other man is thrown in jail. It was a good story. In *High School Jumping.* I have been writing letters and stories of my own, good ones, and sending them in, and I think maybe—"

"It is a *manga?"*

"Hai, Oyabun."

"HEAR. ME. OFFICER. MIYAJIMA?"

"Do you want to keep *your* fingers?"

"Hai! I am sorry to mention it, *sh'tsureishimasu."*

"OFFICER. MIYAJIMA. YOU. HAVE."

"Then why *did* you mention it? And just now?"

"Nothing, no reason. Only that the writer was Miyajima. Same name. Miyajima Yoshinori. *Yumei desu.*"

"Yes," says Kobayashi Miyuki. "He is well known."

"Miyajima, the name is a common one." The old man turns to go.

Captain or ex-Captain Yoshida feels a bolt of lightning through his chest.

"Yoshinori is the son! It is too much of a coincidnce." Yoshida turns toward a uniform. "Put through a call, Miyajima Yoshinori, Yurakucho *gochome,* an apartment—Leopalace? Green Mansion? I forget the address, find out what he drives—"

"Move! Now!" the colonel's wife pushing them, shoving Yoshida, jolting him with the heel of her hard hand. "Make your calls on the *way,* dickhead!"

"COUNT. OF. TEN."

"Exactly." Teshima Oyabun thinks maybe *she* should be Chief of Police, wonders if he has enough influence to install a woman and a foreigner in that slot, dismisses the trivial thought as he concentrates on wedging his bulk into and through the jam of uniforms and patrol cars. All of their little group now, inching, squeezing through the packed vehicles, working their way down the street, moving a little faster in the next block to furthest *patocaa,* one with egress. Yoshida, Donner, the colonel and his wife into that one. The newsgirl and her cameraman sprinting past them to

609

their van, which is blocked on all four sides. Teshima taking her arm, guiding and helping her, trotting with his *kobun* now around the corner, toward the Mercedes and the hideous pink S-Cargo beyond it, trotting fast, the two foolish young *douseiaisha* puffing beside them, Ishimura's bullhorn seeming somehow even louder in the distance, roaring and echoing.

"COUNTING. NOW."

"Oyabun," says Uchiyama. "The *sendenkaa* is out of gas."

"Good," the old man hardly puffing at all, holding the sword. "The little truck is yours, I make you a present of it. The sword is mine. You boys, both of you. I really think you should try to develop other interests. Uchiyama, the foreigner did not ruin your career. You had no career. Find some other work. That is my advice. Learn a trade. And you, Kawakami, the finger. *Sayonara."*

"ONE."

Sunday, 9:10 A.M.

Miyajima Yoshinori, giggling about his soon-to-be-jailed father, then sternly ordering himself to seriousness, composure, before initiating the procedure, the difficult precision job of freeing. Of letting the baby out of the "baby." Of helping her self out of herself. There is not much light, but he doesn't need or want much. He is not some cold surgeon, masked and gloved, aloof and withdrawn. And this is not some brilliant, sterile operating theater. This is life, love, and Yoshinori knows the erotic sequence now by heart. He looks down, at the erection throbbing beneath his garter belt. Throbbing so big it almost hurts. He smiles. Well, doesn't he deserve something, some sweet pain for all his pains? Yoshinori realizes that probably no one else in the world could perform this act so well. And this one, number five, will be special. Very little blood, but still special.

"Ready, Kitty?"

He starts with the tiny hairline cuts, lovingly.

Sunday, 9:11 A.M.

"TEN. ALL. RIGHT. WE. ARE. COMING. IN.

Associate Chief Ishimura nodding to the ram-bearers.

Miyajima clearly insane now, waving his pistol and screaming.

"*Bakayaro!* Don't you see? *He* did it—the kid! He's a fucking murderer!"

Door splintering in, maniac looking down looking up, opening fire, the uniform to Ishimura's right blowing back, a black-red dot appearing in the man's neck then two starred holes in the windshield of Ishimura's official vehicle, ahead and over to his left. Bullets intended for him, the Associate Chief.

Ishimura standing firm, signaling the sharpshooters.

Dots stitching across the chest of Miyajima, who fires once more.

Black dot in Ishimura's rear fender.

Miyajima bending, easing forward, tumbling out, down.

Ishimura knocked flat in the mud by a blooming orange furnace-roar.

Ishimura's pulse, one, two, three, four, and Ishimura scrabbling for the loudhailer scrambling to his feet and even in this emergency taking charge, knowing precisely what must be done.

"MOVE. THE.

But immediately another gas tank, the next *patocaa*, heat now enormous.

"VEHICLES.

Now another.

"APART."

Now three more.

Datsun.

Datsun.

Datsun.

So new, just purchased, now never to be amortized.

Sunday, 10:02 A.M.

Buddy hits the door—wood, solid, but so is he, solid that is, the beef good for something—the door slams in, they're through and into the dark apartment, no light but the television, there, on the floor... Donner sweeps his hand backward for the switches. Pink and white, that smell, and on the floor plastic side by side with... no.

Donner jerks his head away then wrenches it back, forcing himself.

There they are, naked, except that her companion with the knife is wearing a garter belt and a training bra. Donner sees the sturdy little arms, calves, thighs— the red spaces between the joints, and sees the back of her head, he sees the ribbon, the tight pink knot, the threads raveling from one end of the bow, and then he finally has to see the active boy licking, nuzzling, nipping.

See the boy look up, smiling, chewing.

"Isn't she beautiful?"

The boy asks and turns her head, rolling it further from the torso, and there *is* a kind of beauty there, ruby and ivory, as Donner lets his eyes accept the shy little grin, the purple sockets, the tiny skull itself, but then he screams because the floor opens gaping as the bone gully that he never left, and Donner is caught, trapped and breathless, with all the faceless nameless riflemen and scouts and radio operators jumbled and gleaming in the noon sun stinking and ringing like a gong, and he screams, "Mom!"

Teshima Tadao feels behind him for a chair, sits.

Buddy sees the black sparkles quickly form and grow and intersect, hears himself scream, "Donner!" Feels Janey take the weight then nothing.

Yoshinori is spent, serene. So this is the one, then, with the burning ice-blue eyes. "Yoshinori" pulls down the left side of his bra, holds out the knife, like an offering to the killer, the liberator. What is he waiting for?

Kobayashi Miyuki feels the pull of the knife as she dives for it, picks it up, stabs him, the monster, in the scrotum, then rips up through the dripping penis the garterbellt falling away the soft flesh of his abdomen opening blooming like a huge dark rose until the knife

615

catches on his breastbone and jumps from her hand, and Miyuki rolls away holding herself locked in a long shudder.

Where is "Yoshinori"? Who can't protect Yoshinori from... *this,* and Yoshinori's own intestines spilling out, and he holds them not believing there could be pain this big and then finds himself the wrenching center of a deep male bellow.

Yamamoto Hanako rushes from the *ofuro* and into the brightness blinking stumbling but frightened of just only Hanako in there to hear the terrible dark roar alone, more frightened than of the girl who is a boy, and Hanako can see again and she sees the girl who lived in the refrigerator all curled up not curled up now broken all broken and hurt so much, and she sees the girl who is a boy, sees him hurt too and twisting holding roaring, hates him, hates him, sees him red because now everything is red, sees only him, sees only him and the *hocho,* a *hocho* like her mother's cutting the apple-wedges and Hello Kitty *kamaboko* for Hanako, and the *hocho* slides into her hands—both hands Hanako, yes Papa—and she holds it tightly so tightly going up, and coming down.

"Yoshinori" is gone! And Yoshinori is going, burning cellophane curling into nothing, and… who is… now who… *lying on the floor a tiny boy, a baby really, not much older than Hanako, he's been inside the terrible cruel boy, had to hide there, even before the cruel boy hid inside the cold hard one, long before, had to, and very quiet so they wouldn't know. Hello, I'm Yoshi, do you want to play with me? Please don't cut me, please don't stab my eyes. Ah, she sees it, stops, drops the knife. Do you want to come to my house, Hanako? Because now I can go there, and I know. Do you know? I'm not lost and now I know my way home. I'm going home to that light.*

Teshima Tadao comes out of his chair quickly or slowly, before him the blood-flecked baby Hanako, and shining through the child her own great-grandmother: same valentine face, eyes, cheeks, lips—everything. Plum blossoms and blossoms from the mountain cherry on the third and perfect day. He reaches out, touches her face, her hair, as she trots past him and into the arms of the bearded foreigner who resembles DiGiralamo but only very slightly, and Teshima feels a joy and sorrow beyond enduring. Later

617

perhaps he can bear these feelings, but now he must numb himself to the molten joy and sorrow. He bends, retrieves the knife. Joy and sorrow too intense to be borne. And pride.

Janey Nakamura, holding Buddy, avid eyes on the dead monster-boy, nostrils wide, gulping great lungfuls of air but hardly able to breathe because the room is crammed and stretched and supercharged and locked so tight and hot that her head goes back and a high howl, bell-toned and harshly musical, moves through her belly and chest, funnels through her throat and resonates with the room, with the others, touches them where they need to be touched, so that she and they can break out, breathe and move again, shudder back into where and when they are. Panting, hot-cheeked, she looks around, sees the eyes bright, the flicker of pink tongue-tips moving over lips, teeth.

Buddy Nakamura, neck-bristles rippling on his way out of the Namwarp to the skull-near echo-sound of some hellhound belling, Buddy, back now in the land of the living but still physically out of it, half on the floor and half on his wife's lap, she with her arms around him. Buddy blinks, shakes his head to clear it, looks around at this land of the dead. Chopped up baby on the floor, gutted weirdo, blood everywhere sweet rich thick in his nostrils. Old gangster and younger one. Sprawling Donner and live baby and newsgirl, all looking at him—no, looking at Janey, with faces like painted saints, a sort of rapture.

Buddy catches Yoshida's eye, moves his big hand out in an arc.

"Killers," he says.

Yoshida nods. He and Buddy survey the others glumly. Natural killers, got it in their blood, all of them naturals. A secret club. Weeping Donner, like some crucified Christ in the newsgirl's arms, holding the tearful baby and patting her. *There, there.* The newsgirl saying soft things to Donner, kissing and caressing him, soothing him. Her red hand finds Thuong's tooth. *Oh, what's this?* Bloody, all three of them... and Buddy feels—what? Something a lot like envy. At this natural family, this new little family of naturals.

Sunday, 10:57 A.M.

Sawada Ginroku, beached in his lounger, weeping softly, uncontrollably.

"Oh, *Anata*, how could I sleep so late? I was so tired, and I guess—*Anata!* You are still up! Oh, dear, is it your hay fever again?"

Ignoring her, slumped nervelesss as a jellyfish, gaping at the gaping safe.

"*Anata*, you should go to the hospital again for your *butagusa* shots."

Ignoring her, trying not to think what she has done to him.

"And really, *Anata*, you should close your *kinko*. *Anzen dai ichi,* you know. Safety first. Also, shouldn't you put on a shirt? You don't want to catch a cold. *Anata?* Aren't you sleepy? Do you want to watch the *terebi?*"

Ignoring her, observing now his murky reflection in the blank *terebi* screen, a screen as blank as his future.

"Well, *Anata*, I'm going to make us some nice breakfast. Last night was so exciting. No wonder you couldn't sleep. *Tanoshikatta desu,* it was so much fun."

620

Steadfastly ignoring her, drinking Cutty from the bottle, concentrating, as he has been all the long night, on his ruin. What has he left? Nothing. The paper trash on the floor, with a few banknotes mixed in. Those, and his house, and his personalized gold Crown Majesta—no doubt ticketed and towed, but still in Machida somewhere, and still his—and *san oku* yen or so squirreled away here and there. All told, maybe four million dollars U.S. And—and that's all. He is a *binbo* once again, a pauper, with a ragtag of odds and ends, the pitiful wreckage from a lifetime of slaving. The king of Tokyo T's. Well, the king is dead.

Ginroku takes a big gulp, swallows manfully, puts down the bottle, wipes his face again on the handtowel, looks at the towel. Tuxedo Sam, the jolly little Sanrio penguin. Smeared with tears and snot. Sanrio shit, how he hates it. Where did the towel come from? Who bought it? Not Ginroku, that's for sure, and Rumiko hasn't been outside for seventeen years. She must have ordered it. Cute. So cute it makes Ginroku want to puke. Sanrio. More money than God, markets world-wide—*and meanwhile what about the little guy?* He won't have Sanrio in his house, and she knows that. Ginroku has a good mind to storm into the kitchen and beat the living... or at least kick... Teshima or no Teshima...

And this God-damned fucking chair! He lifts his leg and brings his heel down on the vinyl, hard. And again, harder. Now both heels, one after the other, again and again and again. Because Ginroku's chair is giving him the same series of massages, over and over, mindlessly. Ah, fuck it. He doesn't really care. What difference does it make? He raises his left hand, still holding the cigarette lighter, and he looks at it, this gadget which has proven itself to be far from automatic, far from smart. Which has in fact proven itself to be very, very stupid.

"Why?" he asks it, rhetorically.

The old monster was right—Teshima! Here! Ginroku still can't believe it! But he *was* here, and he *was* right. Nothing left, nothing to live for, might as well end it like an old-time *samurai*, which Ginroku sort of is, because hasn't he been a real fighter all these years? No more, however. Now he is battle-weary, and the time has come to rest. He still has his little shops, true. And he has his little T shirt *kojo*, with the three big Toshibas all in a row. He still has his machine operators, his guttersnipe artist, his greedy suppliers, and his city full of scummy contacts. He has his counterjumping *burikko* and has-been rock musicians. He has all these things, but so what? Ginroku is a has-been himself, a dead legend, and that's why he's thinking so seriously now of suicide, *seppuku*, looking at his shapely stomach, all nakedly vulnerable, imagining two horrible dotted lines, an inverted L, that he should cut along...

Hm.

Picturing a flesh-colored T-shirt with such dotted lines. Cut here in the event of severe loss of face or property. The vertical line maybe leaking drops of red, especially in the area of the navel, where there could be a photorepro of some antique *hara kiri* knife, point buried. Maybe even a little gut-bud peeking through. No law against that. And, on either side of the dotted line, *seppuku* instructions, repro'ed right from the old books—*bathe, dry yourself and don a loose-fitting garment, spread the dropcloth, sit* seiza*, still the mind, grasp the knife in both hands with point touching* hara, *then jab, saw up, twist, saw to the right.* All that gory old shit. And printed upside-down, so you could read it while you were doing it. *Nihon-go* on the left, English on the right. English, the language of the world. *Kakko-ii*—neat!... Tits?... Tits on the shirt? Why not, this is the 90s. Big pink rubber nipples for the women, smaller ones for the men—plus a wad of hair there in between... Joke hair? Purple? Green? No, better realistic, lifelike—or, rather, deathlike.

So the concept: a T very much like a naked human torso, with print-graphics giving the effect of tattooing. Sure, could also be some Harley-Davidson wings up there on the right shoulder, or a little dragon, but nothing gaudy or distracting. Yes! *Honto-ni,* the *gaijin* would really go for a shirt like that—Americans especially, they're so fucking sick.

And of course if the Yanks went for it everybody else on the planet would have to have one too. Everybody, not just in Japan, this concept is global, because who doesn't know about *seppuku?* Five thousand yen each, move a million T's—and presto! Ginroku has all his money back, plus a hundred new overseas markets! Really, it's about time he went international, and this is his ticket. Why has it taken him so long to realize this fact? Why has he been thinking so small? Well, he's not thinking small anymore. Fuck the nickle-dime loans, fuck the goons, fuck the penny-ante concert, fuck baby Hanako. Here is the opportunity of a lifetime. And! Added gimmick! Sell the fucker for *six* thousand with a big yellow smile button—Have a Nice Day!—to stick on there. The button would draw blood too… Fangs on it? Fangs on the button? No, play it straight. Better that way. Cheaper too. Ginroku knows where he can get literally a million buttons for next to nothing. Yes! It could be huge!

"Oh, *Anata!* The *terebi,* look—raging out of control, a fire, another one! The engines are blocked and can't get through. In Okubo, a respectable residential district, *taihen desu ne?* And—oh! Terrible! The Healer was murdered! In the hospital! Lying helpless and blinded on his bed, and the killer ripped him open! Oh, Buddha! Disemboweled the poor man, stuffed a sacred rhino hat in his mouth, poured alcohol over his head bandages, and—and set him on fire! Oh, *Anata!* Who would *do* such a thing?"

Could be? *Will* be. *Will* be huge. Ginroku catapults himself from the chair, sends lighter and whiskey bottle and ashtray and still-massaging lounge chair thudding to the lovely green carpet, hardly hearing his wife's high noises of alarm as he scrambles and stumbles with his sweet ample hams and abdomen shim-sham-shimmying this way and that, over to the bookcase for the phone, grabbing it, dropping it, picking it up, punching in the numbers.

The *Seppuku Tskaikata* T.

Okay, you lazy stupid greedy bastards, time to start earning your money.

The king is dead long live the king.

Banzai.

Sunday, 11:04 A.M.

Monday and Wednesday, combustible trash
Tuesday, bottles and other glass items
Thursday, cans
Weekends and Holidays, no garbage pickup.
DOMO ARIGATO GOZAIMASU!

It is the only notice on the board by the roadside *gomitokoro,* a grave-sized concrete pad with low cement-block walls on three sides. Uchiyama Masaaki has been reading this notice with extreme care, the words not penetrating. Unable to glance away, he tries reason once more on stubborn Yukio. "We'll run away. He'll never find us. Or—or cut off someone *else's* finger! Ishimura's probably dead anyway, back there. Fried." They hear the drawn-out wail of fire sirens. "Or at least wait till later. No! Please! Don't do it!"

"Do it," says Hatsue.

She watches the amber shard of whiskey bottle bite between ring and knuckle... deeper, deeper still with a shuddering shove, a hissing intake of breath, the glass much deeper now, another shove, twisting from his

627

hips like a fighter, big shoulders moving too, *and the glass is right through to the wood,* the four-by-four notice board support, blood rilling warmly along the heel of his left hand, wrist, forearm to his elbow, a thicker volume welling on the glass before contacting and being absorbed by the protective wad of *manga* pages at one end, then, at the jagged end, staining the wooden support before streaming down for a few centimeters then branching into three distinct trickles equally wide but lengthening at slightly different rates along the clean white paint—a final grunt and gasp, and Yukio jerks his hand away while most of his left little finger, teetering on the glass, remains.

Hatsue gets the finger.

Masaaki bends for the ring. "Not paid for yet," he mumbles thickly.

They turn to catch Yukio.

Hold him.

Walk him rubberlegged, over to the ugly pink truck.

Help him—*ki o tsukette,* careful now—onto the seat.

"I'm yours," she breathes in his ear. "Forever."

"Why, I wonder." Yukio says muzzily, head between his knees, in the passenger seat of Masaaki's S-Cargo, his blood mixing with Masaaki's on the *oyabun's* handkerchief, wadded now to the stump. "Why send it to Ishimura?"

"Mochiron, the guy's a fucking cop of course. Did you see the way they shoved the *oyabun?* That's death, right there." Masaaki is ill. The *oyabun* was right. Pale and sweat-slicked, he watches his pale and sweat-slicked friend. He and the girl are hunkered by Yukio's open door. *"Daijobu desu ka,* are you okay?

"I can still… make sushi." A tight smile. Tough guy! How would soft little Takeshi do in the same circumstances? Would Takeshi grin and make a hard little joke? Masaaki pictures him, has to smile a little bit himself. But at least Takeshi has a job. Convenience store counter-jumper. Better than nothing. Food, clothes, a roof. Don't sneer too much at Takeshi. Not everyone can be a Yukio.

"Sushi?" the girl says sharply. "Are you a some kind of sushi chef?"

"Only the best in Tokyo. Yukio's got a good trade."

"But no job. I shoved an order of *anago* into a customer's face."

629

"You did what?" This is news to Masaaki. "Why?"

"Thursday."

"Why?"

"Just opened up. It was Yamamoto Koichiro, waddling in, and then—"

"Then you killed him Friday," says Masaaki. "Nice work."

"And then I tried to kill him, and he died, but not because of me."

"Anyway, he's dead," says the girl. "That's the main thing."

"You knew him?" Yukio asks.

"I knew him. He was worse than the capitalists, all talk, a real showman. " She snickers. "So famous for that *minamata* business, those people with mercury poison, rolling around and dying, and you know all he ever actually did? Wrote some letters to the government, very polite. He was proud of that. Some radical. I told him dynamite and Molotov cocktails, he said don't be naive. Poli Sci 101? *Bakamono* gave me an F."

"Yukio's got a good trade. No job, but a great trade. Not me. I couldn't even be a *chinpirra*. All I know is fish."

"What's wrong with fish?" she asks. "I love fish. Raw."

"Masaaki's father owns the best *sakana-ya* in Tamachi."

"Yes, but so what? The place is old, it's falling down, you should see it in the back. The old man is going to sell pretty soon, go retire in Okinawa or some other boring place."

"So buy him out," she says, squinting at the bluish curl of digit in the palm of her hand. "Do we have to send this finger? What will Ishimura do with it?"

"How do I know? But you heard the *oyabun*."

"Ishimura has no use for it. Can I at least keep the nail?"

"I don't know." Yukio looks better. "Sure, I guess."

"I get the handkerchief," says Masaaki. "Blood brothers. Here's your ring back, wear it on your other hand." Then to the girl, "Buy him out?" Masaaki snickers. "With what?"

"With money," she says, still peering at the finger. "You work up the proposal, you take it to the bankers—bloodsuckers, all of them, but necessary— you wait two weeks, and there you are. Or I could do it for you... Tamachi?"

"*Hai.*"

"*Tamachi nan chome,* what area?"

"*Go chome.*"

"Tamachi *go chome!* Prime *tochi.* I've got a little parcel there myself."

"You're not listening—what's your name?"

"Tanaka Hatsue *desu.*"

"You're not listening, Tanaka-*san.* The place has termites, dry rot, it's ready to collapse."

"Great. Give it a kick. Or maybe our friend here could firebomb it."

"There's a family living upstairs, lived there forever. Won't move."

"Move them. Get the building condemned. That's easy, especially if it's wood. It might cost you a case of scotch for *oseibo.* When it's condemned, the lease is automatically void. They have to get out. Then demolish the building. It's the law."

"Anyway, buildings cost money."

"*Chigaimasu,* no they don't—not in Tokyo. Don't you know anything? If you've got the land, you can grow a building on it for free. A big one, new, beautiful. That new *Canada Taishikan?* The Canadians needed a new embassy, but they were broke, of course. My father found out about it, put the deal together, brought in the *zaibatsu*, the conglomerates, unlimited resources, and I helped him with the numbers and the paperwork. My father was the best. Everybody says, Oh, *tochikorogashi*, real estate sharks, they're no good, criminals, and so forth—but really they perform a valuable function."

"What function is that?"

"Have you seen it, the *Taishikan?* Ten billion at least, but it cost the Canadians not one yen, which is good because they all teach English conversation, mostly to each other. It's all they've got, the language. And the land. But that's all they needed. We did the rest, so we—my father, rather, and his friends—could use part of the building. He never saw it, because he... passed away. But it's *kakkoii*, great, right there in Aoyama, in the middle of the money. Same thing with you. Keep the land, let them put up a building, do a double leaseback on the office space for tax purposes, and on the ground floor—

"My shop!"

"Our shop—or rather shops. We'll want a bigger *sakana-ya—"*

"Much bigger," says Masaaki. "Everything stainless steel. Modern."

"And a sushi-*ya* next to it, that's a natural arrangement."

"Yes!" says Yukio. "With a real oak counter, no plastic, no veneer even, the real thing, and Masamoto knives, the best. A customer comes in, I give him a big *Irrashyai!* Like that, really boom it out like a professional. And then I put together some of the best sushi in Tokyo. *Sashimi?* I can do that too, so it's still twitching when you put it in your mouth." The color is back in his cheeks.

"*Oishi so,* that sounds delicious," she says. "You run the sushi shop. And you," turning to Masaaki, "run the fish store, and I—"

"And you wait on the customers and wipe off the tables—"

"And I'll keep an eye on the help. And the cash registers. And the books."

"And maybe sweep—"

"And be *shatchyo.*"

"And—and be the boss, yes, all right, I guess." Masaaki scrutinizes her. "Could you really do... all that?"

"Easily. I've probably got enough myself. And if not there's always my grandmother. Do it right, maybe no need to go near any capitalistic cannibal banker.

The only thing is... love. I love Yukio, *ai sh'teru*. Body and soul."

"Ah, but you see, Masaaki and me. We are homosexuals. Lovers, in fact, since last night."

"Good! That will help keep away the *burikko*. I don't want to be your lover. I just want to be near you, always. And, maybe, beat the *unchi* right out of you once or twice a month with my kendo stick—but I guess you could wear the mask. There wouldn't be any harm in that. I'll have them fix your nose, and you can wear the mask. That's a promise. And the padding. Really, all I want is that feeling, there's nothing quite like it, landing a stroke with everything behind it. It just goes through me, that feeling, and so then I'd probably want to rip off your padding and sort of *hold on...* for a minute or two. That's all I ask. Well?"

"Beat me?"

"*Beat* him?"

"That sounds... reasonable," says Yukio. "Even fun."

"Fun! Yes!"

"Do I get to hit back?"

"Sure you do. If you can."

"Agreed, then."

635

"Agreed," says Masaaki. "Our own place. Let's shake hands like the Americans do. I mean, that *gaijin* brought us together after all, the old bastard."

So they shake on it, the three friends.

"And no fucking foreigners allowed!" says Masaaki.

"Right!" says Yukio. "No *gaijin!* They can go to the sushi-mat."

"They can go to hell!" says Masaaki.

"Honto-ni!" says Hatsue. "No foreigners at all— unless they have money."

"Well, yes, unless they have a lot of money to spend, and then I guess we could let them in, until they spend all they're going to spend, and then we could tell them to go away, or ask them to please come again when they have more money. Or basically just give them a bow and a big smile like my old man does. What the hell, it doesn't cost anything."

"Good manners are just good business," says Yukio.

"And the price is right," says Hatsue. "Zero yen."

"Anyway, that's that!" says Masaaki. "Sometimes you do a little kendo with Yukio—kendo's good exercise—and he makes sushi, and you... be the *shyatchyo* if you want, and I'll be the buyer. Every morning, down there in Tsukiji. They all know me, nobody will try anything *dzurui* on old Masaaki. Buy the best, race back, clean them, put them in the trays. And! Every afternoon I'm out generating business. Right here in the *sendenkaa*—it's mine, you heard him, it just needs a little body work and paint—"

"And a thorough cleaning."

"Yes, scrub it right out, use the steam. It's a very good little truck, a real S-Cargo, they don't make them like this anymore. And there I am, cruising the neighborhoods, which I know as well as I know myself, and maybe giving out some free samples, a few balloons—and playing the tape! The loudspeaker is there, we just have to make a tape! Like, MAIDO ARIGATO GOZAIMASU! UCHIYAMA SAKANA—or should that be 'Tanaka, Kawakami, Uchiyama'?"

"Never change the name," she says. "Keep the good will."

"*Hai, so shimasu,* you're the boss." Masaaki takes a deep breath, tilts his head back, closes his eyes, intones, "UCHIYAMA! ICHIBAN SUSHI! OISHI DESU! UCHIYAMA! UCHIYAMA! UCHIYAMA!"

Sunday, 12:23 P.M.

"Do you mind if I smoke?" Teshima Tadao holds the unlit Camel, looks around owlishly at his *kobun* seated cross-legged around the low table, at Yuuske the chauffeur and the two other domestic soldiers by the door. The soldiers smile. The *kobun* laugh and slap the table. They are home in Ikebukuro, back in his big stone house cut into the hillside, drinking tea in the main room: silk cushions on the fresh *tatami* floors, oiled *hinoki* beams, mounted scrolls on stucco walls. Not so different from the previous century. Or the previous millennium. Teshima thinks of the T-shirt man's wife, of her crazed grace. He pictures her, soothed somehow, in a fine kimono. The old ways, yes. Would she like his garden? He thinks she would like it, would relish the textures, the scents and angles. Would draw comfort from the place as he does. He turns his head. One wall of the room, seemingly invisible, is just a thrice-daily cleaned picture window framing the rocks, the *koi* pond, a little grove of bamboo, and the fieldstone wall. Simple things, natural, no hint of the din and grit nearby, the smoky reek, the panicked ulcerated Tokyo multitudes in polyester, the overpriced drinking dens where you get a draft of oxygen with your draft Heineken's. All that raw urban striving, a world away. Here, freed from her plastic prison, the T-shirt wife could be healed. A woman needs a garden.

But a garden also needs a woman. Well, he has at least the big white-and-copper carp flashing in crystal water. He has the tiny stunted pines and maples, *bonsai*, gnarled and weathered and much older than Teshima himself, set in among the rocks. And he has the rocks themselves. Teshima regards them, selected by himself over a full decade, trucked from as far as Fukuoka, as near as Chiba, each with a history locked in its masses and planes, its breaks and crevices, all those lines of force and destiny. Good colors too, umber and coral and rich grays, streaks of verdegris and ochre. Thick mats of moss. Teshima loves moss— deep, variously green, sparkling with moisture. He has seven varieties, seven greens, from pale chartreuse to profound emerald. Clement mornings and evenings, Teshima walks the pebbled paths with an atomizer, spraying the moss with nutrient minerals. Then he sits on the stone bench, stilling his mind. This garden is real for him even now, in this unreal age. It is a replica of the one he shared with Hanako.

He smokes, viewing his garden at mid-day, pulling high random notes from the old tattooed *shamisen*, giving a full minute's space to each ringing note, letting it linger and twine with the bright smoke curling, curving.

Touch, smell, sound, sight. Life.

But a garden really does need a woman.

Nearly time for lunch. Teshima leans the instrument against the table. He flicks a speck of ash from his tie, extinguishes his cigarette in the *haizara* with one quick jab. He excuses himself, gets up from his cross-legged position with some awkwardness and much effort. As recently as ten years ago he could rise to his feet easily, in one fluid movement. No more. Now he has to press the table, use his arms, and—*and make a real production out of it, as DiGiralamo would say.* And, in another few years...

Teshima Tadao closes the door behind him. In his room there are no windows. Thick drapes, heavy wooden dressers, a small table with its short thick legs planted on the *tatami*. And, on the low dresser, his *butsudan*, a tiny brass and mahogany shrine, with its peaked roof and opened doors. He lights a stick of incense, softly claps, bows. Moriuchi-*sama's* urn. His ashes. And hers. Hanako the great-grandmother of

Hanako but somehow the same person, the light and passion of his life. How terrible was this morning, jagged fragments of the past lodging deep in his heart. The pain of longing and remembering, this time, is too much. He opens the locket, kisses her picture for perhaps the ten thousandth time, closes the locket. Ten thousandth and last.

Teshima emerges, reenters the main room. He is wearing a white silk robe open at the top. In his left hand he is carrying the sushi knife, covering infant Hanako's prints with his own, and in his right the foolish boy's *katana*. Knife and *katana*: two strong hints from the gods. The *kobun* and the soldiers, still open-faced and smiling, turn to regard him, their eyes widening, their smiles fading. Sunlight, *tatami*, the long low table glowing as before. Slender white vase, green stems, three red chrysanthemums. Everything the same, but altered now and for always, absolutely.

"Roll out a cloth." Handing the sword to Eiji, "You are my second."

Paralysis, quickening heartbeats, stunned obedience.

Teshima now kneeling *seiza* on the cloth, knife in both hands, point to *hara*. Soon now. Glance up to Eiji, standing to his right, the *katana* upraised.

"There is an envelope in the *kinko*." Then, "Don't let me suffer too long."

Teshima, breathing, stilling the mind, tasting the air.

Breath.

Breath.

Breath.

Now the final slow deep inhale.

Stilling the mind, stilling it, willing it still as a perfect pool, the pool's surface imperfect, however, roughened by a sudden breeze or twisting carp of thought, a question, insistent now: what would DiGiralamo say? *Fuck this, Tod.* True, that is it exactly. Teshima can hear him. *Fuck this harrycarry shit, Tod. Hey, it'll hurt like hell.* Of course. It is supposed to. It is the way of the brave. *So what? Who do you want to impress? What are you trying to prove? What are you afraid of? This is just stupid. Listen, you're gonna do it, you might as well do it right, have a little fun.* Fun? What are you talking about? What fun? How? *Hey, how should I know? You're the idea man, Tod. You'll think of something. You're the Big Motorcycle.*

Garage. Cool, dark. Smelling of concrete, lubricants, solvents. Overhead light switch by the door.

Ah. To their left the long bench, tools above it on the pegboard. Benz and Lincoln straight ahead, immaculate, facing the big steel roll-door to the outside. A form to their right bulking beneath a tan tarp. Teshima juts his chin at the form. Yuuske whisks away the tarp.

And there it is, the Knucklehead. (*DiGiralamo, tall and hairy-wristed, palm-waved duck's ass pompadour, pencil-line moustache, Pall Mall between his lips and bobbing with his forty-years-ago laughter, Sen-Sen on his breath, wiry arm around Teshima's shoulders, "Hey, hey, he's back! Big Bad Tod on the Ultimate Hog!"*) Ultimate, yes. A mint 1936, the big one, a full thousand of the cubic centimeters. This gleaming two-wheeled tank. Massive, twice as heavy as it has to be, three times as powerful. Finned cylinder heads thicker than your thigh, ribbed rocker boxes, flashing silver. Big headlamp. Swooping lines, risers, mounded tank, fenders like the fenders on a truck, chrome shift-lever. Mudflaps front and back, original, but now clinically clean, the Kanda filth and crusted brick-glass-powder paste long gone. Seat and bags new, moist and supple and glowing with saddle-soap. From the metal all the hundred nicks and dents long since smoothed away, the spokes cut by Tomekichi's bullet long since replaced. By faithful Yuuske. He did it all. Everything, the entire bike, disassembled, repaired, renewed, reground, recalibrated, reassembled. Again and again, years of work. Sandblasted, rechromed, repainted. Ten coats of the bloodiest blood-red imaginable, Yuuske's patient hands rubbing down each coat before applying the next. Simonize. You can look into the fenders, the gas tank, and see yourself. Your past, your future.

Massive, arrogant, at ease on its haunches like some monster cat, some giant man-eater, seeming even bigger than it is, softly pulsing at the heart of its own ruby aura: Harley-Davidson.

Teshima looks at Yuuske, nods, smiles.

"Telephone."

Teshima presses the numbers from memory.

"Kikuno."

"Big Motorcycle! I was just thinking of you. I took in some leathers and a helmet. I was cleaning them. It was fun, two fools—"

"Put them on. We are going for a ride."

"Really? On the motorcycle? Does it still function?"

"Perfectly, I'm sure. The weather is good. Some fresh air for you. We'll go down to Hakone, stop for tea and cakes at that little shop. *Natsu no hana no okashi,* remember? Spring flower sweets."

"Is it still there? Anyway, there's no one in Hakone to visit. Or anywhere. I shouldn't leave the shop. I'm catching a cold. My throat hurts, and—"

"Then we'll visit your dear Tomekichi…"

"Oh."

"And dear Hanako…"

"Oh! Oh, yes!"

"I know the place, a big hill, at the bottom we can meet the barrier at one hundred eighty, meet the ocean much faster than that. There is no risk."

"Yes! Oh, hurry!"

"Should you tell anyone?"

"No, there is only Hatsue, and she is in jail again, or maybe just released. Did you see her on the *terebi?* She bit a *keisatsu.* How I love that child, just like her grandfather. So fierce, and so entertaining—a communist! I love it when she curses me, calls me a cancer on society. That is so much fun. Well, soon she'll be the richest *aka* since Mao!"

"Twenty minutes, perhaps, if traffic is light."

"Wakarimashita, I understand. Oh, Big Motorcycle—hurry!"

The bike invites him. Teshima's big old hands curl around the grips, remembering the ribbed surfaces perfectly. He lifts his right leg, a little stiffly but he lifts it, and swings into the saddle, settles in. His Gentleman's Levi's are capacious. They do not bind him. Nor does the pig man's T-shirt. His old bomber jacket, *zan-nen,* is now a bit too constricting to zip. No matter. Yuuske blows vigorously into the combat helmet. Dust, little clouds. He rubs the helmet with a cloth, proffers it bowing, eyelashes starred with tears. The helmet, old, scratched, olive drab. DiGiralamo's. Also a bit tight. No matter.

"How do I look?"

Well, Tod, it ain't azackly a zoot suit with a reet pleat.

Yuuske, bites his lip, looks down.

Teshima laughs.

Kobun on their knees, sitting on their heels, heads bowed. Statues.

Teshima leans to the right, hits the button. The door rolls up, sunlight floods in, warm and welcoming as remembered brightness: Kanda, Ochanomizu, Akihabara.

He leans slightly left, touches the shoulder of Morinaga Eiji

"Oyabun," he says. Then, more loudly, "Morinaga *Oyabun."* Heads come up. He looks around, meets the eyes, sees the nods, nods himself. To Eiji again, "Hanako," opening the jacket, pointing at her. "You are her safety net."

"Hai, inochi o kakemasu, on my life."

Teshima reaches inside the leather jacket, takes out his aviator sunglasses, hooks the springy earpieces back and around. His *kobun,* his family, kneeling in the green dark. Emerald sunlight beckoning. He plants both old combat boots on the concrete, shoves back, harder, and the bike rolls off its stand. He gets a worn instep on the peg, half-stands, posting like a jockey, snaps his right leg straight sending a jolt through toes crushed so long ago but the bones remembering—*Oh, Jesus, Tod, your foot*—good! A little pain to help him stay alert.

Stand, snap.

The engine catches, coughs, he is too slow with the throttle, the engine dies. He chokes back a fraction, tries again, up, snap, and this time it roars to life, the monster cat roused, thunderingly, deafeningly in the garage. He cranks the throttle, cranks it, feels the power again between his thighs. Buttocks, testicles, thighs, back, shoulders, arms recapturing old sensations on the instant. Stance, balance, attittude—all coming back, vibrations resonating with memories encoded in the old centaur bones and flesh. Rev it. Slow explosions, wonderful. Again. Once more. Rumbling, roaring, echoing and re-echoing. Remembering.

Teshima Tadao relaxes completely, gets his left boot up on the peg, eases the lever into low, more power now, and the clutch—oh, too fast, too much power. No! *Not* too much! Just the right amount! He lets the clutch out all the way, cranks on more power, leans back, tugs lightly on the grips, and the rear wheel squeals just as it used to, the front wheel lifts—*Hey, Tod, reet wheelie*—and in one green rush the sun is all around, he is through the door, into the lane, leaning into the first turn, part of the machine, again, you never forget, never, nothing is ever lost, not ever, because it is all there, forever safe, which you always knew deep down but now that oneness everlasting blossoms up and out and through you in an ecstasy, and you gear up, and up again, and you sob aloud with the joy of it, and you crank on more power, and more... and never—not ever, not at your mother's breast or even in her womb—have you felt so little of yourself, so much of life... and love.

Sunday, 12:23 P.M.

In the considered opinion of Colonel Franklin D. "Buddy" Nakamura, F.X. Donner is more of a flake than ever. Look at him there, sprawled in the a lounge chair, laughing and chattering away nonstop and batting at the tears like a looner. He has no real business in the hospital (except maybe the psychiatric wing). None of them do. Nevertheless, here they all are, in the sunny day-room, which they have to themselves: glass on three sides, Tokyo revving and steaming away out there. In here, scarred and frazzled gum and fig trees in redwood tubs, infant *manga* and coloring books and stuffed toys scattered all over the green and yellow linoleum, framed hygiene propaganda pix on the pale green walls, cupboards and sink and fridge and two-burner range to the right of the door, and, to the left, a rugged-looking big-screen Sony squatting on some black modular stuff. Dinette table and chairs, chrome and Formica, near the center. That waxy-vinegary smell, rustles and static from the intercom. A clean well-lighted place.

Which Buddy doesn't particularly mind, but he's got better things to do than perch here on this dinette chair observing Janey and Donner and Donner's new love-of-his life observing the doctors and nurses observing the baby, Hanako. Nothing wrong with the kid either, she's fine, she's okay, so let's get out of here. Fact of the matter is, Buddy is starving although lunch is over. Lunch: one (1) hot dog, a sort of sadistic mini-hors d'oeuvre for a man of Buddy's bulk and caloric requirements. In fact, Buddy has remembered and is thinking hard about the day-old but still no doubt tasty hero sandwich in the trunk of his car, wedged against the spare tire. Buddy looks down at his own thick spare and sighs. He can't leave the room except for a quick whiz, or Janey would know.

"Forget it, Buddy. You can't have the baby's fruit cocktail."

"I don't want the baby's fruit cocktail." Janey knows anyway.

"I saw you looking at it." Reading Buddy's mind.

"I'm not looking at it." Buddy hates these conversations. They're bad enough between the two of them, but in public forget it. Buddy's a full *colonel.* It's not like he's *afraid* of Janey, that's for god damn sure.

"You're not now, but you were."

"I wasn't, not at any time."

"Okay, Love-Buds"—Buddy hates that name!—
"time for a fat tape."

"No Walkman." Thank God.

"No need. There's a player right under the TV.
Here." She tosses Buddy a cassette tape. "New one.
Guaranteed, super drastic, super potent. Shove it in
there, my man."

"No earphones."

"So what?"

"Janey, for Christ's sake! There's people around!
This is very personal."

"Hey, soldier, we've gone through this all before."

"Fat tapes are intensely personal."

"Well, so is marriage. I'm a woman in my prime. I
don't want some tub of dead guts for a husband. You
know what the doctor said. As of today you are 83
pounds behind schedule, so don't give me any of that,
'Tomorrow Janey for sure' crap. Today. Now. You
want running in place instead? You want sparring?
Hey, if I hafta, I'll punch that flab right off your body.
You're going to work off that hot dog one way or
another. So quit whining. Shove it in, crank it on."

"All right!" Buddy slams in the cassette. "But
there's a time and a place! Here we go, same old shit,
the xylophone boy and then, *'Hel*lo-o-o, friends—'"

"Quiet."

"Hello friends, this is Dr. Jim Abercrombie of Dr. Jim Abercrombie Superlearning Systems, a wholly-owned subsidiary of Dr. Jim Abercrombie International, with our head offices in Dayton, Ohio. We're in the business of positiveness. We're in the business of attitude modification, self-therapy, happiness. We don't recognize problems as such, only challenges. We don't let negativeness get a toe-hold. We face the situation, and we face ourselves, and we dare to imagine and to be all that we can be."

Fucking Donner, look at that smirk.

"Now, friends, some of us have a little weight situation, which is not a problem and therefore nothing to fight against and become stressed about, but which has maybe been a little bit stubborn and hard to resolve in the past, and maybe this has discouraged us to a certain extent, but we shouldn't let it, because, like all challenges, this is an opportunity for new self-awareness and growth."

Growth. Donner, snickering. Buddy'd like to clean his clock.

"Maybe all we need are some stronger, more vivid images. Those, and encouragement from our friends and loved ones, and confidence in our own

capabilities, which, if we only knew, are tremendous. There is untapped potential in each and every one of us, friends, to be the person we can let ourselves become."

"What did you pay for this bullshit?"

"Twenty-nine niney-five, just like all the others."

"Jesus, Janey, can't we just let it go till—"

"Shut up and listen."

"So, really, friends, our little weight problem so-called is really a W-A-I-T wait problem, hehheh, because we naturally want to defer what we subconsciously fear, but of course the good news is that there's nothing to fear because fear and every other negative emotion is the product of our own minds. And who controls our minds? We do. But do we hate our adipose tissue? No indeed, because our tissues, organs, glands, cells—all are a part of ourselves, and we love ourselves. Love is the answer. Try stroking those areas which seem overfull—thighs, buttocks, abdomen—and try talking to these areas. Try it."

"Try it, Love-Buds."

"Fucked if I will."

"Say, for example, Hi there, friend cellulite, I love you because I love myself, but I'd love you more if you

were less. That's it, friends, the key phrase, it really works, because whatever we tell our bodies to do they do. Simple? Yes, but darned effective. I'd love you more if you were less. Try it. I love you, big love-handles, but I'd love you more if there was less to love."

Donner killing himself, doubled up like a stuck bug.

Buddy standing, knocking over his chair, striding over to the window, hands jammed in the pockets of his sweats, damn mad.

"Which is not to say that we can't treat ourselves to a little tough love too. Golly no. We can talk turkey, so to speak, to our subconscious in no uncertain terms. No minced metaphors. Straight talk.

Buddy steaming, looking down on the tollway. There's a sight you don't see every day. Some clown in a bomber jacket and an old infantry helmet, stunting around on a big red Hog. Laying rubber, weaving in and out. Right up on the pegs, got a chick on the back. What an asshole, he's gonna kill 'em both. Well, here come the cops, a whole pod of 'em on white Hondas. Sirens and lights. The guy asked for it, now he's gonna get it… Well, what're they waiting for?… Are they *chasing* the guy or *escorting* him? What a town.

"We can say to ourselves that we are both prisoner and prison, trapped in our fat, yes, and jailer too, all rolled into one, and we can say, darn it, we want out, we want freedom, because this is no way to live."

Dr. Jim Abercrombie, wasp-waisted little faggot, telling Buddy how to live. There's a prior question, as the mayor loves to say at their meetings, God damn her, and Buddy's prior question is, why? Not how but why? Why live at all?

Buddy's feeling that low.

"We can tell ourselves some tough love facts, too, lavish on a few dramatic images. Like those chocolates that we dote on might be better for us if they were big juicy beetles. Like all those cholesterol-drenched buttery dollops would be much less dangerous if they were maggots. Sickening, isn't it? Well, if we could see inside our arteries we'd be truly sickened, and that's not negativity that's fact. Eat fat, get fat. Cheese? You like cheese? Why don't you just inject about 200 ccs of Crisco right into your left ventricle? It would be quicker and cheaper. Fat! Fat, fat, fat, fat, fat, fat, fat."

Live to be thin? Is that why?

"Fat! Great green gobs of greasy grimy gopher guts—remember that one? Well, gopher guts would be

a relative picnic for your own compared to the sort of garbage—you heard me, we're not pulling any punches here—GARBAGE, that you shovel into your gaping maw on a daily basis. Road-kill, how about that? When you love someone you want to keep them alive. When you love yourself you want to keep yourself alive. So how about some fairly fresh road-kill—muskrat, rabbit, it makes no difference. It's a sort of pemmican, as you might say, and a real treat compared to your habitual oil-drooling pork chops and flank steaks. Or how about this? Next time you get the itch for some rich well-marbled meat just think, this isn't a piece of cow or pig, it's a piece of me. This obscenity is human flesh. Yes, and—"

Buddy, yanking out Dr. Jim Abercrombie, crumpling him, pitching him into the corner trailing an arc of tape.

"Twenty-nine ninety-five, Bud." Janey's pissed, too bad. Donner over there with his cutie, kid on one knee cutie on the other. Killer cutie. Saved him. Somehow, she sprung him, dragged him out and pulled him in. And, Buddy just now realizes, Donner's going to do the same for him. Again. If not now, then tomorrow, next week, sometime. Bank on that. Buddy's feeling better. Donner looks over, gives him the old, Well, what the fuck look. Gives him a smile. Okay, Buddy'll bite:

"Donner! Tell me this: what's the fucking point? Why should we—"

"Hanako!" Newsgirl screeching. "Hanako, *nani o yatteru no?*"

"Hanako what are you *do*ing?" Miyuki-*san* exclaims as the baby, imitating Buddy, perhaps, throws her cup toward the corner. Tall and slightly stooped, neatly bearded brown and gray, not really balding though his hair has of late become in places rather fine, sharp-featured but easy-going, not childless (thank God), needing glasses but only to read and drive and brush his teeth, still strong and for his age remarkably agile, Donner swings Hanako to the floor, dashes over to the sink for a wet rag, finds two, and tosses one to Miyuki-*san*.

"We must wipe it up quickly," she says. "Or this will be a sticky-ness."

On all fours they mop toward each other. Their foreheads touch.

"Miyuki-*san,* do you write poetry?"

"Poetry? Me?"

"Haiku."

"Do you kidding?"

657

Donner kisses her.

"Donner-*sensei!* What are you *do*ing?"

"Miyuki-*san,* where should we live?"

"*Mochiron,* Tokyo! Of course!"

"The safest major city in the world?"

"Even if it is not completely safe, yes, Tokyo definitely. Because pardon me, and I'm sorry to say it, but nothing ever really happens out where you are, into the... boonies? Of Kanagawa-ken."

Kanagawa-ken, 2003

About the Author

F.J. Logan has been a Tokyo-based journalist for seventeen years. He has written for most of the major serial publications on the Pacific Rim, including *Kyoto Journal, EastWest Magazine of Hawaii,* and *Tokyo Journal.* His books include *The Point Is the Point* and *Japan Fan.* Mr. Logan lives with his family in Kanagawa, Japan.

Printed in the United States
67473LVS00001B/1